John Richard Green, Charles William Adam Tait

Analysis of English History

Based on Green's short History of the English People

John Richard Green, Charles William Adam Tait

Analysis of English History
Based on Green's short History of the English People

ISBN/EAN: 9783337139278

Printed in Europe, USA, Canada, Australia, Japan

Cover: Foto ©ninafisch / pixelio.de

More available books at **www.hansebooks.com**

ANALYSIS OF ENGLISH HISTORY

ANALYSIS OF ENGLISH HISTORY

BASED ON

GREEN'S SHORT HISTORY

OF THE

ENGLISH PEOPLE

BY

C. W. A. TAIT, M.A.

ASSISTANT MASTER IN CLIFTON COLLEGE

London
MACMILLAN AND CO., Limited
NEW YORK: THE MACMILLAN COMPANY
1897

All rights reserved

RICHARD CLAY AND SONS, LIMITED,
LONDON AND BUNGAY.

First Edition, August 1878. *Reprinted, November* 1878, 1879, 1881, 1882, 1886.
Second Edition, 1890. *Reprinted*, 1897.

PREFACE TO NEW EDITION.

I CANNOT send out this slight attempt to facilitate the study of English History, upon the lines laid down by Mr. Green, without rendering my grateful thanks to Miss K. Norgate, who had the kindness to read over my proof-sheets to the end of the reign of George II.

CLIFTON, *July*, 1890.

ANALYSIS OF THE HISTORY OF THE ENGLISH PEOPLE.

TABLE OF ENGLISH, WEST-FRANKISH, AND FRENCH KINGS.

Year	English	Frankish
800		CHARLES THE GREAT [Charlemagne] (King of the Franks, Emperor of the Romans. Supports Ecgberht of Wessex against Mercia)
814		LEWIS THE PIOUS (Emperor)
836	ECGBERHT (King of West Saxons, finally "Rex Anglorum")	
840	ÆTHELWULF (King of West Saxons)	LOTHAR (King of Italy and Lotharingia, and Emperor) — CHARLES THE BALD (King of West Franks) — LEWIS (King of East Franks)
858	ÆTHELBALD	
860	ÆTHELBERHT (King of Kent and Wessex)	
866	ÆTHELRED I.	
871	ÆLFRED THE GREAT	
877		LEWIS II. THE STAMMERER

ANALYSIS OF THE HISTORY OF THE ENGLISH PEOPLE.

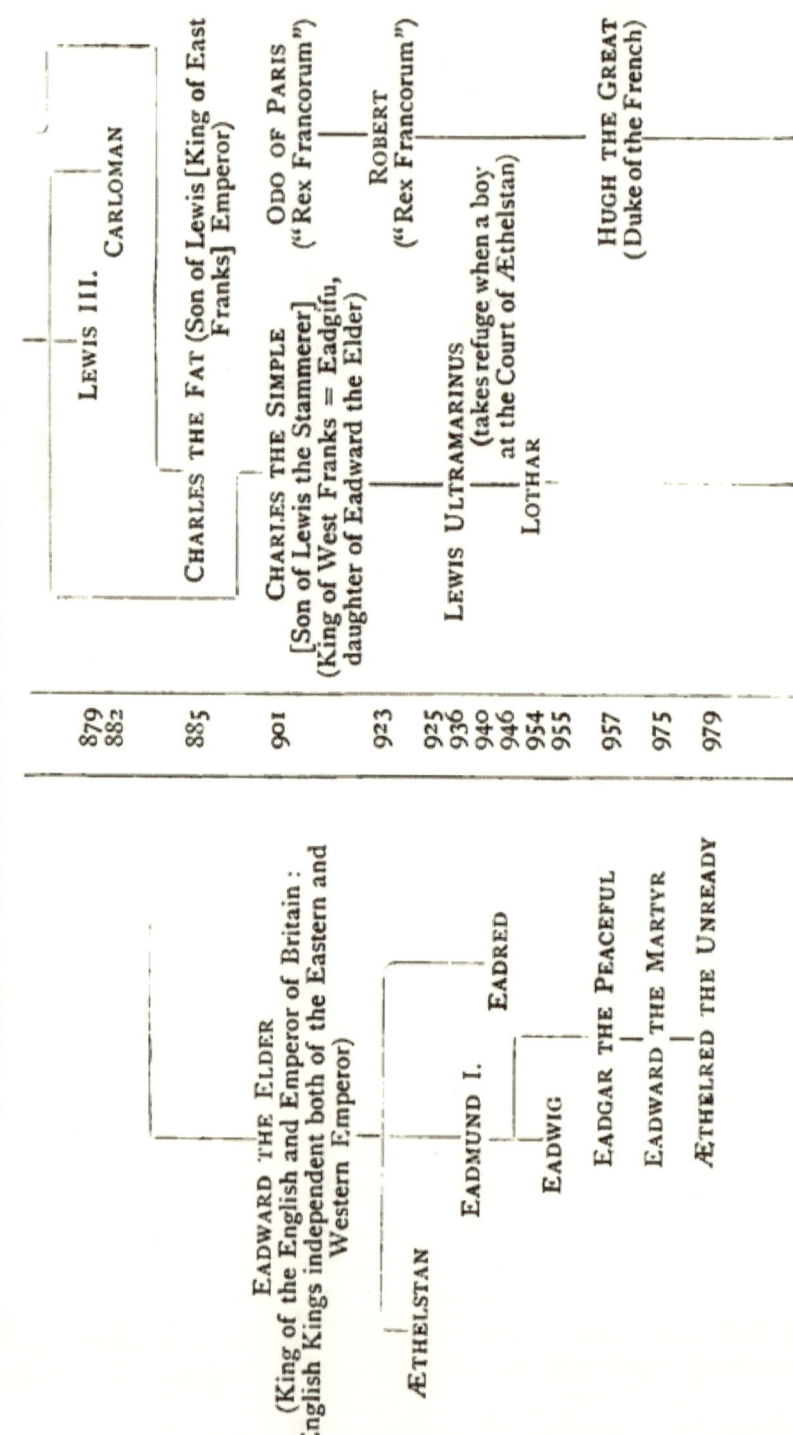

Year	English	Frankish
		Lewis III. ⎤
879		⎬ Carloman
882		⎦
885		Charles the Fat (Son of Lewis [King of East Franks] Emperor)
		Charles the Simple [Son of Lewis the Stammerer] (King of West Franks = Eadgifu, daughter of Eadward the Elder) — Odo of Paris ("Rex Francorum")
901	Eadward the Elder (King of the English and Emperor of Britain: English Kings independent both of the Eastern and Western Emperor)	
		Robert ("Rex Francorum")
923	Æthelstan	
925		Lewis Ultramarinus (takes refuge when a boy at the Court of Æthelstan)
936	Eadmund I.	
940		
946	Eadred	Lothar
954	Eadwig	
955		
957	Eadgar the Peaceful	
975	Eadward the Martyr	Hugh the Great (Duke of the French)
979	Æthelred the Unready	

ANALYSIS OF THE HISTORY OF THE ENGLISH PEOPLE.

Date	English	French
963		Hugh Capet (King of the French)
996		Lewis V. End of the Karlings: *i.e.* of the Kings of the West Franks.
1016	Eadmund Ironside	Robert the Wise
1017	**Danish Kings.** Cnut	
1031		Henry I.
1037	Harold Harefoot	
1040	Harthacnut	
1042	Eadward the Confessor.	
1060	Harold (Son of Godwine).	Philip I.
1066	**House of Normandy.** William the Conqueror	
1087	William Rufus	
1100	Henry I.	
1108		Lewis VI. (helps William Clito, son of Robert of Normandy)
1135	**House of Blois.** Stephen (Grandson of the Conqueror).	

ANALYSIS OF THE HISTORY OF THE ENGLISH PEOPLE.

THE HOUSE OF PLANTAGENET.

HENRY II. = Eleanor of Acquitaine — 1154 — LEWIS VII. = Eleanor of Acquitaine (divorced = Henry II.) 1137

1180 — PHILIP AUGUSTUS

RICHARD I. — 1189
JOHN — 1199

HENRY III. — 1216

1223 — LEWIS VIII.

1226 — LEWIS IX.—Saint Lewis

EDWARD I. = Margaret, daughter of Philip III. — 1270
1272 — PHILIP III.

1285 — PHILIP IV.

EDWARD II. = Isabella, daughter of Philip IV. — 1307

1314 — LEWIS X. (succeeded [after John I., an infant] by his brother)

1316 — PHILIP V. (succeeded by his brother)

1322 — CHARLES IV. End of the elder branch of the House of Capet.

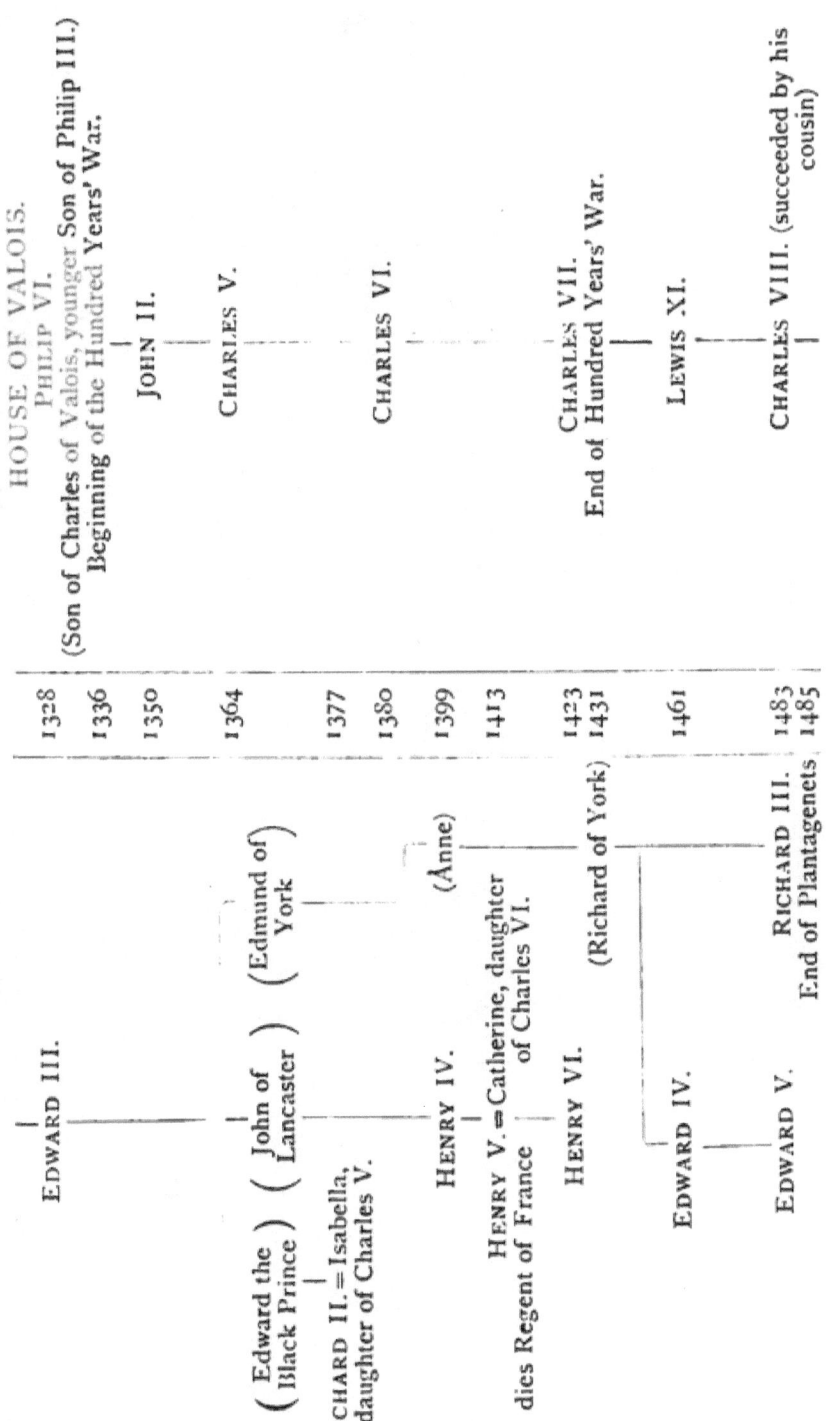

ANALYSIS OF THE HISTORY OF THE ENGLISH PEOPLE.

HOUSE OF TUDOR.
HENRY VII. — 1485

HENRY VIII. — 1509

EDWARD VI. — 1547
MARY — 1553
ELIZABETH — 1558

End of House of Tudor.

THE STUARTS.
JAMES I. — 1603

CHARLES I. = Henrietta Maria, daughter of Henry IV. — 1625

1485	
1498	LEWIS XII.= Mary, daughter of Henry VII. (succeeded by his cousin)
1509	FRANCIS I.
1515	
1547	HENRY II.= Catherine de Medici (obtains Mary Stuart in marriage for his son)
1553	
1558	
1559	FRANCIS II. (claims English crown; succeeded by his brother)
1560	CHARLES IX. (massacre of S. Bartholomew) [succeeded by his brother]
1572	
1574	HENRY III. (by his assassination the line of Valois becomes extinct) [succeeded by his cousin]
1589	HOUSE OF BOURBON. HENRY IV. (Edict of Nantes, 1598.)
1603	
1610	LEWIS XIII.
1625	
1643	LEWIS XIV.

xii

ANALYSIS OF THE HISTORY OF THE ENGLISH PEOPLE.

1649	**COMMONWEALTH.**	
1653	OLIVER CROMWELL, Protector.	
1660	CHARLES II.	
1685	JAMES II.	
1689	MARY II. = WILLIAM III. (of Orange).	
	(James, Old Pretender)—1715	
1702	ANNE	
	(Charles Edward Young Pretender)—1745 End of the Stuarts.	
1714	**HOUSE OF BRUNSWICK.** GEORGE I.	
1715	(Rising for the Old Pretender.)	LEWIS XV. (Great Grandson of Lewis XIV., Duke of Orleans, Regent.)
1727	GEORGE II.	
1745	(Rising under the Young Pretender.)	

ANALYSIS OF THE HISTORY OF THE ENGLISH PEOPLE.

English	Year	French
GEORGE III.	1760	
	1774	LEWIS XVI. (Grandson of Lewis XV.)
	1793	REPUBLIC.
	1799	NAPOLEON BUONAPARTE—First Consul.
	1804	NAPOLEON BUONAPARTE—Emperor.
	1814	LEWIS XVIII. [brother of Lewis XVI.]
(Edward Duke of Kent)	1820	
GEORGE IV.	1820	
	1824	CHARLES X. (brother of Lewis XVIII.)
WILLIAM IV.	1830	HOUSE OF ORLEANS. LOUIS PHILIPPE (cousin to Charles X.)—King of the French.
VICTORIA.	1837	
	1848	REPUBLIC.
	1851	Coup d'État.
	1852	LOUIS NAPOLEON.—Emperor.
	1870	REPUBLIC.

xiv

ANALYSIS OF ENGLISH HISTORY

ANALYSIS OF ENGLISH HISTORY

ENGLAND BEFORE THE NORMAN CONQUEST.

A **Britain and the Roman Occupation. A.D. 50–410.**
    I. Considerable material and industrial prosperity; order ensured; corn raised and exported; tin (Cornwall), iron (Forest of Dean), and lead mines (Somerset and Northumberland) worked.
    II. To a great extent, however, Britain was little more than a military colony.
        a Walled towns (Castra) connected by roads.
        b The country population remained mainly unaffected by Roman influence, and British in feeling.
        c Hence may be inferred a severance in feeling between Town and Country, and most probably alliances between the Country folk and the unsubdued Picts.

B **Resistance of Britain as a free Province to the attacks of Picts, Scots** (*from Ireland*), **and Saxon pirates. 410–449.**

C **The English Conquest. 449–579.**
449–500. I. The Conquest of the Saxon Shore (Littus Saxonicum—from Southampton Water to the Wash).
    449. *a* The *Jutes* under Hengest and Horsa called in against the Picts (landing at Ebbsfleet in Thanet). Quarrels between Jutes and Britons.
    455. Jutish march from Thanet upon the Medway Valley and victory at Aylesford. Last rally of
    457. the Romanized Britons, and repulse of Jutes.
    465. Decisive victories of the Jutes at Wippedsfleet
    473. and at Portus Lemannis (Lymne); and foundation of the Kingdom of Kent, **465–473**. Jutish advance checked by the Andredsweald and by the fortifications of London.

477.   *b* Landing of *Saxons* under Ælle at Selsey. Siege
491.   and destruction of Anderida (Pevensey) 491.
           Foundation of Kingdom of Sussex. Further
           advance checked by the Andredsweald.
480-500.   *c* Descent of *Saxons* upon districts north of the
           Thames and capture of Camulodunum (Colchester). Advance inland checked by forests,
           of which Epping and Hainault forests are
           survivals. Foundation of Essex.
480-500.   *d* Landing of *Angles*. Settlement of the North-folk and South-folk, and conquest of East
           Anglia.
495-577. II. The Conquests of the Saxons.
  495-519.   *a* Descents of Saxons known as Gewissas upon
             Southampton Water.
  519.   *b* Decisive battle of Charford, and establishment
             of Kingdom of Wessex.
  520.   *c* Saxon advance westward checked at Mount
             Badon (Badbury upon the Frome in Dorsetshire).
  530.   *d* Conquest of the Isle of Wight, and settlement of
             Jutes in it.
  552.   *e* Capture of Sorbiodunum (Old Sarum), and settlement in Wiltshire.
  556.   *f* Capture of Cunetio (Marlborough), battle of Barbury Hill, and settlement in Berkshire.
  540-568.   *g* Capture of Verulamium (S. Albans), and of
             London by the East Saxons.
  568.   *h* Collision between Jutes of Kent, set free by the
             fall of London to advance westward, and West
             Saxons at Wimbledon. Victory of West Saxons,
             and consequent settlement in Surrey.
  571.   *i* Victory of West Saxons over British at Bedford,
             and consequent settlement in Bedfordshire,
             Bucks, and Oxfordshire. Advance Northwards
             barred by the Angles.
  577.   *j* West Saxon advance upon the Severn Valley.
             Victory of Ceawlin of Wessex at Deorham (between Bath and the Bristol Channel); occupation of Bath, Gloucester, Cirencester—separation of the Britons south of the Bristol Channel
             from those to the north, and settlement of the
             West Saxons (as Hwiccas) along the lower
             Severn, on the Cotswolds, and by the Avon.
500-579. III. The Conquests of the Angles.
  500.   *a* Anglian advance along the coast and capture of
             Lindum (Lincoln).

500-520. *b* Fresh descents of Angles. Foundation of the Kingdom of the Deirans in the (Yorkshire) Wolds. Capture of Eboracum (York), and conquest of country up to the Tees.

500-547. *c* Settlement of Angles in the Basin of the Tweed.

547. Kingdom of the Bernicians set up at Bamborough by Ida.

547-580. *d* Occupation of Sherwood and the wooded country between the Trent and the Don. The North English or Southumbrians.

c. 550. *e* Occupation of the Soar, and capture of Ratae (Leicester). The Middle English.

c. 560. *f* Occupation of the head waters of the Trent, near Lichfield, Repton, and Stafford. The West English or Mercians, *i.e.*, Men of the March, or Borderers.

D **Nature of the English Conquest, and characteristics of the Conquerors.**

 I. Not so much a conquest as a migration of three nations, slowly, independently, but fully accomplished.

 II. Complete displacement (not necessarily extermination) of the native British, and disappearance of Christianity.

 III. English social and political life.

  a Though the "mark" system (*i.e.* the cultivation of land in common by a body of kindred freemen) had mainly passed away, the social unit was still the Homestead or Family. Clusters of Homesteads made the Town, clusters of Towns the Hundred or Wapentake, clusters of Hundreds the Tribe.

[*Note upon the Hundred, or (in districts occupied by the Danes) the Wapentake.*

 A. The Hundred of the "Germania."

  i. Centeni (pedites) ex singulis pagis sunt; idque ipsum inter suos vocantur, et quod primo numerus fuit, jam nomen et honor est.

  ii. Centeni singulis (principibus) ex plebe comites, consilium simul et auctoritas, adsunt.

B. Different views of the relation of the territorial hundred to this hundred of the Germania.
   i. A division of 100 hides of land (*i.e.* the extent of land allotted to 100 families).
   ii. A district furnishing 100 warriors to the host.
   iii. The land originally allotted to 100 warriors (the inequality of size accounted for by geographical and political causes, *e.g.* mountains, rivers, remains of British independence).

878-893.   C. Adopted (possibly) by Ælfred as a basis for rating. (Hence the tradition that the arrangement into hundreds was devised by Ælfred). Adopted by
959-975.   Eadgar as a basis for securing the pursuit and capture of criminals.

D. Hundred Courts.
   i. Composed of landowners, priest, reeve, and four or ten best men of each township.
   ii. The judges were first the whole body, then a representative body of twelve.
   iii. Their function—to declare folk-right, try criminals (in the first instance), settle disputes, witness transfer of land, and when
1008.   necessary collect taxation (as in Æthelred's reign for the fleet).
   iv. The meetings held monthly.

E. Side by side with the Hundred Courts were Franchises, or Liberties, in which the jurisdiction was in private hands (Sac and Soc), subject, however, like the Hundred Courts, to the general organization of the Shire.]

b The Land.
   1. Remains of the "mark" system of common cultivation.
      a Woodland and pasture land undivided.
      b Meadow-land undivided from hay harvest to spring.
   2. Beginnings of personal property. The plough-land permanently allotted in equal shares of corn-land and fallow-land to the families of "ceorls," *i.e.*, freemen. This was termed "alod," "odal," or sometimes "yrfe and" (*i.e.*, heir land).

3. The rest of the land, after sufficient allodial allotments had been made, remained as Folkland, from which grants were made to individuals by the King and his Witan: land thus granted was called "book-land," its possession being secured by book, *i.e.*, charter.
4. All land was held under condition of—
    a Service in the host ("fyrd ").
    b Contributing to the repair of bridges, "bricg-bot."
    c Maintenance of fortifications, "burh-bot." These conditions first specified as Trinoda Necessitas about A.D. 700.

c Organization of the State.
  1. Each Township represented in the Hundred-moot by its priest, reeve, and four or ten "best men."
  2. The Folk-moot, in which all freemen (*i.e.* all possessed of land) appeared in person or by representation.
  3. The Witan, not a representative body, but an assembly of leading men to advise the chief or King.

d Gradation of ranks.
  1. The slave, his owner's chattel.
  2. The Free.
     a The landless freeman or "læt," the tiller of another man's land; personally free but compelled to have a lord.
     b The landed freeman, "ceorl," the base of the community. It was as an owner of land that the freeman had rights and duties.
     c The "Eorl," or "Ætheling," the man of noble blood and of large holding (including pasture and meadow-land as well as plough land).
     d The King: the title of King, apparently unknown until landing in Britain, due to the necessity for a common leader.
     e The "Gesith" (companion) or personal comrade and dependant of the king, contributing to form a nobility of service, and scarcely distinguishable from the later "Thegn."

E The Formation and Struggle of the three groups.

593.
I. Main prominent English settlements — Kent (Jutish), Sussex, Essex, Wessex, East Anglia, Northumbria, Mercia, grouped (about 593) into three great masses; 1, North; 2, South; 3, Central England.

591-607. II. Supremacy of Kent, and preaching of Latin Christianity.

584. *a* West Saxon advance upon the upper Severn Valley. Storm of Uriconium (at the base of the Wrekin). Defeat by the British at Faddiley (near Nantwich), and loss of the upper Severn Valley, followed by internal strife among the West Saxons, and the defeat of Ceawlin by the combined forces of British and
591. Hwiccas at Wanborough (Vale of the White Horse.)

588. *b* Creation of Northumbria by the Conquest of Deira by the Bernicians.

591-597. *c* Establishment of supremacy of Æthelberht of Kent to Humber (in spite of his defeat by the West Saxons, 568), excluding Wessex.

597. *d* Landing of Augustine in the Isle of Thanet, consequent upon marriage of Æthelberht to Bercta, daughter of the Christian West Frankish King, Charibert. The Kentish Kings the first to issue written codes of laws (due possibly to the influence of the Roman missionaries).

607. *e* Fall of national supremacy of Kent, though still ecclesiastically predominant, and rise of Rædwald of East Anglia to supremacy over Mid-Britain.

617-627. II*a*. Supremacy of Northumbria.

603. *a* Victory of Æthelfrith at Dægsastan (Dawston in Roxburghshire) over the Scots, and capture of Chester.

617-625. *b* Conquest by Eadwine of Northumbria, brother-in-law of Æthelfrith,' of the Forest of Elmet, Anglesea, and Man; extension of supremacy over Mid-Britain after death of Rædwald.

626. *c* Extension of Northumbrian supremacy over Wessex.

625.
627.
d Marriage of Eadwine to Æthelburh, the daughter of the Kentish King; preaching of Paulinus, and acceptance of Christianity by Northumbria.

ANALYSIS OF ENGLISH HISTORY.

627-655. III. The Heathen struggle.
    628. *a* Rise of Penda, King of Mercia, victory over the West Saxons, and probable annexation of lower Severn basin (the country of the Hwiccas).
    633. *b* Struggle with Eadwine for the possession of East Anglia. Eadwine defeated and slain by Penda and his Welsh allies at Hatfield on the Don.
    635. *c* Defeat of Penda's Welsh allies under Cadwallon at Heaven's Field near Hexham by Oswald of Bernicia. Union of Northumbria under Oswald. Establishment of the Irish form of Christianity at Lindisfarne under Aidan from the Columban Monastery at Iona.
    642. *d* Defeat of Oswald by Penda at Maserfield (probably in Shropshire, near Oswestry), and ravaging of Northumbria.
    655. *e* Struggle between Penda and Oswiu for supremacy in East Anglia ; Penda slain at Winwædfield (near Leeds). Conversion of the Mercians to the Irish form of Christianity.
    IV. The struggle between the opposing forms of Christianity.
        a Notice with regard to Irish Christianity—
            i The great activity of its missionaries (Aidan, Cuthbert, Chad).
            ii Its want of organization (the bishops being numerous and without special sees).
            iii The clannish system of its Monasteries, clustering round some one individual.
            iv Its dissent from the rest of Christian Europe with regard to the time of observing Easter, and the shape of the tonsure.
    664. *b* The Irish party defeated at the Synod of Whitby.
    669. *c* Theodore of Tarsus named Primate by the Pope.
669-678.   Creation of new sees in South and Central Britain, and their subordination to Canterbury.
    673.
    678. First Church Council called at Hertford. This organization of the Episcopate extended to Northumbria. Followed during the course of the next hundred years by the organization of
678-800. the parish system, settled clergy taking the place of missionaries.
659-825. V. The revival of Northumbria under Ecgfrith, and of Mercia (now Christian) under Wulfhere and Æthelred.

659–661.	*a* Mercian supremacy re-established in Mid-Britain and extended over Essex, Surrey, and Sussex.
675–709.	*b* Industrial and moral progress seen in reclaiming the country and founding abbeys—Peterborough, Ely, Crowland, Evesham.
670–675.	*c* Conquest of Northern Lancashire and Lake district and of Pict-land to the north of the Forth by Ecgfrith of Northumbria.
675–679.	*d* Struggle between Northumbria and Mercia for Lindsey, terminated by mediation of Archbishop Theodore, and surrender of Lindsey to Ecgfrith
685.	*e* Ecgfrith and his army slain by the Picts at Nectansmere in Fife. End of the political importance of Northumbria. **685.**
673–767.	*f* Literary importance of Northumbria during the next century: Schools at Jarrow and at York: Cædmon, Bæda, Ecgberht and Alcuin of York. (See Green, pp. 27-29, 38-41, 43.)
652–829.	VI. Revival and final supremacy of Wessex.
652–658. 682–710. 685. 688–694.	*a* Growth of Wessex westward to the Parret, to the Quantocks **682**, to the Tone **710**; growth eastward, Conquest of Sussex and Isle of Wight, of Essex, Kent, London.
710. 715.	*b* Publication of the earliest West Saxon code of laws. Repulse of the Mercians in the vale of the White Horse.
728–733. 733–754. 754.	*c* West Saxon defeat by Æthelbald of Mercia, and capture of Somerton. Æthelbald's title: "King of the Southern English." Defeat of Æthelbald by the West Saxons at Burford.
758–796.	*d* Offa, King of Mercia. **758–796.**
775. 779. 779.	(1) Mercian recovery of Kent, Essex, London, of Oxfordshire and Buckinghamshire. Capture of Pengwern (Shrewsbury). Building of Offa's dyke from the mouth of the Dee to the Wye, and drawing up of Offa's laws to settle the relations between the English and Welsh: but no attempt made at over-lordship of all England.
802. 808.	(2) Friendly relations between Offa and Charles of the West-Franks (Charles the Great). Charles' Court, however, a refuge for all English exiles, in hopes, possibly, of recovering England for the Empire. Ecgberht (driven out by civil war **787**) restored as King of Wessex, and Eardwulf as King of Northumbria by Frankish influence.

825-829.	*e* Ecgberht, King of Wessex, finally over-lord from the British Channel to the Forth.
815-823.	(1) Conquest of Cornwall by Ecgberht, and close of contest with Britons. **815-825.**
825.	(2) Defeat of Mercians at Ellandun, near Wilton.
825.	(3) Recapture of Kent and Essex.
828-829.	(4) Submission of Mercia and Northumbria.

The results of the consolidation of Britain into these three great groups—

(1) The growing importance of the King as the kingdom increased in extent. Less seen by the people, therefore, more mysterious.

(2) The elevation of the Thegns, *i.e.*, the nobility of service, enriched by frequent grants from folkland.

(3) Loss of power of the Folk-moot, owing to the difficulty of enforcing obedience to its awards. Justice became the "justice of the King"; peace, "the King's peace."

(4) Change of character in the Witenagemot from a national to a royal council (consisting on ordinary occasions of the King and some of his family, some bishops (say nine) some ealdormen (say five), summoned by the King, and about fifteen thegns).

(5) The title of Bretwalda (assigned by the Anglo-Saxon chronicle to eight Kings ending with Ecgberht) seems to point to growing claims of substantial hegemony, though the title was not probably derived from the Roman Cæsarship.

F The Coming of the Danes.

Five stages in Danish Conquest.

787-855.	I. Simple plundering raids.
855-878.	II. Raids followed by settlement.
878-954.	III. No fresh inroads. Struggle of the West Saxon Kings with the Danes already settled in Britain.
954-980.	IV. Period of cessation in the Danish Struggle.
980-1042.	V. Period of political conquest. Attempt of the Kings of all Denmark to make themselves Kings of England as well.
787-855.	I. The plundering raids.
794-840.	*a* Descent of the Northmen upon Ireland and settlements there.

837-845.	*b* Attacks upon Wessex from Ireland, assisted by the rising of the West Welsh, checked by Ecgberht at Hengest-dun in Cornwall (Hingston Down) **837**, by Bishop Ealhstan of Sherborne and Osric the Ealdorman, at the mouth of the Parret. **845**.
851. 853.	*c* Attacks of Northmen upon the East Coast, checked by Æthelstan near Sandwich, and Æthelwulf at Aclea (Ockley) in Surrey. Victory of Æthelwulf over Roderic of North Wales.
855-878.	II. Raids followed by settlement. The first appearance of the Danes from Denmark. The making of the Danelaw.
855.	*a* "This year the heathen men, for the first time, remained over winter in Sheppey."
856.	*b* Journey of Æthelwulf to the court of Charles the Bald, King of the West Franks, to concert operations against the Northmen and marriage with his daughter Judith.
866-870. 867.	*c* Danish conquest of East Anglia. Attack on Northumbria and conquest of York.
870. 871.	*d* Mercia tributary to the Danes. Danish attack upon Wessex. Victory at Reading and encampment upon Ashdown (commanding vale of the White Horse). Victory of West Saxons at Ashdown under Æthelred and Ælfred. The Danes, however, had to be finally bought off.
874.	*e* Danish conquest of Mercia.
876. 877.	*f* Second Danish attack upon Wessex and seizure of a neck of land near Wareham in Dorsetshire. Defeat of Danes at Exeter, oath taken "upon the holy ring" to leave the king's land.
878.	*g* Third Danish attack upon Wessex; Ælfred driven to take refuge behind Selwood in fortress at Athelney. Ælfred's victory over the Danes at Edington (near Westbury-upon-Avon). The peace of Wedmore; all England south of the Thames and west of Watling Street (from a little east of Reading as far north as the Ribble) left in Ælfred's hands.

Notice the 3 divisions of the Danelaw—

(1) In Danish Northumbria a complete division of the land south of the Tees among the conquerors, and political re-organization.

ANALYSIS OF ENGLISH HISTORY.

           (2) In Danish Mercia; the confederacy of the Five Boroughs, Derby, Leicester, Lincoln, Nottingham, Stamford; and complete division and organization of our Lincolnshire; elsewhere the settlement less complete.

           (3) In East Anglia, the local institutions remained English, and Christianity prevailed undisturbed.

878-954. III. Period of struggle between the West Saxon Kings and the Danes already settled in Britain.

878-901. *a* Reign of Ælfred after treaty of Wedmore.

878-884.   (1) Years of peace. Re-construction of the military system, all owners of five hides of land subjected to thegn-service (a well-armed permanent force subject to the King's command thus created); the rest of the national force by turns to take service in the field, and to guard the fortifications of their own townships. Development of a naval force. [The hide variously reckoned from 30 to 120 acres, possibly 30 acres in four common fields, but also varying with local custom.]

885-886.   (2) Renewal of the struggle with invading Northmen at Rochester, and with the Danes in East Anglia. Ælfred's capture of London. **886.** Second treaty between Ælfred and Guthrum; the boundary between Guthrum's and Ælfred's dominions, "up on the Thames, and then up on the Lea, and along the Lea to its source, then right to Bedford, and then up the Ouse into Watling Street."

886-893.   (3) Years of peace. Ælfred's efforts to revive learning by means of schools, translations, introduction of learned foreigners. The beginning of the continuous English Chronicle, based upon the Bishops' Roll of Winchester.

893-897.   (4) Renewal of the Danish attack upon South Britain.

893.   *a* Landing of Danes from Frankland at Lymne (in Kent), and establishment in Andredsweald.

894.   *b* Rising of the Danelaw, and invasion of Wessex; defeat of the Danes, who had passed up the Thames to the Severn, at Buttington (in Shropshire).

896-897.	c Alliance between the invaders and Welsh. Danish occupation of Chester. English capture of the Danish fleet in the Lea, and close of the war.
901.	Death of King Ælfred.
901-925.	b Eadward the Elder.

Eadward (King of the Angul-Saxons, *i.e.*, of Mercia and Wessex).

Æthelstan. Eadmund. Eadred. Eadwine. Eadgifu = Charles the Simple of the West Franks.

Lewis Ultramarinus.

Eadgyth = Otto the Great. Eadhild = Duke Hugh of Paris.

	(1) Attack by Eadward and Æthelred and his wife Æthelflæd of Mercia upon Guthrum's Kingdom and the Five Boroughs.
907.	a Strengthening of Chester to protect northern part of English Mercia.
913.	b Conquest by Eadward of Southern Essex and Hertford.
913.	c Occupation by Æthelflæd of the valley of upper Trent and Avon. Building of forts at Tamworth, Stafford, Warwick.
917.	Attack upon the Five Boroughs.
918-921.	d Complete conquest by Eadward of East Anglia, Essex, and the Fens.
922.	e Death of Æthelflæd. Submission of Mid-Britain to Eadward.
923-924.	(2) Preparations for attack upon Danes in Northumbria. Building of forts at Manchester, Nottingham, and in the Peak. Submission of the Northern league (including the King of Scots) to Eadward as "father and lord."
925.	Death of Eadward.

ANALYSIS OF ENGLISH HISTORY. 13

925-940. *c* Æthelstan.
  (1) Completion of his father's conquests.
925-926.   Submission of the league of the North and of the Welsh. Æthelstan, King of North-
933.   umbria. Adoption of supreme royal and imperial title as "Rex Anglorum" or, as in one charter, "Angul-Saxonum necnon et totius Britanniæ rex."
  (2) Growth of public order.
   a Frequent "witenagemots" (including all parts of Britain) to advise as to regulations for order. **931-934.**
   b The "Frith-gild" accepted as the means of enforcing order (known afterwards as frank-pledge). [The complete system of Frank-pledge or Tenmannetale not earlier than the Norman Conquest, though based upon successive legislation by Æthelstan, Eadgar (959-975) and Cnut (1016-1035), that every man should have a security. By Frank-pledge every man was compelled to belong to a *tithing*, *i.e.* an association of ten men. The men of each tithing were bound to produce any of their number when called upon by law, or in default to pay for his wrong-doing unless able to clear themselves of all complicity in it.]
   c Every landless man to be under the protection of a lord.
   d Beginning of the extension of the shire system, with the shire-reeve as the King's financial officer, and the shire-moot, under the ealdorman and bishop (to declare law in civil and spiritual cases), from Wessex over East Anglia and Mercia.
  (3) Foreign alliances proceeding from the fear of the Norman settlement at the mouth of the Seine, under Hrolf, **912-927**, and his son William Longsword. **927-943.** Marriage of Æthelstan's sister Eadgyth to Otto (son
925.   of the German King Henry) **925**, and of
926.   his sister Eadhild to Duke Hugh of Paris. [The policy of marriage alliances against a common foe first seen in the marriage of Ælfred's daughter Ælfthryth to Count Baldwin of Flanders.]
  (4) Revolt of Northumbria supported by the

937.	Northern league. (Olaf the Dane with Ostmen from Ireland, Constantine of Scotland, the Welshmen of Strathclyde.) Æthelstan's victory at Brunanburh. Northumbria, however, not fully subdued, retaining its own under-King.
936-938.	(5) Support given to Lewis from over-sea, Æthelstan's nephew (son of Charles the Simple and Eadgifu) as King of the West Franks, to check still further the growing power of William Longsword and the Normans.
940.	Death of Æthelstan.
940-946.	*d* Eadmund the Magnificent.

Eadmund.

Eadwig.   Eadgar.

941-944.	(1) The rising of the Danelaw and its re-conquest.
945.	(2) Cumberland harried by Eadmund, and given to Malcolm, King of the Scots, "on the condition that he should be his fellow-worker as well by sea as by land." Murder
946.	of King Eadmund at Pucklechurch.
946-955.	*e* Eadred.
947-954.	(1) Revolts of Northumbria. **947-948-952.** The under-kingdom of Northumbria turned into an Earldom, and final submission of,
954.	the Danelaw. Eadred " Cæsar of all Britain."
	(2) Influence of Dunstan (Abbot of Glastonbury) upon the revival of English learning. (See Green, pp. 55-57.)
955.	Death of Eadred.

f Effects of the long struggle with the Danes.
1. Growth of kingly authority, the King becoming the lord or patron of the people.
2. Growth of a military aristocracy; the ceorls superseded by the thegns.
3. Gradual disappearance of "folkland" and conversion into "bookland," *i.e.*, private estates guaranteed by charter, or into "heir-land."
4. Gradual disappearance of the "ceorl" or freeman, owing to the necessity of finding protection against attack; land held more and more by tenure service; passing of the "ceorl" into the "villein."
5. Destruction of learning and decline of religion.

ANALYSIS OF ENGLISH HISTORY. 15

954-980. IV. Period of cessation in the Danish struggle.
955-959. *a* Eadwig.
956-958.   Party strife. Banishment of Abbot Dunstan. Revolt of Mercia, and recognition of Eadgar
958.   as Mercian King.
959.   Death of Eadwig.
959-975. *b* Eadgar the Peaceful.

   Æthelflaed = Eadgar = Ælfthryth
     | |
   Eadward. Æthelred.

  (1) Rise in the power of the great Ealdormen of East Anglia, Mercia, Essex, and of the Earl of Northumbria (seen already in the revolt against Eadwig).

959.   (2) Dunstan, Archbishop of Canterbury. Union of the King and primate in the government of the realm.

   a Chief attention confined to maintenance of order in Wessex. The "Hundred" adopted as a basis for securing the pursuit and capture of criminals. The Danelaw and the great Ealdormanries left practically to their own laws.

   b Educational impulse given by Dunstan. Revival of monasticism, and gradual displacement of secular by regular clergy. The Chronicle of Worcester, and rise of Worcester as a historical school.

973.   (3) Coronation of Eadgar by the primates of Canterbury and York, and recognition as over-lord of Britain.
975.   Death of Eadgar.
975-978. *c* Eadward the Martyr. Renewed contest between the nobles and the crown.

978-1042. V. The Danish political Conquest.
978-1016. *a* —Æthelred the Unready.

Ælgifu = Æthelred the Unready = Emma of Normandy, sister of Richard the Good.

Eadmund. Eadwig. Eadgith = Eadric Streona. Eadward. Ælfred. Goda = Eustace of Boulogne.

991.   (1) Descent of Norwegians upon Essex (possibly under Olaf Tryggvesson) and victory in

992.	battle of Maldon: Money paid to the Norwegians on condition of their settling in the land as allies. (Danegeld.)
994.	(2) Joint attack of Swein (driven from Denmark) and Olaf Tryggvesson upon Eastern coast of England. Olaf detached from Swein. **994.** Other attacks, and peace again bought. Swein restored to throne of Denmark. **1000.**
997-1001.	
1002.	(3) Marriage of Æthelred to Emma of Normandy, and massacre of the Danes (probably those who had fought against the English and remained in the land). Nov. 13.
1003-1007.	(4) Wessex and East Anglia harried by Swein.
1008.	(5) A great fleet collected by Æthelred, possibly owing to the influence of Eadric Streona (now Ealdorman of Mercia). This ship levy being raised by a land-tax upon the whole country, and the Danegeld are noteworthy as the beginning of National taxation. Fresh attacks of the Danes.
1009-1012.	
	(6) Final attack of Swein upon England. **1013.** Flight of Æthelred to Normandy.
1014-1016.	**1014.** Death of Swein, and return of Æthelred. **1014.** Struggle between Cnut (son of Swein) and Æthelred, and desertion of Eadric Streona.
1016.	Death of Æthelred.

    b   Eadmund Ironside.

Eadmund Ironside = Ealdgyth.
                 |
    ┌─────────┴─────────┐
  Eadward.   Eadmund.

1016.	Fierce struggle between Eadmund and Cnut; final victory of Cnut at Assandun (in Essex). Division of England as in reign of Ælfred, Eadmund retaining Wessex and English Mercia. Death of Eadmund, and election of Cnut as King of all England. **1016.**
1016-1035. *c*	Cnut.

Ælfgifu of Northampton, = Cnut = Emma of Normandy,
daughter of Earl Ælfhelm. | widow of Æthelred.
                          |
                      Harthacnut. Gunhilda = Henry III.
                                              (Emperor).
┌─────┴─────┐
Swein.   Harald.

1017.	Eadwig (brother of Eadmund) and Eadric Streona killed by order of Cnut (the latter "very justly").
	Cnut's policy to make England the head and centre of a Northern Empire.
1018.	(1) Government according to national laws and customs. Eadgar's laws received both by Danes and English.
	(2) Local organisation retained, but central power strengthened. England divided into four Earldoms to supersede the Ealdormanries. The Earls nominees of the King. The King's chaplains formed into a body of clerks for administrative purposes.
1018.	(3) The greater part of Cnut's army dismissed, but the hus-carls retained as a permanent body-guard.
	(4) The foundation of religious houses, and encouragement of trade.
	(5) Foreign policy.
1027.	(*a*) Pilgrimage to Rome, to strengthen the bond between his new Empire and Western Christendom. Freedom from toll obtained for the Saxon School at Rome. Marriage of his daughter to Henry (afterwards Henry III., Emperor.)
1028.	(*b*) Conquest of Norway by Cnut, "with fifty ships of English Thegns."
1031.	(*c*) Malcolm II. King of Scots confirmed in possession of Lothian upon terms of homage.
1035.	(*d*) Cnut set free from fear of struggle with Normandy by the strife among the Norman nobles which followed upon the death of Duke Robert.
1035.	Death of Cnut.
1035-1042.	*d* Harald and Harthacnut.
1035.	Harthacnut supported by Earl Godwine from a wish to carry on Cnut's policy of a united Northern Empire. Harald, however, chosen as King at Oxford. Blinding of Ælfred
1036.	Ætheling on his visit to England from Normandy.
1037.	Supremacy of Harald and submission of Godwine.
1040.	Death of Harald.
1042.	Death of Harthacnut.

G The Eve of the Norman Conquest. 1042-1065.

I. Table of the Dukes of the Normans.

Hrolf, **911-927** (Land on either side Seine and the Bessin, *i.e.* the country round Bayeux.).

William Longsword, **927-943** the Cotentin (occupied by a colony of Danes) and the Channel Islands added.

Richard the Fearless **943-996** (gradual but complete change from a Norse settlement to a feudal Christian State).

Richard the Good, **996-1026**.   Emma = (1) Æthelred II. of England.
   = (2) Cnut of England and Denmark.

Richard III. **1026-1028**.   Robert the Magnificent, **1028-1035**.

William the Conqueror, **1035-1087**.

II. William of Normandy born **1027**.

1045. *a* Influence of Lanfranc, Prior of Bec, over William, dating from **1045**.

1047. *b* Victory of Val-ès-Dunes over the rebels of the Bessin and the Cotentin, and Establishment of William's power in Normandy.

1048. *c* William's assistance to French King against Geoffrey Martel of Anjou. Capture of Alençon and Domfront.

1049. *d* Proposed Marriage with Matilda of Flanders, forbidden by Council of Rheims (possibly owing to the prompting of Bishop Duduc of Wells, the English envoy) as against the law of the Church.

1051. *e* Visit to England. Alleged promise of succession from Eadward the Confessor.

1053. *f* Marriage with Matilda during the imprisonment of Leo IX. by the Normans in southern Italy, in spite of the veto of the Church.

1054.
1058. *g* Invasion of the French stopped by victory at Mortemer and of the French and Angevins by victory at Varaville, near Caen.

1060-1064. *h* Conquest of Maine.

ANALYSIS OF ENGLISH HISTORY. 19

1064 ? *i* Visit of Harold, who took part with William in his Breton War. Harold's pledge, possibly an engagement, to marry William's daughter, and doing of homage to him as his future father-in-law.

III. Family of Earl Godwine.

Godwine = Gytha.

Swein, Earl of Hereford, Gloucestershire, Earl of Somersetshire, Berkshire, and Oxfordshire. 1045.	Harold, Earl of East Anglia. 1045, then of Wessex. 1053.	Tostig, Earl of Northumbria and Northamptonshire. 1055.	Gyrth, Earl of East Angles. 1057.	Leofwine, Earl of Essex, Hertford, Bucks, Middlesex, Kent, Surrey. 1057.

Wulfnoth.	Eadgyth = Eadward the Confessor.	Gunhild.	Ælfgifu.

IV. Events of Eadward's reign.

1045. *a* Marriage of Eadward to Eadgyth, daughter of Godwine. Jealousy aroused by the supremacy
1048-1049. of Godwine and his family—all England S. of a line drawn from Bristol Channel to the Wash being in the hands of Godwine, Swein, Harold and Beorn (nephew of the wife of Earl Godwine)—increased by the crimes of Swein.

1050. *b* Strife between the King and Godwine about the primacy. Robert de Jumièges, a Norman,
1051. appointed. Marriage of Tostig, son of Godwine, to Judith, sister of Baldwin of Flanders.

1051. *c* Visit of Eustace of Boulogne (the King's brother-in-law). Riot at Dover. Refusal of Godwine to punish the town. Outlawry of Godwine, and visit of William of Normandy to England. Alleged promise of succession.

1052. *d* Restoration of Godwine and his family. Flight of Robert de Jumièges and "the Frenchmen" (Robert de Jumièges Archbishop of Canterbury and Ulf Bishop of Dorchester); Robert deposed from the Primacy by the Witan, and Stigand of Winchester appointed Archbishop.

1053. *e* Death of Earl Godwine.
1054. *f* Victory of Siward of Northumbria over Macbeth of Scotland.
1055. *g* Death of Siward. Tostig appointed Earl of Northumbria. Henceforth Northumbria fully absorbed into England.
1057. *h* Death of Eadward the Ætheling (son of Eadmund Ironside) in London. The possible commencement of Harold's designs upon the Crown.
1057. *i* Death of Leofric of Mercia, redistribution of Earldoms, Ælfgar (son of Leofric), Earl of the Mercians (succeeded by his son Eadwine, 1062); Herefordshire added to Harold's Earldom of Wessex; Gyrth, Earl of East Angles and Oxfordshire; Leofwine, Earl of Kent, Surrey, Hertfordshire, Bucks, and Essex. London not under any earl.
1063. *j* Invasion and ravaging of Wales by Harold. The dominions of Gruffydd of Wales divided among two of his kinsmen to be held as dependencies of the English crown.
1065. *k* Revolt of Northumbria against Tostig. Morkere (son of Ælfgar of Mercia, and brother of Eadwine) elected Earl. Banishment of Tostig. Waltheof made Earl of Northamptonshire in place of Tostig.
1065-1066. Consecration of Westminster Abbey and death of Eadward the Confessor.
1066. V. Harold = Eadgyth (sister of Eadwine and Morkere).

| Godwine. | Eadmund. | Magnus. | Gytha. | Gunhild. |

(Children of Harold and Eadgyth Swan-neck.)

JAN. 5-6. *a* Election and Coronation of Harold.
JAN. 15. *b* The right to present himself for election claimed by William of Normandy. His claim based partly upon his nearness of kin to Eadward, partly upon Eadward's bequest, partly upon Harold's alleged perjury.

c William's expedition against England sanctioned by Alexander II. as a crusade to reform the ecclesiastical abuses of England, especially the deposition of Robert de Jumièges and the appointment of Stigand.

May–Sept.	*d* Tostig's invasion of England with William's consent. Application for aid to Harald Hardrada of Norway. Defeat of Eadwine (of Mercia) and Morkere (of Northumbria) at Fulford, near York, by Harald Hardrada. Sept. **20**.
Sept. **25**.	*e* Victory of Harold over Tostig and Harald Hardrada at Stamford Bridge. Tostig and Harald Hardrada slain in the battle.
Sept. **27**.	*f* Sailing of William from S. Valery. Landing at Pevensey, Sept. **28**. Norman encampment at Hastings; and plundering of the country.
Oct. **1-5**. Oct. **5-11**.	*g* March of Harold from York to London. The army joined by men of Wessex, East Anglia, East Mercia, and Kent. (Half-heartedness of Eadwine and Morkere.)
Oct. **13**.	*h* Harold's encampment upon the Hill of Senlac to cover London and stop the Norman ravages.
Oct. **14**.	*i* The Battle of Senlac, and death of Harold.

VI. The Interregnum.

Oct. **15**– Nov. **1**.	*a* Election of the Ætheling Eadgar (grandson of Eadmund Ironside) as King by a Gemót in London upon the news of the defeat. Withdrawal of their forces from London by Eadwine and Morkere.
Oct. **20**.	*b* Occupation by William of Romney, "quam placuit poenam exegit pro clade suorum."
Oct. **21**– Oct. **29**.	*c* Surrender of Dover to William. Dover town accidentally burned, compensation given by William for the damage.
Oct. **29**.	*d* Surrender of Canterbury.
Nov.	*e* Sickness of William at Canterbury. Submission of Winchester.
Dec.	*f* March upon London, Dec. **1**. Burning of Southwark; march of William up the right bank of the Thames and crossing of the river at Wallingford; northward march to Berkhampstead in Hertfordshire.
	g Submission of Eadger Ætheling, Ealdred Archbishop of York, Wulfstan Bishop of Worcester and others to William at Berkhampstead. Invitation to William to assume the crown.
Dec. **25**.	*h* Coronation of William as elected King of England by Ealdred Archbishop of York. Alarm of the Norman guard and burning of the houses round the West Minster.

1066-1087. WILLIAM THE CONQUEROR. 1066-1087.

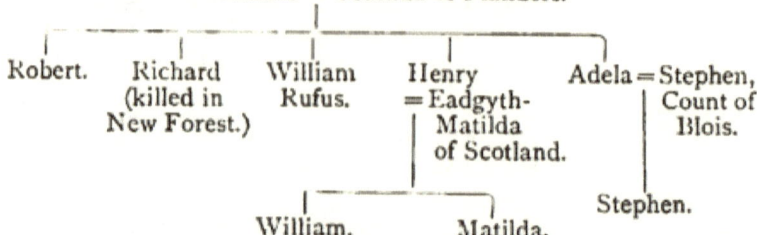

1067-1071. A The Completion of the Conquest.

MARCH-DEC. 1067.
1. Oppressive government of the Regents (Odo and William Fitz-Osbern) during William's absence in Normandy.

DEC. 1067-FEB. 1068.
2. The conquest of the West. DEC. 1067-MARCH 1068. Offer of Exeter, where Gytha (Harold's mother) had found refuge, to pay tribute while retaining the independence of the town. Capture of Exeter.

1068.
3. First conquest of Central and Northern England. Submission of Eadwine and Morkere. SUMMER and AUTUMN.

1069-1070.
4. The revolt and final conquest of the North.

AUTUMN 1069.
(1) Arrival of assistance to English and Eadgar Ætheling from Swein of Denmark. English capture of York and massacre of Normans.

(2) Movements against the Normans in the West, and on the Welsh border.

(3) The Danish fleet bribed by William to withdraw.

WINTER 1069.
(4) The harrying of the country by William from York to the Tees.

FEB. 1070.
(5) Capture of Chester and harrying of Cheshire.

1070-1071.
5. The revolt of the Fen country, gallant resistance of Hereward. Revolt of Eadwine and Morkere. Death of Eadwine, submission and imprisonment of Morkere.

1068.
1070.
1072.
6. Reception of Eadgar Ætheling and his sisters, Margaret and Christina, by Malcolm III. of Scotland. Marriage of Malcolm to Margaret leading to a plundering expedition into England and a counter expedition of William into Scotland, upon which Malcolm swore fealty to William at Abernethy.

7. William's conquests consolidated by building castles and planting Norman garrisons, *e.g.*, Exeter, Warwick, Nottingham, York, Lincoln, Cambridge, Huntingdon, Pontefract, Chester, Stafford.

1074.   7. Eadgar Ætheling received by William in Normandy.

B Feudalism.

1. Origin of Feudalism on the Continent. Feudalism as a system arose from the union of the personal tie of commendation and the beneficiary grant of lands.

   a The practice of "commendation," at first a purely personal relation between the weaker and the stronger implying no change in the ownership of land, but consisting of an act of homage and oath of fealty.

   b The system of "beneficia" *i.e.* (1) Lands granted by the Kings out of their own estates; (2) "Alodial" estates surrendered by lesser to more powerful proprietors and received back by their original possessors as tenants. Both classes of "beneficia" were commonly held upon terms of military tenure.

   To this must be added:—

   c The grant of powers of full jurisdiction within the "beneficium" which was thus withdrawn from any national judicial system.

2. Traces of Feudalism in England before the Conquest.

cc. 700-800.   *a* Creation of a nobility of service enriched by grants from the Folkland. (The "Gesith" passing into the "Thegn.")

925-950.   *b* Every landless man to be under the protection of a lord.

900-950.   *c* Growth of a military aristocracy, and gradual disappearance of the "ceorl" or freeman; land being held more and more under military service. (The "ceorl" passing into the "villein.")

cc. 958, cc. 1045.   *d* Rise of the great "ealdormen," then of the great earls.

3. William the Conqueror and Feudalism.

   a Vast confiscation consequent upon the English resistance. The soil largely occupied by the Normans on condition of military service.

        b William's checks upon the Norman Baronage.
          i. The great earldoms suppressed.
          ii. The Sheriff of each shire nominated by the King.
          iii. The estates of a great noble not continuous but scattered over different parts of the country. Only Kent, Cheshire, Durham, (and practically Shropshire), left as counties Palatine for the sake of the national defence.
          iv. The old courts (*e.g.*, the Hundred Court and the Shire Court) maintained so as to prevent military rule and to secure central judicial authority.

1085-1086.   v. The extent and value of all royal dues from property ascertained by Domesday Book.

1086.   vi. Under-tenants as well as tenants-in-chief did homage to the King personally for their holdings, and became the King's men. AUGUST 1.

C William and the Church.
1070.   I. Lanfranc made archbishop in place of Stigand. Co-operation of Lanfranc and William in carrying out the reforms of Gregory VII. with regard to the celibacy of the Clergy and the suppression of Simony.
      II. English Bishops and Abbots replaced by learned foreigners.
      III. Opposition of William to Gregory's claim of papal supremacy.
        a Oath of fealty to the pope refused. **1077-1078.**
        b No royal tenant to be excommunicated without the King's leave.
        c No synod to legislate without the King's previous assent and subsequent sanction.
        d No papal letters to be received in the realm except with the King's permission.
      IV. Establishment of distinct ecclesiastical courts for ecclesiastical cases, whereas till now bishop and ealdorman or sheriff had presided jointly in the Shire Court to declare law in spiritual and civil cases.

D William and the Norman Barons.
1073.   1. Revolt of Maine suppressed by William at the head of a force largely composed by English.

1075.	2. Rising of Roger, Earl of Hereford, and Ralph, Earl of Norfolk, to restore the system of the great earldoms. Confession of complicity made before the outbreak of the rising by Waltheof, Earl of Northumberland (the last great English noble left). Aid sought by the rebel earls from Denmark. Trial and unjust execution of Waltheof.
1076.	
1077-1080.	3. Revolt of William's eldest son Robert, claiming to be Duke of Normandy in his father's lifetime. Battle of Gerberoi, and reconciliation between William and Robert.
1082.	4. Pride and oppression of Odo, Bishop of Bayeux and Earl of Kent, who was aspiring to the papacy and collecting money and arms. Arrested not as Bishop but as Earl of Kent. [After the death of Odo Kent ceased to be a county Palatine.]
1080. 1081.	5. Security gained upon the Scottish and Welsh marches by the foundation of Newcastle-upon-Tyne, and by a Welsh campaign. [Beginning of the severe Forest laws **1069**, and making of the New Forest by the devastation of thirty miles of country (between **1071** and **1080**)].

E The King's Last Years.

1083.	1. Death of Matilda and of his son Richard.
1083-1085	2. Great invasion of England planned by Saint Cnut, King of Denmark; the Danegeld reimposed (**1084**) and the sea-coast laid waste by William as precautionary measures. The danger removed by a mutiny in the Danish fleet and the murder of Saint Cnut.
1085.	
1086.	
MIDWINTER. 1085.	3. William induced by this danger to order a great survey of the kingdom. Domesday Book.

    a The inquiry conducted upon the oaths of the men of each district, French and English, (*i.e.* the sheriffs and barons, the parish-priest, reeve, and six villeins of each township) to discover the extent of each holding in the reign of Eadward and in that of William, and the title by which it was held.

        (1) To see that the Danegeld of **1084** had been duly paid.

        (2) To register the King's grants of land, and to ascertain the military strength and financial resources of the country.

	b The King considered by the Survey as the grantor of all land.
1086.	*c* Great Gemót on Salisbury plain on the conclusion of the Survey. All landholders "whose men so ever they were" obliged to pay homage to the King and so become "his men." AUG. 1.
1097. 4.	War with France as to the possession of the Vexin, and death of the King.
AUGUST.	*a* Invasion of the Vexin by King William, and burning of Mantes where the King received his death-wound.
SEPT.	*b* Death of the King. SEPT. 9. Desertion of the dead body. Strange scene at the funeral.

F Effects of the Norman Conquest.

1. England brought into contact with the Romance speaking nations of the Continent. Till now so far as English isolation had been broken it had been by a Scandinavian connexion.

2. Strengthening of the power of the Roman see over the English Church and nation (*e.g.* the struggle between Henry I. and Anselm as to the right of Investiture, and the commencement of the practice of appeals to Rome.) [An illustration of both these tendencies (1 and 2) may be seen in the share taken by England in the Crusades. (Robert of Normandy, **1096.** The Saladin Tithe, **1188.** Richard I., **1189-1192.** Richard of Cornwall, **1240.** Edward, **1268.**)]

3. Introduction of foreign prelates and consequent claim for the exemption of churchmen from the jurisdiction of the national courts. [Growth of English canon law from the reign of Henry III. to that of Henry VIII.]

4. Effect upon language.

	a French the home-speech of the higher ranks, English of the lower. Latin the official language.
1100-1215.	
1215-1363.	*b* Use of French in official documents (French being used as the most common language among nobles and statesmen, and being no longer considered as a mark of a foreign
1268.	conqueror). The Provisions of Oxford published in Latin, French, and English.

1349-1363. *c* English taught in schools; pleading in the higher courts of law conducted in English.
1380-1400. Rise of "the King's English" as the literary standard.

    d The final effect upon the English language was to destroy inflexions, to introduce an infusion of French words, to entail the loss of the power of making new native words, but to leave the bulk of the vocabulary and the spirit of the grammar English not French.

5. Increase of the royal power. The King not only universal ruler, but universal landlord (see above). This increase necessitated the building up of an elaborate administrative system.

6. Introduction of the Jews not as citizens of the country but as the King's chattels, subject at will to tallage but under the King's protection as regarding all but himself.

7. The Norman Conquest and villenage.

    [*a* The word "villenage" often ambiguously used as implying (i.) land tenure by customary service; (ii.) dependent personal status of tenant.]

    b The origin of villenage as a mode of land tenure may possibly be traced in the servile holdings of the conquered British, especially in the west and south-west where the progress of the English Conquest was milder and more gradual.

    c The origin of villenage as implying inferiority of personal status may be traced in the legislation due to the pressure of the Danish invaders and conquerors that every man have a lord.

TENTH CENTURY.

    d Direct effect of the Norman Conquest.
Dependent free men, or men holding land by customary tenure (villani) gradually confounded with men personally unfree (servi), partly owing to the increase of feudal principles which followed upon the Conquest, partly from the carelessness of the Normans in discriminating between the degrees of English dependence. Thus the dependent free man (villanus) lost, while eventually the serf (servus) gained.

TWELFTH CENTURY.
 e By **1100** the position of the tillers of the land was that of "irremovable cultivators," under the power of a lord, although under the protection of the law with regard to all other oppression. The power of the lord, though great, was limited; the villein had his house, his land, certain customary rights on his lord's demesne, and an appeal against him in the King's Court.

 f Subsequent mitigations of villenage.

FROM **1159**.
  i. Commutation of customary service for money rent as proprietors found a need of money to meet the demand of scutage.

EDWARD THIRD.
  ii. As armies ceased to be feudal and became raised by contract serfs often gained admission into them, and at the end of their service got some wage-paid labour.

  iii. A residence of a year and a day in a chartered town conferred freedom (if no claim was made meanwhile by the lord).

  iv. The influence of the Church in preaching the duty of manumission and in admitting the sons of villeins into orders. (An attempt to stop this latter made by the Constitutions of Clarendon, **1164**.)

1348-1349.
 g This movement towards freedom checked by the Black Death. (See Richard II., Peasant Revolt.)

1087-1100.   **WILLIAM RUFUS. 1087-1100.**

1. Conspiracy of Norman nobles (including Odo, now released from prison, and Roger, Earl of Shrewsbury) against William, in favour of his elder brother Robert, crushed by the loyalty of the English to William and largely by means of an English force.

1088.

1089. 2. Death of Archbishop Lanfranc. Rise of Flambard, afterwards Bishop of Durham, as the King's adviser (appointed Justicier, **1094**.) Flambard's policy;

 a To strengthen the central power and create a royal revenue by imposing heavy feudal obligations and dues on the nobles.

 b To keep vacant sees empty and confiscate the revenues to the royal revenue.

1089-1091. 3. Foreign wars of William for the possession of Normandy and Maine; Treaty of Caen between William and Robert that on the death of either the whole of his dominion should pass to his surviving brother.

1091.

1091-1092. 4. Renewal of homage by Malcolm, annexation of Northern Cumberland, restoration of Carlisle (destroyed by the Danes, c. 877), and transportation of peasants from the South of England to people the country.

1093. 5. William's illness at Gloucester. Anselm appointed to the see of Canterbury, vacant since death of Lanfranc.

1095. 6. Defeat of Robert Mowbray, Earl of Northumberland, and capture of Bamborough Castle. Campaign in North Wales.

1096. 7. Departure of Robert of Normandy on the First Crusade. The Duchy of Normandy mortgaged to William for £6,000.

1097. 8. Quarrel between William and Anselm as to the right of investing bishops, and as to the recognition of Urban II. as Pope in opposition to Clement, who was supported as anti-Pope by the Emperor Henry IV. Departure of Anselm and seizure of the estates of his see by the King. Building of Westminster Hall. Campaign in Wales, the border strengthened with castles.

1098. 9. Edgar, son of Malcolm, made King of Scotland as an English vassal.

1100. 10. Death of William in the New Forest.

1100-1135.   **HENRY I., 1100-1135.**

Eadgyth-Matilda of Scotland. = Henry. = Adeliza of Louvain.

William.   Henry V. = Matilda = Geoffrey of Anjou.
            Henry II.

Descent of Matilda of Scotland from Eadmund Ironside.

Eadmund Ironside.

Eadmund.   Eadward.

Eadgar Ætheling.   Margaret. = Malcolm   Christina.
                              of Scotland.

Eadgyth-Matilda.

A 1100-1106. Establishment of Henry upon the Throne.

1100.
1. Charter of Liberties issued, renouncing the evil customs of the last reign, *e.g.* the excessive exactions from the feudal baronage, and the delay of election to vacant sees. Imprisonment of Flambard. Recall of Anselm. Marriage to Eadgyth, her name changed to Matilda.

1101.
2. Henry thrown upon the English for support against his brother Robert, who claiming the fulfilment of the terms of the Treaty of Caen invaded England with the acquiescence of the Feudal Baronage (possibly wishing to retain their estates in England and Normandy), and

1102.
against Robert of Belesme, Earl of Shrewsbury, Robert's chief partisan, **1104**; banishment of William of Mortain, nephew of Odo of Kent.

1106.
Battle of Tenchebrai, capture and imprisonment of Robert till his death (**1134**) and conquest of Normandy.

1102.
3. Synod of Westminster, including laymen as well as clerics, called by Anselm; celibacy made binding on all churchmen of the rank of sub-deacon and upwards; decree passed condemning the Slave Trade. Contest between the King and Anselm on the question of

1103-1107.
investitures. Final settlement that the investiture of a bishop was to come from the Pope, but homage was to be done by the bishop, as

1107.
by a feudal baron, to the King.

B Henry's Rule.

1. Growth of an official administrative nobility.
   - (*a*) The Justiciar: the King's chief agent, and his representative in his absence. At first the office confined to ecclesiastics.
   - (*b*) The Chancellor: the head of the clerks of the Chapel Royal who had gradually been formed, dating from the reign of Cnut, into a body of royal secretaries.
   - (*c*) The Treasurer: who received the accounts of the sheriffs.
   - (*d*) The Chamberlain: auditor in chief.

   Contrast with these *ministerial* offices of State the *feudal* or Court offices of High Steward, Constable, and Marshal.

2. The great officers of state, and others summoned by the King, formed into a Supreme Court of the Realm, "Curia Regis."

(*a*) To act as a Royal Council to revise, register and attest laws.

(*b*) To act as the highest Court of Appeal.

(*c*) To assess and collect Royal Revenue, and to make visitations of the Shires to settle disputes as to assessment. In this capacity known as Court of Exchequer.

The sources of Royal Revenue at this time were:—

a Danegeld or Land-Tax.

b The rent from the Royal domains in the Shires.

c Fines proceeding from the King's pleas in the local courts.

d Feudal reliefs and aids.

C Progress of the Nation.

1. Grant of charters to towns situated in the royal demesne, securing exemption from jurisdiction of the sheriff (*i.e.*, freedom to raise their own taxation, and, in the case of London, freedom from immediate jurisdiction of any tribunal not of their own appointing).

2. Similar but slower advance in towns not situated in the royal demesne (*e.g.*, S. Edmundsbury).

3. Survival of old English traditions of freedom (free right of meeting, condemnation or acquittal by oath of neighbours).

4. Disappearance of slavery; but gradually increasing depression of the condition of the "villani," the ancient "ceorls" or freemen.

1128-1132. 5. Introduction of the Cistercian order into England, and foundation of Cistercian monasteries (*e.g.* Fountains Abbey.)

D Events between 1107 and 1120.

1111-1113. 1. War of Gisors between Henry and Lewis VI. (the Fat) of France; final imprisonment by
1112. Henry of Robert of Belesme; peace of Gisors,
1113. homage paid to Henry by Fulk of Anjou for Maine.

1114. 2. Marriage of Matilda, Henry's daughter to the Emperor Henry V. Expedition of Henry to Wales (repeated successfully in **1121**).

1116–1120. 3. War against Baldwin of Flanders and Lewis VI., supporters of William the Clito (son of Robert of Normandy).

1119. 4. Marriage of William, the King's son, to Matilda of Anjou.

1120–1135. **E Difficulties of Succession.**

1120. 1. Loss of the King's son William at sea and extinction of the Conqueror's male line.

1121. 2. Henry's second marriage to Adeliza of Louvain.

1123.
1125. 3. William the Clito again supported as heir to the crown by Lewis VI. of France, Fulk of Anjou, and Norman barons. Death of the Emperor Henry V.

1126. 4. Exaction of oath of fealty from the barons to Matilda as future Queen. Marriage of Matilda
1128. to Geoffrey the heir of Anjou to detach him from William the Clito. Discontent of Norman barons—

    a at the novelty of female succession;
    b at the prospect of an Angevin ruler;
    c at the marriage being effected without assent of the baronage.

1128. 6. Death of William the Clito in Flanders.

1125–1135. 7. Discontent of the people at the strictness of the royal taxation, increased by the famines and calamities that prevailed during the last ten years of the reign.

1135. 8. Intrigues of Geoffrey with the Norman barons to secure Normandy for himself. Death of the King.

1135–1154. **STEPHEN. 1135–1154.**

Genealogical Table.

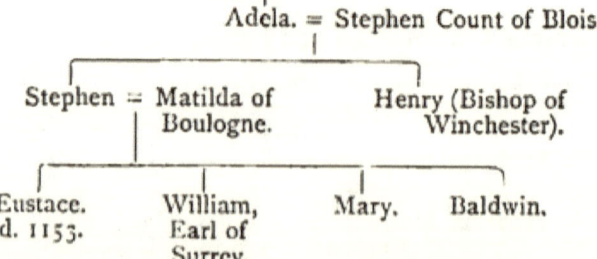

1135-1139. A Accession of Stephen, the Scottish Wars, and the Beginnings of Misrule.

1135. 1. Stephen, the nearest male heir after his brother Theobald, elected King by "the Aldermen and wise folk of London," owing to the fear of Angevin (*i.e.* foreign) rule.

1135. 2. Invasion of Normandy by Geoffrey of Anjou. War with Geoffrey till **1137**.

1136. 3. Issue of a charter by Stephen at Oxford basing his claim upon his ecclesiastical rather than civil election, upon his consecration and the confirmation by the Pope.

1136. 4. Invasion of England by David of Scotland the uncle of the Empress Matilda. Carlisle and Cumberland ceded to David.

1138. 5. Second invasion of England by David. The Scots defeated by the barons and commons of the North at Northallerton, in the battle of the Standard.

1138. 6. Defiance of Stephen by Robert of Gloucester, brother of the Empress Matilda, at Bristol. The beginnings of the misrule;

> *a* Introduction of Flemish mercenaries by Stephen.
>
> *b* Creation of fiscal earldoms by Stephen, *i.e.* earldoms supported by grants from the treasury.
>
> *c* Building of castles at their pleasure by the barons (the number of these "adulterine," *i.e.* unlicensed, castles amounting before **1154** to the probable number of 375).

1139. *d* Arrest of the Justiciar (Roger, Bishop of Salisbury), and of his nephew Alexander (Bishop of Lincoln), and seizure of their castles. Nigel, Bishop of Ely, (also a nephew of the Justiciar,) driven from his post as treasurer. Collapse of the administrative system established by Henry I. and alienation of the Church.

1139. 7. Henry of Scotland, son of David, invested with the Earldom of Northumberland with the exception of Newcastle, Bamborough, and the Church lands of Durham and York.

1139-1153. B The Civil War.

 1139-1145. 1. Gradual Conquest of Normandy by Geoffrey of Anjou.

 Sept. 1139. 2. Landing of the Empress Matilda and Robert of Gloucester at Portsmouth.

 1141. 3. Capture of Stephen at Lincoln. Election of Matilda at Winchester as "Lady of England," with the support of Henry, Bishop of Winchester, Stephen's brother.

 1141. 4. Refusal of Matilda to grant the Londoners their customary privileges, "the laws of King Eadward", and quarrel with Henry Bishop of Winchester. Flight of the Empress Matilda to Oxford; Capture of Robert of Gloucester and exchange with Stephen. Siege of Oxford by Stephen and escape of the Empress.

 1143. 5. Matilda supported by the West of England, Stephen by London, and the East.

 1147. 6. Death of Robert of Gloucester, and withdrawal
 1148. of the Empress to Normandy.

 1147-1152. 7. Pause of five years in the war. All country north of Tyne in the hands of the Scots. The rest of the North of England in the power of the Earl of Chester and the Earl of Aumâle.

 1152. 8. Refusal of Archbishop Theobald to accept Eustace, Stephen's son, as King along with his father.

 1153. 9. Landing of Henry, son of the Empress Matilda, in England.

 1153. 10. Conference between Stephen and Henry at Wallingford, death of Eustace, and Treaty concluded at Winchester securing the destruction of the "adulterine" castles, the dismissal of the Flemish mercenaries, the recognition of Henry as heir to the crown.

 1154. 11. Death of Stephen.

  C The Church.

   1. Three great schools or divisions of the higher clergy.

    a The official administrative clergy, *e.g.*, Roger of Salisbury.

    b The ecclesiastical professional clergy, *e.g.*, Henry of Winchester.

    c The devotional spiritual clergy, *e.g.* Anselm.

ANALYSIS OF ENGLISH HISTORY. 35

2 The power of the Church as the one organized body shown in the alternate depositions of Stephen and Matilda (**1141**) and in the arrangement of the Treaty of Wallingford. (**1153**.)

3. Revival of religious devotion throughout the nation commencing in the reign of Henry I. and due largely, especially in the north, to the efforts of the Cistercian monks. One hundred and fifteen monasteries built during Stephen's reign; one hundred and thirteen more in that of Henry II.

1154–1189.   **HENRY II. 1154–1189.**

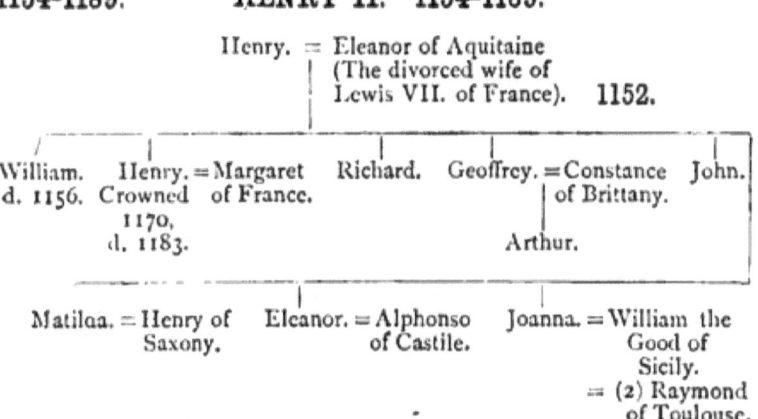

Two distinguished illegitimate sons, William, Earl of Salisbury, and Geoffrey, Bishop of Lincoln and Chancellor, afterwards Archbishop of York.

A **Henry as an English King.** His policy all through his reign to establish a strong kingly rule, administered by royal servants, over all orders and classes.

1154–1158.   I. Restoration of order in the land.

    1154. *a* Appointment of Thomas Becket as Chancellor to co-operate in the work.

        b Banishment of foreign mercenaries, restoration of "Curia Regis" and exchequer (under the Justiciar De Lucy and the Chancellor Thomas), demolition of the "adulterine" castles, resumption of royal demesne which had been alienated, displacement, in part at least, of the "fiscal" earls, and reform of the coinage.

D 2

1155. *c* Submission of the Count of Aumâle, of Roger of Hereford, Hugh Mortimer, William of Warrenne, Hugh Bigod. Homage paid by
1157. Malcolm IV. and surrender by him of Northumberland and Cumberland. Expeditions into
1157–1158. Wales.

1162–1170. II. Extension of central authority over the Church.

a Appointment of Thomas Becket as Archbishop:
1162. Becket's resignation of the Chancellorship: Resistance of Becket to a change in the collection of the land-tax proposed by the King: Refusal of Becket to submit criminous clerks
1163. to the punishment of the lay courts.

b The "customs" of Henry I. upon disputed points
1164. between Church and State codified in the Constitutions of Clarendon (near Salisbury).

(1) In bulk a re-enactment of the previous system of William I. and Henry I.

(*a*) No tenant-in-capite to be excommunicated save by the King's leave.

(*b*) No bishop to leave the country without the King's permission.

(*c*) Election of bishops and abbots to take place before Justiciar or officer appointed by the King, in the King's chapel, and with the King's consent (a survival possibly of the English practice of nominating the bishops in the Witan).

(*d*) Bishops to do homage to the King and hold their lands from him.

(2) Special clauses with reference to ecclesiastical jurisdiction.

(*a*) In the case of a suit between a clerk and a layman the decision whether it belong to the King's Courts or to the Church Courts to rest with the "Curia Regis."

(*b*) Clerics accused of a crime, to appear first in the King's Court; a royal officer to watch the proceedings in the Church Court; clerks after conviction and degradation in their own courts to be handed over for punishment to the lay courts.

(*c*) An appeal from Archbishop's Court to "Curia Regis," but not beyond, without the King's assent.

(*d*) The Sheriff and a jury of twelve legal men of the vicinity to assist the Ecclesiastical Courts in criminal causes or in cases of disputed claims to land.

(*e*) No villein's son to be admitted into orders without his lord's consent.

1164-1170. *c* Contest between the King and Becket.

1164. 1. Retractation by Becket of the consent he had given to the Constitutions: charges of embezzlement while Chancellor (**1154-1162**) brought against him at Northampton.

1166. 2. Bitter contest from **1164** to **1170**. Becket appointed Papal Legate for England.

1170. 3. Coronation of the King's son Henry by the Archbishop of York. Reconciliation of the King and Becket, and return of Becket to England; excommunication by Becket of the Bishops who had taken part in the coronation.

Murder of Becket DEC. **29, 1170**.

III. Extension of central authority over the Baronage.

1157. *a* Every two knights bound to service ordered to furnish for the Welsh campaign one knight to serve in their place as long as the King required.

1159. Scutage introduced in the war of Toulouse. (A tax of two marks on the knight's fee accepted as commutation of personal military service.) The King was thus provided with means to raise a hired army *for foreign war*.

1170. *b* The Inquest of Sheriffs upon Henry's return from his long absence. **1166-1170**. The office of Sheriff transferred from the feudal nobility to officers of the King's Court. ["Such an act of absolute authority had no example in the history of Europe since the time of the Roman Empire, except possibly in the power wielded by Charles the Great."]

1173. *c* Revolt of the young King Henry supported by France, Scotland, and the counts of Flanders, Blois, and Boulogne: rising of Richard commander of the forces in Aquitaine, and Geoffrey lord of Britanny (at the instigation of their mother Queen Eleanor), and of discontented Feudal Baronage in England.

JULY 12, 1174. (1) Public penance of Henry at the tomb of Becket; defeat and capture of Scotch King, William the Lion, at Alnwick by the
JULY 13.   Justiciar, Ranulf de Glanvil. Dispersion of the French and Flemish Fleet which was lying off Gravelines for the invasion of Kent.

1174. (2) Submission of the revolters in England. JULY.

(3) The end of the revolt abroad. Submission of Henry's sons at Gisors. SEPT.

(4) Acknowledgment of English suzerainty over Scotland: English garrisons in chief Scottish fortresses. Queen Eleanor remained confined as a close prisoner. DEC.

d Demolition of castles held against the King, and exaction of oath of fealty from all classes at
1176.   the Assize of Northampton.
1181. *e* The Assize of Arms. Every freeman to bear arms according to his means. Re-organization of the old English "fyrd." The armed force of the whole nation thus placed at the King's disposal for war *at home*, while scutage made him independent of the barons for war *abroad*.

IV. Legal reforms.

1166. *a* The Assize of Clarendon.

1. Revival of the system of frankpledge: sureties to be given for the good behaviour of strangers.

2. Twelve lawful men from each hundred and four from each township to present reputed criminals in the county court to the sheriff for trial by ordeal. Abolition of compurgation by the oath of neighbours.

Development of the Jury System.

1. First used in England as a means of collecting correct information (as in **1070** to discover the ancient customs, and in the Domesday Survey, **1086**, to discover the extent and liabilities of estates). Probably adopted by the Normans from the Inquisitiones of the Frankish k'ngs.

2. By the Great Assize (between **1154** and **1164**) the recognition of twelve sworn knights was admitted as an alternative for trial by battle to settle disputed claims to land (the origin of the civil jury).

3. The jury for the presentment of reputed criminals established by this Assize of Clarendon. **1166.**

4. Abolition of ordeal by the Lateran Council. **1216.** Establishment of a second jury ("petty jury") to confirm or disallow the presentment of the first jury ("grand jury").

5. Addition to the sworn jurors of persons well acquainted with the particular matter in hand (Edward I.).

6. Severance of these two classes of jurors, the additional jurors becoming sworn witnesses, the original jurors becoming judges of the fact after hearing evidence (Edward IV.).

1170. *b* The Inquest of Sheriffs. Officials of Exchequer appointed as sheriffs.

1176. *c* The Assize of Northampton (at the close of the revolt of **1173**).

(1) Division of England into six circuits, primarily for financial purposes, each with three justices representing the Court of "our sovereign lord the King."

(2) Less power placed in the power of the sheriff, and more in those of the justice, and abolition of feudal exemptions from the jurisdiction of the justices.

(3) Oath of fealty exacted from all classes.

1178. *d* The number of justices sitting in "Curia Regis" limited from eighteen to five, two clerks and and three laymen. The "King's Bench" thus separated as a Committee of "Curia Regis." Before long the name of "Curia Regis" was exclusively applied to this new Court of Appeal. A further appeal from this Court of King's Bench to the King himself in Council.

Table illustrating the development of the "King's Courts."

The King's Council of Magnates with the right to advise the King on Questions of Policy.

- Great or Common Council to which all Magnates who could conveniently come were summoned (developing afterwards into the Parliament of the Nation).
- Permanent or Continual Council:—
  i. Called Curia Regis, or Aula Regia.
  ii. Composed of great Officers of State, e.g. Justiciar, Chancellor, Treasurer, Chamberlain, The Earl Marshal, Constable; of the two Archbishops; of any others whom the King wished to appoint.
  iii. Its powers.
      a. Executive.
      b. Partially legislative.
      c. Judicial, gradually separated into

A
Judicial powers delegated to separate Committees or Courts.

- Court of Exchequer to receive taxes and decide Placita de Scaccario (Revenue Cases).
  - Under Chief Baron (Ed. I.)
- King's Bench of 5 Judges, for Placita Regis (1178).
  - Under Chief Justice (Ed. I.)
- Court of Common Pleas for Placita Communia (Cases between subjects) fixed at Westminster (1215)
  - Under Chief Justice of Common Pleas (Ed. I.)
- The Chancellor in his Court of Chancery for Cases of Equity, "When there was too great might on the one side, and unmight on the other," or where the technical rules of law did not apply. (Ed. III, c. 1256).

These four Courts (Exchequer, King's Bench, Common Pleas, Chancery) now consolidated into the Supreme Court of Judicature.

- High Court of Justice.
  a. Chancery division.
  b. Queen's } Bench division.
     King's
  c. Probate division.

Court of Appeal.

B
Judicial and appellate power retained by Council whence sprang

a. Star Chamber.
b. Council of North.
c. Council of Wales.
d. The existing Judicial Committee of the Privy Council, representing the *decisions* of the King on the *advice* of his Council upon cases connected with—
   a. Education.
   b. Ecclesiastical
   c. Colonial   } Matters.
   d. Indian

ANALYSIS OF ENGLISH HISTORY. 41

1181-1189. B **The last years of the King's reign.**
- **1183.** 1. Death of the young King Henry while in revolt against his father.
- **1187.** 2. Capture of Jerusalem by Saladin. Imposition of
- **1188.** the Saladin Tithe, the first tax levied upon personal property.
- **1189.** 3. The last revolt of the King's sons, supported by Philip Augustus of France. Death of Henry.

C **Henry as a foreign King.**
1. Duke of Normandy, Count of Anjou, Maine and Touraine, Count of Poitou, Duke of Aquitaine, Suzerain Lord of Britanny. Anjou, Maine and Touraine derived from his father Geoffrey. Normandy from his mother Matilda. Poitou, Aquitaine, and Gascony from his wife Eleanor. Britanny further secured by the marriage of his son Geoffrey to Constance, daughter of Conan IV. native prince of Britanny.
2. His possessions, large though they were, and though he tried to add to them the county of Toulouse, **1159**, and Wales, were held together by no common bond of language or nationality.
3. From the foreign policy of Henry II. can be dated the beginning of the hostility between England and France, and of the sympathy between England and her mediæval allies— The Empire, Spain, Flanders—(in spite of the share taken by the Count of Flanders in the revolt of **1173**).

D **Henry and the Conquest of Ireland.**
- 1. Conversion of Ireland by S. Patrick and possible
- c **432.** codification of the Brehon Law.
- **600-800.** 2. Period of activity of Irish missionaries and renown of Irish monastic schools.
- **852.** 3. Descent of the Ost-men. Settlements made in Dublin, Wexford, Waterford; but Irish life in the main unaffected.
- **1000.** 4. Temporary union of the Irish under Brian Boru against the Ost-men. Irish victory at Clontarf,
- **1014.** and death of Brian Boru. Power of the Ost-men weakened but not destroyed.
- 5. Five great Irish Provinces or Kingdoms: Ulster, Meath, Leinster, Munster, Connaught.
- 6. Amongst distinctive Irish customs are to be noticed,

(*a*) Tanistry, by which the succession to the chieftaincy of a tribe or of a sept devolved upon the eldest and most worthy of the same blood.

(*b*) Gavelkind, by which upon the death of a member of the sept a fresh division of the land of the sept was made.

(*c*) Coshery and Bonaght: Coshery being a practice of the chiefs analogous to the English "purveyance"; Bonaght being the right of the chiefs to quarter their fighting men upon the people.

(*d*) Gorsipred, *i.e.* Compaternity, and Fosterage "a stronger alliance than blood."

(*e*) The independence of the Irish Church with regard to the Pope.

1152. 7. Four archbishops appointed over Ireland in order to bring Ireland into closer connection with the Roman See.

1155. 8. The Bull of Adrian IV. (an English Pope), handing over the sovereignty of Ireland to Henry II. in exchange for the payment of Peter's Pence. Henry dissuaded from the Conquest of Ireland largely by the influence of his mother, the Empress Matilda.

1166. 9. Flight of Diarmait Mac Murchadha, King of Leinster, to Henry in Aquitaine, requesting restoration to his kingdom, and paying homage for it.

1160-1170. 10. Landing of Robert FitzStephen, Maurice FitzGerald, and Richard de Clare, Earl of Pembroke, in Ireland. Conquest of the S.E. seaboard of Ireland and defeat of a fleet of Northmen. Death of Diarmait and succession **1171.** of Richard de Clare as Earl of Leinster.

1171-1172. 11. Landing of Henry II. in Ireland. Henry acknowledged as Lord of Ireland. Attempt at a permanent settlement of the Island. Henry recalled by the troubles which led to the revolt of **1173**. [For two hundred years no English King set foot in Ireland.]

1185. 12. Second attempt of Henry at a permanent settlement in Ireland. His son John formally appointed as King, and sent over. The invaders by this time divided into three hostile groups —the Normans, the English, and the men of the Welsh Border. Refusal of the native princes, irritated by John's arrogance and petulance, to do fealty to him. Departure of John from Ireland. The English power limited to the Pale with Dublin as its centre and fluctuating boundaries, which fell back rather than advanced.

1189-1199.   **RICHARD LION HEART. 1189-1199.**

Richard = Berengaria of Navarre.

In one sense he can hardly count as an English King, as he was only five months in England, Sept.-Dec., **1189**, and March 13-May 12, **1194**.

1189. Sale of offices, fortresses, charters (as Winchester and Lincoln), and of the supremacy over Scotland, to raise money for the Third Crusade.

1189. Hugh Puiset, Bishop of Durham, and William Longchamp, Bishop of Ely, left as regents. Exactions and arrogance of Longchamp; the feeling against him increased by the intrigues of John. Arrival of Walter de Coutances, Arch-
1191. bishop of Rouen, with full powers from Richard. Exile of Longchamp.

1192. Richard's return and seizure by the Duke of Austria. Imprisonment. Rebellion of John supported by Philip Augustus of France. Richard released upon payment of ransom and
1194. doing homage to the Emperor.

1194. Suppression of John's rebellion. Second Coronation. War with Philip of France. Money raised to hire mercenaries by Hubert Walter, Archbishop and Justiciar.

The importance of this period upon self-government shown by the employment of the jury system to assess the taxes; the basing of the grand jury of each county upon the choice of elected knights; the removal of the King's pleas from the hands of the sheriff to those of the coroner—an officer elected in county court; and by the rising of the craftsmen of London, under William of the Beard, against the exclusive power of the Merchant Guild. **1196.**

1196-1199. Richard's wide-reaching combination of the Counts of Chartres, Champagne, Boulogne, the Bretons, Flanders, and his nephew Otto, King of the Germans, against France. *Beginning of the break-up of the Angevin empire.*

Building of a fortress (Château Gaillard) above Rouen to secure Normandy.

1198. Resistance by Hugh, Bishop of Lincoln, to the imposition upon the clergy of a carucage (a tax upon every hundred acres of land), really a revival of the Danegeld (which had been dropped since **1163**).

1199. Death of Richard.

1199-1216.   **JOHN. 1199-1216.**

Hawisia (Isabel) of Gloucester = John = Isabella of Angoulême.

| Henry. | Richard of Cornwall. | Joan = Alexander II. of Scotland. | Eleanor = (1) William Marshal. = (2) Simon de Montfort. | Isabel = Emperor Frederick II. |

A   The Loss of Normandy.   1199-1205.

1199.   1. John (Duke of Normandy) recognized as King of England at a conference between Archbishop Hubert and the baronage at Northampton, after a solemn promise to redress grievances.

1199.   2. Coronation of John as elected King of England, ASCENSION DAY. Arthur, son of Geoffrey, recognized as Count by Anjou, Touraine, Maine, garrisoned for him by Philip of France. Aquitaine loyal to Queen Eleanor, John's mother.

1200.   3. Agreement between John and Philip, and marriage between Blanche of Castile, John's niece, and the Dauphin Lewis. MAY.

     4. Divorce by John of his wife, Hawisia of Gloucester, and marriage to Isabella of Angoulême. AUG., **1200**.

1202.   5. John summoned by Philip to answer before the Peers of France the charges brought against him by the Poitevins: on non-appearance declared to have forfeited his possessions in France.

     6. Attack by Arthur upon Queen Eleanor at Mirebeau. Capture (JULY) and death of Arthur, **1203.** APRIL **3, 1203**.

1203.   7. Second sentence of forfeiture pronounced upon John as Arthur's murderer. Capture by **1204.**   Philip of Château Gaillard. MARCH. Completion of the conquest of Normandy, and submission to Philip of Anjou, Touraine, Maine. Death of Queen Eleanor, followed by the loss to John of most of Aquitaine. APRIL **1**,

1205. 8. Attempt of John to recover Normandy and Anjou. Abandoned on the protest of Archbishop Hubert and William Marshal.

B John's Quarrel with Pope Innocent III. 1205-1213.

1205. 1. Death of Archbishop Hubert Walter. Election by the younger monks of Canterbury of the Sub-Prior Reginald. JULY 12.

1205. 2. Appeal to the Pope as to the right of election, by the King, the bishops of the province of Canterbury, and the monks of the Cathedral. Meanwhile John's nominee—John de Grey, Bishop of Norwich—elected and enthroned by the King's orders.

3. Decision of the Pope; the right of election with the monks of Canterbury, but the election of Reginald informal and invalid. • Stephen Langton elected at Rome by the proctors of the monks upon the Pope's recommendation.

1207. Consecration of Langton in spite of John's refusal to accept him. JUNE. Retaliation by John upon the property of the monks of Canterbury.

1208. 4. England laid under Interdict. MARCH 12 John's defiance of the Church and oppression of the baronage.
   (*a*) A thirteenth of all property seized. **1207.**
   (*b*) Hostages demanded from the barons as pledges of allegiance. **1208.**
   (*c*) Continued exactions from the Church. **1209-1210.**

5. Activity of John.

1209-1211.   (*a*) Homage and tribute exacted from Alexander II. of Scotland. **1209.**
   (*b*) Successful campaigns in Ireland, **1210**; and Wales, **1211.**

1212. 6. Bull of deposition issued by the Pope, and execution of sentence committed to Philip of France. Philip's action checked by the burning of Dieppe and ravaging of French coast by the
1212. Earl of Salisbury, but upon a fresh attack from Wales, forces raised for invasion of Wales had
1212. to be disbanded owing to the secret conspiracies of the barons. Flight of the chief of the conspiring barons to France.

1213. 7. Submission of John to the Pope, represented by Pandulf. Surrender of his realms, which were given back to him as a tributary vassal of the Roman see. MAY 15.

C Quarrel with the Barons. 1213-1215.

    1. Measures against France.

1213.   (*a*) Burning of the French fleet by the Earl of Salisbury.

    (*b*) Summoning of the baronage to Poitou to attack Philip from the south, while the Emperor Otto, John's nephew, invaded France from the north. Refusal of baronage to follow till the removal of the Excommunication.

JULY.   2. Arrival of Langton. Removal of the Excommunication, and formal absolution of the King. Persistence of the northern baronage in their refusal to follow or serve the King except within
AUG.   the four seas. The King's march to the North.

    3. Assembly of S. Albans, under the Justiciar, Geoffrey Fitz-Peter, (of bishops, barons, and
AUG. 4.   the reeve and four men from each township upon the Royal demesne), to assess the damages due to the plundered clergy. Appeal to the laws of Henry I.

    4. Council of barons at S. Paul's. Production by
AUG. 25.   Archbishop Langton of the Charter of Henry I. as a basis for the needed reforms.

    5. Death of the Justiciar, Geoffrey Fitz-Peter, and appointment of Peter des Roches, Bishop of
OCT.   Winchester, to succeed him. The King's assent to the Charter of Henry I. demanded by Langton.

1214. 6. Departure of John for Poitou. FEB. Removal of
JUNE 29.   the Interdict. Victories of John south of the Loire neutralized by the total defeat of Otto at
JULY 27. OCT. Bouvines. Return of John to England.

    7. Rising of all classes of the baronage (with the exception of John's personal adherents, his ministers, and William Marshal, Earl of Pembroke), including

    a The northern barons, originally lesser tenants in chief, who had risen into importance after the fall of the Mowbrays. (**1095**.)

    b The old feudal barons.

    c The ministerial baronage created by Henry I. and Henry II.

NOV.   Meeting at S. Edmundsbury. Presentation of
1215. JAN.   demands to the King by the barons in arms.

8. Attempts of John between January and Easter to divide or disable his opponents.
   a Freedom of election to bishoprics offered to the Church.
   b Allegiance and fealty, and surrender of castles demanded.
   c Assumption of the Cross to shield himself from violence as a Crusader.

MAY. 9. March of the barons in arms, under Robert FitzWalter, from Stamford to London. Voluntary surrender of Exeter and Lincoln. Promises of aid to the barons from Scotland and Wales.

JUNE 15. 10. Meeting of John and the barons at Runnymede.

D **The Great Charter.**
   1. The freedom of the Church : freedom of election to bishoprics reasserted (Clause 1).
   2. Redress of feudal grievances ; reliefs, *i.e.* payments upon succession, fixed as to amount (Clause 2). Extortion and waste prohibited during wardship (3–5) ; heirs to be married "without disparagement" (*i.e.* disparagement by unequal marriage); widows to receive their dowry without delay or oppression, and not to be compelled to a second marriage (6–8). Debts due to the Crown or to the Jews to be collected in accordance with justice (9–12).
   3. The Constitutional Clauses.
      a No scutage or aid to be imposed, but by the Common Council of the realm, except for the King's ransom, and for the making the King's eldest son a Knight, and for marrying the King's eldest daughter once; and for these purposes a reasonable aid to be required (12). Similar limitations upon aids due to barons by feudal tenure (15).
      b Prelates, abbots, earls, and greater barons to be summoned to the Common Council severally by Royal writ ; tenants *in capite* by a general writ addressed to the sheriff: the cause of the summons to be stated : forty days' notice of the assembly to be given (14).
   4. The Judicial Clauses.
      a Common Pleas not to follow the King's Court, but to be held in a fixed place (17).
      b Two justices (with four knights of every county, chosen by the county court) to take assizes in the county court four times a year (18.)

c Freemen, merchants, and villeins only to be amerced "salvo contenemento suo" (*i.e.* in accordance with their degree), and by the oath of good men of the neighbourhood (20). Barons to be amerced by their peers (21). Clerks only upon their lay-fee (22).

5. Restrictions upon Royal officers.

  a No sheriff, constable, coroner, nor Royal bailiff to hold the King's pleas (24). The farms of counties to the king not to be increased: debts due to the Crown from tenants deceased to be collected by the sheriff in the view of lawful men (26). Goods of intestates to go to their natural heirs by the view of holy Church (27). Royal officers not to take corn or goods without payment (28), nor to take money in place of service for castle-guard when service is offered (29); nor to take horses, carts, or wood without consent (30, 31).

6. Clauses for removal of general exactions and encroachments, and for security of trade.

  The writ called "Præcipe," *i.e.* command to a freeman to do some act or show why he should not be compelled, not to be issued beyond the limits of the jurisdiction of the county court. Uniformity of measures insured (35). Writs of inquest concerning life or limb to be given freely (36). Merchants to come in and go out of England, buy and sell, without evil toll (41). Leave to all to leave the kingdom and return, saving their allegiance to the King, except in time of war (42). All afforestments of the present reign to be at once disforested, and fenced rivers thrown open (47). Inquests to be held in every county into evil customs of forests or fencing of rivers, by twelve sworn knights (48).

7. General Clauses for the administration of justice.

  a No Royal officer to compel a trial by his bare word without witnesses (38).

  b No freeman to be taken, nor imprisoned, nor disseized (*i.e.* dispossessed), nor outlawed, nor exiled, nor destroyed in any manner; nor will we go upon him, nor send upon him, but by the lawful judgment of his peers, or by the law of the land (39).

c To none will we sell, to none will we deny or delay right and justice (40).
d We will not make justices, constables, sheriffs, nor bailiffs, but of such as know the law and will keep it (45).

8. Special temporary clauses.
   Hostages and charters in the King's hands to be surrendered (49). All foreign knights, slingers, serjeants, and soldiers, who have come with horses and arms to the nuisance of the realm, to be dismissed immediately after the pacification, "post pacis reformationem" (51). Justice to be done to the Welsh (57, 58), and to Alexander, King of Scotland, "as we do with our other barons of England, by judgement of his peers in our court" (59).

9. Guaranteeing clauses.
   Five-and-twenty barons to be chosen by the whole baronage, to guard the liberties of the Charter; any breach of them to be reported to the King by four of the number; in case of his refusal to amend the grievance the five-and-twenty barons, "cum communâ totius Angliæ," may distress the King by all the ways they can, to wit, by seizing on his castles, lands, and possessions, till it be amended as they shall adjudge; saving the King's own person, the person of his Queen, and the persons of his children (61).

E Attempts of John to evade the Charter. JUNE, 1215—OCT. 1216.

AUG. 25. *a* Appeal of John to Innocent III. as over-lord.
DEC. 16.   The Charter annulled. The Barons excommunicated. Langton suspended. Departure of Langton to Rome:
            b The crown offered by the barons to Lewis of France: successes of John's mercenary army,
NOV.   capture of Rochester, NOV.: conquest of the south of England: northward march to
1216. JAN. Berwick and into Scotland, JAN.: the Midlands subdued by the Earl of Salisbury for John.
MARCH.   Capture of Colchester by John.
            c Acceptance of the crown by Lewis, and arrival
MAY   in England, MAY. Refusal of John's French mercenaries to fight against Lewis. Retreat of John to Wales: John's last effort, the relief of
SEPT.   Lincoln, SEPT. 22. Disaster on the shores of
OCT.   the Wash: death of the King at Newark, OCT. 19.

HENRY III. 1216-1272.

Henry III. = Eleanor of Provence.

| Edward I. | Edmund of Lancaster. | Margaret = Alexander III. of Scotland. | Beatrice = John of Britanny. |

A 1216-1227.   The King's Minority.   1216-1227.

1216. 1.   *a* Coronation of Henry at Gloucester, OCT. The Great Charter re-issued at Bristol (the clauses regulating taxation and defining the nature of the Great Council being suspended). William Marshal declared "Governor of the King and Kingdom."

NOV.

1217.   *b* Truce with Lewis for the Christmas season. Successes of Lewis in the east of England: defection of English barons to the side of Henry: defeat of Lewis's adherents at Lincoln by the Earl Marshal. Defeat of French fleet bringing support to Lewis, by Hubert de Burgh. Departure of Lewis upon payment of £5,000 and promise of a larger sum, and general pardon to his adherents. Third issue of the Charter (the clauses regulating taxation and defining the nature of the Great Council being omitted). Charter of the Forest disafforesting the encroachments made under Richard and John: no man to lose life or limb for poaching.

MAY. 20.

AUG. 24.

SEPT.

1218.   *c* Gualo succeeded as Legate by Pandulf. Death of William Marshal.
1219.

2. Ministry consisting of Peter des Roches, guardian of the Royal person; Pandulf, the Legate; Hubert de Burgh, Justiciar; Langton, Archbishop of Canterbury.

1220-1224.   *a* Second coronation of the King, and demand for the restoration of the Royal castles, MAY. Submission of William of Aumâle, **1220-1223**; of the Earl of Chester, **1223**. Capture of Bedford and banishment of Faukes de Breauté, **1224**, JUNE–AUG.

1221.   *b* Resignation of Pandulf. Concession by the Pope that no Papal Legate be sent to England during Langton's life. Arrival of the Dominican Friars, **1221**; of the Franciscans, **1224**.

1224.

1225.	*c* Grant of a subsidy of one-fifteenth upon moveable property for the recovery of the possessions in France, in consideration of the fourth issue of the Charter " *bonâ voluntate nostrâ.*"
1226.	The nomination of some prebends in each Cathedral church claimed by Pope Gregory IX.
1227.	*d* Declaration of the King's majority; all Charters sealed during the King's minority to be invalid until confirmed by the King. JAN. **1227**.

B The King's Personal Administration. 1227-1258.

1. Events till the fall of Hubert de Burgh. 1227-1232.

1228. 1229.	*a* Death of Archbishop Langton. **1228**. Confirmation of Richard le Grand as his successor purchased from Pope Gregory IX. by a subsidy of a tithe of all moveables.
1229.	*b* Rejection of the invitation sent by the Norman barons to invade Normandy. Collection of troops at Portsmouth for a campaign in Poitou. Abandonment of the expedition owing to want of transport and supplies. SEPT.-OCT. Quarrel between the King and Hubert de Burgh.
1230.	*c* Expedition under the King to Britanny and Poitou. MAY-OCT.
1231.	*d* Riots in consequence of the Papal exactions: the outbreak ascribed by the Pope to the influence of Hubert de Burgh.
1232.	*e* Hubert de Burgh deprived of the Justiciarship, and of his estates. The end of the great Justiciarships.

2. Events till the King's marriage. 1232-1236.

1233.	*a* Peter des Roches, Bishop of Winchester, the King's chief adviser. Remonstrance of the barons under William Marshal (the younger) against foreign advisers.
APRIL.	*b* Intrigues of Peter des Roches against William Marshal, Earl of Pembroke: flight of Pembroke to the Welsh, then to Ireland, **1234**, where he died from wounds.
	c Des Roches removed from Court owing to the renewed remonstrance of the barons under the new Archbishop, Edmund of Abingdon, a few days previous to the death of William Marshal.

1235.	Marriage of Isabella, the King's sister, to the Emperor Frederick II.; and of the King to Eleanor of Provence. JAN.
1236.	

3. Events from the King's marriage till **1258**.

1237.	*a* Pressure of the Royal debts. A thirtieth of all moveables granted to the King, on promise of control by the Royal Council over its expenditure, and in consideration of a fresh confirmation of the Charter.
1238.	*b* Marriage of Eleanor, the King's sister, widow of William the younger, Earl Marshal (in spite of her vow of perpetual chastity after her widowhood), to Simon de Montfort.
1237-1241.	*c* Visit of Cardinal Otho, as Papal Legate, to reform the Church; large sums exacted for the Pope, **1240**; and from the Jews. **1239-1241.**
1239-1241.	
1242.	*d* Refusal of the Great Council to grant further subsidies. JAN. Disastrous expedition of the King to Poitou. JULY.
1244.	*e* Visit of Master Martin to collect money for the Pope from the clergy, and to seize vacant benefices. Meeting of the Great Council at Westminster. Proposals of De Montfort—

      i. Justiciar, Chancellor, Treasurer, to be elected in the Council;

      ii. A perpetual Council of twelve barons, including De Montfort and Richard of Cornwall, to attend the King;

stopped by a prohibition from the Pope.

1245.	*f* Boniface of Savoy (the Queen's uncle) consecrated Archbishop of Canterbury. Peter of Savoy, another uncle, created Earl of Richmond. **1241**.
1246-1247.	*g* Protests addressed by the Great Council to the Pope about exactions.
1248.	Condemnation of the King's administration and repeated demand for the appointment of the great officers in Council.
1248.	*h* De Montfort appointed Seneschal of Gascony. Complaints of the severity of his rule there, and quarrel between the King and De Montfort. Return of De Montfort to England.
1252.	
1253.	

ANALYSIS OF ENGLISH HISTORY.   53

1253. **1253-1254.** **1254.** **1255.**	*i* The Charter again confirmed. Expedition of the King to France. [Knights of the shire, elected in the county court, summoned to an assembly for granting an aid as representatives of the smaller tenants.] Request by the Jews for permission to leave England to avoid exactions; the whole body of Jews in England assigned by the King to Earl Richard of Cornwall as security for a loan. Renewed demand for the appointment of Justiciar, Chancellor, Treasurer in the Council to be removed only by consent of Council.
1254.	*j* The offer of the kingdom of Sicily accepted by the King from Pope Innocent IV. for his second son Edmund. [Sicily to be conquered from Frederick II., the King's brother-in-law.]
1255-1257 **1257.**	*k* Unsuccessful expeditions against Llewelyn of Wales. Aid refused by Parliament, but one-tenth, 52,000 marks, exacted from the clergy for the Sicilian expedition. Severe famine.

C   Years of Eclipse. 1258-1265.

1258.   1. Fresh grants demanded for Sicily. The patience of the barons exhausted. Consent of the King to put all reforms into the hands
MAY.   of a committee of twenty-four barons. Meet-
JUNE 11.   ing of the Parliament at Oxford. The Provisions of Oxford drawn up by the twenty-four barons.

   i. The reform of the Church placed in the hands of the twenty-four barons.

   ii. A body of fifteen chosen by four out of the twenty-four to advise the King as a Permanent Council.

   iii. A second body of twenty-four chosen to deal with aids and financial matters.

   iv. A third body of twelve chosen as representing the community to confer with the Perpetual Council three times a year, in February, June, and October.
   [The principal men elected on all these four committees, De Montfort, Richard de Clare Earl of Gloucester, Roger Mortimer Lord of Wigmore.]

   v. Royal proclamation of assent to the Provisions published in Latin, French, and English.

1259.	2. Domestic policy of the Council. The Provisions of Westminster. OCT.
	i. Four knights to be elected in each shire to guard against encroachments of sheriff.
	ii. Tenants protected by the regulation of legal procedure in the feudal courts.
	iii. Nobles and prelates, however, exempted, "*nisi specialiter eorum præsentia exigatur,*" from attendance at the Sheriffs' courts.
OCT.	
	3. Foreign policy of the Council.
	i. Prohibition of further aids to Rome, secular or ecclesiastical.
	ii. Notification to the Pope of the abandonment of the Sicilian expedition.
	iii. Abandonment of claim to Normandy, Anjou, Maine, and Touraine, for a grant of money. Poitou to be delivered to the English King after the death of Lewis.
OCT.	
1260.	4. Quarrels between the Earl of Leicester (supported by the King's son Edward) and Gloucester (supported by the King).
1261. JUNE. FEB.	5. Papal Bull releasing the King from his oath to the Provisions. (The Tower of London already seized by the King, and preparations made for defence.)
1262.	6. Death of Richard de Clare, Earl of Gloucester. Confirmation of the Provisions by the King.
1263.	7. Open hostilities, WHITSUNTIDE. Rising of London against the King. The question of the Provisions referred to Lewis IX. of France. DEC.
1264.	8. The Mise of Amiens. JAN.
	i. The Provisions of Oxford annulled.
	ii. The appointment and removal of officers to be in the hands of the King.
	iii. The King in all matters to have full and free power as in time past.
	iv. All Charters issued before the Provisions to remain valid.
	9. The War.
MARCH.	i. Open resistance of London.
APRIL–MAY.	ii. Successes of Henry: capture of Northampton, Nottingham, Tutbury, relief of Rochester.
MAY 14.	iii. Defeat and capture of the King at Lewes.

JUNE.   iv. Supreme power placed in the hands of the King assisted by a Council of nine appointed by the Bishop of Chichester, the Earl of Leicester and of Gloucester (the younger).

v. Attempts of the Queen and the King's son Edmund to procure foreign aid for the King. Seizure and destruction at Dover of the Pope's Bull of Excommunication against the barons.

1265.   vi. Parliament at Westminster composed of the adherents to the Provisions, twenty-three barons, one hundred and twenty ecclesiastics, two knights from each shire, *two burghers from each town.*

JAN.   Leicester appointed Justiciar. Liberation of Edward from his confinement at Wallingford, his residence in "free custody" fixed at Hereford. Quarrel between Gilbert de Clare the Earl of Gloucester and De Montfort. Escape of Edward. Rising of Edward, Gloucester, and Roger Mortimer in Cheshire and Shropshire, and capture of Gloucester.

MAY. 28.

AUG. 4.   Defeat and death of the Justiciar at Evesham.

D **The Results of the Struggle and the Last Years of the Reign. 1265-1272.**

  1. Parliament at Winchester; the adherents of De Montfort disinherited. Submission of Dover and the Cinque Ports to the King.

  2. Efforts of Edward for conciliation.

    a Friendly negotiations with Simon de Montfort the younger.

NOV.

1266.   *b* The Ban of Kenilworth (*Dictum de Kenilworth*) drawn up by a commission under Gilbert, Earl of Gloucester, and passed by Parliament.

      (1) None to be utterly disinherited, but possessions in all cases redeemable by fines.

      (2) The liberties of the Church and the Great Charters to be observed.

      (3) The restoration of the House of De Montfort left to the Royal will.

OCT.

Nov.	3.	The last resistance. Surrender of Kenilworth. Nov. Appearance of Gilbert of Gloucester in arms in London to secure the execution of the Ban of Kenilworth. Reduction of the isle of Ely. JULY, **1267**.
1267. Nov.	4.	Statute of Marlborough, re-enacting most of the reforms of the Provisions of Oxford and Westminster, but reserving to the King the appointment of officers of State.
1270-1272.	5.	Departure of Edward to the Crusade under Lewis IX.; and quiet at home till the death of the King. Nov. **16, 1272**.

EDWARD I., 1272-1307.

Eleanor of Castile = Edward I. = Margaret of France.

| Edward. | Thomas. | Edmund, Earl of Kent. | Eleanor = Henry of Bar. | Margaret = John of Brabant. | Elizabeth = (1) John, Count of Holland. | Johanna = Gilbert, Earl of Gloucester. |

(1) Sir Thomas Holland = Johanna = (2) Black Prince.   = (2) Humphry de Bohun.

[Seven others, who died young.]

A Events till Edward's arrival in England.

1272. 1. Order for the proclamation of the King's peace, and appointment of a Regency.

1273. 2. Visit of Edward to the Pope to obtain permission to levy one-tenth upon Church revenues for the three coming years; allegiance paid to Philip III. for the possessions in France; reduction of Gascony to order.

1274. 3. Coronation. AUGUST.

1275-1280. B The early Legislative and Financial Measures.

1275. 1. First Statute of Westminster, enacted by the King
APRIL. *par son Conseil* and with the assent of the prelates, abbots, priors, counts, barons, and commonalty of the land being thither summoned.

    a Summary and codification of previous enactments, contained in Great Charter, Statute of Marlborough, and others.

    b Provision made for freedom of election, and for limitation of the amount of feudal aids. APRIL.

2. Grant of custom on wool, woolfells, and leather (half a mark upon each sack of wool, half a mark for every 300 woolfells, one mark upon every lading of leather, exported from the kingdom). *Custuma magna et antiqua.* APRIL. One-fifteenth voted upon movables by clergy and laity. AUG.

1278. 3. *Quo warranto* inquest, based upon Commission of Inquiry into territorial franchises, appointed 1274. Resistance to the inquest by Warrenne, Earl of Surrey.

1278. 4. All freeholders possessed of an estate of £20 a year, of whatsoever lord they held, to receive knighthood or to pay a fine *pro respectu militiæ* for respite of knighthood.

1279. 5. The opposition of the Church and Statute of Mortmain.

 a Council at Reading called by Archbishop Peckham; canon passed ordaining that a copy of Magna Charta (which guaranteed the liberties of the Church) should be annually posted upon all cathedral and collegiate churches. AUGUST.

 b The clergy of the Southern Province ordered by the Archbishop to declare publicly the sentence of excommunication issued against all who obtained royal writs to obstruct ecclesiastical cases, or who neglected to carry out sentences of ecclesiastical Courts.

 c The Archbishop compelled to rescind his order and to remove the copies of Magna Charta.

 d The Statute *de viris religiosis* or Mortmain, forbidding the alienation of land to religious bodies in such wise as to come into Mortmain, and so cease to render its due service to the King. All land so bestowed to be forfeited to the immediate lord of the fee; in the case of his neglect, to the next superior *proximo capitali domino feodi* and ultimately to the Crown.

1277-1284. C The Welsh Campaigns.

1. Consolidation of a central authority in Wales by
1194-1240. Llewelyn ap Jorwerth.

2. Turbulence of the great barons upon the Welsh Border—Mortimers, Bohuns, Marshalls, Clares.

1273-1276. 3. Refusal of Llewelyn ap Gruffydd to present himself for homage.

1277. 4. Removal of the courts of law to Shrewsbury, and invasion of Wales. English annexation of the coast as far south as Conway; submission of Llewelyn and marriage to Eleanor de Montfort, daughter of the late Earl Simon.

1277-1282. 5. Peace with Wales. Rebellion of Llewelyn and his brother David. MARCH, **1282.** Second removal of the law courts to Shrewsbury;

1282-1283. capture and death of Llewelyn. DEC. Capture of David. JUNE, **1283.** Trial of David for treason at Shrewsbury by an assembly of nobles and representatives of towns (summoned by separate writs and not through the sheriffs), and execution. SEPT.

[Statute of Merchants passed by this assembly, enabling traders to get their debts by imprisonment of the debtor and distraint of his goods.]

1284. 6. The Statute of Wales. Introduction into Wales of the English law of inheritance, and of the English criminal law. Sheriffs appointed for Anglesey, Caernarvon, Merioneth, Flint. The rest of the country left to the jurisdiction of the Lord Marchers.

D Financial Expedients to raise Money for the Welsh Campaign of 1282-1283.

1282. 1. John Kirkby sent to negotiate with the counties and boroughs separately for a subsidy. JUNE.

2. Writs issued to the sheriffs and the two Archbishops to call provincial assemblies of the two estates (the nobles being with the King in Wales) at Northampton and York. The sheriffs to summon four knights of each shire and two representatives of each city, borough, and market town. The Archbishops to summon heads of religious houses, and proctors of the cathedral clergy. NOV.

E Judicial Reforms (during these early years).

1. A distinct staff of judges assigned to each of the tribunals of the King's Court.

Court of Exchequer for causes in which royal revenue was concerned.

Court of Common Pleas for suits between private persons (under a chief Justiciar).

Court of King's Bench for "pleas of the Crown," and all matters affecting the sovereign (under chief Justiciar).

2. Establishment of an equitable jurisdiction side by side with that of the common law.

   a The correction of all breaches of law which the common law courts had failed to repress reserved for the King's Council.

   b Cases in which the common law courts gave no relief dealt with by the King's Chancellor (acting for the King), according to fairness or *equity*. " Matters of grace and favour."

F Fresh Legislation of 1285.

1285. 1. Statute of Westminster (the second).

a De donis conditionalibus. Tenants of lands under conditional grants (*i.e.* grants limited in their terms, and intended to confine the estate to a particular line of succession—*e.g.* to heirs male,) to possess only a limited and *inalienable* estate (a fee tail, *feodum talliatum, hoc est limitatum*), whereas till now the fulfilment of the condition, *e.g.* the birth of an heir male, had enabled the tenant to alienate, *i.e.* make a fresh grant, to another person, in whose hands the land became a complete fee simple, conferring possession in the widest sense.

b Two sworn judges, in conjunction with one or two knights of the shire, to take assizes thrice a year—in July, September, and January. Cases to be tried at Westminster, unless the sworn justices held their visitation before a fixed day. Hence the title Justices of Nisi Prius.

2. Statute of Winchester.

a Suit to be made after robbers and felons from town to town and from country to country.

b Hundreds to be answerable for felonies and robberies done and also the damages.

c Police regulations—the gates of towns to be closed from sun-setting to sun-rising ; towns to be watched all night; highways to be enlarged by clearing of the underwood for 200 feet on either side of the way ; each man to have in his house harness for to keep the peace after the ancient assize (*i.e.*, the Assize of Arms, 1181); two constables to be chosen in every hundred to make the view of armour and report to a justice assigned for the purpose. [The origin of Justices of the Peace.]

3. *Cicumspecte Agatis*, limiting jurisdiction of Spiritual Courts to matters merely spiritual, *e.g.*, matrimonial and testamentary cases, and offences for which penance was due.

G 1286-1290. Events till 1290, the close of the first, *i.e.*, the Legislative Period of the reign.

1286-1289. 1. Absence of Edward in France, and ordering of affairs in Gascony. Outbreak of private war upon the Welsh Borders between the Earls of Gloucester and Hereford. Grant of money refused by the Lords till the King's return.

1289. 2. Inquest into the conduct of judges and sheriffs during the King's absence.

1290. 3. Reconciliation of Gloucester and Hereford; marriage of Gloucester to the King's daughter Johanna.

4. Statute of *Quia Emptores*. "Every free man may henceforth dispose at will of his land or tenement, or any part thereof, but so that the taker hold it of the same chief lord, and by the same services." Meant to prevent the loss of the feudal profits of wardships and reliefs to the chief lords by the growing practice of subinfeudation, and to stop the creation of new manors. [Chiefly, however, important as having tended to increase the division of estates and transfer of land. "One of the few acts of legislation which, being passed with a distinct view to the interests of a class" (*i.e.*, the landlords, and above all the Crown), "have been found to work to the advantage of the nation generally."]

5. Expulsion of the Jews.

a Jewish traders established by the protection of William the Conqueror in separate quarters, or "Jewries," in large towns: not citizens of the country, but the special property of the King; protected by the Crown therefore against popular dislike (*e.g.*, privileged with a separate tribunal and justiciars), but protected as a source of revenue (*e.g.*, the whole body of the Jews assigned to Earl Richard of Cornwall by Henry III., as security for a loan. **1255**).

b Increasing dislike of the Jews: partly religious; partly from their own insolence and defiance; partly from their usury and speculation and pecuniary oppression of the natives; partly from the jealousy of exceptional jurisdiction and of exemption from the common burthens of the realm. The dislike not merely popular: the Jews expelled from France by S. Lewis **1252**, and their expulsion from England demanded by Bishop Grosseteste and Simon de Montfort.

c Usury forbidden to the Jews, under pain of death, by the Statute *de la Jeuerie*, probably in **1275**; their trade also crippled by the rivalry of the bankers of Cahors (in the reign of Henry III.), and of the bankers of Florence and Lucca (in the reign of Edward I.).

d Edward's consent to their final expulsion obtained by a grant of "a fifteenth" of moveables "from clergy and laity" and a tenth of spiritual revenues over and above. The Jews permitted to take their personal wealth with them. JULY, **1290**.

H The Scotch Succession.

1. The Kingdom of Scotland an aggregate of four distinct countries: Pictland, north of the Forth and Clyde; Scotland proper, in South-west Argyle; Cumbria or Strathclyde (Galloway); Lothian, the Anglian settlement between the Forth and the Tweed.

2. Earlier relations of English and Scotch Crowns.

924. *a* Submission and "Commendation" of Northern League (including the King of Scots) to Eadward the Elder.

945. *b* Grant of Strathclyde (Cumbria) to Malcolm I. by Eadmund the Magnificent, on condition that he should be his fellow-worker as well by sea as by land.

1031. *c* King of Scots, Malcolm II., confirmed by Cnut in possession of Lothian.

d The Kings of Scots regarded as representatives of the old English dynasty, and claimants to the English throne, in consequence of the

1070. marriage of Malcolm III. to Margaret, sister of Eadgar Ætheling. This danger finally removed by the marriage of Henry I. to

Nov. Matilda (daughter of Malcolm and Margaret).

e Grant of lordships within England to Scot kings or their sons; *e.g.*, of Northumberland and

1139. Huntingdon. Capture of William the Lion

1174.
1174-1189.
at Alnwick; the Scotch Crown held of England.

3. Condition of the Scotch Succession, **1290**.

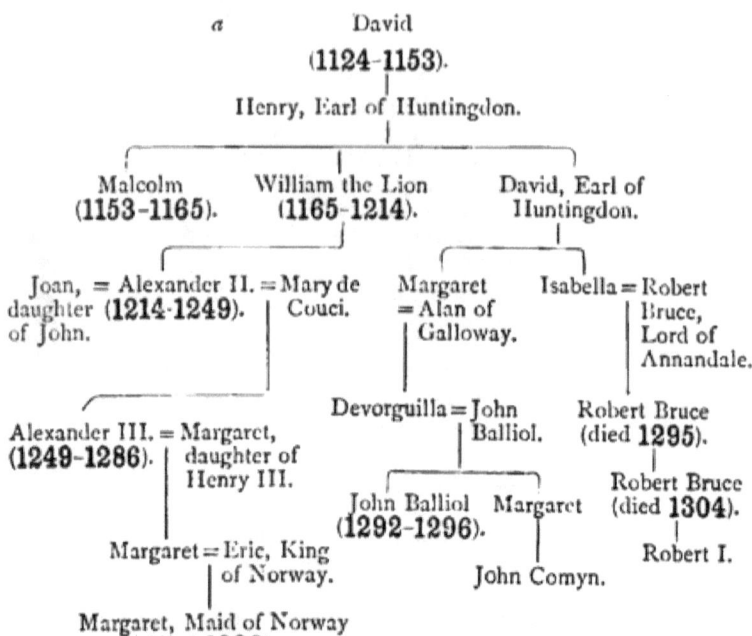

1290. *b* Proposal of marriage between the son of Edward I. and the Maid of Norway: Scotland to remain a separate and free kingdom; no military claim to be made by English King, nor appeal allowed to English Court. Death of the Maid.

1291. *c* Edward acknowledged as over-lord of Scotland: the castles delivered up to him, and his peace sworn through the land. JUNE. Decision, after recognition of the claims of John Balliol and Robert Bruce, in favour of Balliol. NOV. Homage done by Balliol for the whole of Scotland. DEC. [The external greatness of Edward here reached its height.] Two points however remained unsettled, from which after troubles ensued.

1292.

i. Whether the Scotch King was bound to do service in English warfare or contribute to English aids.

ANALYSIS OF ENGLISH HISTORY. 63

   ii. Whether Scotland was to remain judicially independent.

1293. *d* Balliol summoned to Westminster to answer complaints of his subjects.

The French Attack and its Consequences.

1293. *a* Hostilities between the mariners of the Cinque Ports and the Normans: great defeat of the Normans. APRIL. Hostilities also between the Gascons and French. Edward summoned to Paris as a vassal by Philip the Fair to answer for the wrong-doing of his dependents. Guienne ceded by Edward to Philip for forty days as an acknowledgment of his supremacy.

1294. *b* Edward declared "contumacious," his fiefs forfeited to the French crown. FEB.—MAY.

  c Edward's preparations for war.
   i. Summons to the Scotch barons to follow him in arms to Guienne [disregarded, the Scotch being encouraged in their resistance by promises of French aid].
   ii. A permanent staff of officials appointed over all the portmen and mariners of the King's dominions.
   iii. The whole body of knightly tenants summoned to meet in arms at Portsmouth on SEP. **1**. (Action however postponed till **1295**: firstly, owing possibly to bad weather; secondly, owing to revolt in Wales, OCT., **1294**—MAY, **1295**.)
   iv. Activity in collecting money.
    a The wool of the merchants seized, released upon payment of three to five marks the sack. JULY. (Possibly granted by an assembly of merchants.)
    b Assembly of the clergy called and half the ecclesiastical revenue demanded upon pain of outlawry. SEP.
   v. Summoning of a Parliament of nobles and knights of the shire. NOV.

  d Increasing difficulties.

1295. i. Attack upon Dover by the French. AUG.
   ii. Twelve peers appointed by the Scotch nobles to act as guardians of the realm, and arrangements made for the marriage of Edward Balliol to Johanna of France. OCT. Application of John Balliol to the Pope for absolution from his fealty to Edward.

e The great Parliament of **1295**, consisting of the nobles; heads of chapters, archdeacons, one proctor for each cathedral, two proctors for the clergy of each diocese; two knights of each shire, two citizens of each city, and two burghers of each borough *ut quod omnes tangit ab omnibus approbetur.*

f The first conquest of Scotland.

1296. Capture of Berwick (consequent ruin of the town as a seaport). MARCH. Formal renunciation of allegiance by Balliol. Capture of Edinburgh, Stirling, Perth. Surrender and imprisonment of Balliol (till **1299**). JULY. Government intrusted to John de Warrenne at the head of an English Council of Regency.

g The confirmation of the Charters.

  i. Publication by Pope Boniface VIII. of the Bull *Clericis Laicos* forbidding the clergy to pay taxes upon the revenues of their churches **1296.** [intended to act as a check upon war in general, which was largely carried on at the expense of the clergy]. FEB.

  ii. Consequent refusal of the clergy to contribute; the clergy put out of the King's **1297.** protection, *i.e.* outlawed. JAN.

  iii. Assembly of the baronage at Shrewsbury. Refusal of Humfrey de Bohun of Hereford (Constable) and of Roger Bigod of Norfolk (Earl Marshal) to undertake service abroad, except in attendance upon the King. (The King proposing to go to Flanders, while the nobles were to undertake the war in Gascony.)

  iv. The clergy recommended by the Archbishop of Canterbury (Winchelsey) to act on their own responsibility and make, if they will, separate bargains, *salvet quisque animam suam.* MARCH.

  v. Seizure by the King of all the wool and woolfells in the kingdom which were weighed and mainly paid for by tallies.

  vi. The military force summoned to meet. JULY. Continued refusal and dismissal from office of the Constable and Marshal. Solemn pacification between the King and Archbishop at St. Paul's, accompanied however with a fresh demand for money and a promise in exchange to confirm the Charters. JULY.

    vii. Departure of the King for Flanders. Statement of his case published by the King under letters patent as an appeal to the people. Bill of Grievances presented to the King by Hereford and Norfolk. AUG.

    viii. Upon the King's departure, collection of taxes forbidden by Hereford and Norfolk until the confirmation of the Charter.

    ix. Magna Charta, the Charter of the Forest, and certain supplementary articles contained in the Bill of Grievances confirmed by the younger Edward as Regent, OCT., and by the King at Ghent. NOV.

    [These supplementary articles exist in two forms—Latin and French. The Latin forbidding "tallage or aid to be taken without the will and consent" of Parliament: the French merely declaring that the recent exactions shall not be made precedents and "that no such exactions (including the maletote on wool) shall be taken without the common consent of the realm," with no mention of "tallage," and in addition saving the King's right to the ancient aids, prises, and customs on wool. The Latin is known as *de tallagio non concedendo*, and is referred to in the Petition of Right; but the French is probably the authentic form (see Stubbs' *Select Charters* and *Const. Hist.* ii. *in loc.*)].

    x. The Confirmation repeated in **1298, 1299, 1300, 1301,** but the Constitutional articles of the Magna Charta **(12-14)** omitted in **1216** not replaced.

1298.   *h* Truce followed by peace with France and the marriage of the King to Margaret, sister of Philip the Fair (Queen Eleanor having died **1290**).

J The National Resistance in Scotland: Second Conquest and Settlement.

    i. Rising of the Scotch peasants, especially those on the east coast north of the Tay, under William Wallace.

1297.   *a* Defeat of Warrenne near Stirling. SEPT. **10.**

    b Wallace, "Guardian of the Realm," in Balliol's name.

1298.   *c* Defeat of Wallace by the King in person at Falkirk. JULY **22.**

1299. *d* Upon the release of Balliol from imprisonment the struggle for independence continued by Robert Bruce and John Comyn. Edward's action crippled

    i. By the jealousy of the English barons who resented his attempt to add an evasive saving clause to his confirmation of the Charters (**1299**).

1300.   ii. By the claim advanced by Pope Boniface VIII. to feudal superiority over Scotland, (though the Papal demand summoning the King to prove his right of interference in Scotch matters was boldly resisted by the English baronage).

    iii. By the encouragement given by France to the Scotch.

1303. *e* Quarrel of Philip the Fair with Pope Boniface, restoration of Gascony by France to England, and abandonment of Scotland to Edward's mercy. Second conquest and
1304.   settlement of Scotland.

    i. General amnesty to all concerned in the resistance. Wallace, who refused to surrender, captured and executed as a traitor.

    ii. Ten representatives assigned to Scotland in the Common Parliament.

    iii. The laws of the Highlanders and Welsh of Strathclyde replaced by the laws of King David with additions, and the country divided into four judicial districts, each under two justiciaries, one English, one Scotch.

K The Last Years and Troubles.

1302.   i. *Custuma nova* paid to the King by alien merchants; the King driven by want of money to call a *colloqium* of native merchants, and try
1303.   to obtain from them a similar increased duty upon wine, wool, and merchandise. The grant refused, but collected from those who were willing to pay it. [This "new custom" so called in contrast to that of **1275**, the origin of our import duties.]

  ii. Appeal of the King to Pope Clement V. to obtain absolution from the confirmation of the
1305.   Charters in order to evade the fulfilment of the clauses of the Forest Charter.

iii. Statute passed against Trailbâtons or Clubmen (afterwards known as Sturdy Beggars). Quarrel between the King and Archbishop Winchelsey. The suspension of Winchelsey procured from Pope Clement V.

1306-1307. iv. The intrigues of Robert Bruce with the Bishops of St. Andrew and Glasgow, the murder of Comyn, the coronation of Bruce at Scone, MARCH; advance of the King from Carlisle (where he had just held his last Parliament) towards Scotland, death of the King at Burgh-upon-Sands. JULY **7, 1307.**

NOTE UPON THE GROWTH OF THE ENGLISH TOWNS.

i. The historic township, *villata* or *vicus*, is either

    a A body of alodial owners who have advanced beyond the stage of community of land (*i.e.* the mark) but still retain vestiges of it (*e.g.* the common land of the township, power of determining by-laws), or,

    b A body of tenants of a lord who are regulated upon principles derived from the ancient mark organization.

    This body, when assigned as a district to a priest, appears ecclesiastically as the "parish."

ii. The "burh", borough, only different from the village township by being larger, more defensible, more organized: in privileges and constitution similar to a "hundred."

iii. From the time of Aethelstan (**925-940**) and Eadgar (**959-975**), townships, like the rest of the country, were required to be under a lord. The majority were known as in the demesne of the King, and were under the jurisdiction of the King's reeve; the remainder in the hands of great thegns. But though externally subject to their lords (*e.g.* in tolls and fees) internally free (*e.g.* in participation in the administration of justice, in the right of meeting and deliberation about the affairs concerning the town).

iv. Stages in the external development of the towns thus subjected to jurisdiction.

    a A distinct valuation obtained of the dues to the lord or sheriff.

  b The collection of these dues taken out of the hands of the lord or sheriff by the obtainal of a Charter letting the town to the burghers upon a rent, *firma burgi*.
  c Purchase of further privileges as to regulation of trade and internal government (*e.g.* exemption from the Norman custom of trial by battle, and from the judicial administration of the sheriff) by the *communitas civitatis* i.e. the original purchasers of the *firma burgi*.
  d Obtainal of the right to elect their own magistrates (most commonly found in the Charters of the reign of John).
 v. Stages in the internal development of the towns. The townsmen held together by confraternities or guilds.
  a The religious guild in honour of God and the local saint.
  b The "frith guild" or peace guild for mutual responsibility and mutual defence (dating as far back in London as the time of Aethelstan).
  c The Merchant guild or Hansa (dating at least from the Norman Conquest) with the power of making by-laws (*i.e.* town-laws), owning property, and claiming monopoly of local trade.
  d Struggles of the inferior trades to obtain royal charters for the formation of guilds of their own known as "craft guilds" (dating from the reign of Henry I.).
  e Struggle between the craft guilds and merchant guilds for commercial and municipal power seen most in London (under William of the Long Beard, **1196**), and in the support given to Simon de Montfort by the Craft guilds in the Barons' War, **1264**.

EDWARD II. 1307-1327.

Edward II. = Isabella of France.

| Edward III. | John. | Eleanor. | Joan = David II. of Scotland. |

A Struggle between the King and the Baronage (attempt of **1307-1312**. the King to rule by a minister wholly dependent upon the Crown.)

ANALYSIS OF ENGLISH HISTORY.

1307. **1.** Pier Gaveston of Gascony recalled from banishment (to which he had been sent by Edward I. at the beginning of the year) made Earl of Cornwall, and appointed Regent during the
1308. King's absence for his marriage.

    2. Gaveston again banished from the realm by demand of Parliament, but made by the King Regent of Ireland.

    3. Thomas, Earl of Lancaster, the head of the baronage in opposition to Gaveston and the Court.

TABLE OF THE HOUSE OF LANCASTER.

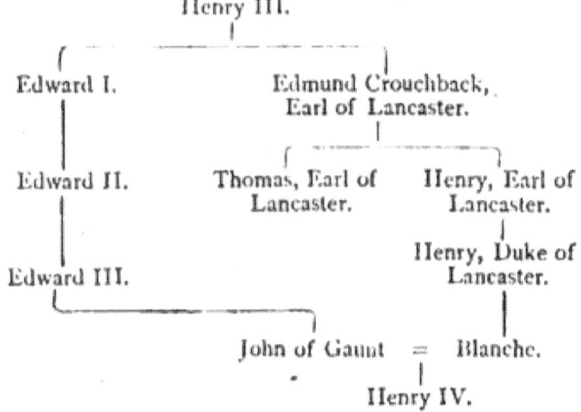

1309. **4.** Presentment of articles to the King complaining of

    1. Purveyance.

    2. The new custom taken by Edward I. from the alien merchants.

    3. The uncertainty of the value of the coinage.

    4. The mal-administration of officials.
Acceptance of the articles by the King and return of Gaveston from Ireland through the intervention of the Pope. Withdrawal of Lancaster, through offence at Gaveston's conduct, from the Council. OCT.

1310. **5.** Fresh complaints of the nobles. The Government entrusted from MARCH, **1310**, to MICHAELMAS, **1311**, to twenty-one lords ordainers (among them Archbishop Winchelsey).

1311. 6. The ordinances.
  i. Alienations from the royal demesne forbidden without the consent of the ordainers.
  ii. The "new custom" (notwithstanding its illegality) to be collected by native officers that the King may live of his own.
  iii. Perpetual banishment and forfeiture of Gaveston and expulsion of other foreign favourites.
  iv. Provisions for the proper administration of Government and observation of the Charters.
  v. The great offices of State to be filled with the counsel and consent of the baronage.
  vi. The consent of the baronage necessary to the levying of forces, declaration of war, or absence of the King from the realm.
  vii. Parliaments to be held once or twice every year.

7. Consent of the King to the ordinances. OCT. The articles broken by him, and Gaveston recalled. FEB.

1312.

1312. 8. Excommunication of Gaveston by Archbishop Winchelsey. Appearance of the barons in arms. Capture of Gaveston at Scarborough, MAY, and execution near Warwick, JUNE. Pardon granted by the King to the barons. DEC.

1312-1322. B The Scotch War of Independence to the Battle of Bannockburn; Supremacy and Fall of Lancaster.

1311-1313. 1. Successes of King Robert in Scotland. Capture of Linlithgow, Perth, Roxburgh and Edinburgh.

1314. 2. March of King Edward (the Earl of Lancaster and other nobles refusing to follow him because the barons had not been consulted) to raise the siege of Stirling. Defeat of the English at Bannockburn. JUNE 24.

1313-1315. 3. Misery produced by succession of famines. Lancaster made chief of the Council and practical ruler of the kingdom. Attack made upon Ireland by Edward Bruce. Defeat of Bruce at Dundalk. A new permanent Council appointed after the Scotch capture of Berwick.
1316.
1315.
1318.
1318.

1319-1321. 4. Unpopularity of Lancaster (partly through his refusal to co-operate for the re-capture of Berwick from the Scots.) Accusation brought by Lancaster against the King's new favourites, the Despensers, for receiving royal gifts (*e.g.* the county of Glamorgan given to the younger Despenser by marriage) without consent of the Council. Armed attack threatened upon Despenser by Mortimer Earl of March, and Bohun Earl of Hereford.

5. TABLE OF THE DESPENSERS.

Hugh Despenser (Justiciar, killed at Evesham, **1265**).
|
Hugh the Elder.
|
Hugh the Younger = Eleanor (daughter of Earl Gilbert and co-heiress of Gloucester).

1321. 6. Attack made in Parliament upon the Despensers. Their forfeiture and exile. AUG.

7. Appearance of the King in arms in consequence of an insult offered to the Queen at Leeds. OCT. Surrender of Mortimer.

1322. JAN. **1322.** Defeat of Lancaster at Boroughbridge. MARCH 16. Execution at Pontefract. MARCH 22.

1322-1327. C **The Policy of the Despensers, and the King's Fall.**

1322. 1. Parliament at York (including for this occasion representatives from Wales). Proceedings against the Despensers annulled; the Ordinances repealed; the principle asserted that "matters touching the realm be established in Parliament by the King and by the consent of the prelates, earls, barons, and the *commonalty of the realm*, as hath been hitherto accustomed."

[This marks the popular feeling against the attempt of the baronage to monopolize all legislative action, and gives the clue to the policy of the Despensers—to strengthen the Crown by supporting the power of the Three Estates against the separate action of the Baronage.] MARCH-MAY.

1323. 2. Truce with the Scots for thirteen years. King Robert suffered to adopt title of king in the negotiations.

ANALYSIS OF ENGLISH HISTORY.

1322. 3. Troubles with France. The King summoned upon accession of Charles IV. to do homage for Ponthieu and Gascony. Upon his delay to do so Gascony atttacked by the French. Visit of Queen Isabella to France to bring about arrangement. Ponthieu and Gascony transferred by the King to his eldest son (who did homage for them). League formed by the Queen, Edmund Earl of Kent, (the King's brother), and Mortimer Earl of March, who had taken refuge in France, for the overthrow of the Despensers. Negotiations for the marriage of the King's son Edward to Philippa of Hainault, and preparations for the invasion of England.

1324.
1325.

1326.

4. Landing of the Queen at Orwell. SEPT. Capture and execution of the elder Despenser at Bristol. OCT. The younger captured along with the King on his way to Ireland and executed at Hereford. NOV.

1327. 5. Deposition of the King. Parliament called at Westminster. JAN :—

    i. For incompetence to govern, being led by evil counsellors, and neglecting the business of the kingdom.

    ii. For the loss of Scotland, Ireland, and Gascony.

    iii. For putting to death, exiling, imprisoning many noblemen of the land.

    iv. For breaking his coronation oath.

    v. For being incorrigible and without hope of amendment.

Death of the King at Berkeley Castle. SEPT.

Edward III. 1327-1377.

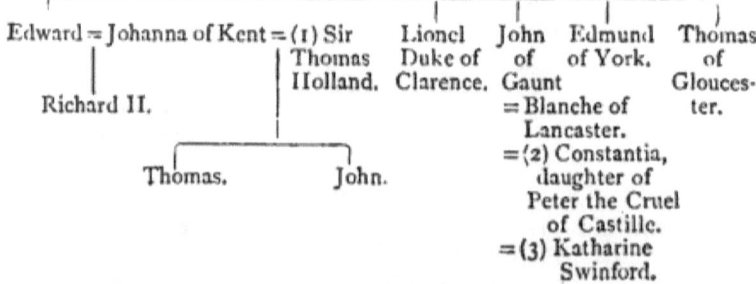

ANALYSIS OF ENGLISH HISTORY. 73

1327-1330. A The Rule of Isabella and Mortimer.

    1327. 1. Henry Earl of Lancaster appointed by Parliament Head of a Council of Regency.

        2. Reception at the Court of Edward Balliol as vassal-King of Scotland. Scotch invasion of
1328. England leading to Treaty of Northampton.
i. Claim of feudal superiority over Scotland renounced, and Robert Bruce acknowledged as King. ii. Restitution of forfeited estates promised by Robert to Scotch nobles who had sided with England. iii. Marriage arranged between Johanna and David Bruce.

        3. Unsuccessful attempt of Henry Earl of Lancaster, Thomas Earl of Norfolk, and Edmund Earl of
1328-1329. Kent (uncles of the King), and Bishop Stratford to assert the power of the Council of Regency against Mortimer, and bring him to account for the murder of Edward II., the seizure of the lands of the Despensers, and for the dishonourable peace with Scotland.

    1330. 4. Arrest, trial, and execution of Edmund Earl of Kent through Mortimer's influence. MARCH. Mortimer arrested by Edward at Nottingham, condemned without a hearing and hanged. Queen Isabella pensioned and confined for life at Castle Rising.

E Renewal of the Scotch War and Progress of Events to the Outbreak of the Hundred Years' War.

    1329. 1. Death of King Robert; dissatisfaction both among English and Scotch nobles owing to the delay in compensation and the non-restitution of
1332. estates. Successful landing of Edward Balliol (son of John Balliol) on the coast of Fife. AUG. Balliol's coronation at Scone (SEPT.), and acknowledgment of English suzerainty, NOV.; his expulsion from Scotland. CHRISTMAS.

    1333. 2. Advance of Edward to Scotland to enforce his suzerainty: defeat of the Scots at Halidon Hill and capture of Berwick, JULY. All Scotland south of the Forth ceded to England, Balliol proclaimed vassal-King of the country north of
1333-1334. the Forth. Opposition of Scotch nobles under Robert the Steward and Earl Randolph of Moray to Balliol. Expeditions of Edward to
1336. Scotland, **1334. 1336.**

1335-1337. 3. Intervention of the French King, Philip VI., with whom David Bruce had taken refuge, in the Scotch quarrel. French descents upon the English coasts.

C The beginning of the Hundred Years' War.

1. Causes of the war.

   a The support given by Philip VI. (of Valois) to the Counts of Flanders against the rising power of the towns which were closely connected with England, as it supplied the raw material for the cloth-trade.

   b The support given by Philip VI. to David Bruce against Edward in his struggle for independence.

1337. *c* The renewal by Philip VI. of the attempt of Philip the Fair to change the Feudal superiority of the King of France over Aquitaine into actual possession (in spite of homage paid by Edward, **1331**).

   d Consequent assumption by Edward of Title of King of France.

TABLE TO ILLUSTRATE EDWARD'S CLAIM.

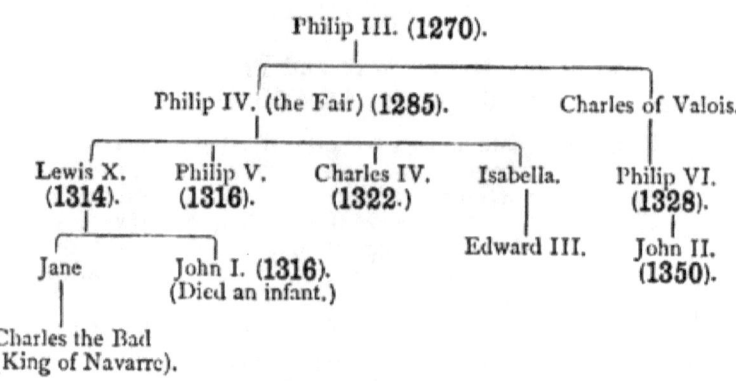

2. Summary of the history of the war.

   a **1337-1340.** Attempt of Edward to form a foreign confederacy against the superior power of France.

   b **1340-1342.** Failure of the confederacy and truce with France.

c **1341-1345.** War of succession in Britanny between John of Montfort and Charles of Blois (supported respectively by England and France).

d **1345-1347.** Renewal of the General War. English successes in Guienne, victory of Crecy, capture of Calais.

e **1347-1355.** Truce, originally for a few months, then extended owing to the exhaustion produced by the Black Death.

f **1355-1357.** Renewal of the English attack in Normandy and from Guienne. English victory at Poitiers.

g **1357-1360.** Truce. Exhaustion and anarchy in France. Revolt in Paris. Treaty of Bretigny.

h **1360-1369.** Truce, though the Treaty of Bretigny was not carried out. Campaign of the Black Prince in Spain in defence of Pedro the Cruel.

i **1369-1374.** Appeal of the barons of Aquitaine to the French King Charles V. Renewal of the war ending in the loss of Guienne to the English.

j **1374-1396.** Desultory warfare upon the whole unfavourable to the English.

k **1396-1415.** Marriage of Richard II. to Isabella (daughter of Charles VI.) and truce concluded for 25 years.

l **1415-1420.** Renewal of the war by Henry V. English victory of Agincourt, capture of Rouen. Treaty of Troyes.

m **1422-1437.** First period of the loss of English possessions in France. The maid of Orleans. Defection of the Burgundians from the English alliance, death of the Duke of Bedford, and loss of Paris.

n **1437-1446.** Growth of a peace party in England, and marriage of Henry VI. to Margaret of Anjou.

o **1447-1453.** Loss of Normandy, Guienne, and all English possessions in France except Calais.

D The First Years of the War and Constitutional Crisis of 1340-1341.

1337.
1. Attempt to form a confederacy of the Emperor Lewis IV. (married to the sister of Queen Philippa, and excommunicated by Pope Benedict XII. owing to the influence of Philip VI.), and of the imperial vassals to the north-east of France, (the Duke of Brabant, the Count of Hainault (Edward's father-in-law), the Count of Gelders, and the Markgrave of Juliers).

1338. 2. Attack upon the Agenois (on the Garonne) by France and open declaration of war, Edward recognized as Vicar-General of the Emperor west of the Rhine; seizure of Cambrai by the French, 1338, and ineffectual siege by the Confederates 1339. Gradual dissolution of the Confederacy.

1339-1340.
1340.
3. Fresh Confederacy between Edward, the Duke of Brabant, and the great Flemish commercial towns, negotiated mainly by Van Arteveldt of Ghent. English naval victory at Sluys, securing the command of the Channel, JUNE **24**. Unsuccessful siege of Tournai (upon the lower Scheldt, intercepting the commerce between Brabant and Flanders). JULY-SEPTEMBER. Truce with France for a year, continued till OCT. **1342**.

1339.
1340.
1340-1341.
1341.
4. Rising discontent in England against the expenses of the war. Conditions made before grant of money. The Royal right of Tallage finally abolished. No attempts to be made to deal with the merchants apart from the Houses of Parliament. Return of Edward to England from Tournai and summary removal from office of Archbishop Stratford, the treasurer, and some of the judges. Appointment for the first time of a lay Chancellor. Publication of Edward's complaints against Archbishop Stratford, in "Libellus Famosus." Contention of the Archbishop that he can only be tried by his Peers conceded—after a struggle—by the King. Further concession of the King to the Commons.

   i. Commissioners to be appointed for the audit of accounts.

   ii. The Chancellor and other great officers to be appointed in Parliament, sworn to obey the law, and to be accountable for all grievances. [From this time may be dated the clear division of Parliament into two houses— Lords and Commons.]

1342. 5. Revocation by Letters Patent of the Statutes passed in 1341, as prejudicial to the Prerogative, and only assented to in order to prevent worse confusion. [Henceforward may be noticed Edward's jealousy of Parliament.]

1341-1347. E Edward triumphant.

1341. 1. Outbreak of the war of succession in Britanny between Charles of Blois, cousin of the King of France, and John of Montfort (supported by England).

1345. 2. Murder of Jacob Van Arteveldt at Ghent owing to internal dissensions in the Flemish towns, and consequent failure of the design to proclaim the Prince of Wales as Count of Flanders. Ruin of the chief Italian bankers owing mainly to the large loans made to Edward. Successes of Henry of Lancaster (Earl of Derby) in Guienne, where he had been appointed governor.

1346. 3. Expedition of Edward to France, originally designed to support Derby, now hard pressed in Guienne, then diverted to La Hogue and Normandy. Advance on Paris. Consequent recall of the French forces from Guienne. March of Edward to join the invading Flemish at Gravelines; his halt at Crecy in Ponthieu. The battle of Crecy, AUGUST 26. [For map of Route see Public Schools Historical Atlas.] Defeat and capture of David II. of Scotland, at Neville's Cross, near Durham, OCT. 17.
1347. Siege of Calais, which surrendered AUGUST 1347.

1347. 4. The death of the Emperor Lewis IV. Edward
1350. elected Emperor in his place; compelled however by Parliament to decline the offer.
1349 or 1346. Foundation of the Order of the Garter.

1349-1360. F The Black Death and subsequent events till the treaty of Bretigny.

1348. 1. Repeated complaints in Parliament; the Commons decline responsibility for the war "as being so ignorant and simple."

1348-1349. 2. First visitation of the Great Pestilence. Its effects.

    a Diminution of the population by one half. (The population being estimated at from three to five millions.)

    b The rate of labour-wages doubled.

    c A consequent change in the management of lands. The modern system of "letting" gradually introduced, owing to the difficulty of getting lands cultivated. Commencement of a permanent distinction between the farmer and the labourer.

    d A series of attempts to fix the rate of wages and to bind the labourer to the soil (beginning with the Statute of Labourers, **1349** and **1351**), leading to discontent of those who lived by manual labour, which finally broke into rebellion, **1381**.
To these may be added:—

    e Great mortality among sheep, upon whose wool the King largely depended as a source of revenue.

1351-1353. 3. The Parliaments after the Pestilence.

1351-1352.   *a* Appearance of jealousy between the Commons and the royal Council. Demand that the reasonable petitions of their estate be granted, confirmed, and sealed before the departure of Parliament; and complaints against the legal interference of the Council with the business of the Common Law Courts.

1351.   *b* The First Statute of Provisors—against the right claimed by the Popes to present (often aliens) to English benefices.

1352   *c* The Statute of Treason. Treason declared by Edward (at the request of Parliament), to consist in—

    i. Compassing death of King, Queen, or their eldest son.

    ii. Levying war upon the King in his kingdom, or adhering to the King's enemies.

    iii. Counterfeiting the Great Seal, or bringing false money into the land.

    iv. Slaying the Chancellor, Treasurer, or Judges, "being in their place doing their offices."

1353.   *d* The First Statute of Præmunire, against referring any matter belonging to any jurisdiction outside the realm. [Aimed at the claims of the Court of Rome, though not directly stated so in the Statute.]

1353.   *e* The Statute of the Staples.
   i. Appointment of Staple Towns (*i.e.*, markets for the sale of the chief commodities of England—wool, woolfells, leather, lead, tin). All merchants, except merchants of the Staple, forbidden to buy or export these goods.
   ii. Importance of the Statute—
      a As a means of collecting the customs.
      b As a means of insuring the quality of exports.
      c As a means of bringing the Merchants of the Staple under the control of the Parliament, and preventing the King dealing with them in a separate "colloquium," after the fashion of Edward I.
   iii. The most important of these Staple towns:—London, York, Bristol, Newcastle, Exeter, Lincoln, Norwich. For Ireland: Dublin, Cork, Waterford, Drogheda. For Wales: Caermarthen. For foreign merchants: Calais.

1357.   *f* [Publication by the King of an ordinance for the better estate of the land of Ireland.]

   4. The resumption of the war.

1355.   *a* Attempt to support Charles the Bad of Navarre (who had lands in Normandy) against John II. of France. Failure of the expedition through bad weather. Plundering campaign of the Black Prince up the Garonne.
   King Edward recalled from Calais by the Scotch recapture of Berwick.

1356.   *b* Second expedition, under Henry of Lancaster, (now Duke) opposed and driven to Cherbourg by the French King John. John recalled to the defence of Paris by advance of Black Prince from Guienne. The Prince out-manœuvred and intercepted by the French army at Poitiers. English victory at Poitiers, and capture of King John. SEPT. 19.

1357. Expedition of King Edward into Scotland, re-capture of Berwick, and ineffectual ravaging of S. E. Scotland. "The burnt Candlemas." Restoration of David II. to Scotland upon ransom; truce and equal trade settled for ten years.

1357. *c* Truce concluded with France for two years.
1358. Rising of Paris against the Regent, Charles of Normandy, and of the peasantry against their lords; the country devastated by Free Companies of soldiers.

1359. *d* Rejection by the French, in spite of their exhaustion, of terms proposed by John II. (a prisoner in England), ceding Maine, Touraine, and Poitou in the South, Normandy, Ponthieu and Calais in the North, to the English. Resumption of hostilities. France
1360. compelled to accede to the Treaty of Bretigny:—
  i. English claims on the Crown of France and Duchy of Normandy waived.
  ii. Aquitaine and Gascony (including Poitou, but excluding Auvergne), Ponthieu, Guines, Calais, made over to the King of England as absolute possession without any reservation of homage. [See Map in Public Schools Historical Atlas.]

1361-1370. G Events from 1360 to the renewal of the War.

1361-1362. 1. Re-appearance of the Pestilence, Henry Duke of Lancaster among those who died. Increasing discontent in England with the King's expenses and luxury [see the Letter of Archbishop Islip].

1362. 2. Proceedings in Parliament.
  a Besides attempts to enforce the Statute of Labourers, were enacted—
    i. The use of English in Courts of Law.
    ii. No subsidy to be set on wool without the consent of Parliament (re-enacted **1371**). Grants by "colloquium" of merchants illegal.
    iii. Renunciation by the King of the right of purveyance (*i.e.*, the right of demanding provisions at prices fixed by the royal officers) except for personal needs of King or Queen. Purveyors to change their name to buyers. Payments to be made not by tallies, but in money.

ANALYSIS OF ENGLISH HISTORY. 81

1365.   *b* Second Statute of Præmunire (with definite mention of the jurisdiction of the Papal Court) forbidding questionings of judgments rendered in the King's Courts under pain of outlawry, imprisonment, or banishment from the land.

1366.   *c* Unanimous refusal of the Parliament (Bishops, Lords and Commons) to pay to Urban V. the tribute of 1000 marks promised by King John, **1213** (in arrears since **1333**).

3. Edward's policy of accumulation of great fiefs in his family.

1342.   *a* Marriage of Lionel to Elizabeth de Burgh, heiress of Ulster.

1361.   *b* Marriage of the Black Prince to Johanna of Kent, daughter of Edmund of Woodstock.
1359.   Marriage of John of Gaunt to Blanche, daughter of Henry Duke of Lancaster (heiress of Lancaster, Derby, Leicester, Lincoln).

1362.   *c* Bestowal of title of Duke on Lionel and John of Gaunt.

d Marriage of Philippa, daughter of Lionel Duke of Clarence, to Earl Mortimer of March.

e Marriage of Eleanor and Mary Bohun (heiresses
1381.   of Hereford, Essex, and Northampton) to Thomas of Woodstock and Henry of Bolingbroke (son of John of Gaunt.)

1362-1369. 4. The Black Prince as Governor of Aquitaine.

a Discontent of the nobles of Aquitaine at the transference of their fealty from France to England.

1365.   *b* Co-operation of France in crusade declared by Pope Urban V. against Pedro the Cruel of Castile for the murder of his wife. Flight of Pedro to Bordeaux, and re-establishment
1367.   by the Black Prince after a victory at Navarete.

c Consequent heavy taxation upon Aquitaine,
1369.   and appeal of the nobles to Charles of France. The Black Prince summoned as a French vassal to Paris to answer for his conduct.

d Renewal of the war with France in conse-
1370.   quence. Capture and sack of Limoges by the Black Prince.

G

1369-1377. H The Last Years of the Reign.

        1. Family Troubles. Death of Lionel Duke of
1368-1371.   Clarence, **1368**, of Queen Philippa, **1369**. Return of the Black Prince from Guienne owing to illness (originally contracted in his Spanish campaign.) **1371**.

        2. Foreign difficulties.

1371.   *a* David II. of Scotland succeeded by Robert the Steward his nephew (not by an English Prince as David II. had proposed to the Scotch Parliament—naming Lionel Duke of Clarence, **1363**). Renewal of the alliance between Scotland and France.

     b France secured from attack on the north-east by the marriage of Margaret (heiress of Flanders) to Philip Duke of Burgundy, brother of Charles V. of France.

     c Refusal of the Castilians to recognize John of Gaunt's assumption of the title of King of Castile upon his marriage to Constantia,
1370-1371.   daughter of Pedro the Cruel.

1372.   *d* Defeat of the English at sea by the Castilian fleet, off Rochelle. Communication thus cut off between England and Guienne. JUNE.

     e Ineffectual march of John of Gaunt from
1373.   Calais to Bordeaux, with much loss in the Mountains of Auvergne. Complete loss to the English of all Southern France, except
1374.   Bordeaux and Bayonne.

        3. Internal troubles.

     a Growth of an anti-clerical party among the baronage (strengthened by the influence of Wyclif's preaching and the increasing impatience of lax discipline, pluralities, and other clerical abuses).

1371.   i. Suggested proposal to resume the temporalities of the clergy in time of war as the common property of the nation.

        ii. Removal of William of Wykeham and other clerical ministers from office. Inexperience of the new lay ministers shown by their calculation of the parishes in England at 40,000, though in reality between 8,000 and 9,000.

ANALYSIS OF ENGLISH HISTORY.

1373.
b Growing dissatisfaction at the expenses and conduct of the war. Upon fresh demands for money after Lancaster's unsuccessful expedition (**1373**), a conference with a committee of the Lords demanded by the Commons, and a petition added to the subsidy which was finally granted that the money be spent on the war and on that only.

1374-1375.
c The discontent increased by the apparent failure of the negotiations conducted at Bruges to come to a settlement with the Pope as to the question of Provisors and Freedom of Election. [A private compromise seems to have been made between the King and the Pope to the profit of both at the expense of the nation.] Scandal occasioned by the interference of Alice Perrers with State affairs and the administration of justice.

1376.
d The good Parliament.
    i. Peter de la Mare elected Speaker. Demand made for the audit of public accounts.
    ii. Impeachment of Lord Latimer, the King's chamberlain, and Richard Lyons, the King's agent with the merchants, for extortion and malversation of money. [The first instance of impeachment.]
    iii. Attack upon Alice Perrers. No woman to interfere in the courts of law under pain of forfeiture.
    iv. (Upon the death of the Black Prince, JUNE 8), a petition that Richard of Bordeaux, his son, be presented to Parliament as next heir.
    v. Petition for the election of an administrative council (William of Wykeham, two other prelates, and nine lords in addition to the ordinary Council).
    vi. Various petitions (140 in all). Especially notable are—
        a Petition for annual parliaments (none had met since **1373**).
        b Petition that the knights be elected by the better folk of the shires, not merely nominated by the sheriff.
        c Petition that the sheriffs be elected, not appointed at the Exchequer.

  d Petitions that the Statute of Labourers be enforced, and the abuses of Papal provisions and "of the Brokers of the sinful city of Rome" removed.

  e The work of the Parliament undone by John of Gaunt.

   i. Not one of the petitions enrolled as a statute.

   ii. The additional members of Council dismissed.

   iii. Latimer, Lyons, and Alice Perrers recalled to court and influence.

   iv. Peter de la Mare imprisoned; William of Wykeham accused of malversation, and his estates confiscated; with difficulty included in the Jubilee Pardon.

1377.   v. Another Parliament called to confirm John of Gaunt's measures [the first instance of a packed Parliament]. First imposition of a poll-tax (a groat a head on all over 14). [N.B. The exertions of Convocation to prosecute Wyclif; the attack on the Savoy; and on the other side the mixture of Lollard feeling with opposition to constitutional reform.]

  f Death of the King, JUNE 21 (five months after his Jubilee), and the antagonism of the Londoners to John of Gaunt.

RICHARD II. 1377–1399.

Richard II. = (1) Anne of Bohemia = (2) Isabella of France.

A The Early Years and the Peasant Revolt.

1377. 1. Withdrawal of John of Gaunt from the court upon his father's death; release of Peter de la Mare from prison, and election as Speaker of the Commons. Action of Parliament (in pursuance of the work of the good Parliament).

  a Petition for the appointment of treasurers to superintend the due application of the subsidy. William Walworth and John Philipot, London merchants, appointed accordingly.

  b Petition for the election of ministers by the Lords in Parliament during the King's minority.

  c Petitions that the annual assembly of Parliament be defined by law ; and that petitions granted by the Crown be changed into statutes without modification by the Royal Council.

1377. 2. Disastrous course of the war. The Isle of Wight ravaged, and Hastings burnt by the French. Unsuccessful expedition of John of Gaunt against St. Malo. Parliament called at
1378. Gloucester owing to the hatred of John of Gaunt in London. Heavy taxation, though insufficient for the necessities of the war, still further increased by the expense of garrisoning Cherbourg and Brest (ceded temporarily by Charles of Navarre and the Duke of Britanny).
1379. Second poll-tax, graduated according to income, from 6*l*. 13*s*. 4*d*. to a groat per head.
1380. Third poll-tax, also graduated, from sixty groats to one per head (with a provision that the richer should help the poorer).
1381. 3. The revolt. JUNE 5—JUNE 30.
  a The causes.[1]
   i. The revolt seems a result of the general discontent organized by the associations formed to defeat the Statutes of Labourers ; by religious preachers ; and by discharged soldiers and country artisans out of work owing to the continuance of the war or the restrictions of the gilds.
   ii. The main grievances were two.
    a Political ; the poll-tax (bringing home the expense and mismanagement of the war), especially in Kent.
    b Social ; the revival of villenage and customary service (the demand for which had become more strict and exacting since the Great Pestilence). [See William I. (note upon the Conquest and Villenage.)]
   As subsidiary causes may be added—
    c Discontent at the prosperity of the Flemish who had come over to England.
    d Hatred of, or sometimes belief in, John of Gaunt.
    e A vague socialism stirred up by religious preachers.

---

[1] See *Dictionary of English History*. Wat Tyler's Rebellion. (Cassell.)

b History of the Revolt.

    i. Almost simultaneous outbreak in Kent, owing to political; in Essex and Hertfordshire, owing to social grievances. — JUNE 5.

    ii. Entry of the Kentish rebels into London, destruction of John of Gaunt's palace of the Savoy, of Temple Bar, and massacre of lawyers and Flemings. The men of Essex at Mile End, the men of Hertfordshire at Highbury. — JUNE 13.

    iii. Interview between the King and the Essex rebels at Mile End. Their demands. — JUNE 14.
        a Abolition of villenage.
        b General pardon.
        c Liberty to buy and sell untolled in all fairs and markets.
        d Rent of land to be fixed at 4*d.* an acre (*i.e.* money commutation of villein services). Retreat of the Essex and Hertfordshire men upon promise of Charters and receipt of letters of manumission.

    iv. Forcible entry of the Kentish men into the Tower during the King's absence. Murder of Simon Sudbury, Archbishop of Canterbury and Chancellor, Richard Lyons, the late King's Agent with the Merchants, and Sir R. Hales, the Treasurer. — JUNE 14.

    v. Meeting of the King with the Kentish men in Smithfield. Scuffle and death of their leader Wat Tyler. Loyalty of the Kentish men to the young king, and retreat upon receipt of letters of pardon. — JUNE 15.

    vi. Revolt in Suffolk, Norfolk, Cambridge and Huntingdon under John Lytstere (the dyer) "the king of the Commons," crushed by armed force by Henry Spencer Bishop of Norwich. The revolts in the other parts of the country, in the south as far as Devonshire, and in Yorkshire, more easily dispersed.

    vii. The measures after the immediate suppression of the rising. The letters of manumission — unconstitutional indeed from the first — revoked; severe and cruel trials of the rebels chiefly under Sir Robert Tresilian, the Chief Justice. Fifteen hundred said to have been executed, seven thousand in all to have perished. — JULY 2.

4. Effects of the Revolt.

NOVEMBER. *a* Unanimity of the Parliament, while divided upon the political grievances and pressing economy upon the King, on the retention of villenage ; no villein's son to be apprenticed in a town, or placed at school. [From this rising however dates the final decay of villenage.]

b Gradual disappearance of John of Gaunt from a conspicuous place as a political leader.

1381.
1382.
1383.
  c Religious reaction, increased by Wyclif's denial of Transubstantiation. Wyclif's principal adherents in Oxford induced to recant, his doctrines condemned by a Council of the Province of Canterbury at Blackfriars, MAY. Examined in person before another Council at Oxford, NOVEMBER. Death of Wyclif, 1384.

1382-1389. B The King's Minority after the Peasant Revolt.

1. The continuance of the war.

1382. *a* French victory at Rosbecque over Philip van Arteveldt and the Flemish towns.

1383. *b* Unsuccessful expedition of Henry Spencer Bishop of Norwich to Flanders (nominally a crusade on behalf of Urban VI. against the anti-Pope Clement VII.). MAY—OCT.

c Truce with France. JAN. **1384**—MAY, **1385**.
1385. French expedition to Scotland, and Scotch invasion of England ; the invasion repelled, and Edinburgh burnt. Capture of Ghent by the French, and threatened invasion of England. **1385-1386**.

1386. *d* Departure of John of Gaunt with an English expedition to Castille, to assert his claim to the Castilian throne.

1387. *e* Capture of a fleet of Flemings, French, and Spaniards by Richard Fitz-Alan, Earl of Arundel. MARCH. Retreat of John of Gaunt from Castille to Gascony.

1388. *f* Close of John of Gaunt's designs upon Castille by the marriage of his daughter Katharine to Henry of Castille.

1389.   *g* Truces with France. **1389-1392. 1392-1393. 1394** for four years. **1396** for twenty-five years, upon the King's marriage to Isabella of France.

1382-1389. 2. Progress of internal affairs.

a The King's friends and advisers. His half-brothers, John and Thomas Holland (sons of Johanna of Kent by her first marriage with Sir Thomas Holland) created Earls of Huntingdon and Kent. Robert de Vere, Earl of Oxford; Sir Simon Burley; Michael de la Pole, son of a Hull merchant.

1383.   *b* Michael de la Pole made Chancellor.

1384.   *c* Thomas of Woodstock and Edmund of Langley, the King's uncles, created Dukes of Gloucester and York; Michael de la Pole, Earl of Suffolk.

1385.   *d* Death of Johanna, the King's mother. De Vere created Marquess of Dublin, receiving as an appanage the whole territory and lordship of Ireland. Haughty refusal of the King to allow Parliamentary annual enquiry.

e Party of baronial opposition to de Vere and de la Pole as favourites, under the Duke of Gloucester and Henry of Bolingbroke (son of John of Gaunt), including Thomas Beauchamp, Earl of Warwick; Thomas Mowbray, Earl of Nottingham; Richard Fitz-Alan, Earl of Arundel; Archbishop Courtenay, and the Bishop of Ely (brother of the Earl of Arundel).

1386.   *f* De Vere further created Duke of Ireland. OCT. Outbreak of the storm; dismissal of the Chancellor demanded by Parliament, the King's haughty refusal; the King threatened with deposition by the Duke of Gloucester and the Bishop of Ely (acting as envoys). The Chancellor (de la Pole, Earl of Suffolk) removed from office, and charged with malversation, corruption, and neglect to relieve Ghent: sentenced to fine and imprisonment. A Continual Council, under Gloucester, nominated for a year to regulate the realm and the royal household.

1387.   *g* Suffolk liberated by the King at the close of Parliament. Formation of a royal party—

Sir Simon Burley, Archbishop Neville (of York), the Duke of Ireland, Chief Justice Tresilian, Sir Nicholas Brember ex-Lord Mayor of London. Attempt of the King to raise an armed force by means of the Sheriffs, and to exclude his opponents from the next Parliament. Opinion obtained from five of the judges that the Continual Council was contrary to the prerogative; that the King's servants could not be removed by Parliament; that the sentence on Suffolk was erroneous. The King however compelled, by Gloucester's armed force, to receive the Petition of Complaint against his advisers. NOV.

1388. *h* The Duke of Ireland, Neville, Suffolk, Tresilian, Brember, "appealed" in Parliament on a charge of high treason by Gloucester, Henry of Bolingbroke (Earl of Derby), Warwick, Nottingham, Arundel (hence called "The Lords appellant"). FEB. Suffolk and Vere condemned to death (but had already escaped); Tresilian and Brember executed; Neville translated by Pope Urban VI. to St. Andrews (which acknowledged the anti-Pope Clement VII). The judges who had condemned the Council banished for life to Ireland. Sir Simon Burley and three others of the royal household found guilty of high treason and executed. "The merciless Parliament."

1389. *i* The King declared himself of age. MAY 3

1389-1395. C The King's Constitutional Rule.

1. Moderation of the King. The Lords appellant removed from the Council, but neither de Vere nor the banished judges recalled (Suffolk died this year in France). Return of John of Gaunt to England, and reconciliation between the King and Gloucester. The Lords appellant

1390. restored to the Council. John of Gaunt made Duke of Aquitaine for life. Archbishop William of Wykeham Chancellor. **1389-1391**. Archbishop Arundel. **1391-1396**.

2. Activity of Parliament.

a Statute of Provisors (third) re-enacting statutes
1390. of **1351** and **1362** against Papal claims of presentation.

1390.		*b* Statute against interference with due course of justice by livery and maintenance.
1391.		*c* The Statute of Uses. Forbiddal of the practice of granting lands to a layman in use for the Church, and thus evading the Statute of Mortmain.
1391.		*d* The King's consent refused to the petition of the Commons that villeins be not allowed to acquire lands or put their sons to school " to advance them by means of clergy," *i.e.* scholarship.
1393.		*e* The great Statute of " Præmunire facias."

      i. The right of recovering the presentation to a church benefice declared to belong only to the King's Court.

      ii. The Papal practice of translation condemned.

      iii. The pursuance in the Court of Rome of such translations, processes, excommunications, bulls, &c., to be punished with forfeiture of goods.

On the other hand should be noticed, as a condemnation of political opposition—

1390-1391.   *f* Declarations of Parliament that the Prerogative of the King is unaffected by the legislation of his reign or of his progenitors (including that of Edward II.).

    3. Pacific influences.

      a Moderating influence of John of Gaunt and of the Queen, "the good Queen Anne."

      b Absence of Henry of Bolingbroke (Earl of Derby) from England, on a pilgrimage to Jerusalem and a crusade with the Teutonic knights against the heathens in Prussia.

1394-1395.   4. Growth of Lollardry. Twelve Lollard articles presented to the Parliament at York (during Richard's absence in Ireland) complaining of the secular power of the clergy, the idolatry of the mass, multiplication of chantries, auricular confession, and celibacy of the clergy.

Upon Richard's return from Ireland an oath of abjuration of heresy imposed.

1394-1395.   5. The King's expedition to Ireland to vindicate the power of the crown.

1395-1398. D **The change to Absolutism.**

1. The first symptoms of change of temper in the King. The Earl of Arundel, who had quarrelled with John of Gaunt, struck by the King on the occasion of the funeral of Queen Anne.

1394.

2. Marriage of Richard to Isabella of France. Truce with France for twenty-five years. Cherbourg surrendered to the King of Navarre and Brest restored to the Duke of Britanny. Increased extravagance of the Court.

1396.

3. Complaint of the Commons as to the administration and defence of the realm, and the number of bishops and ladies maintained at the Court. The Commons compelled to surrender the name of the proposer of the Bill—Haxey—and to apologize. Recall of the banished judges from Ireland. Arrest of the Earl of Warwick and Duke of Gloucester (the latter sent in custody to Calais). Surrender of the Earl of Arundel.

1397.

4. Meeting of a second and packed Parliament. The King's vengeance for **1388**. The pardons of Gloucester, Warwick, and Arundel revoked. Archbishop Arundel impeached and banished, being translated by the Pope (Boniface IX.) to S. Andrews. Trial and execution of the Earl of Arundel. Death of Gloucester in prison at Calais. Confession and perpetual imprisonment of Warwick.

1397.

5. Aggrandisement of the House of Lancaster, and of the King's adherents. The Beauforts, children of John of Gaunt by Katharine Swinford, acknowledged as members of the royal family. Henry of Bolingbroke Earl of Derby created Duke of Hereford (at the same time Mowbray Earl of Nottingham, the fifth of the Lords appellant, created Duke of Norfolk; Edward (son of Edmund of York) created Duke of Aumale; the Hollands, Dukes of Surrey and Exeter.

1395-1397.

6. The Parliament of **1398**.

    i. The Acts of the Parliament of **1388** declared void.

    ii. The customs on wool, wool-fells, and leather granted for the King's life.

       iii. The powers of a Parliament delegated to a standing committee of eighteen members (ten lords temporal, two earls as proctors for the clergy, six members of the Commons.)

       iv. A bull procured, by request of Parliament, from Pope Boniface IX. confirming these proceedings and declaring them irreversible.

[The King's victory was thus complete, and his absolutism acknowledged by the nation.]

1398-1399. E **The Fall of the King.**

1397-1398.   *a* Recriminatory quarrel between the newly-created dukes of Hereford and Norfolk. The quarrel referred by the Permanent Committee to settlement by single combat at Coventry. The combat forbidden by the King; Hereford banished for ten years, Norfolk for life.

1399.   *b* Death of John of Gaunt. Seizure of his estates by the King with the sanction of the Permanent Committee. Departure of the King for Ireland to avenge the defeat and death of Edmund Earl of March, and return of Hereford from France, owing to the influence of Archbishop Arundel, for the recovery of his estates.

    c Landing of Hereford (Henry of Lancaster) at Ravenspur, JULY **4**; Henry joined by Earls of Northumberland (Percy) and Westmoreland (Neville) and Edmund Duke of York, the regent, at Berkeley Castle. March upon Cheshire. Dispersal of the King's forces commanded by the Earl of Salisbury (John de Montacute). Capture of Bristol by Henry. JULY **29**.

    d Landing of the King at Milford Haven, JULY **25**, to find himself deserted. Submission of the King to Henry at Flint. The King brought to London. SEPT. **2**.

    e Parliament summoned by the King to meet upon SEPT. **30**. Resignation of the crown (SEPT. **29**) presented to Parliament on its meeting. The resignation accepted, and articles of accusation presented against Richard complaining of

ANALYSIS OF ENGLISH HISTORY. 93

 i. His unjust conduct to Henry of Lancaster, Archbishop Arundel, and the Duke of Gloucester.

 ii. His breaches of the Constitution, tampering with the judges (**1387**), and appeal to the Pope (**1398**).

 iii. His illegal taxation, especially the extortion of money from seventeen counties for pardons (**1399**), non-payment of loans, and alienation of crown lands.

 iv. His claim to the absolute right of legislation.

Sentence of deposition pronounced. SEPT. **30**.

1399-1413.   **HENRY IV.**   1399-1413.

Henry = (1) Mary de Bohun, = (2) Joan of Navarre.

| Henry. | Thomas. | John, Duke of Bedford = (1) Anne of Burgundy, = (2) Jacquetta of Luxembourg. | Humphrey, Duke of Gloucester. = (1) Jacqueline of Holland, = (2) Eleanor Cobham. | Blanche = Lewis, of Bavaria, eldest son of the Emperor Rupert. | Philippa = Eric of Denmark. |

A Nature of Henry's Claim, and Measures to Consolidate his Throne.

 1. Henry's claim to the throne.

  a As being descended by right line of blood, coming from the good Lord Henry the Third.

  b The right that God has sent with the help of kin and friends.

  c The realm was in point to be undone for default of governance and undoing of the good laws.

 2. The claim accepted by Parliament. The Lancastrian title therefore Parliamentary, in contrast to the hereditary claim of the House of Mortimer.

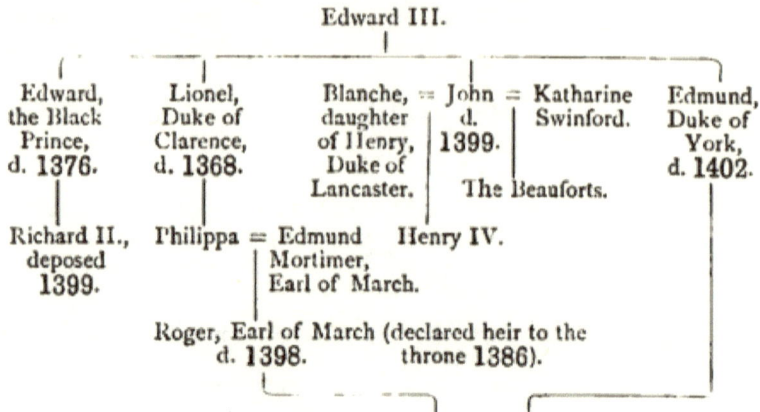

3. Supremacy of Parliament recognized throughout this reign more fully than before.
4. The support of the Church confirmed by the statute De Hæretico Comburendo for the suppression of Lollardism. Sautre burned, **1401**. Badby burned, **1410**.
5. The support of the nobles confirmed by the prospect of the renewal of the French war.

B Relations with France.

1. France divided between two factions, that of John, Duke of Burgundy and Count of Flanders, (inclined to peace with England on account of the industrial connection between Flanders and England), and of Louis of Orleans (succeeded after his murder, by the Count of Armagnac father-in-law of one of his sons).

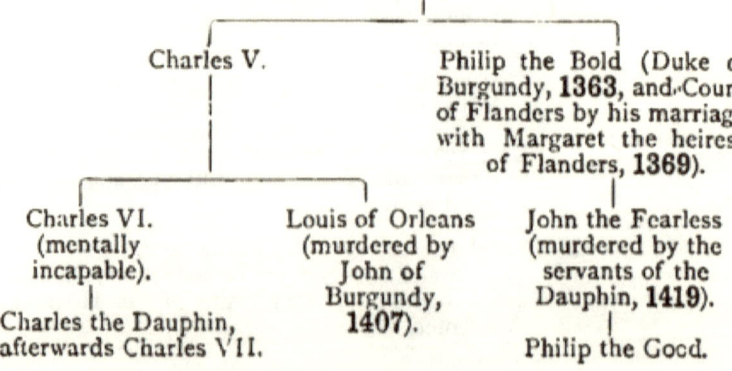

Scotch invasions encouraged by France. Battle of Homildon Hill near Wooler, in Northumberland. SEPT. **1402**. Desultory fighting in the Channel. **1403-1404**. Owen Glyndwr recognized by the French as Prince of Wales. **1404**. French aid sent him. **1405** and **1407**.

C Revolts against Henry.

1400.
1. Plot of the Earls of Huntingdon and Kent, (the half-brothers of Richard II.,) the Earl of Salisbury and Lord Despenser to release Richard and murder the King, betrayed possibly by the Earl of Rutland (degraded from being Duke of Aumale), and followed by the death of Richard.

1400-1410.
2. Revolt of Wales under Owen Glyndwr (reputed a descendant of Llewelyn, the last native Prince of Wales). **1400**. Defeat and capture of Edmund Mortimer, uncle of the Earl of March. **1402**. Glyndwr joined by Henry Percy (Hotspur) and Thomas Percy, Earl of Worcester, owing possibly to Henry's remissness in ransoming Edmund Mortimer (Henry Percy's brother-in-law), or to his claim upon the Scotch prisoners taken at Homildon, or to his tardiness in repaying their loans; defeat of the confederates at Shrewsbury. **1403**. Glyndwr, however, recognized by the French as Prince of Wales. **1404**. Supported by French aid. **1405** and **1407**. Crippled by defeat, **1409**. Glyndwr's death probably about **1410**.

3. Rising in the North by Henry Percy the elder, Earl of Northumberland, Mowbray, Earl of Nottingham (son of the Lord Appellant), Scrope, Archbishop of York: articles of accusation against the King, and of reform to be laid before Parliament. Execution of Archbishop Scrope and Mowbray. **1407**.

4. The last rising of the Earl of Northumberland. Defeat and death at Bramham Moor, in Yorkshire. **1408**.

D Turn of the Tide. 1405-1409.

1405.
1. Capture of James, Prince of Scotland (son of Robert III.), on his way to the French Court. Detained in England till **1424**, married to Joan Beaufort.

1407.   2. France occupied by the civil strife following upon the murder of Louis of Orleans by John of Burgundy.

1408-1409.   3. Defeat and death of Northumberland, **1408**; and first decisive defeat of the Welsh. **1409**.

1401-1410.   E Claims put forward by Parliament.

1401.   1. Freedom of Speech in Parliament affirmed. Petition that redress of grievances should precede supply of money refused by the King, but in practice secured by postponing the grant till the last day of the session.

1404.   2. Attack upon the constitution of the Royal household, and petition against aliens (in consequence of Henry's second marriage). The names of the Royal Council to be published. In a second Parliament of this year called the Unlearned, because lawyers were excluded, proposed confiscation of the temporalities of the clergy for one year, and resumption of all grants since **1367**.

1406.   3. The defence of the Channel to be intrusted to a body of merchants in exchange for the receipt of tonnage and poundage. Sixteen Members (including two Commoners) appointed in Parliament as a Continuous Council to advise the King till the next Parliament. Audit of accounts claimed by the Commons and granted. Thirty-one articles of reform in expenditure and management presented to the King by the Commons, and sworn to by the Council.

1407.   4. All grants of money to be declared only by the mouth of the Speaker of the Commons, not to be altered by House of Lords, nor discussed in the presence of the King.

1410.   5. Renewed proposals for the permanent confiscation of part of the temporalities of the Church for the purposes of State rejected.

1411-1415.   F The last years of the King's Reign.

1. Gradual decline of the King's health from **1406**.

1411.   2. Resistance of the King to the growing claims of Parliament and power of the Continuous Council. Support given by the Prince of Wales and the Beauforts to the Burgundian party in France and expedition to France.

1412.	Dismissal of the Prince of Wales from the Council; the appointment of the Continuous Council annulled; change in foreign policy and support of the Armagnacs by a force under Clarence. Parliament, at their own request, declared "loyal" by the King.
1413.	Death of the King. MARCH. Notice the extreme poverty of the nation, the amount of treason and disaffection, and the strength of the Commons throughout the reign.

1413-1422.   HENRY V.   1413-1422.

Henry V. = Katharine of France = Owen Tudor.
 | |
Henry VI.   Edmund, Earl of
                              Richmond.
                                    |
                              Henry VII.

1413-1415.   A The Years before the War.

1413.	1. Appointment of Henry Beaufort, Bishop of Winchester as Chancellor in place of Archbishop Arundel. Condemnation of Sir John Oldcastle
1413. 1414.	for Lollard opinions, and suppression of the apprehended Lollard rising. JAN. Escape of Oldcastle, afterwards captured in the Welsh Marches and burnt, **1418**.
1414.	2. Last great Constitutional victory of the Commons; statutes to be made without altering the petitions on which they are based.
1416.	3. Final and complete confiscation (on the petition of the Commons) of the alien priories, *i.e.* of houses depending upon foreign monasteries, to the Crown.
1414-1418.	4. Council of Constance: healing of the schism caused by the rival Popes, John XXIII., Gregory XII., and Benedict XIII., and election of Martin V. as Pope through the co-operation of Henry and the Emperor Sigismund. Condemnation of John Huss for preaching heretical doctrines.
1415.	5. Plot of Richard, Earl of Cambridge (son of Edmund, Duke of York) in favour of his brother-in-law, Edmund, Earl of March. Execution of the conspirators, Cambridge, Lord Scrope of Masham, and Sir Thomas Grey.

H

The French War. 1415–1422.

1414. 1. Restoration of Henry's rights as King of France demanded, JUNE. Aquitaine offered by the French, but the compromise rejected.

2. Sailing of the expedition, AUG. **11.** Capture of Harfleur, SEPT. **22.** Great sickness in English camp. March towards Calais through a hostile country (Normandy, Picardy, Artois), OCT. **8.**
1415. Attempt to cross the Somme near Abbeville, OCT. **13.** Passage of the Somme by night at Péronne, OCT. **20.** Battle of Agincourt, OCT. **25.** Arrival at Calais, OCT. **29**; at Dover, NOV. **17.**

1416. 3. Visit of Emperor Sigismund to England and attempt to mediate in the war. Offensive and defensive alliance concluded between him and Henry. Organization of English army and fleet by Henry. Struggle with France for the mastery of the Channel. Open alliance between John, Duke of Burgundy, and the English.

1417. 4. Activity of Henry in shipbuilding. Ordinances issued for the fleets and armies. [This may be regarded as the basis of the English law of the Admiralty.] The commencement of loans for the war by Cardinal Beaufort. Capture of Caen, Bayeux, and other Norman towns.
1418. Isolation and siege of Rouen. Expulsion of the Armagnacs from Paris by the citizens.

1419. 5. Capture of Rouen. Henry's attempt to settle the government of Normandy.

6. Murder of John, Duke of Burgundy at Montereau,
1419. in the presence of the Dauphin, followed by the Treaty of Troyes (due mainly to the determination of Philip the Good, Duke of Burgundy and master of Paris, to exclude the Dauphin from the Throne). Henry acknowledged as
1420. Regent of France during Charles's life, and as his successor on the throne: marriage of Henry with Katharine, Charles's eldest daughter: England and France to retain their own laws, and neither to be in any way subject to the other.

1421. Henry recalled from England to the war by the defeat and death of Clarence at Beaugé, in Anjou. MARCH.
Capture of Dreux and **(1422)** of Meaux. Death of the King, AUG. **31, 1422.**

Notice the general popularity of this war, and the share of the clergy in promoting it, possibly from fear of confiscation. There could however be little legitimate claim to France by a King whose title was mainly parliamentary and who certainly was not "heir general" to Edward III.; the one excuse for the war being the constant support given by France to all risings in England against the House of Lancaster.

1422-1461. **HENRY VI.** 1422-1461 (died 1471).

Henry VI. = Margaret of Anjou.
|
Edward = Anne Neville.
killed at
Tewkesbury,
1471.

1422-1435. A **Progress of affairs till the death of Bedford** (marking the close of the first period in the loss of France), **1435.**

1422. 1. Supreme authority in France given to John, Duke of Bedford; Humphrey, Duke of Gloucester, to act as his representative and as head of the Council in England.

1422.
1423.
2. Consolidation of the conquest of northern France by a marriage between Bedford and the sister of Philip of Burgundy, and by a Treaty with John, Duke of Britanny.

1424.
3. Release of King James I. of Scotland from imprisonment, and return to Scotland with his wife Joan Beaufort. Defeat of the French and Scots at Verneuil. AUG. Success neutralised by the invasion of Hainault by Gloucester, to assert the claims of his wife, Jacqueline of Hainault, (the divorced wife of the Duke of Brabant); the Burgundian forces withdrawn from Bedford to oppose Gloucester. OCT. First blow to the Burgundian alliance.

1425.
4. Return of Bedford to England to mediate between Gloucester and Henry Beaufort, Bishop of Winchester, who were disputing for supremacy in the Council.

1426. 5. The Parliament of Bats (Clubs); pacification and resignation of the Chancellorship by Beaufort. Beaufort made Cardinal and Papal Legate for the Hussite Crusade. Alarm at this in England. Cessation of war in Hainault.

ANALYSIS OF ENGLISH HISTORY.

1428. 6. Bedford thus able to resume the offensive. Siege of Orleans by the English, to open the road to Bourges, the court of the Dauphin.

1429. 7. The appearance of Jeanne Darc. Relief of Orleans by her. APRIL. Talbot defeated at Patay. JUNE. The Dauphin crowned as Charles VII. at Rheims. JULY. Beaufort's troops raised for Hussite Crusade sent by him to France instead of to Bohemia.

1430. 8. Capture of Jeanne Darc at Compiègne, sold to the Burgundians, and handed over to English. Tried and burned for witchcraft at Rouen, MAY, **1431.** [For estimate of her character and work in arousing moral enthusiasm in France, see Green, pp. 274-278.]

1431. 9. Coronation of Henry at Paris. DEC. Bedford's efforts however mainly confined to securing Normandy, re-establishing order there, and binding it closely to England. Henry's court at Rouen for a year.

1430-1434. 10. Cardinal Beaufort now supreme in the Council and the director of English diplomacy with Scotland and Burgundy.

1432. 11. Death of the Duchess of Bedford, and second marriage of Bedford to Jacquetta of Luxemburg without obtaining the consent of Duke of Burgundy, her feudal superior. The second **1433.** blow to the Burgundian alliance.

1435. 12. Congress of Arras, through the diplomacy of Beaufort, to arbitrate between France and England. Offer of the French to cede Normandy and Guienne, upon homage, on condition of surrender of all English claims and possessions in France (including Calais). Refusal of the English. Death of Bedford, and final defection of Burgundy from the English alliance. SEPT.

1435-1449. B **Course of events till loss of Normandy.**

1436. 1. Renewal of the struggle between Gloucester and Cardinal Beaufort. Recapture of Paris by the French. Henry's dominions in France limited to Normandy, Picardy, and Maine.

1436-1437. 2. Success of Richard Duke of York as Regent in Normandy.

1437. 3. York succeeded as Regent of France by Richard Beauchamp, Earl of Warwick, then by John Beaufort, Earl of Somerset.

1440. 4. Recapture of Harfleur and ravaging of Picardy by Somerset and his brother, Edmund Beaufort, during the conspiracy of the Dauphin against Charles VII. Re-appointment of York as Regent.

1441. 5. Condemnation of Eleanor Cobham (wife of Gloucester) to imprisonment for life in the Isle of Man for practising witchcraft against the King's life. Retirement of Gloucester from public life.

1442. The King of age.

1444. 6. Truce with France. York superseded as Regent by Edmund Beaufort, Marquis of Dorset. The Beaufort policy to secure the Lancastrian succession by the King's marriage carried on in the Council (owing to the age of Cardinal Beaufort) by William de la Pole (Earl of Suffolk), who had come into political prominence after Gloucester's retirement.

1445. 7. Marriage of Henry to Margaret of Anjou; Maine to be surrendered to her father (possibly only a verbal promise).

1447. 8. Re-appearance of Gloucester as head of the war-party. His arrest and sudden death. FEB. Death of Cardinal Beaufort. APRIL.

1448. 9. Surrender of Maine by Marquis of Suffolk to avoid war with France and to make it easier to hold Normandy and Guienne.

1449-1450. 10. Invasion and conquest of Normandy by the French attributed by the English nation to the incapacity of the Regent, Edmund Beaufort (now Duke of Somerset).

1449-1451. C **Course of events till the loss óf Guienne.**

1. National discontent at the issue of the war and the feeble government at home.

1450. *a* Murder of the Bishop of Chichester at Portsmouth by the sailors, while paying the soldiers going to France.

b Accusations of treason and malversation brought against Suffolk. Upon submission to King's mercy banished for five years. [This was the last impeachment till **1621**.]

1450. Murdered at sea while leaving the kingdom. MAY **2**.

1450. *c* Unsuccessful revolt of Kent under John Cade (calling himself "Mortimer"). The "complaint of the Commons of Kent" laid before the King, demanding—

(1) Resumption of the gifts from the royal demesne.

(2) Return of the Duke of York to court.

(3) Punishment of the Suffolk party for the death of the Duke of Gloucester and Cardinal Beaufort, and for the loss of Normandy.

(4) Abolition of abuses (*e.g.* undue interference with elections, heavy taxation, promotion of favourites).

The King's forces defeated at Sevenoaks, JUNE **18**. Entry of Cade into London, JULY **3**. Seizure and execution of Lord Say, the Treasurer, JULY **4**. Cade defeated at London Bridge, JULY **5**. Dispersal of most of the rebels on the receipt of sealed pardons; the prisons however opened by Cade, who formed the prisoners into a new force. Cade finally killed in Kent by a force under the sheriff, Iden.

1451. 2. Guienne conquered by the French. Final expulsion of the English from France (excepting Calais) due partly to the contest between the Commons (demanding the removal of Somerset from the Council) and the King.

1451-1461. D Course of events till the accession of Edward IV.

1452. 1. Appearance of York (who had been Lieutenant of Ireland **1449-1450**) in arms demanding the trial of Somerset. Failure of the attempt, the nation not yet prepared for civil war.

1452-1453. 2. Disastrous attempt under Talbot, Earl of Shrewsbury, to recover Guienne. Birth of the Prince of Wales. Two consequences—

(*a*) The Queen, not Somerset, the head of the party of the Lancastrian succession.

(*b*) York's hope of succeeding at the death of Henry crushed.

1454. Madness of the King. Somerset sent to the Tower. York appointed by the Lords "Protector and Defender of the Realm."

1455. 3. Recovery of the King. Somerset restored to power. York summoned to submit to arbitration at Leicester. Appearance of York and the Nevilles (Earls of Salisbury and Warwick) in arms. Somerset slain and King captured at St. Alban's.

1455. 4. Return of the King's illness and second Pro-
1456–1458. tectorate of York. Recovery of the King, and
two years of comparative quiet.

1458 5. Apparent reconciliation of the rival parties
1459. at St. Paul's. Attempted arrest of the Earl of
Salisbury checked by his victory at Bloreheath,
but followed by flight of the Nevilles to Calais,
of which Warwick was captain, and of York to
Ireland, and by the attainder of York and the
Nevilles in a Parliament at Coventry.

1460 6. Return of York and the Nevilles. Defeat of the
Royal army and capture of the King at
Northampton. JULY. The crown claimed by
the Duke of York as the representative of
Lionel of Clarence. Compromise by Parliament, Henry to be King for life, and York
recognised as his heir. OCT.

1460. 7. Rising in the North for the Lancastrian succession. (The industrial and commercial classes
being chiefly in favour of York from a desire
for a strong rule.) Battle of Wakefield. DEC.
29. Defeat of York who was killed in the
battle, and execution of the Earl of Salisbury.

1461. Victory in the West at Mortimer's Cross by
Edward of York. FEB. 3.

Victory of the Northern Lancastrian army
advancing upon London over Warwick at St.
Alban's. FEB. 17. Retirement of the vic-
torious Lancastrians northwards. Entry of
Edward into London and acknowledgment as
King. MARCH 1–4. Utter defeat of the Lan-
castrians at Towton Field (near Tadcaster).
MARCH 29

E Decline of Parliament in this Reign.

1. Sanction of Parliament still considered necessary
for legislation. The power of granting and
controlling subsidies and impeaching ministers
retained by the Commons as well as the security
already obtained that statutes, when drawn up,
should correspond exactly to petitions **(1414)**.
But powers of Parliament encroached upon by
Royal Council. During the minority the Council was a Council of Regency, in possession of
the power of the Crown, and thus independent
of Parliamentary control. After **1437** the right
of appointing members claimed and exerted by
Parliament **(1402, 1406, 1410)** was resumed
by the King.

2. Increased power of the Royal Council which during this period, Richard II.—Henry VI., reached the highest point of its authority, independent both of the Crown and of Parliament.

 a Tenure of office. Under Richard II. and Henry IV. for one year. Afterwards for the King's life.

 b Authority of the Council with reference to the Crown.

  (1) The King could appoint or dismiss individuals, but he could not dispense with a Council altogether. A Royal Council must exist.

  (2) Certain non-ministerial officials, *e.g.*, the Marshal, and the Archbishops, had an *ex-officio* claim to a seat.

  (3) The King, though not bound to take, was bound to receive the advice of the Council.

  (4) Every writ issued by the King had to be sealed with the Great Seal which—except under Edward II. and Richard II.—was in the hands of the Chancellor. Partly to protect the King against hasty grants which might be prejudicial to his prerogative, partly to protect the Chancellor—by showing that he had warrant for his act—partly to secure that the Council should be consulted, a theory grew up, most fully expressed by the enactment that every writ or grant should be endorsed,

1389.

   i. By the Signet,
   ii. By the Privy Seal,
   iii. By the Great Seal.

  Thus the Chancellor or Council could interpose remonstrance.

  (5) The highest point of the authority of the Council with reference is marked by two enactments.

1406.
   i. That all letters containing orders to the Chancellor be under the cognizance of the Council.

1444.
   ii. That all grants should be under the cognizance of the Council.

  (6) This great authority of the Council during the first half of the fifteenth century may be ascribed to

   i. The doubtful claim and bad health of **Henry IV.**

ii. The absence of Henry V. from England.

iii. The long minority of Henry VI. But after **1437** the appointments to the Council were made solely by the King.

c Change in name. The Royal Council under the minority of Henry VI. was a Council of Regency, and thus there grew up within the Council a smaller and more authoritative body. This change may be considered as coinciding in time with the rise of the name "Privy Council."

d Functions of the Council.

(1) Revenue and finance. Review of the whole royal outgoings (whether private expenditure, or public expenses) and consideration as to best means of raising money.

(2) Dealings with aliens as being under the protection of the Crown or of treaties, the extent and validity of which could only be decided by the Council.

(3) Dealings with trade, *e.g.*, in the appointment of staple towns, impressment of labourers, and issue of proclamations dispensing in individual cases with the restrictions upon trade.

1400-1444.
(4) Dealings with the Church, *e.g.*, in granting dispensations from the Statutes of Mortmain, and in making ecclesiastical appointments, though the contest between England and the Pope was but slight during this period, as the Lancastrian policy was to court the Church, and the Statutes of Præmunire were frequently transgressed.

(5) The preservation of the King's peace, not only by suppressing riots, but judicially by trying rioters.

(6) Equitable judicial power. Regarded with much jealousy by Parliament ; *e. g.*

1400. Petition that all personal actions be tried at common law.

1422. Petition that no one be brought before Council or Chancery unless unable to get right at common law.

But on this point the general feeling in favour of the equitable jurisdiction of the Council and Chancellor was of real value to justice. [It was the lawlessness of nobles that men feared rather than the arbitrary power of the Crown.] Thus even the Commons, in the alarm excited

ANALYSIS OF ENGLISH HISTORY.

1453.
 by Cade's rebellion, passed an act enhancing the judicial powers of the Council. [For the substance of this note see "Privy Council," by A. V. Dicey. Macmillan & Co.]

 e In the reigns of Edward IV. and Richard III. the Council was tending to become a committee of Royal Nominees; its records a blank. [For continuance of this note see Henry VII. F, and Edward VI. E.]

F Comparison of the House of Lancaster and York; (*a*) with reference to Title, (*b*) with reference to Constitutional Government.

 a Title (see Tables at the beginning of reigns of Henry IV. and Edward IV.). The Yorkist House was undoubtedly in the position of "heir-general," the Lancastrian on the other hand was in the position of "heir-male."

 b Constitutional Government.
  The rule of the House of Lancaster was in the main constitutional, especially under Henry IV. and Henry V.; that of the House of York unconstitutional.

  i. The Lancastrian rule.
   a The growth of independence in the Parliament, and especially in the Commons.

1401.
1407.
1401.

1404-1413.

1414.
1433.

   Freedom of speech without interference of the King in the deliberations; money grants to be declared by the Speaker of the Commons; even the request that answers to petitions should precede supply, though refused by Henry IV., practically secured by postponing the grant to the last day of the session; grants appropriated for special purposes, in some cases permanently (*e.g.* tonnage and poundage for the fleet, and part of the subsidy on wool for Calais); the expenses of the household separated from those of the realm; all matters of public interest, even foreign policy, laid before the Commons (*e.g.*, the Treaty of Troyes, **1420**); the Commons secured in the right that acts when drawn up should correspond exactly with their petitions; the right of auditing the accounts acknowledged **1407** and **1433**.

   b Authority of Parliament over the nomination of the Royal Council claimed, **1404, 1406. 1410**, though the nomination was resumed by the King, **1437**.

- *c* The action of the King checked by the influence of the Royal Council (see note upon Royal Council).
 ii. The Yorkist rule.
    - *a* Suspension of Parliamentary action. No Parliament called between **1475** and **1483** (except in **1478** for the attainder of the Duke of Clarence). Income granted by the early Yorkist Parliaments to King Edward IV. for life. No instance of impeachment after **1450**. Poverty of national legislation in the Parliaments called by Edward IV.
    - *b* Taxation by benevolences (declared however illegal "as new and unlawful inventions" under Richard III. **1484**).
    - *c* Levy of armed forces by Commissioners of Array, not by authority of Parliament, under Edward IV. and Richard III.
    - *d* Increased rigour of law-courts, *e.g.*, use of torture; unconstitutional authority of John Tiptoft, Earl of Worcester, as Constable, in cases of high treason, "summarily and plainly, on simple inspection of fact."
    - *e* Rise of a new nobility composed of the King's friends, and depending upon his support.
    - *f* The character of the Royal Council materially modified, tending to become an irresponsible Committee of Royal Nominees.
1. The Lords losing hold over the nation owing to their factions, their lust for gold, and selfish scramble for power.
2. The Commons ceasing to be representative; the right of choosing members often confined to the Common Councils of towns or a select body of them.
    - *a* Borough freedom limited by boroughs obtaining charters of incorporation (to protect the civic property from strangers) and thus becoming close bodies; the right of voting confirmed by these charters, but mostly only for the Common Council of the Borough or for a select portion of it.
    - *b* The county franchise restricted by the fixing of a freehold of 40*s*. as the qualification for voters.

1430.

108   ANALYSIS OF ENGLISH HISTORY.

G Causes of the fall of the House of Lancaster in spite of the constitutional character of its rule.

1. The want of success abroad.
2. The weakness of the government at home, shown by the frequency of illegal usurpations upon private property, private wars, "grants of livery" by the great nobles, and failure to enforce the sentence of the law.
3. Want of economical management of the finances.
4. The close connection of the Lancastrians with the clergy.
5. The unpopularity of the Queen, owing to her strong partisanship and supposed connexion with the enemies of the realm—Irish, Scots, French.
6. Weariness of the scramble for power among the Baronage, and desire for a strong government giving protection for life and property.

1461-1483.   EDWARD IV. 1461-1483.

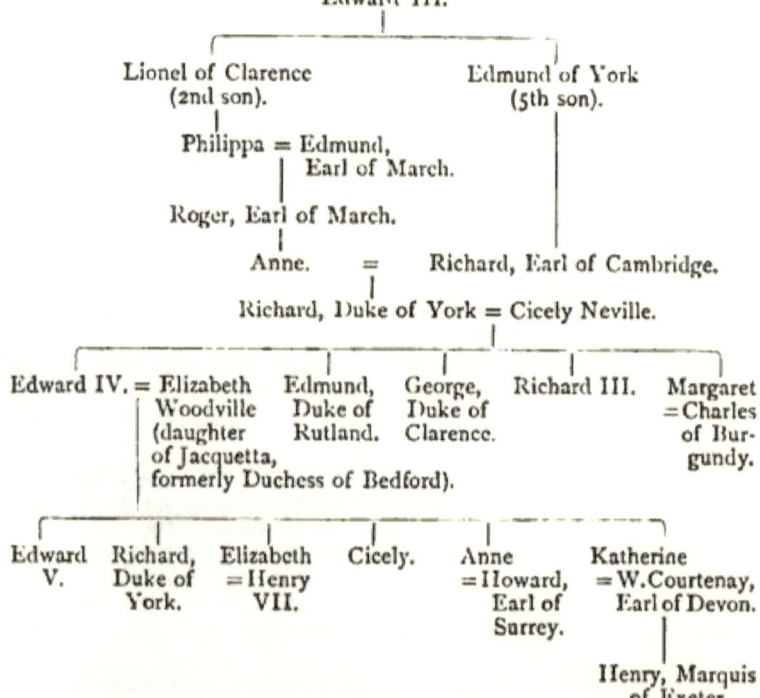

1461-1464. **A Power of the Nevilles.** Richard Neville, Earl of Warwick and of Salisbury, Captain of Calais and Dover, Admiral of the Fleet in the Channel, Warden of the Western Scottish Marches, Lord Chamberlain and Steward; his brother Richard, Lord Montague, Warden of the Eastern Scottish Marches; his brother George, Archbishop of York and Chancellor. This power lasted supreme in the state till the Lancastrian power was finally crushed at the
1464. battle of Hedgley Moor and Hexham, in Northumberland, APRIL and MAY, and till the capture of King Henry.

1464-1471. **B Struggle between the King and Warwick.**

1464. 1. Warwick's policy to secure an alliance with France by the King's marriage to the sister of the queen of Lewis XI. Edward's avowal of his marriage with Elizabeth Grey, daughter of Sir R. Woodville and Jacquetta, widow of John, Duke of Bedford.

1464. 2. Commencement of struggles at court between the Woodvilles and the Nevilles.

3. Divergence in foreign policy between Warwick
1467. and the King. Question of the marriage of Margaret, the King's sister, with a French prince, or with Charles the Bold, Duke of Burgundy. The French alliance supported by Warwick, the Burgundian favoured by the merchants on account of the trade with Flanders. Archbishop Neville superseded as Chancellor during Warwick's absence in France to negotiate a French alliance. Alliance concluded between Edward and Charles of Burgundy.

1468. 4. Proposed invasion of France in conjunction with Burgundy. Margaret married to Charles of Burgundy. JULY.

1469. 5. Marriage between Isabel Neville (Warwick's daughter) and Duke of Clarence, the King's second brother. Rising in the north of discontented peasantry under Robin of Redesdale, supported by Clarence and Warwick. The King for a time a prisoner after the fight at Edgecote near Banbury. JULY. Issue by the King of a general pardon. DEC.

1470. 6. Clarence and Warwick denounced by the King, and forced to take refuge in France. MARCH. Reconciliation between Queen Margaret and Warwick. Marriage of Prince Edward to Anne Neville (Warwick's daughter). Consequent dissatisfaction of Clarence.
Landing of Clarence and Warwick at Dartmouth and flight of Edward to Flanders. SEPT.-OCT

Henry VI. restored to the throne. OCT.

1471. Landing of Edward nominally to recover his hereditary duchy. MARCH **14.** Joined by Clarence at Warwick. MARCH **30.** Admitted into London by Archbishop Bourchier. Warwick and Montague defeated and slain at Barnet. APRIL **14.** Rising for the House of Lancaster in the West under Somerset and Jasper Tudor. Landing of Queen Margaret at Weymouth. APRIL **14.** Her army overtaken by Edward at Tewkesbury on its march up the Severn Valley towards the North. Defeat of Margaret and death of Prince Edward. MAY **4,** King Henry found dead in the Tower. MAY **21,**

C Foreign Policy.

1473-1474. 1. Preparations for war with France in conjunction with Charles of Burgundy. Large grants in Parliament, and first collection of "Benevolences."

1473. 2. Secret defection of Charles of Burgundy. Betrothal of Mary of Burgundy to Maximilian (son of Emperor Frederick III.) in the hopes of securing for Charles the imperial crown.

1475. 3. Treaty of Pecquigny between Lewis XI. and Edward. Expenses of war paid and pension of 50,000 crowns promised to Edward, and the Dauphin Charles betrothed to Edward's daughter Elizabeth. AUG. **29.**

1477. 4. Death of Charles of Burgundy. Marriage of Mary to Maximilian. Edward faithful to the French alliance, but neutral in the war between Lewis and Maximilian.

1478. [Clarence accused and attainted of high treason for his complicity with the Lancastrians in **1470.** His death possibly due to the enmity of Gloucester, with whom he had quarrelled since Gloucester's marriage with Anne Neville. **1472.**]

1482. 5. Expedition of Gloucester in support of the claim to the Scotch throne by the Duke of Albany against his elder brother James III. (upon a promise by Albany to hold Scotland as a fief of England.) Capture of Edinburgh by Gloucester and Albany. Betrothal of Albany (though he had two wives living) to Cicely, Edward's daughter (previously betrothed to Prince James of Scotland). Berwick again an English possession.

1482-1483. 6. Breach by Lewis of the treaty of Pecquigny. The Dauphin betrothed to Margaret of Austria (daughter of Maximilian and Mary of Burgundy). **1482.** Preparations for war with France.

1483. Death of the King. APRIL 9.

EDWARD V. APRIL 9—JUNE 22, 1483,
and
RICHARD III. JUNE, 1483—AUGUST, 1485.

Richard III. = Anne Neville.
|
Edward, d. **1484.**

A Attack by Richard of Gloucester upon the Queen's party, the Woodvilles and Greys.

1483. King Edward taken from their guardianship at Stony Stratford; Lords Rivers and Grey having been arrested at Northampton, Gloucester appointed by the Council Protector of the King and kingdom. APRIL 29—MAY 4.

B Attack upon the New Nobility created by Edward IV. and against the Succession of his Family.

JUNE, **1483. 1.** Lord Hastings (most prominent of the new nobility) arrested in Council and executed, though he had supported Richard against the Woodvilles.

2. Petition of nobles and "notable persons of the Commons" declaring Edward's children illegitimate, those of Clarence (Edward and Margaret) disabled from the succession by their father's attainder, and Gloucester the undoubted heir of Richard, Duke of York. JUNE **24.**

3. Disappearance and probable murder of Edward V. and Richard of York, between JUNE and OCT. Execution of Lords Rivers and Grey at Pontefract. JUNE or JULY.

C Revival of the Lancastrian Hopes.

1. Support given to Henry Tudor, a refugee in Britanny, by Buckingham (head of the elder baronage, discontented with Richard for refusing him the succession to the Earldom of Hereford, and possibly plotting for himself), and Morton, Bishop of Ely, also a refugee, who was planning a marriage between Henry and Elizabeth of York.

2. Table showing descent of Buckingham and Henry Tudor.

a.

```
                    Edward III.
                         |
                 Thomas of Woodstock.
                         |
                   Anne = Edmund Stafford,
                        | Earl of Buckingham.
                        |
              Humphrey, Duke of Buckingham,
                   killed at Northampton,
                           1460.
        _____|_____
       |                   |                   |
Humphrey, = Margaret Beaufort,   Henry = Margaret Beaufort,
  killed at   daughter of Edmund,  Stafford    Countess of
  St. Alban's   Duke of Somerset.              Richmond.
    1455.
       |
   Henry, = Katharine Woodville.
   Duke of
 Buckingham.
```

b.

```
                    Edward III.
                         |
 Blanche of = John of Gaunt = Katharine Swinford.
 Lancaster |                 |_____
           |                                    |
       Henry IV.                         John Beaufort,
           |                             Earl of Somerset.
           |                                    |
     Henry V. = Katharine = (2) Owen      John Beaufort,
               of France. |   Tudor.     Duke of Somerset.
                          |                     |
                   Edmund Tudor,      =   Margaret (after-
                   Earl of Richmond.   |   wards married to
                                       |   Henry Stafford).
                                       |
                                 Henry Tudor.
```

Oct. 1483. 3. Suppression of the rising of Henry Tudor, (whose arrival had been delayed by storms) and Buckingham. Execution of Buckingham at Salisbury. Nov.

D **The King's Measures of Defence.**
  1484. 1. Apparent reconciliation between Queen Elizabeth (widow of Edward IV.) and Richard. MARCH, 1484.
  2. Summoning of Parliament, and appeal for national support as the restorer of the old liberties. Statutes forbidding "benevolences" (broken however next year, 1485), and seizure of goods before conviction of felony, and fixing forty shillings freehold as qualification for jurors. Statute of Fines, imposing a limit on suits for recovery of lands; forbiddal of "secret feoffments"; enactments for protection of trade. Royal orders manumitting unenfranchised bondmen upon the royal demesne, and endowing religious houses.
  3. Armistice with Britanny and threatened renewal of the war with France (possibly to increase his popularity), and truce for three years with Scotland: the fleet also strengthened.
  4. Disafforestment of lands enclosed under Edward IV.
  1485. 5. Arrangement of marriage with Elizabeth of York.

1485. E **The Fall of the King. 1485.**
  1. Gathering indignation at the reputed murder of the princes.
  2. Collection of benevolences against statute of 1484.
  3. Landing of Henry Tudor at Milford Haven. Treachery of Thomas, Lord Stanley (third husband of Margaret Beaufort), and his brother, Sir W. Stanley, and defeat of Richard at Bosworth Field. AUG. 22, 1485.

1485-1509.   **HENRY VII. 1485-1509.**

Henry VII. = Elizabeth of York.

| Arthur = Katharine d. of Aragon. 1502. | Henry VIII. | Margaret = (1) James IV. of Scotland. = (2) Earl of Angus. = (3) Lord Methven. | Mary = (1) Lewis XII. of France. = (2) Charles Brandon. Duke of Suffolk. |

A Summary of Causes that led to the "New Monarchy"
(begun under Edward IV. and completed under the Tudors).

1. The elder baronage had become impoverished, reduced in numbers (especially in the greater houses), demoralised by the struggle for power, and had lost influence by their violent defiance of law (shown in the "grants of livery" to their retainers, and the maintenance of quarrels in return for service). The newer baronage, as in the case of Edward IV.'s nobility, depended upon the favour of the crown. The constitutional power of the House of Lords superseded by the Council, now a body of royal nominees.

2. The clergy were lacking in moral enthusiasm and in intellectual vigour, and the papacy under Sixtus IV. (**1471**), Alexander VI. (**1492**) and Julius II. (**1503**), was becoming more of an Italian and less of an universal power. The higher clergy (*e.g.*, Morton, Fox, Warham) were becoming mere officials of the royal administration.

3. The House of Commons was less representative and independent, owing to the restrictions in the franchise both in boroughs (owing to the charters of corporations, making the burgesses a close body) and in counties (owing to the legislation of **1430** restricting franchise to 40*s.* freeholders).

4. Growth of wealth and industry among the smaller landowners and the burgess class in the cities increased the desire for settled rule. Weariness of the political struggle.

5. Growth of pauperism, "of the sturdy beggars," (due to the consolidation of small into large holdings, the introduction of sheep-farming upon a large scale, and the break-up of the military households of the nobles), led to desire for a strong rule to repress social disorder and preserve from social anarchy.

6. The crown was the only remaining political power: further strengthened by the union of family titles through the marriage of Henry to Elizabeth of York, and by the wealth accruing from confiscations; rendered independent of Parliamentary subsidies by the cessation of foreign war, and made irresistible in the field by the sole possession of the artillery.

1485–1487. B Establishment upon the Throne.

1485. 1. Henry's title Parliamentary, although he claimed the crown by title of "inheritance," as well as "by the true judgment of God in giving him victory over his enemies." Confirmed by a Bull of Innocent VIII. (**1486**).

1485. 2. Imprisonment of the Earl of Warwick (son of the Duke of Clarence) in the Tower.

TABLE TO ILLUSTRATE THE YORKIST RISINGS.

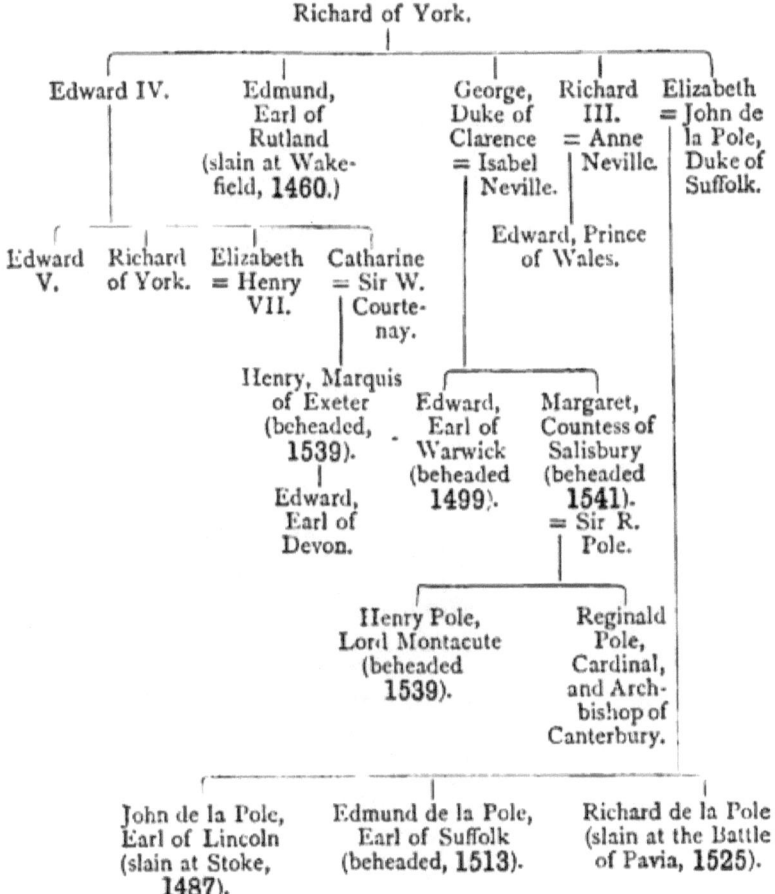

1486. 3. Marriage with Elizabeth of York. JAN. **18**. Postponement of her Coronation: consequent irritation of Yorkists.

4. Revolt of Lord Lovel, and Humphrey and Thomas Stafford, cousins of the Duke of Buckingham, in Worcestershire.

1487. 5. Lambert Simnel personating Edward Earl of Warwick, well known to be a prisoner in the King's hands, recognised by Gerald Fitzgerald, (Earl of Kildare), John de la Pole (see Table) and Margaret, Duchess of Burgundy; defeated at Stoke (near Newark).

1487. 6. Coronation of the Queen. Nov. 25.

C Henry's Government at Home.

1. Continued suspension of Parliamentary life. Parliament only twice called between **1496** and **1509** (**1497** and **1504**).

1486. 2. Extension of the criminal jurisdiction of the Royal Council by the foundation of the Court of Star Chamber as a remedy for the evils of maintenance, the misconduct of sheriffs, riots, and unlawful assemblies. (The Court to consist of the Chancellor, Treasurer, Privy Seal, taking to themselves a bishop, a lord temporal, and the two chief justices.) [See note at the end of the reign.] Re-enactment and enforce-
1504. ment of the statute against "granting of livery."

3. Accumulation of treasure.

   a By obtaining subsidies for wars subsequently evaded (**1488** and **1492**). Resumption of royal grants to the House of York. **1497**.

   b By confiscations, and fines after revolts.

   c By benevolences. (**1492. 1497. 1504.**)

   d By exactions for breach of obsolete statutes upon the information of "promoters" (*e.g.*, Richard Empson and Edmund Dudley).

4. Statutes for the security of property from vexatious attacks.

1489. *a* Statute of Fines, fixing a term of five years after proclamation of a fine in court as a prescriptive title to land barring suits for recovery.

1496. *b* No person rendering service to the King of the land for the time being to be convicted of high treason.

Foreign Policy.

1485-1492. 1. The early policy, **1485-1492**, centred round Britanny.

ANALYSIS OF ENGLISH HISTORY.

1487. *a* Duke Francis of Britanny openly attacked by Charles VIII. of France. Anne of Britanny betrothed to Maximilian of Burgundy.

1488. *b* Volunteers raised in England for the defence of Britanny. Death of Duke Francis.

1490. *c* League between Henry, Maximilian, and Spain, for the defence of Britanny if attacked.

1491. *d* Britanny attacked by France, but not defended by the League. French capture of Nantes, and marriage of Charles VIII. of France and Anne of Britanny. Consequent annexation of Britanny by France.

1492. *e* Expedition of Henry VII. to Boulogne; treaty of Etaples; Henry bought off by a payment of £149,000, and Charles VIII. left free for his expedition for the conquest of Naples (long in dispute between the Houses of Aragon and Anjou).

1492-1498. 2. The policy from **1492-1498.** Mainly connected with Perkin Warbeck, who claimed to be Richard, Duke of York, and was supported by Margaret of Burgundy (sister of Edward IV.), Charles VIII. of France, James IV. of Scotland, and by the popular feeling in Ireland in favour of the House of York.

1492. *a* Perkin deserted by France after the treaty of Etaples.

1494. *b* Order enforced among the English in Ireland by Sir E. Poynings. All existing English laws to be in force in Ireland; no Parliament to be held in Ireland without the sanction of the King and Council; the King and Council to have power to disallow statutes passed by the Irish Houses. The Earl of Kildare won over by being appointed Royal Deputy in Ireland. Ireland thus shut to Warbeck.

1496. *c* Commercial treaty with Burgundy, the "Great Intercourse," securing freedom of trading and mutual expulsion of rebels. Warbeck obliged to leave Flanders. [The Great Intercourse renewed **1506,** on the occasion of Duke Philip being driven by a storm into Weymouth, when Edmund de la Pole, Earl of Suffolk, was also given up by Philip on condition of his life being spared. Suffolk consequently imprisoned in the Tower, till his execution by Henry VIII. **1513.**]

	d League of Spain, the Empire, the Pope (Julius II.), Milan, Venice, for the mutual preservation of States, (joined by Henry, though he would contribute neither men nor money). [The first enunciation of the idea of Balance of Power.]
1497.	*e* Treaty concluded with Scotland, where Warbeck had been received by James IV., and married to Katharine Gordon. (Warbeck obliged to leave Scotland, JULY. Treaty, SEPT.)
1497.	[Rising for Warbeck in the West, Devon and Cornwall; capture and imprisonment of Warbeck. Attempted escape of Warbeck. JUNE, **1498.** Execution of Warbeck along with Edward, Earl of Warwick. NOV., **1499.**]

    3. Marriage alliances and proposed alliances.

      a For himself, after the death of Queen Elizabeth. **1503.** Margaret of Austria (daughter of Maximilian), Johanna of Castile, Louisa of Savoy (mother of Francis I.), Katharine of Aragon (his own daughter-in-law).

      b Marriage of Arthur the King's eldest son to Katharine of Aragon, (thus strengthening England by an alliance with Spain against France,) delayed by Henry's caution till

1501.	France was occupied by the invasion of Italy.
1502.	*c* Upon the death of Arthur, Katharine betrothed to his brother Henry; the betrothal sanctioned (conditionally) by Pope Julius II.
1502.	*d* Marriage of Margaret of England to James IV. of Scotland.
1509.	Death of the King. APRIL **21.**

E Notice the importance of the reign as marking the **transition from Mediæval to Modern History**; the transition from separate national development to the idea of national aggrandisement and the counter-idea of Balance of Power, which, though first formally conceived by Henry IV. and Sully (**1603**), is the key to political action from **1500** to **1800**. Influences that led to this political change.

1422-1483.	i. Concentration of power in the royal hands in France under Charles VII. and Lewis XI., due mainly to the pressure of the long struggle with England.
1469.	ii. The union of Castile and Aragon by the marriage of Isabella to Ferdinand, and the
1491.	conquest of Granada from the Moors.

	iii. The union of all Austrian hereditary possessions under Maximilian of Austria, and his
1477.	marriage to Mary of Burgundy, bringing with it the County of Burgundy, *i.e.*, Franche Comté and Flanders.
	iv. The weakness of the German national Kingship owing to the claim of the German King to the Universal rule of the Holy Roman Empire. (The power of the Emperor in Germany becoming mainly nominal.)
1471.	v. Attempts of the Popes from the papacy of Sixtus IV. to gain territorial jurisdiction in Italy, entailing finally the loss of their position as a mediating power.
1520.	vi. Rise into importance of Sweden by its separation from Denmark, under Gustavus Vasa.

Note upon the Star Chamber.

1. The Court as constituted by Henry VII. was really a Committee of the Council, but by the end of the reign of Henry VIII. this special Commission no longer existed, but criminal powers, analogous although far larger, continued to be exercised by a Court retaining the same name of Star Chamber and mainly identical with the Council itself.

2. Methods of procedure before the Star Chamber.

    a The proceeding "Ore tenus." The accused privately arrested, examined (no information being given either as to accuser or nature of charge), and judged, or, in case of refusal to confess or answer questions, remanded.

    b Procedure by Bill of Complaint addressed to the Council and signed by a Councillor. The accused compelled to answer the bill on oath; after the answer of the accused witnesses were privately examined by the Council. Torture could also be used to extract confession (as in the cases of Anne Askew and Guido Fawkes).

3. Penalties. Fines (sometimes however apparently not enforced and intended to serve as a mark of severe condemnation), whipping, the stocks, the pillory, branding, and any penalty short of death.

4. Sphere of Jurisdiction.

    a Accusations of treasonable or seditious acts and words.

  b Cases of libel.
  c The regulation of printing.
  d Accusations of breach of royal proclamation.
  e Cases where individuals acted in a way which the law could not punish but which morality condemned.
  f Cases transferred from the Law Courts, "taken by the King into his own hands."
  g Summoning and fining of Juries for erroneous verdicts.
  h The right of interference claimed not only in criminal but in civil cases, and the right of arrest claimed further not only by the Council collectively but by its members individually.

(See "The Privy Council" by A. V. Dicey (Macmillan & Co.)
For the growth and influence of the New Learning, the chief progressive movement of the reign, see Green, pp. 303—320.

1509-1547.   HENRY VIII.   1509-1547.

Henry VIII. = (1) Katharine of Aragon.   = (2) Anne Boleyn.   = (3) Jane Seymour.   = (4) Anne of Cleves.
                            = (5) Katharine Howard.
  Mary.   Elizabeth.   Edward.
                            = (6) Katharine Parr.

1509-1511.   A. Early years.   1509-1511.

  1. Popularity of the King and hopes of "a new order" at his accession.

1509.   2. Trial and execution of Empson and Dudley for high treason. Statute limiting action upon penal suits to within three years after alleged offence.
1510.

  3. Marriage to Katharine of Aragon upon advice of Council (in spite of opposition of Warham),
1509.   for security against the growing power of France.

1511-1525.   B. Foreign wars.

1511-1514. 1. The Holy League between Ferdinand of Spain, Henry VIII. of England, Pope Julius II., and the Republic of Venice to protect the Papacy and drive the French out of Italy, though the Pope had co-operated with France and the Emperor Maximilian in the League of Cambrai, **1508,** for the dismemberment of Venice, as being the only Italian power likely to unite Italy.

1512.	The French driven back in the north of Italy, and Navarre seized by Spain. The Scots defeated
1513.	at Flodden Field (upon the Till) and Terouenne and Tournai taken by Henry. AUG.—SEPT.
1514.	2. Truce for a year between Lewis XII., Maximilian, and Ferdinand. Anger of Henry VIII. at his desertion by Ferdinand, and conclusion of an alliance between England and France sealed by the marriage of Mary Tudor to Lewis XII.
1515. 1516-1518.	3. Death of Lewis XII. Invasion and reconquest of the Milanese by Francis I. counterbalanced by the accession of Charles of the Netherlands to the throne of Spain as Charles I., and of Naples as Charles IV. Confederacy between England, France, and Spain.
1519.	4. Death of Maximilian. Election of Charles of Spain as Emperor (Charles V.). [The beginning of the rivalry between France and the House of Hapsburg.]
1520.	English alliance courted both by France and Spain. Conference between Charles V. and Henry at Canterbury, between Francis I. and Henry on the plain of Ardres, "the Field of the Cloth of Gold." English alliance with
1521.	Spain: Charles betrothed to Mary (Henry's daughter), and Buckingham (heir to the throne next to Mary) executed to secure her succession.

```
              Edward III.
                  |
         Thomas of Woodstock.
                  |
          Anne = Edmund Stafford, Earl of
                    Buckingham.
                  |
          Humphrey, Duke of Buckingham,
                    killed at Northampton, 1460.
                  |
          Humphrey = Margaret Beaufort, daughter
                    |  of Edmund Duke of Somerset.
                  |
          Henry, Duke of Buckingham, = Katharine
               executed 1483.        |  Woodville.
                                     |
                              Duke of Buckingham.
```

1522-1525.	5. War declared upon France, and English claims upon France revived.
1522.	*a* Money raised by benevolences.

1523. *b* Parliament summoned: a property tax of 20 per cent. demanded by Wolsey: his visit in state to the Commons to receive their answer. Deliberation suspended during his presence. Half the demand voted.

  c Cooling on both sides of the friendship between Charles and Henry.

1525. *d* France crushed at the battle of Pavia. England drawn towards France to counteract the excessive power of Spain.

C Internal Affairs.

1525. 1. Concentration of power in Wolsey's hands.

Wolsey, Dean of Lincoln, Almoner, Member of the Council, Dean of York (**1509-1513**), for his able management of the preparations for the campaign of **1513** made Bishop of Tournai, then (in addition) of Lincoln (**1514**), then (in addition) Archbishop of York. Made Cardinal (**1515**) and Legatus a Latere by Leo X. (**1517**), besides being entrusted with the administration of the See of Bath and Wells, and of the temporalities of the Abbey of S. Alban's. Chancellor (**1525**), Bishop of Winchester (**1528**).

2. Features of the government at home under Wolsey's advice and administration.

  a Parliament not called between **1515** and **1523**.

  b Unconstitutional taxation by benevolences (**1522**) and (**1525**), though abandoned in the latter year owing to very general resistance to the demand.

  c Immense industry in the Court of Chancery, subordinate courts created to expedite justice.

1524. *d* Visitation of the monasteries: bull obtained from Pope (Clement VII.) for the suppression of forty of the smaller (having less than seven inmates), and for the conversion of the Monastery of S. Frideswyde in Oxford into a college: the endowments of the suppressed monasteries used for the new Cardinal College (afterwards Christ Church) in Oxford, and for a new college at Ipswich (which last however was dissolved and confiscated by Henry upon Wolsey's fall).

  e Gentle treatment of heresy.

D The Question of the Divorce and Fall of Wolsey.

1526. 1. Attempt made by the English Envoy at Rome to procure the divorce of Katharine of Aragon.

1527. 2. Question of the legality of Henry's marriage with Katharine raised in Wolsey's Court, as Legate, by a collusive action (a complaint being preferred against the King for having lived eighteen years with his brother's wife).

1528. 3. Legatine Commission granted to Campeggio and Wolsey by Clement VII. Delay of their proceedings.

1529. 4. Opening of the Legatine Court. Adjournment of the Court for two months when a decision was expected. JULY. The cause called to Rome by Clement VII., under pressure from Charles. OCT.

Treaty of Cambrai formed between France and the Emperor. AUG.

Fall of Wolsey owing to these combined causes. Accused under Statute of Præmunire of receiving Bulls and Legatine authority from Rome. OCT. The bill for Wolsey's impeachment thrown out in the Commons through the efforts of Thomas Cromwell, but Wolsey's property declared forfeited to the Crown according to the Statute of Præmunire. Wolsey allowed to retire to his see at York. Arrest of Wolsey (**1530**) for high treason, and death on the road to London. NOV. **29**.

1529. 5. Wolsey succeeded in power by Charles Brandon, Duke of Suffolk (President of the Council), Thomas Howard, Duke of Norfolk (Lord Treasurer), and Sir Thomas More (Chancellor). Parliament summoned. NOV., **1529**. [The long Organic Parliament of the reign.]

E The Breach with Rome and establishment of the Royal Supremacy over the Church.

1529. 1. Profits of the Bishops' Courts in cases of probate reduced, and discipline more strictly enforced upon the lower clergy by Act of Parliament.

1530. 2. Measures of Norfolk to get over the marriage difficulty.

a. By negotiations with the Imperial Court.
b. By an appeal to the Universities.

1531. 3. The clergy held liable to the penalties of Præmunire in submitting to Wolsey as Legate. Fined £118,840 by Convocation. Acknowledgment of the King as "Supreme Head of the Church, as far as the law of Christ will allow." (This assumption of title did not imply independence of Rome, but was a warning to the Pope and the clergy that the clergy were dependent upon the King.)

1532. 4. Withdrawal of More from the Chancellorship (succeeded by Audley). MAY. Conditional discontinuance of the payment of annates (the first year's revenue upon election to a see) to the Pope.

Petition of Convocation that Church legislation be henceforth only with the King's assent. [The Statutes of Uses (passed **1536**) and of Wills (passed **1540**) rejected by the Commons.]

1533. 5. Secret marriage with Anne Boleyn. JAN. **25.** Death of Archbishop Warham, and appointment of Cranmer as Archbishop by Papal Bull. MARCH.

The marriage between Henry and Katharine declared by Cranmer in Court null and void from the beginning, and the marriage with Anne Boleyn good and lawful. MAY. Reversal of the sentence by the Pope: Henry's appeal to a general Council. Avowal of the marriage with Anne Boleyn and her Coronation. JUNE. Appeals to Rome forbidden by Statute. APRIL. Act of Succession, settling the crown upon the children of Anne Boleyn.

1534. 6. Statute transferring the payment of annates from the Pope to the crown. A new Statute of Appeals making the final reference (not as before to the Archbishop, but) to the King in Chancery. A new Statute of Annates, empowering the King to nominate Bishops; Chapters subjected to the penalties of Præmunire for non-election of the royal nominee mentioned along with the Congé d'Elire.

Statute granting the petition of Convocation (**1532**) that Church legislation henceforward be only with the King's consent.

The Act of Supremacy, vesting authority over all ecclesiastical matters in the crown,

Denial of any of the King's titles declared treason.
Execution of Elizabeth Barton (the Nun of Kent) for high treason. MAY 5.

1535. 7. Assumption by the King by Letters Patent of the title of " on earth supreme Head of the Church of England." Execution of Fisher (Bishop of Rochester), Sir Thomas More, and three brethren of the Charterhouse, under the Statute of Treason of **1534**. Cromwell appointed Vicar-General ; visitation of the monasteries. Study of the Canon Law forbidden at the Universities.

1536. 8. Suppression of all monasteries and nunneries (380 in number) under £200 of yearly revenue. Their revenues to be administered by a Court of Augmentations.

Negotiations between Henry and the Lutheran princes forming the League of Schmalkald. Publication of Ten Articles basing the faith of the Church of England upon the Bible, the Three Creeds, and the first Four Councils, limiting the sacraments to Baptism, Penance, and the Eucharist, condemning the abuses of the Church (*e.g.* pardons, and masses for the dead), but retaining most of its ceremonies, and approximating to the Confession of Augsburg in the acceptance of the doctrine of justification by faith.

Trial and execution of Queen Anne for treason and adultery, MAY **19**, and marriage with Jane Seymour, MAY **20**.

The succession re-settled upon the issue of Jane Seymour, and failing that and the issue of any other lawful wife left to the King to make over and bequeath at his pleasure.

1537. 9. Rising in Lincolnshire, followed by the rising in Yorkshire called the Pilgrimage of Grace, and by a Parliament of the North at Pomfret, demanding the fall of Cromwell, the acknowledgment of Mary as legitimate, and the restitution of the goods of the Church.

1537. The promise of consideration of grievances in a free Parliament at York, made to the leaders by the Royal Commissioners (the Earl of Shrewsbury and the Duke of Norfolk), but recalled in consequence of a subsequent rising

MARCH. in the North and Somersetshire. Many cruel executions. Death of Jane Seymour. **1537.**

1538. Royal licence given to Coverdale's translation of the Bible.

Negotiations begun with the Lutheran princes forming the League of Schmalkald, but abandoned.

Excommunication of Henry by Pope Paul III. Refusal of France and Spain to execute it.

1539. Execution of the Marquess of Exeter and Lord Montacute, and imprisonment of the Countess of Salisbury (executed MAY **27, 1541**) upon the charge of high treason (as privy to the plans of Cardinal Pole).

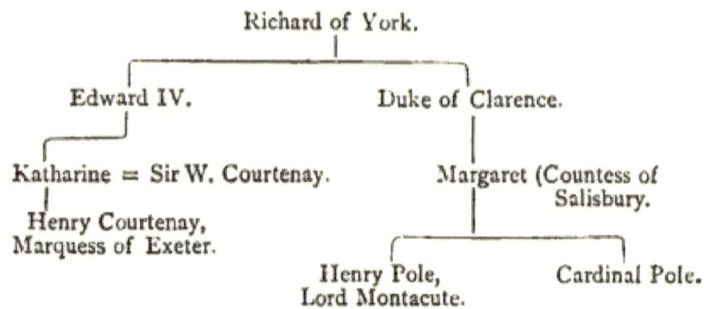

1539. Dissolution of the larger monasteries (645 in number), and disappearance of the mitred abbots from the House of Lords.

Act "for abolishing diversity of opinions in certain articles concerning Christian religion," commonly called "The Six Articles," declaring transubstantiation, communion in one kind, celibacy of the clergy, monastic vows, private masses, auricular confession and the binding power of vows of chastity to be agreeable to the law of God, and fixing burning as the penalty for the denial of transubstantiation, and on a second offence for an infraction of the other five doctrines (due to the reaction against the violence of the "Lutheran" or "Protestant" Party).

Statute empowering the King to appoint new bishops by his letters patent. Bishops appointed for Oxford, Peterborough, Gloucester, Bristol, Chester, Westminster.

1540. Attempt of Cromwell to unite Henry with the German Lutheran princes against the Empire by the marriage with Anne of Cleves, niece of the Elector of Saxony (head of the League of Schmalkald). Dissatisfaction of the King with his wife and with the irresolution of the German princes.

Cromwell accused of treason, attainted without being heard in his own defence, and executed, JULY, **1540.** (For the character and policy of Cromwell see Green pp. 331-348.)

Cranmer's Bible, known as the "Great Bible," appointed by royal command to be read in churches.

F **Indirect Political Effects of this exaltation of the Royal Power.**

1. The change was the result of the action of Parliament. Abandonment of the practice of ruling without Parliament, which had prevailed since the reign of Edward IV.
2. Parliament however as yet mainly a tool to strengthen the royal supremacy.

1529.   *a* Remittal by statue of the loans of **1523-1528**, (*i.e.*, the King released from his debts), and again in **1544**;

1534. 1536.   *b* The succession to be limited according to the King's discretion.

c The creation of new treasons. **1534, 1537, 1541**, and **1544.**

1536.   *d* Statutes passed during a King's minority liable to be rescinded by him when of the age of twenty-four.

e No opposition to the severities practised after Pilgrimage of Grace, **1537**, or to the acceptance of the Ten Articles in **1536** and the Six Articles in **1539.**

1539.   *f* The larger monasteries dissolved without debate.

1539.   *g* Proclamations made by the King and Council to have the force of statutes, so that they do not infringe existing laws or be not prejudicial to any person's liberty or property.

3. That Parliamentary life however was not extinct may be seen by

1536.   *a* The "great debate" upon the suppression

1539.   *b* The limitations upon the statute giving proclamations the force of laws.

    4. The creation of a new nobility (*e.g.* Russells, Cavendishes, Wriothesleys, Fitzwilliams) enriched by grants of the estates of the Church, tended to increase the strength of the aristocracy.

    5. The treatment of religious dissent as political treason ended finally in the revolt of Puritanism against the monarchy under the Stuarts.

1541-1546. G **Return of Norfolk to power; efforts for a General Council (in co-operation with Charles V.) for the purification of Catholic Christianity.**

1540.   1. Divorce from Anne of Cleves, who was pensioned off, and marriage with Katharine Howard, niece of the Duke of Norfolk. JULY 28.

1541.
1542.   2. Katharine Howard tried and executed upon charge of adultery. FEB. Norfolk's influence partially superseded by that of Gardiner, Bishop of Winchester; policy however unchanged towards an Imperial alliance and a General Council.

1542.   3. Opposition of France to the English and imperial policy in order to keep the Empire disunited. War declared by France against the Emperor, and hostility against England stirred up in Scotland. Surrender of the Scotch army on the banks of the Esk (Solway Moss), NOV. 25. Death of James V. of Scotland, succeeded by Mary (an infant), under the regency of James Hamilton, Earl of Arran. NOV. and
1542.   DEC. **1542.**

    4. Increasing violence of the religious contest abroad.

        i. Failure of the assembly at Ratisbon for devising union between the Catholics and
1541.   Lutherans, owing to the opposition both of Luther and the Pope (Paul III.).

        ii. A General Supreme Court of Inquisition established at Rome owing to the influence of Cardinal Caraffa (afterwards Paul IV.).

        iii. Papal sanction given to the Society of Jesus
1543.   (bound to chastity, poverty, obedience).

1543. 5. Proposal by Henry of a marriage treaty between Mary Stuart and his son Edward ; alliance with the Emperor against France, FEB. ; Henry's hopes of union with Scotland foiled by Cardinal Beaton and the Queen-Mother (Mary of Guise), who formed alliance with France, annulling the marriage treaty already concluded with England.

1544. 6. Sack of Edinburgh and Leith by Hertford. Capture of Boulogne by Henry. Treaty of Crépy made with France by the Emperor in order to deprive the German Lutheran princes of French assistance. SEPT. Exhaustion of the Treasury ; the King set free from his debts ; any sums he had paid ordered to be returned.

1545. Continued war with Scotland and France. Resistance to a fresh demand for "benevolences ;" suppression of chantries and hospitals, their funds granted by Parliament to the Crown. First sittings of the Council at Trent, their decisions unfavourable to doctrinal union.

1546. 7. Murder of Cardinal Beaton at St. Andrew's ; peace with France and Scotland. Boulogne to be retained by Henry for eight years or till the debt due by Francis was paid.

H Measures for the security of the Succession and Religious
1544-1547. Union at Home (Norfolk's hopes of a general religious union having failed).

1544. 1. The succession fixed upon Edward, Mary, Elizabeth, and their issue ; the King empowered to make further disposition by will.

1544. 2. Revision by Cranmer of an English litany for processions. Publication of the "King's Prymer," containing the English translation of
1545. the Creed, Lord's Prayer, and Commandments, several Canticles and Collects.

3. Rise into power of a new nobility enriched by the spoils of the monasteries, pledged to break with Rome, and inclined to an alliance with the Lutheran princes, under John Dudley, Lord Lisle (afterwards Duke of Northumberland), and Edward Seymour, Earl of Hertford. (Their influence seen in Henry's offer of aid to the League of Schmalkald, 1546, which was however refused.)

4. Henry however far from Protestant doctrinally. Anne Askew, for denying Transubstantiation, racked to make her, if possible, inculpate Katharine Parr (whom the King had married, **1543**) and burned.

1546.
1547.
5. Norfolk and his son, the Earl of Surrey, sent to the Tower upon the charge of quartering the royal arms, and using treasonable language. Execution of Surrey, JAN. **19**, and attainder of Norfolk. JAN. **27**.

Death of Henry, JAN. **28, 1547**.

[In this reign the Principality of Wales was incorporated with England, all Wales made shireground, English laws introduced, and Parliamentary representation granted. **1536. 1543. 1544.**]

Notice also the change in the Land Laws by the Statute of Uses (**1536**), by which the "use" carried the legal estate, the person named for the "use" becoming the feudal tenant, *i.e.* the legal owner; and the Statute of Wills (**1540**) allowing a man to divide half his land by will, if the other half, left to his heir, secured the King in his feudal rights.

1547-1553.   **EDWARD VI. 1547-1553.**

1547. A The Will of Henry VIII.

1. The Will.

    a In default of issue by his children, the crown bequeathed to the descendants of his younger sister, Mary. **1544-1545**.

    b A Council of Regency appointed to preserve if possible the religious union at home.

2. Modification of the Will by the new Protestant nobility in their own favour.

    a Gardiner, Bishop of Winchester, not included in the Council of Regency (possibly struck out by Hertford and Lord Lisle).

    b Hertford nominated Protector of the Realm.

    c Hertford created Duke of Somerset, Lisle Earl of Warwick, and others of their party elevated presumably to carry out the King's directions for the repair "of the decay of the old English nobility."

3. In the Coronation service the Coronation oath put by Cranmer *after* and not before the expression of popular assent [thus destroying the conditional character of the assent].

B The chief points in which the Reformed Religion was opposed to the old Religion. (See Hallam, *Const. Hist.* chap. ii.)

1. Substitution of English for the old Latin ritual.
2. Removal of images from churches (often accompanied with wanton destruction).
3. The rejection of the worship of the Virgin and saints, and of masses for the dead.
4. Disuse (though without formal condemnation) of auricular confession.
5. The sacrament to be administered in both kinds.
6. Rejection of the doctrine of Transubstantiation in the Mass. The reformers divided between three theories.
    a The theory of Luther — Consubstantiation. The two substances so united that the elements may either be called bread and wine or the body and blood.
    b The theory of Zwingle and the Calvinists — the Lord's Supper a commemoration, the bread and wine merely symbols.
    c The theory of Bucer (and apparently that of the Church of England now)—Christ's body and blood not locally present in the elements, but really, and without figure, received by the worthy communicant through faith. A real but not a corporeal presence.
7. Release of the priesthood from the obligation to celibacy.
8. Resistance to the sacerdotal claims of the clergy, and to the interference of the priest in the family.

1547-1549. **C The Protectorate of the Duke of Somerset. 1547-Oct. 1549.**

1. Somerset's active policy to advance the new religion.

1547. *a* A new patent of Protectorate granted by Edward to Somerset, making his authority independent of the Council.

    b The Six Articles repealed: bishops to be nominated by the King *quamdiu se bene gesserint.*

    c Invasion of Scotland to enforce the marriage treaty (of **1543**) between Edward and Mary Stuart. Defeat of the Scots at Pinkie Cleugh (near Musselburgh), and consequent alliance between Scotland and France, followed by the departure of Mary Stuart to France and marriage to the Dauphin Francis.

1547.

1548

    d The use of English in Church services made compulsory, and images ordered to be removed.

    e The sacrament of the altar to be administered in both kinds.

    f The Vagrant Act; vagrants to be branded, and in case of attempted escape to be sentenced to slavery (directed possibly against the expelled monks).

1547.

    g The revenues of the suppressed chantries devoted by Parliament to the foundation of grammar-schools and support of preachers; mainly however squandered by the Government.

1548.
1549.

    h "The Order of Communion" drawn up for temporary use. Publication of an English book of Common Prayer; the first prayer-book of Edward VI. The Virgin still mentioned, and prayers for the dead included, as well as the use of the "chrisom" and a form of exorcism at Baptism. [Victory of the Emperor Charles V. over the League of Schmalkald (APRIL, **1547**), and flight of Protestant refugees to England.] Bishop Gardiner imprisoned.

1549.

    i Passing of the Act of Uniformity. JAN. Removal of Bonner from the see of London.

  2. The arbitrary measures of Henry VIII.'s reign to some extent reversed. Repeal of the Statute of **1539** giving proclamations in Council the force of laws, and of the new treasons created in that reign.

  3. Fall of the Protector.

    a Lord Seymour, the High Admiral (Somerset's brother who had married Katharine Parr,

1549. Henry VIII.'s widow), accused of an attempt to overthrow the Protector, and of projecting a marriage with the Lady Elizabeth; attainted of high treason, condemned without a hearing and executed. MARCH 27.

b Revolt in Cornwall and Devon for the restoration of the old Liturgy (the Mass and the Six Articles).

c Discontent caused by enclosures and evictions (increased by the rise of rent upon the old Church lands, the rise of prices due to the inflow of gold and silver from America, and the debasement of the coinage).

Sympathy of the Protector with the sufferers, and issue of Commission to inquire into grievances. Rising in Norfolk under Robert Ket for the removal of evil counsellors, for a prohibition of enclosures, and for redress of grievances of the poor, suppressed by the Earl of Warwick. AUG.

d Continued debasement of the coinage, which had begun under Henry VIII. Exhaustion of the Treasury; Boulogne threatened by the French and war declared against France; recovery of castles in Scotland by the Scots.

e Unpopularity of Somerset caused by his having grown rich upon Church property, and having pulled down churches and the cloister of S. Paul's to make room or supply materials for his palace—"Somerset House."

f Want of foresight in the multiplicity and haste of his plans.

g Opposition to Somerset in the Council; attempt of Somerset to declare the Council treasonable. Authority resumed by Warwick and the Council. Somerset sent to the Tower. OCT.-DEC. **1549.**

1549-1553. D **The Supremacy of the Earl of Warwick in the Council.**

1550. 1. Surrender of Boulogne upon payment of 400,000 crowns and peace with France and Scotland.

2. Committee appointed for the revision of the Prayer-book. Bucer and Peter Martyr consulted.

1551. 3. Cranmer ordered by the Council to frame Articles of Religion as a formal standard of faith.

4. Removal of Gardiner from his see of Winchester. Vain attempt to force Mary to obey the act of Uniformity, or to adopt the new Prayer-book. Her attempted flight to Flanders. Reluctance to proceed to extreme measures against her on account of her popularity, and fear of her cousin Charles V. Further deprivation of Bishops—Day, Heath;

5. Warwick made Duke of Northumberland; bestowal of honours and Church property on his party (amongst others William Cecil, his secretary, knighted).

6. Reaction in favour of Somerset, who had been released from the Tower, FEB. **1550**; his arrest, DEC. **1551**, and execution. JAN. **22, 1552**.

1552.

7. *Reformatio legum*, or a revision of the Canon Law (executed by Peter Martyr) attaching perpetual imprisonment or exile to heresy, blasphemy, and adultery (left unfinished at the death of Edward).

8. Discontent at the want of uniformity and even decency in ritual; at the repeated debasement of the coinage, increase of expenditure, and wasteful gifts of Crown lands. Northumberland reduced to "pack" Parliament by summoning members from villages in the west by royal prerogative. [Treaty of Passau, securing both Protestants and Catholics in Germany in their existing rights and possessions.]

1552.

9. Publication of the second Prayer-book of Edward VI., adding the introductory portion of Morning and Evening Prayer and the Ten Commandments to the Communion Service; abolishing vestments except the surplice, and fixing the position of the priest at the north side of the table.

Issue of Forty-two Articles of Religion (based largely upon the Lutheran Confessions) ordered to be signed by all clergymen, churchwardens, and schoolmasters.

Opposition even of a "packed" Parliament to Northumberland's "wilful misgovernance." Increasing bad health of Edward; marriage of Guildford Dudley, Northumberland's fourth son, to Jane Grey. Northumberland's "plan" for settling the succession upon Jane Grey (passing over her mother) approved by the Council and judges, and signed by Cranmer.

Henry VII.

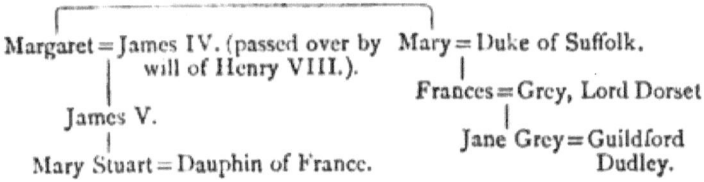

Death of the King. JULY **6, 1553**.

E The Royal Council in the Reign of Edward VI.

1553. 1. The Council of Edward VI. composed of forty members, divided into five Commissions, *i.e.* Committees—

   a For the hearing of suits which were wont to be brought before the Council.

   b For the punishing of breaches of laws and proclamations.

   c For the State.

   d For the review of all the Courts, especially the newly-created Court of Augmentations.

   e For the bulwarks.

2. All matters to be brought under the King's notice, and the Secretaries to be a channel of communication between the King and the Council. [Change in position of the Secretary from a clerk to a royal minister. From the time of Henry VIII. the secretaries take rank as barons, and are "ex officio" Members of the Council.]

3. Decline of the baronial element in the Council. Of the forty members twenty-two were Commoners.

4. Admission into the Council of "ordinary Councillors" such as Judges, who act merely on particular Commissions without belonging to the Commission for the State.

5. Throughout the reigns of the Tudors the Royal Council remains dependent on the Crown, instead of being a check upon it. Due to the depression of the Nobles and of the Church.

[See "The Privy Council" by A. V. Dicey. (Macmillan and Co.)].

1553-1558.   **MARY.**   **1553-1558.**

Mary = Philip I. of Naples and Milan and II. of Spain.

JULY, **1553**-FEB., **1554**. A **The Reign till the Suppression of Wyatt's Rising.**

1. Failure of Northumberland's "plan" owing to the loyalty of the nation and jealousy of his colleagues in the Council. Submission of Northumberland. JULY **21**. Executed. AUG. **22**. Imprisonment of Jane Grey.

2. Release of the Duke of Norfolk and Bishop Gardiner from the Tower. Gardiner appointed Chancellor. Restoration of the deprived bishops (Gardiner, Bonner, Day, Heath) to their sees. Imprisonment of Bishops Latimer and Hooper and of Archbishop Cranmer. Foreign Protestants ordered to leave England. Sentences upon Cranmer, Lady Jane Grey, and Guildford Dudley, pleading guilty of treason, not executed. NOV.

3. Remonstrance of Parliament against the proposed marriage between Mary and Philip, (accompanied with the cession of the Netherlands to the issue of the marriage) : fear of an Austrian line upon the throne of England. Political attraction of Mary to the marriage, in order to secure herself against the claims of Mary Stuart and France, hence her rejection of Gardiner's advice to marry Courtenay, Earl of Devon. (See Table at beginning of Edward IV.)

4. Projected rising of the Protestants in arms. Premature rising of Kent under Sir Thomas Wyatt in favour of Elizabeth and Edward Courtenay, Earl of Devon, crushed by the courage of the Queen. JAN., **1554**.

5. Execution of Jane Grey, her father (Duke of Suffolk), her uncle Thomas Grey, Guildford Dudley and Wyatt. FEB.-APRIL, **1554**.

    Courtenay and Elizabeth sent to the Tower. MARCH.

FEB., **1554**-NOV., **1558**. B **Attempted Reconciliation with Rome.**

1. All married clergy expelled from their cures; deprivation of nine Bishops appointed in Edward VI.'s reign.

1554. **2.** Marriage to Philip in Winchester Cathedral. JULY.

3. Submission of Bishop Gardiner, till lately the advocate of a National orthodox Church, to Rome as the only means left of preserving religious unity.

4. Absolution granted to Parliament by Cardinal Pole (his attainder having been reversed) NOV. **30.** Repeal of all ecclesiastical statutes passed against the Apostolic see since **1529**, but laymen confirmed in the possession of ecclesiastical property.

1555. **5.** Revival of the Persecuting Statute of Henry IV., and commencement of persecution. Martyrdom of Rogers at London, Bishop Hooper at Gloucester, Lawrence Saunders at Coventry, Bishop Ferrar at Carmarthen, Bishops Latimer and Ridley at Oxford.

6. Philip's proposal to marry Elizabeth to the Duke of Savoy. Disappointment of Mary's hopes of an heir. Departure of Philip to take possession of the Netherlands and Spain upon his father's abdication. Improved position of Elizabeth.

7. Accession of Cardinal Caraffa (founder of the Order of Jesuits and suggester of the Supreme Court of Inquisition at Rome) to the Papacy as Paul IV. Demands of the Pope for the restoration of Church lands by laymen, and for payment of Peter's pence. Restoration of annates to the Church after much opposition. Death of Gardiner. NOV.

1556. **8.** Cardinal Pole (Papal Legate) Chief Minister in place of Gardiner. Cranmer convicted of heresy by the Papal see and burnt at Oxford. MARCH. Growing indignation of the people.

9. Re-establishment of the Abbey at Westminster. NOV.

1557. **10.** Return of Philip to England. Revolt of Sir Thomas Stafford, grandson of the late Duke of Buckingham, "to deliver his country from foreign tyranny", fomented by France. (See Table Henry VIII. B.) War declared against France in support of Spain. Spanish victory of S. Quentin, with the assistance of English troops. AUG. **10.**

1558. 11. Capture of Calais by the Duke of Guise. JAN. Spanish victory of Gravelines (JULY), with the assistance of English fleet. Discontent in Ireland owing to the plantation of the country of the O'Connors as shire-land (King's and Queen's Counties). Negotiations for peace at Cambrai. Refusal of the French to restore Calais. Pole deprived of his office as Legate by Paul IV. who had been allied with France against Spain. Death of the Queen. NOV., 1558.

1558-1603. ELIZABETH. 1558-1603.

1558-1559. A Years of Settlement.

1. The Queen's difficulties.
   - a France mistress of the Channel. Civil strife in Ireland. Social discontent at home. Spain apparently her only possible ally.
   - b Difficulties in the way of religious union. The Protestants made fiercer by the persecution; the Catholics more closely bound to Rome.
   - c The style and arms of English sovereigns adopted by Mary Stuart and her husband, Francis VIII. of France. **1559.**
   - d Exhaustion of the Treasury by the misgovernment under Edward VI., increased by the expenses of the restoration of the annates and the Church lands, in the possession of the Crown, to Rome, and of the French war under Mary.

2. The Queen's measures.

1558.
   - a The Council chiefly unchanged. Cecil and Nicolas Bacon added to it.
   - b The Lord's Prayer, Creed, and Commandments again permitted to be used in English. Alarm of the bishops. Only one, Bishop Oglethorpe of Carlisle, officiated at Coronation **(1559)**.
   - c Announcement of her accession to the Pope (Paul IV.). Elizabeth summoned to submit her claims to him.

1559.
   - d Meeting of Parliament. The legitimacy and title of Elizabeth recognised. The royal supremacy over the Church limited; the Queen styled not "supreme head" but "supreme governor."

    e Peace of Cateau Cambrésis between France, Spain, and England. France to restore Calais after eight years; Francis and Mary to recognize Elizabeth's right to English throne. Philip's proposal of marriage refused by the Queen.

    f The Prayer Book restored (with some alterations *e.g.* the ornaments in use in 1548 recognised). The Act of Uniformity passed. APRIL.

    g A Court of High Commission established to enforce the Act of Supremacy. (MAY.) The oath cautiously administered, several clerical members replaced by laymen (OCT.), the Commission suspended. DEC.

    h Activity in creating an English fleet, and in recruiting the financial and military resources of the kingdom.

    i Appointment of Parker as Archbishop of Canterbury to restore order and discipline in worship. DEC.

1564.   *k* Thirty-eight Articles (of Edward's forty-two) constituted as the standard of doctrine.

1559-1568. B Difficulties with Scotland and France. 1559-1568.

1555-1557. 1. Reception of English Protestant refugees in Scotland by the Regent, Mary of Guise, owing to her hostility to Mary Tudor. Consequent increase of Protestantism and signature of the
1557. First Covenant by the Scotch nobles.

1558. 2. Arrival of French troops in Scotland, and demand by Mary of the "Crown Matrimonial" for her husband. Alarm of the Scotch reforming nobles at the prospect of annexation to France, and appeal to Elizabeth.

    3. Division of opinion as to the expedience of entertaining the Scotch appeal, and aiding the Lords of the Congregation.

Arguments for doing so,
    i. Help to the Scotch the best way to defeat the schemes of the Guises, who hoped to acquire England and Scotland by means of Mary.
    ii. If the Lords were defeated Scotland would be free to attack England. These arguments pressed by Cecil, who urged Elizabeth to marry James Hamilton (Earl of Arran,

140 ANALYSIS OF ENGLISH HISTORY.

Duke of Chatelherault, and Regent of Scotland from **1542** to **1554**), and thus unite the two kingdoms.

Arguments against Cecil's advice,

  i. Danger of France and Spain uniting to prevent Scotland and England from becoming one kingdom.

  ii. Elizabeth felt that she could not rely upon the unity of the Scotch.

  iii. Elizabeth objected to set the example of aiding rebels

  iv. Elizabeth objected to the severe Calvinism of Knox and the Scotch reformers, and was afraid of alienating her Catholic subjects, at present kept quiet by the influence of Philip and the possible hope of Elizabeth's conversion.

  v. The majority of the Royal Council were opposed to the scheme.

1560. 4. Despatch of English fleet to the Forth. Siege and capitulation of Leith. Treaty of Edinburgh: the French to withdraw from Scotland, Francis and Mary to acknowledge Elizabeth's title to England, and to leave the settlement of the religious question in Scotland and the government of the country to a Council of the Lords. Refusal of Francis and Mary to ratify the treaty.

5. Death of Francis II. **1560.** Progress of Huguenot doctrines in France, and demand for a National Council. **1561.**

6. The House of Guise, and of Bourbon.

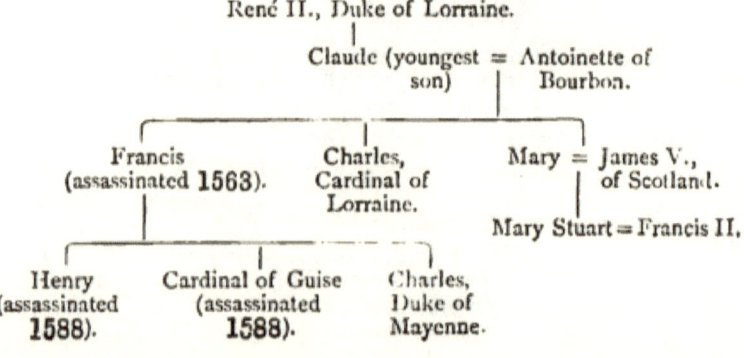

1560. Failure of the Huguenot plot to seize the French Court at Amboise.

Power divided between—
  a The queen-mother Catherine de Medicis.
  b The Guises, with a policy aiming at
    i. The suppression of Protestantism.
    ii. The recognition of Mary Stuart as Queen of England.
  c The house of Bourbon (the next of kin to the house of Valois).

```
                    Charles, Duke of Vendôme.
                              |
       ┌──────────────────────┼──────────────────────┐
Antoine = Jeanne d'Albret,   Charles, Cardinal    Louis, Prince
  |      heiress of Navarre.   of Bourbon.          of Condé.
  |
Henry IV.   Supported by the Constable de Montmorency, and
            Coligny, Admiral of France.
```

1561. 7. Landing of Mary in Scotland. AUG. Promise of religious toleration to the Scotch. Amicable pressure of claim to be recognised as Elizabeth's successor. Keener struggle both in England and France between Catholicism and Protestantism.

1561. *a* Refusal of Elizabeth to take part in the Council of Trent. MAY.

1562. *b* Catholics forbidden, by a prohibition from Rome, to be present at the New Worship. Absentees thereupon fined for "recusancy."

1562. *c* Outbreak of religious war in France. Assistance sent by Elizabeth to the Prince of Condé (the Huguenot leader in Normandy), upon the terms of the occupation of Havre. Victory of the Catholics at Dreux, and capture of Rouen. Siege of Orleans by the Duke of Guise.

1563. *d* The oath of the Royal Supremacy and abjuration of the temporal power of the Pope exacted from all holders of office, except peers, under the penalty of Præmunire for the first refusal, and high treason for the second (due to the fear caused by the victory at Dreux, and afterwards not fully enforced).

1563. *e* Assassination of the Duke of Guise, and pacification of Amboise between the religious parties, and capture of Havre from the English by the reunited French parties.

1564. 8. Thirty-eight Articles constituted as a standard of doctrine.

1564. **9.** Peace between England and France. Appeal of
1565.   Mary Stuart, disappointed by the failure of the Guises in France, to the English Catholics, by her marriage with Lord Darnley.

James IV. = Margaret Tudor = (2) Earl of Angus.
    | |
James V.   Margaret Douglas = Earl of Lennox.
    | |
Mary Stuart   =   Henry Stuart, Lord Darnley.

    Appearance of Earl of Murray (Mary Stuart's half-brother) and the reforming Scottish nobles in arms; their defeat and flight to England. Demand of Mary for recognition as Elizabeth's successor; abandonment of Mary's moderate measures and determination to re-establish Catholicism in Scotland.

1566. 10. Murder of Rizzio through the jealousy of Lord Darnley, and restoration of the Earl of Murray to his old power. Reconciliation of Mary and Darnley. Birth of their son James. Vexation of Elizabeth and fear in England of a league between Mary, the Guises, and Philip.

1566. 11. Meeting of the English Parliament (after an interval of four years). Business of supply voted to go hand-in-hand with that of the succession, and the Queen's marriage. [The Lords however inclined towards Mary Stuart, the Commons towards Katharine Grey, as successor.] The debate stopped by the Queen; acquiescence of the Lords, remonstrance of the Commons under Paul Wentworth.

    With reference to this Parliament, notice
    i. The advance of Parliamentary independence in the assertion of its right to give advice for the public safety.
    ii. The tact of Elizabeth in her reconciliation with the Parliament after a hot burst of anger.
    iii. The peculiar way in which Parliament has often gained its privileges by being satisfied with the mere record of their violation. "Heaping precedent upon precedent they gradually honeycombed the prerogative of the Crown."

ANALYSIS OF ENGLISH HISTORY. 143

1567. 12. The murder of Darnley, and marriage of Mary Stuart with James Hepburn, Earl of Bothwell, his reputed murderer. Indignation of the country; Elizabeth made safe on the side of Scotland. Flight of Bothwell and imprisonment of Mary at Loch Leven. James VI.
1568. crowned. Her escape and defeat at Langside (near Glasgow). Escape of Mary to Carlisle.

13. Four courses open to Elizabeth—

(*a*) Cecil's plan—to hand Mary over unconditionally to Murray.

(*b*) To restore her to her throne under English control. Politic for Elizabeth, but impossible without public refutation of her imputed crimes.

(*c*) To permit her a passage to France. Impossible without inviting French intervention in Scotland.

(*d*) To keep her in England. This was the worst, and into this Elizabeth drifted.

14. Attempts of Elizabeth to effect a compromise between the Earl of Murray (Regent of Scotland) and Mary Stuart, by a Commission opened at York, SEPT., removed to London, and sitting till JAN. **1569.**

1567-1572.   C Danger of Internal Revolt.

1567. 1. Danger of Elizabeth owing to the orthodox zeal of Pius V. (Pope, **1565**), and the presence of the Duke of Alva with his army to stamp out heresy and restore order in the Netherlands. AUTUMN.

1568. 2. Political strife in England: Cecil advising a Protestant League, war in the Low Countries against Alva, and the surrender of Mary to the Scots. The Duke of Norfolk, backed by many of the merchants fearing the ruin of the Flemish trade, demanding the dismissal of Cecil, and a steady peace with Spain. Vacillation of Elizabeth.

1569. 3. The Queen denounced as a heretic by Pius V. (FEB.). Defeat of the Huguenots at Jarnac (Prince of Condé killed) MARCH, and at Moncontour. OCT.

4. Mary a centre of plots in England. Intrigues (including Protestants, such as Leicester, Sussex, and Throgmorton, as well as Catholics) to bring about marriage between the Duke of Norfolk and Mary Stuart on condition of her conforming to Anglican ritual. Conversion of Norfolk to Catholicism. His vacillation and arrest. OCT.

5. Rising of the Earls of Northumberland and Westmoreland (encouraged by the news of Moncontour and by the news of a Bull of Deposition) defeated and sternly repressed. NOV. —DEC., **1569**.

1570. 6. Assassination of the Regent Murray of Scotland. The Bull of Excommunication and Deposition published. Success of the Huguenots under Coligny, and close of the Religious War in France. Proposed marriage of Elizabeth with the Duke of Anjou (brother of the French King).

1571. 7. Severe Statutes for the Queen's security passed against Roman Catholics, the signature of the Articles (now definitely thirty-nine in number) made compulsory upon all magistrates and public officers; reconciliation with the Roman Church declared treason concerning faith and doctrine. (Notice the strong expression of Puritan feeling in this Parliament.)

1571. 8. The discovery of the Ridolfi Plot for the deposition of the Queen, and the marriage of Norfolk to Mary Stuart by means of a Spanish force; MAY.

1571-1572. Second arrest of Norfolk (SEPT.) and execution, JUNE. Execution of Northumberland, AUG.

D Development of England.

1. Elizabeth and Constitutional Government.

   a The system of the "new monarchy" not abandoned but modified.

   (1) Arbitrary taxation confined to taxes upon cloth (imposed by Mary), and sweet wine (imposed by Elizabeth). Benevolences abandoned. Loans, though not quite voluntary, punctually repaid.

   (2) The ordinary course of justice left undisturbed; the jurisdiction of the Council mainly asserted against Roman Catholics.

(3) Proclamations confined mainly to the maintenance of Unity in Worship, the regulation of Trade, or temporary supplemental legislation.

(4) Trials for treason and seditious writing still conducted unjustly (*e.g.*, the cases of Stubbe, 1579, and Udal, 1592).

b Elizabeth and the Houses.

(1) Growth of independence both among the Nobility and the Commons. The seats for the "boroughs" passing into the possession of non-resident burgesses, who adopted a bolder attitude towards the Crown.

(2) Gradual abandonment of attempts to "pack" Parliament, but on the other hand Parliaments called at intervals of three or even of five years in order to avoid conflict with the Crown upon matters of Trade, Religion, and State (still claimed as belonging to the Royal Prerogative).

(3) Instances of this growing conflict.

1562. (i.) Petition of the Houses for declaration of successor and advising marriage.

1566. (ii.) Business of supply voted to go hand-in-hand with that of the succession. The Queen's forbiddal of the discussion [the more justifiable as the Lords were in favour of Mary Stuart, the Commons in favour of Katharine Grey]. The liberties and privileges of Parliament pleaded by the Commons. The Queen's order of silence softened into a request, which was complied with.

1571. (iii.) Strickland's Bill for a new Confession of Faith and a more Puritan Liturgy. Strickland forbidden to proceed by the Council.

1571. (iv.) Protest against the licenses to sell granted by the Crown, checked by a royal message.

2. Steps towards the removal of the old social and agrarian discontent.

1560. *a* Restoration of the currency; the base money called in.

1562. *b* The mayor of each town and churchwardens to draw up lists of inhabitants able to contribute towards the relief of the poor, and payment, in case of refusal, to be assessed and made compulsory.

L

1572.	*c* All inhabitants of towns and country districts assessed by the mayor or justices: the impotent poor to be settled in fitting habitations. Overseers appointed to superintend their labour. Houses of Correction established in each county for obstinate vagabonds.
	3. Improved methods of Agriculture (requiring the employment of a greater number of hands); beginning of Manufactures in the North of England as well as growth of them in the South; influx of industry and capital owing to the troubles in the Netherlands; opening of new Trade routes (to Russia, Africa, Newfoundland); increasing well-being of the country shown by the change in the architecture of dwelling houses, and the general demand for domestic comfort. (See Green pp. 394-397.)
	4. Religious change: growth of Protestant conviction, and increase of Puritanism. Cartwright, a famous Puritan preacher, appointed Lady
1571.	Margaret Professor of Divinity at Cambridge, although expelled, for the violence of his opinions, the same year. Publication of Cartwright's "Admonition to Parliament," attacking
1572.	Episcopacy. (See also Strickland's Bill as above, **1571**.)

1572-1579. E The Netherlands, Spain, and France.

1572.	1. Victory of the King of Spain at Lepanto, danger from the Turks removed. Alliance proposed by Catherine de Medicis against Spain and the House of Guise, to be cemented by marriage of Elizabeth to Henry Duke of Anjou.
	2. Seizure of Brill by a body of Netherland privateers, driven from refuge in England by Alva's request. The commencement of the revolt of the Netherlands.
	3. Promise of aid by Charles IX. to Coligny and the Huguenots to conquer Netherlands from Spain.
	4. Catherine de Medicis, through pique at being set aside, driven to the side of the Guises: Charles IX. alarmed by fear of the ambition of Coligny: massacre of Coligny and the Huguenot leaders at Paris, followed by similar massacres in other towns, known as the Massacre of S. Bartholomew. AUG. **24**,

1574.	5. Unwillingness of Elizabeth to help the Netherlands : proposal of Requesens (Alva's successor) that they should submit to the Church in exchange for the restoration of their constitutional privileges, urged upon them by Elizabeth.
1575.	6. Refusal by Elizabeth of the protectorate of Holland and Zealand.
1576.	7. Arrival in England of the "Seminary Priests" from Douay. Alarm of the nation: revival of the Catholic persecution: execution
1577.	of Cuthbert Mayne, for having denied the Queen's supremacy, and celebrated Mass. [Mayne condemned upon presumption only, without actual proof.]

8. The States of the Netherlands united by the Pacification of Ghent, in consequence of the plunder of Antwerp by the Spanish after the death of Requesens.

Proposal of Don John of Austria (half-brother of Philip of Spain and the new governor of the Netherlands) to maintain the liberties of the States and to withdraw the Spanish troops from the Netherlands at the end of three months, by sea (with the intention of attacking England and marrying Mary of Scotland). Insistence of the States that the Spanish should retire at once and by land.

9. Renewal of the war in the Netherlands. Money, ships, and men sent by Elizabeth to help the States.

1578.	Success of Don John. JAN.
1578.10.	Death of Don John. Arrival in the Netherlands of Alexander, Prince of Parma (nephew of Philip II.). Secession of the Catholic States from the Pacification of Ghent. The seven remaining Protestant States formed by William of Orange into a new confederacy by the Union
1579.	of Utrecht.
1581-82. 11.	The protectorate of the United Provinces (from despair of adequate help from England) offered to and accepted by Francis Duke of Anjou. Alarm of Elizabeth, and negotiations for her marriage with Anjou.
1583.12.	Attempt of Anjou to surprise Antwerp for himself. Indignation of the States, and flight of Anjou.

1579-1581. F The Papal Attack.

Threefold attempt of Pope Gregory XIII. to bring about—(1) a Catholic revolt in England, (2) a Catholic revolution in Scotland, (3) a Catholic insurrection in Ireland.

    1. Attempt to bring about a Catholic insurrection in Ireland.

1579.   *a* Landing in Ireland of a force of Spaniards (projected **1578**) under James Fitzmaurice, brother of the Earl of Desmond.

1580.   *b* Revolt of the Earl of Desmond; reinforcements of Italian and Spanish soldiers: capitulation of the invaders at Smerwick. Nov.

    2. The Catholic revolution in Scotland.

1579.   *a* Despatch of Esmé Stuart, Count d'Aubigné (created Duke of Lennox, **1581**), to Scotland to act as the King's adviser.

(1) James IV. = Margaret Tudor = (2) Earl of Angus.

    James V.
    | Margaret = Earl of   John.
    Mary.   Lennox.
    |
    James VI.   Esmé
                Darnley.   Charles.

1581.   *b* Morton, formerly regent, tried and executed for sharing in Darnley's murder. JUNE.

1582.   *c* James seized by Alexander Ruthven, Earl of Gowrie, and Esmé dismissed. (James regained his freedom, and procured the execution of Ruthven and banishment of his confederates. **1584.**)

    3. Attempts at a Catholic revolt in England.

1580.   *a* Despatch of a Jesuit Mission under Campian and Parsons. JULY. Conversions among the English nobility (*e.g*, Lord Oxford, Cecil's son-in-law.)

1581.   *b* Alarm of the nation. Parliament assembled: Act to retain the Queen's Majesty's subjects in due obedience, forbidding the saying of Mass even in houses: penalties of high treason attached to converters and converts to Roman Catholicism.

    c Flight of Parsons: arrest, torture, and execution of Campian. **1581.**

    d Abandonment of Elizabeth's former policy of conciliation. Continued persecution till the end of the reign (confined however to priests). (For its indirect effects upon liberty of conscience, see Green p. 410.)

1580. 4. The Papal attack rendered powerless by the occupation of Philip in the annexation of Portugal.

G England and Spain. (The popular feeling replacing diplomatic and political action.) (For the blighting effect of the Spanish power see Green p. 411.)

    1. The balanced and "political" neutrality of Elizabeth not shared by the country.

1562.   *a* Letters of Marque from the Prince of Condé and the Huguenots accepted by the seamen of the southern coast.

1572.   *b* Assistance given by English volunteers to the struggle against Spain in the Netherlands, **1572**, and onwards.

    c Attacks upon the "Spanish Main" in America, after the suspension of the Huguenot strife in France. Drake's voyage. **1577-1580.**

1580. 2. The power of Spain increased by the annexation of Portugal, and the gain of the Portuguese possessions in Africa and the East (thus compensating for the loss of the United Provinces).

    3. The negotiations for the marriage with Anjou strongly resisted by the Puritans. The marriage broken off by the selfish but unsuccessful attempt of Anjou to seize Antwerp, and his consequent flight from the States.

    4. Spanish designs against England encouraged by

1584.   *a* The assassination of William of Orange.

1585.   *b* The formation of the League in France (in close connexion with Spain) to exclude Henry of Navarre, become next heir to the throne by the death of Anjou (**1584**).

1585.   *c* The capture of Antwerp by the Prince of Parma.

1584. 5. Catholic plots in England. Arrest, torture, and execution of Throgmorton. Formation of an association to punish with death any attempt on the Queen's life, and to exclude from the throne any in whose favour such attempt be made.

1585. 6. Alarm of Elizabeth at the fall of Antwerp. Despatch of Leicester with a force to the States, and departure of Drake to the West Indies and the Spanish Main. Treaty defensive and offensive between Elizabeth and James VI.
1586.   of Scotland.
1586. 7. Plot of Savage, Ballard, Babington and others to kill the Queen and set Mary Stuart upon the throne. The plot discovered and Mary's knowledge and approval of it. Trial of Mary Stuart. OCT. Execution of Mary Stuart. FEB. 8,
1587.   1587. Elizabeth's anger with her ministers due to the feeling that Philip could now claim the succession to the crown as the nearest in blood of the Catholic faith.
1587. 8. Philip delayed from immediate action by the victory of Henry of Navarre over the league at Coutras, and the descent of Drake upon Cadiz and Corunna.
1588. 9. Appearance of the Duke of Guise in Paris. Rising of the people in his favour, the King (Henry III). in the power of the league. MAY. Sailing of the Armada to join the Prince of Parma in Flanders, and with a united army of 40,000 to invade England. Parma kept in Flanders by the Dutch ships. No rising for Philip among the English Catholics. The failure and scattering of the Armada. JULY-OCT. (The Armada off the Lizard ; THURSDAY, JULY 28. First engagement with the English fleet ; SUNDAY, JULY 31. Cannonade off Portland ; TUESDAY, AUG. 2. The Armada at Calais ; SATURDAY, AUG. 6. The despatch of the Fire-ships and panic of the Spaniards ; SUNDAY NIGHT, AUG. 7. Attack upon and disorganization of the Armada ; MONDAY, AUG. 8. Flight of the Armada northwards ; WEDNESDAY, AUG. 10.)

[10. The events which brought on the crisis of the Armada may be briefly stated as
 (1) Battle of Lepanto—relieving Philip from danger on the side of the Turks. 1572.
 (2) Drake's voyage and attack upon the Spanish Main. 1577-1580.
 (3) Jesuit intrigues in Ireland, Scotland, and England. 1579-1581.
 (4) Throgmorton's conspiracy. 1583
 (5) Babington's conspiracy. 1586.
 (6) Execution of Mary Stuart. 1587.]

11. Results of the defeat of the Armada.
   (1) The Roman Catholic reaction checked.
   (2) The independence of the seven United Provinces assured.
   (3) Commencement of the decadence of Spain as a political power.

1588-1603. H The Conclusion of the Foreign Struggle.

1588-1595. 1. Close of the religious strife in France.

1588. *a* The assassination of the Duke and Cardinal de Guise. Philip's hold on France weakened. DEC.

1589 [*b* Expedition under Drake and Norris to assist Don Antonio to recover the throne of Portugal. Failed in its object.]
c Henry III. assassinated before Paris by Jacques Clement. AUGUST. Succeeded by Henry of Navarre as Henry IV. Cardinal de Bourbon proclaimed King by the League as Charles X., and Philip of Spain recognised as Protector of France.

1590. *d* Victory of Henry IV. at Ivry, and siege of Paris. The siege raised at the advance of Parma from Flanders. Death of the Cardinal de Bourbon (Charles X.).

1591. *e* Despatch of aid from England to Henry IV. to win Normandy and Britanny from the League. Siege of Rouen by the combined force. Advance of Parma and abandonment of siege. **1592.**

1593-1595. *f* Conversion of Henry IV. to Catholicism. **1593.** Submission of Paris to him. **1594.** Henry absolved by Pope Clement VIII. **1595.**

1595-1603. 2. Close of the struggle with Spain and final conquest of Ireland.

1596. 1. Alarm of a second Armada. Descent of the English fleet upon Cadiz, and capture of Cadiz by Essex. JUNE-AUGUST.

1597. 2. Wreck of Philip's second Armada in the Bay of Biscay.

1598. *g* Toleration granted to the Huguenots by the Edict of Nantes (APRIL). Henry IV. recognised by Philip. **1598.**

1598. 3. Triple league between England, France, and the United Provinces. Death of Philip of Spain, and of Cecil (Lord Burleigh).

1598-1603. 4. Revolt of Ulster under Hugh O'Neill (Earl of Tyrone). Defeat of the English at Blackwater. **1598.** Failure (if not treachery) of Essex. **1599.** [Intrigues of Essex against Robert Cecil. **1600.** Attempt to raise the people of London for the deliverance of the Queen from intriguers and for the settlement of the succession. Trial and execution of Essex. **1601.**] Revolt of Munster under the Earl of Desmond. Landing of Spaniards at Kinsale. **1601.** Capitulation of Kinsale, submission of Tyrone, and conquest of Ireland completed. **1603.**

Internal condition of England from 1572 to the end of the reign.

1. Advance of Parliament.
    - *a* Assertion of the freedom not only of members, but of members' servants, from arrest except by permission of the House. **1575.**
    - *b* Assertion of the right to punish and expel members for crimes against the House. **1581.**
    - *c* Assertion of the sole right of the House to determine contested elections. **1586.**
    - *d* Freedom of debate on the part of individual members not yet insisted on (Peter Wentworth imprisoned by the House, **1575**, and again by the Council without interference from the House. **1588**).
    - *e* Bill for the Abolition of Monopolies pressed in spite of the opposition of the Ministers (claiming the direction of Trade for the Queen and Council). Withdrawal by the Queen of all monopolies granted. **1601.**
2. Growth of Puritanism, and of a consequent reaction in favour of the Church system.
    - *a* "Prophesyings" *i.e.* meetings of the clergy for prayer and exposition without the use of the Service-book (begun at Northampton, **1570**), encouraged by some of the bishops (with Grindal, Archbishop of Canterbury, **1575**, at their head), and members of Council, but suppressed by the Queen. **1577.** Grindal suspended from his functions as Archbishop. **1572-1582.**
    - *b.* Formation of a permanent Court of High Commission (claiming to sit under the Act of **1559**). **1583.**

        i. Composed of forty-four persons, twelve of whom were to be Bishops.
        ii. Empowered to inquire into all manner of Ecclesiastical offences.
        iii. The evidence of the accused used against himself or his friends by the "ex-officio" oath.
        iv. Articles of questions drawn up and presented to all suspected clergymen.
    c A desire among clergy and laity to leave certain matters of Ritual voluntary.
        (1) The use of the Surplice.
        (2) The sign of the Cross in Baptism.
        (3) The use of the ring in Marriage.
        (4) The Kneeling posture at the Communion.

1593.   *d* Severe statutes however passed against open Sectaries (especially Brownists). The first Act passed in the reign of Elizabeth against Protestants of any kind. This re-action in favour of the Church due partly to the popularity of the Queen after the defeat of the Armada, partly to the violent language used by the Puritans, *e.g.*, The Martin Mar-Prelate libels.

    The Queen's displeasure with the rising manifestations of popular feeling shown

1583.   *a* By the establishment of the High Commission as a permanent court (**1583**).

1585.   *b* By the restriction of printing to London and the two Universities, and the supervision of printers and publishers. **1585.**

    3. The rivalry between William Cecil leading the peace party, and Robert Devereux (Earl of Essex) leading the war party, after the death of Burleigh.

1599.   *a* Exclusion of Essex from public life after his failure in Ireland.

1601.   *b* Attempt of Essex to raise the people of London for the deliverance of the Queen from intriguers and the settlement of the succession. His arrest, trial, and execution. **FEB. 1601.**

1601.   4. The settlement of the old agrarian and social difficulty by the Poor-Law. The collection of the poor-rate transferred from the justices to the parochial overseers of Pauper Labour appointed by them; powers given them to give relief to the destitute, and impose work upon the idle in the Houses of Correction. Each parish thus made responsible for its own poor.

[Previous legislative attempts for the relief of the poor.
  i. Impotent beggars to find a maintenance in the place where they were at the passing of the Act or within their native hundred. **1388**.
  ii. Collections ordered in the churches for the poor who were not able to work. **1535**.
  iii. Bishops empowered to proceed in their Courts against such as should refuse to contribute for the relief of the poor, or dissuade others from doing so. **1547**.
  iv. The alms collected in church put into the hands of appointed collectors.
  v. Mayors and Churchwardens to draw up lists of inhabitants able to contribute, and payment, in case of refusal, to be assessed and made compulsory. **1562**.
  vi. All inhabitants of town and country districts to be assessed by the Mayors or Justices. The impotent poor to be settled in fitting habitations, under the superintendence of Overseers. Houses of Correction established in each county for obstinate vagabonds. **1572**.]

5. Advance of Commercial Enterprise (colonization of Virginia by Raleigh, **1584**. His voyage to Darien, **1592**, to Guiana, **1595**. Charter granted to Merchants trading to the East Indies, **1600**).

1603. Death of the Queen, MARCH, **1603**.

J. Summary of events in Ireland, from the departure of John. **1185**.
  1. Campaign of John in Ireland and division of the English Pale (consisting, roughly speaking, of the districts of Drogheda, and Dublin, Wexford, Waterford, and Cork) into counties. **1210**.
  2. Invasion of Ireland by Edward Bruce, who was crowned King. **1315**. English victories at Athenree, **1316**, and at Dundalk. **1318**.

3. Anarchy among the English settlers. Avowed independence of the family of de Burgo, in Connaught, **1333**, and of practical independence of the Fitz Maurices (Earls of Desmond) in Munster. Adoption by both families of Irish language, apparel, and laws.
4. Attempt to stop this evil by the Convention at Kilkenny, **1342**, and the statute of Kilkenny forbidding
    a The adoption by any man of English blood of the Irish language, name or dress.
    b Intermarriage with the natives, such customs as tanistry, gossipred, fosterage, and the adoption of the Brehon Law.
    c. The waging of war upon the Irish. **1367**.
5. Attempt of the Lord Deputy (William de Windsor) to force the English settlers to send representatives to England with power to assent to taxation. **1374**.
6. Expeditions of Richard II. to Ireland to enforce the power of the Crown. **1394, 1399**.
7. Subjugation of the Irish supporters of the House of York by Sir E. Poynings (Deputy for Henry, Duke of York).

"Poynings' Act,"
    a All English laws to be in force in Ireland.
    b No Parliament to be held in Ireland without the sanction of the King and Council.
    c The Irish Parliament to treat of no matters save those first approved by the King and Council. **1495**.
    The Earl of Kildare made Lord Deputy of Ireland. Continued defiance of royal authority by the great lords of the Pale (Butlers, Geraldines, De la Poers, Fitzpatricks).
8. Revolt of the Leinster Geraldines crushed by Skeffington, their castles demolished, and their house annihilated. **1535**. The power of the Crown established over all Ireland. **1535-1542**. Attempt to "make Ireland English" by guaranteeing the chiefs in possession of their lands and of their tribal authority on condition of paying tribute, giving a pledge of loyalty (involving the acceptance of an English title and the education of a son at the English Court), of abstinence from private wars and exactions.

9. The Reformation in Ireland. **1535-1558**.
   a. Quiet acceptance of the Royal supremacy by the Catholics of the Pale, **1536-1537**, and of the dissolution of the Monasteries.
   b. Strife upon the attempt to force the new practices and Liturgy upon the Irish. **1535-1551**.
   c. Restoration of Catholic worship under Mary. The church lands, however, not restored, and the Royal supremacy exercised. **1553-1558**.
   [A new cause of quarrel however appeared in the making of the country of the O'Connors into shire-land for English settlers as King's and Queen's Counties. **1556-1558**.]
10. Ireland under Elizabeth.
    a Election of Shane O'Neill by "tanistry" as chief of the O'Neills (now Earls, of Tyrone). Visit of Shane to Elizabeth his return to Ireland, after making submission and receiving pardon, and his supremacy over the North of Ireland. Defeat and death of Shane. **1567**.
    b A form established by which Irish lords might surrender their lands, and receive them back under English tenure. **1570**. Landing of Spaniards in Kerry and the revolt of the Earl of Desmond; capitulation of Smerwick, massacre of the invading garrison, followed by a war of extermination in Munster. **1579-1580**.
    c Revolt of Ulster under Hugh O'Neill (Earl of Tyrone) and O'Donnell (Earl of Tyrconnell); the revolt suppressed and the work of the Conquest of Ireland completed. **1598-1603**.

1603-1625.   **JAMES I.**   **1603-1625.**

James I. = Anne of Denmark.

| Henry, d. **1612**. | Charles I. | Elizabeth = Frederick, Elector Palatine. |

| Rupert. | Maurice. | Sophia = Elector of Hanover. |

George I.

TABLE OF POSSIBLE CLAIMANTS TO THE ENGLISH THRONE.

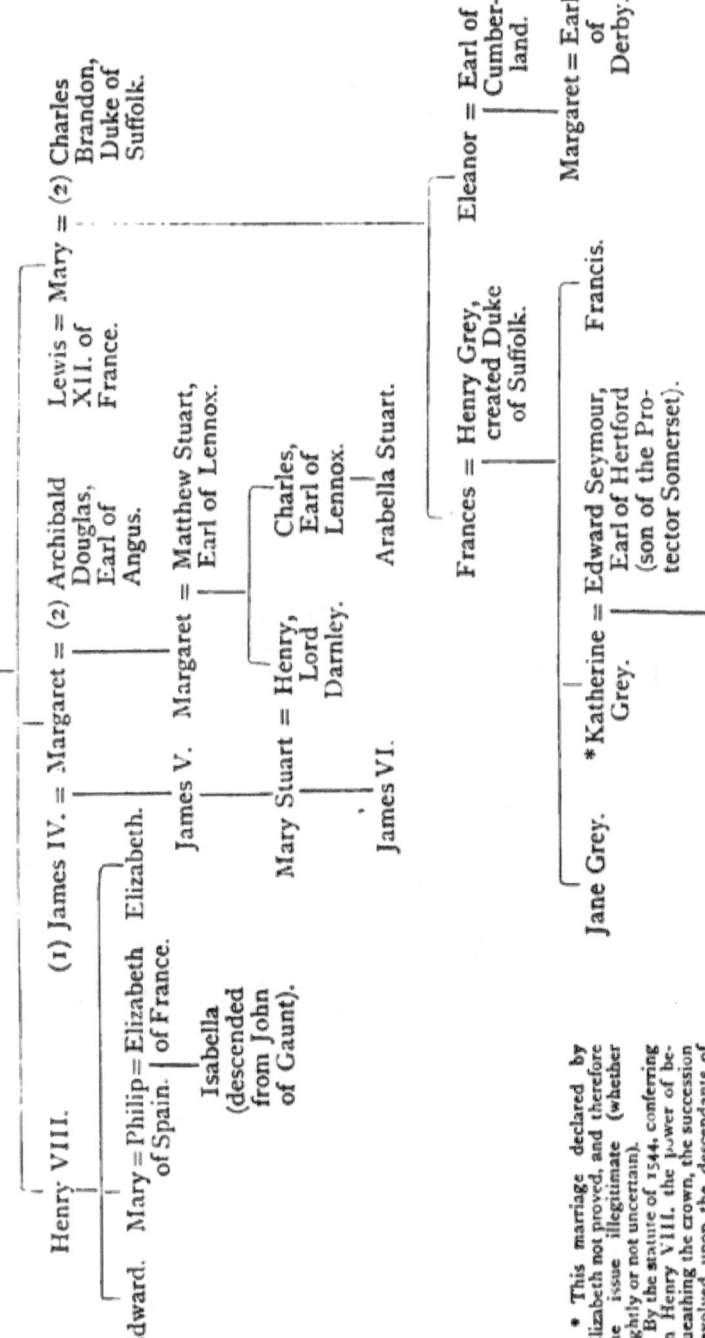

* This marriage declared by Elizabeth not proved, and therefore the issue illegitimate (whether rightly or not uncertain). By the statute of 1544, conferring on Henry VIII. the power of bequeathing the crown, the succession devolved upon the descendants of the Duchess of Suffolk, *i.e.*, Lord Beauchamp, or, if decided to be illegitimate, upon Margaret, Countess of Derby.

A The reign of James to the discovery of the Gunpowder Plot.

1. James and the Puritans.

1603.   *a* Presentation of the Millenary Petition by the Puritan Clergy for the removal of superstitious usages from the Prayer-book.

1604.   *b* Conference of Hampton Court between the Archbishop of Canterbury (Whitgift), eight bishops, seven deans, and two other clergymen, on the one side, and four Puritan clergymen, Reynolds, Chaderton, Sparks, Knewstubs, on the other. No material change made in the Prayer-book, but a new Translation of the Bible ordered. JAN.

1604.   *c* Bills of Church reform (in the direction of Puritanism) passed through the Commons, but rejected by the Lords owing to Court influence.

1604.   *d* A book of Canons accepted by Convocation. Beneficed clergy required to subscribe not only the Articles of Faith and Doctrine (as in 1559), but also those of Rites and Ceremonies. (The Canons not sanctioned by Parliament, and therefore not binding upon the laity.)

1605.   *e* Expulsion of 300 Puritan clergy from their livings for nonconformity with the rubrics.

2 James and the Roman Catholics.

1603.   *a* Promise of James to the leading Roman Catholics to remit the fines for "recusancy."

1604.   *b* Increase of "recusancy." Jesuits and Seminary priests ordered by Royal Proclamation (March) to leave the realm, but not put in force by the Government till Nov., and statutes against recusants re-enacted by Parliament. (JUNE—JULY.)

1605.   *c* Fines for "recusancy" generally levied upon the Roman Catholic laity. FEB.

3. The Plots against James.

1603.   *a* Failure of Watson's plot to seize the King; Cobham's plot to put Arabella Stuart upon the Throne. (Sir Walter Raleigh implicated, condemned, and sent to the Tower.)

1604-1605.   *b* The Gunpowder Plot (due to the disappointment of the Roman Catholics) to blow up the King and Parliament, and put the Princess Elizabeth on the Throne as a Catholic Queen. Discovery of the Plot. Nov. 5. **1605.**

B **James and his First Parliament. 1604-1611.**

1604. 1. First Session of Parliament.

    a Re-establishment of the principle that the House of Commons is "a court of record, and judge of returns," *i.e.* the judge of its own elections (in the case of Goodwin).

    b Proposals sent by the Commons to the Lords as to the new Book of Canons and Compulsory Ceremonies.

    c Conference between the Houses as to the right of purveyance and incidents of feudal tenure (aids, wardship, and marriage).

    d Address of the Commons to the King against the King's claim to "absolute" power in religion, asserting their right to be a Court of Record, and claiming their privileges as of right.

    e Appointment of Commissioners to confer with the Scots as to the union of the two Kingdoms.

1604. 2. Peace concluded with Spain, and commercial treaty with France.

1606. 3. The Second Session of Parliament.

    a Severe statutes against Roman Catholics. Subsidies voted sufficient to extinguish the royal debt (mainly incurred owing to the Spanish war). [A subsidy was an income-tax of 4*s*. in the pound upon the annual value of land worth 20*s*. a year, and a property-tax of 2*s*. 8*d*. in the pound upon the actual value of all personal property worth 3*l*. and upwards. Double the amount was exacted from aliens. To this must be added the subsidy from the clergy. The whole amount about 70,000*l*. To the subsidy was generally added a tax upon moveables (originally a fifteenth in the counties, a tenth in the boroughs), settled by a valuation made in the reign of Ed. III. The amount at this time about 29,000*l*.]

    b Decision of the Court of Exchequer (in the case of Bates) that the right to levy customs duties belongs to the King's "absolute power."

1607. 4. The Third Session of Parliament.
- *a* Opinion of the law-officers of the Crown that all Scotchmen born after the King's accession to the English throne were naturalized by their allegiance (given as a judgement in Chancery JUNE, **1608.**)
- *b* Objection of the Commons to the doctrine that nationality depends upon relation to a King. Proposals of the Commons,
  - (1) To naturalize *all* Scotchmen by statute; excluding Scotchmen from certain official positions.
  - (2) To abolish all hostile laws between England and Scotland, and to provide that criminals be tried in their own country.
- *c* Resistance of the King to naturalization by statute: the proposals of the Commissioners for Freedom of Trade (excepting Cattle and Wool), dropped, owing to the opposition of the Merchants.

1607–1610. 5. Cecil's attempts to get money to meet the King's extravagance by means of new Impositions (*i.e.* taxes on imports and exports other than wool, leather, tin); inclosure of Commons; riots in Northamptonshire and the Midlands.

1610. 6. Fourth Session of Parliament.
- *a* Cecil's proposal of the Great Contract. Feudal rights of the Crown to be abandoned in exchange for an annual revenue of £200,000.
- *b* Remonstrance of the Commons against the Royal proclamation of Impositions; against the newly established jurisdiction of the President and Council of Wales, including Gloucester, Worcester, Hereford, Shropshire; against the increased jurisdiction (in spite of the Prohibitions of the judges) of the Ecclesiastical Courts; and against Royal proclamations.
- *c* Suppression of Cowell's "Interpreter" or Law Dictionary, on the remonstrance of the Commons.
- *d* Refusal of the King to make any concession as to ecclesiastical jurisdiction.
- *e* Abandonment of the Great Contract owing to the wish of the Commons to make it depend upon redress of grievances, and owing to the King's increased demands. Dissolution of Parliament. FEB. **1611.**

C The Plantation of Ulster.

1605-1608. 1. Sir Arthur Chichester Lord Deputy. Attempt to introduce English customs, justice and religion.

    a The chiefs reduced to landowners, the tribal holdings of the tribesmen converted into copyholds.

    b Trial by jury instituted.

    c Attempt to introduce Uniformity of Worship.

1607. 2. Flight of the Earl of Tyrone (Hugh O'Neill) and of the Earl of Tyrconnell (Rory O Donnell) from Ireland.

3. Divergence of view between Chichester and the English Council as to the plantation of Estates escheated by the flight of the Earls.

    a Chichester's plan. To satisfy the natives and retired civil and military servants of the Crown in Ireland with grants of land, and then to throw open to English and Scotch Colonists whatever was left undisposed of.

1608-1609. *b* The decision of the Council. To allot 150,000 acres to English and Scotch "undertakers," who were forbidden to have Irish tenants or alienate their lots to Irishmen ; 45,500 acres to the servitors of the Crown, a certain number of Irish tenants being allowed to remain ; 70,000 acres reserved for the natives.

1610-1611. *c* The decision of the Council carried into effect and the Irish removed.

    d Material prosperity of the new plantation. Sullen discontent of the natives.

    e The part of Ireland affected by these changes —Tyrone, Coleraine, Donegal, Cavan, Armagh, Fermanagh. (In Fermanagh, however, there were no English or Scotch settlers, the land being divided between the ancient servants of the Crown and the natives.)

1611-1616. D **James's Government to the disgrace of Chief Justice Coke. 1611-1616.**

    1. Religious war threatening abroad. Attempt
1606   of the Emperor Rudolf to force Catholicism upon the Duchy of Austria. Alarm of the Calvinistic States (Hesse, Baden, the Palatinate), not being guaranteed by the Treaty of

		Passau (**1552**) (Calvinism having arisen since the Treaty). Formation of the Calvinistic "Protestant Union," and of the Catholic League under Maximilian of Bavaria.

1608.
1609.

1609. 2. Truce for twelve years concluded between Spain and Holland mainly through Cecil's
1610. mediation. The town of Juliers recovered from Archduke Leopold by the action of Holland, England and France, but the question as to the disputed succession to the duchy of Cleves left unsettled owing to the assassination of Henry IV. of France.

1611. 3. Beginning of the change of English Foreign Policy. Negotiations begun by James for a Spanish marriage, between the Infanta Anne and the Prince of Wales.

4. Imprisonment of Arabella Stuart upon her marriage with William Seymour (see Table) till her death, **1615**.

1611-1612. 5. Marriage arranged by Cecil between the King's daughter Elizabeth and Frederick the Elector Palatine. Death of Cecil, FEB., and of the Prince of Wales, NOV. **1612.**

1613. After Cecil's death the advice of the Royal Council gradually superseded by that of Carr, created Earl of Rochester.

1613. 6. Lord Essex divorced from his wife who was then married to Rochester. Murder of Sir Thomas Overbury. Rochester created Earl of Somerset.

1611-1613. 7. Sale of peerages and of patents of hereditary knighthood (baronetcies, created (**1611**) avowedly to provide a fund for the defence of the new English settlement in Ulster) in order to raise money and avoid the summoning of Parliament.

1614. 8. Parliament summoned by the advice of Bacon, and in trust upon the pledges of "undertakers" to secure compliance.

9. Meeting of Parliament. Unanimous remonstrance against "Impositions." Remonstrance against interference in elections. Dissolution. Wentworth, Hoskins, Neville, Chute, sent to the Tower. "The Addled Parliament." APRIL 5-JUNE 7.

1614. 10. Recourse to a "benevolence" to raise money.

1616. 11. Somerset and his wife accused and found guilty of the murder of Sir Thomas Overbury. Pardoned by the King, but banished from the Court.

Nov. 12. Dismissal of Chief Justice Coke from his office owing
    a To his decision that royal proclamation can only declare and not alter the law of the land, and cannot create offences. **1610**.
    b To his objection to "particular and auricular taking of opinions" from judges. (Case of Peacham. **1615**.)
    c To his refusal to admit the right of the King to consult with the judges before a decision in matters ecclesiastical. (The particular case at issue concerning a living held by the Bishop of Lichfield "in commendam.") **1616**.

E The Spanish Marriage.

1616–1619. 1. The rise of George Villiers, created Earl **1617**, Marquis **1618**, finally Duke of Buckingham (**1623**), as chief adviser. **1616**.

1617. 2. Negotiations with Spain for the marriage first formally opened.

1617–1618. 3. Unsuccessful expedition of Raleigh to Guiana upon security that he will not injure Spain. Return and execution upon his old sentence.

    4. Outbreak of revolt in Bohemia against Ferdi-
1618.   nand. MAY. First successes of the Bohemians. Situation altered by the death of the Emperor
1619.   Matthias and the election of Ferdinand.

Table to illustrate the origin of the Thirty Years' War.

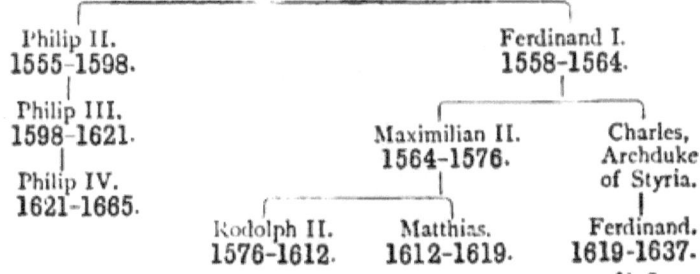

1619. 5. Acceptance of the Crown of Bohemia by Frederick the Elector Palatine, head of the Calvinistic Union and son-in-law of James.

      6. Frederick urged by James to leave Bohemia and trust to the mediation of England and Spain. **1619.**

1620. 7. Departure of English volunteers under Sir Horace Vere to support Frederick. March of the Spaniards upon the Lower Palatinate (between the Mosel and the Neckar) in order to secure the road by land to the Spanish Netherlands. Treaty of neutrality between the Protestant Union and the Catholic League. Frederick ejected from Bohemia. Nov. **1620.**

1621. 8. Parliament summoned. James however still bent upon diplomacy. Vexation of the Commons.

    a Attack upon the revival of the monopolies (especially the patent for inns, for alehouses, and for the manufacture of gold and silver thread; the last having been taken into the King's hands from the original patentees, **1618**). Royal proclamation forbidding eighteen monopolies. Prosecution and degradation of Sir Francis Mitchell, degradation and outlawry of Sir Giles Mompesson.

    b Revival of the practice of impeachment (dormant since reign of Henry VI.). Lord Chancellor Bacon attacked for corruption in taking gifts from suitors before the settlement of their suits. Submission of Bacon and disappearance from public life.

    c Lord Digby sent to Vienna to negotiate for peace upon the terms of Frederick's restoration to the whole of the Palatinate, and of due submission by him to the Emperor. Failure of the mission. Expulsion of Frederick by the army of the Catholic League from the Upper, *i.e.* Eastern Palatinate.

1621.   *d* Second session of the Parliament. Nov. The King's request for money for the war met by

        (1) A resolution after debate to vote a subsidy (76,000*l.*) to support Mansfeld's army through the winter.

        (2) A petition by the Commons that war be directed against Spain, as the moving cause of the strife.

        (3) A petition that the Prince of Wales be married to a Protestant princess.

        (4) A petition that laws against recusants be strictly enforced.

    e Prorogation (followed by dissolution) of Parliament upon the protest of the Commons against the King's command not to meddle with mysteries of State, and against his threat to interfere with freedom of speech. The protest torn from the journals by the King's own hand. DEC.

1622.   *f* Imprisonment of Coke; Pym ordered to confine himself to his own house in London.

1623. 9. Journey of Prince Charles and Buckingham to
FEB.   Madrid to secure the Spanish match. Suspension of penal laws against Catholics sworn to by the Council. Return of the Prince, OCT. Marriage negotiations finally broken off on the refusal of the Spaniards to fight against the Emperor, for the recovery of the Palatinate.

1624. 10. Parliament summoned DEC. **1623.** Sits FEB.—MAY, **1624.**

    a The Spanish negotiations laid before Parliament.

    b Three subsidies and three-fifteenths (300,000*l.*) voted for
      i. The defence of this realm.
      ii. The securing of Ireland.
      iii. The assistance of the States of the United Provinces.
      iv. The setting forth of the Royal Navy; and final breach with Spain. MARCH.

    c Impeachment of Cranfield, Earl of Middlesex, Lord Treasurer.

    d Monopolies declared contrary to law.

    e Negotiations opened with the Lutheran princes of North Germany, and for a triple alliance between England, France, and Holland.

    f Alarm of the Commons at the King's plan for a French marriage. Promise exacted from the King that no pledges of toleration to the Roman Catholics be given. APRIL.

  11. Marriage treaty settled between Prince Charles and Henrietta Maria of France (in the recess of Parliament). Secret pledges of toleration given in spite of the promise to Parliament. NOV.

1625. 12. An army of 12,000 men impressed by the King to co-operate with the French for the recovery of the Palatinate, under the command of Count Mansfeld (although the subsidy had been voted for a naval war with Spain). Failure of the expedition through want of supplies.

Discouragement of James at the failure of all his plans. Death of the King. MARCH, **1625.**

Notice in this reign in spite of the activity of the Royal Council in levying customs, issuing proclamations, stretching its authority under the presidency of the King himself in the Star Chamber, its decline in real importance.

a The necessity for a strong rule to restore order, administer justice, guard against invasion or conspiracy, had passed.

b The resistance of the lawyers to its powers, especially as exercised in the Star Chamber, increased. The powers of the Star Chamber considered as founded on unconstitutional encroachments of the Crown.

c The growth of independence in Parliament was incompatible with the authority of the Council.

d The Council had become unequal to its work.

e On the other hand the activity of the Council was never so great; Customs were levied by it; the force of Proclamations never stretched so far; the King himself resumed the custom of presiding at the sessions of the Star Chamber.

1625-1649.   **CHARLES I.**   **1625-1649.**

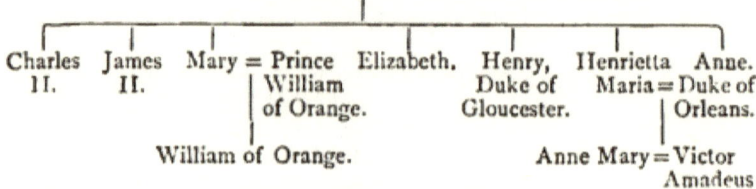

1625-1629. A Charles and his First Three Parliaments. 1625-1629.

1625. I. First Parliament. JUNE-AUG., **1625.**

   1. Committal by the Commons of Dr. Montague to the charge of the Serjeant-at-Arms for his book, "Appello Cæsarem."

2. Two subsidies only (£140,000) voted as supply, owing to the indignation of the Commons at the breach of faith about the last subsidy, and their distrust of Buckingham. Grant of Tonnage and Poundage limited to one year (instead of life) to leave time for the settlement of the vexed question as to Impositions. The Houses adjourned to Oxford on account of the Plague, JULY 11.

AUG. 3. Meeting of the Houses at Oxford. Montague declared a royal chaplain, and the decision of his case claimed for the King. Conflict in the Commons as to further supply demanded by the King and the foreign policy of Buckingham. Dissolution, AUG. 12.

1625. II. Interval between First and Second Parliament. AUG., **1625**—FEB., **1626.**

1. Buckingham's departure to Holland to conclude an alliance against Spain and Austria.

2. Additional supplies raised by general loan, and fleet despatched to intercept the Spanish Plate fleet from America. Failure through the incompetence of commander, Lord Wimbledon. **1625.**

3. Attempt to crush opposition by appointing Coke, Wentworth, Seymour, Phelips, sheriffs in their counties: refusal of writ of summons to Williams, Bishop of Lincoln, and Digby, Earl of Bristol, who were opposed to Buckingham.

1626. III. Second Parliament. FEB., **1626.**

FEB.-MAY. 1. Articles of accusation presented by Sir Dudley Digges and Sir John Eliot against Buckingham for corruption, incompetence, and support given to France against the Huguenots.

MAY. 2. Imprisonment, by royal order, of Digges and Eliot. Recriminations of Bristol and Buckingham in the Upper House.

3. Reply of Buckingham to the accusations of the Commons. Petition for his dismissal. Consequent dissolution by the King, although the subsidies were not voted. JUNE 16.

4. Defeat of the Protestants under Christian IV. of Denmark at Lutter, mainly owing to the failure of the English subsidies. AUG. 27.

1626-1628. IV. Interval between Second and Third Parliament. JUNE, **1626**—MAR., **1628.**

1626-1627. 1. Demand of a free gift, (that failing) of a forced loan (in open defiance of the law). Resistance throughout the country. **1626-1627.**

2. Difficulties with France, leading finally to war.

1625. (*a*) Double-dealing of the King with reference to the ships promised by James 1. for the reduction of La Rochelle, which by its revolt prevented the operation of the league between England, France and Holland against Spain and Austria.

1625-1626. (*b*) The delay in the fulfilment of the promises of toleration to the Catholics.

(*c*) The seizure by the English of French ships, charged with carrying war-material to the Spaniards.

(*d*) Encouragement of La Rochelle to refuse the terms of Pacification.

(*e*) Dismissal of Henrietta Maria's French household. JULY, **1626.**

1627. 3. War declared against France, and help sent to La Rochelle. Buckingham's expedition to the Ile de Rhé, and disastrous retreat. JUNE—OCT.

1627. 4. Refusal by the judges of writ of "habeas corpus" to Hampden and four others of those imprisoned for non-payment of forced loan, on the ground that the imprisonment was by special command of the King, no particular cause being specified. NOV.

1628-1629. V. Third Parliament. MAR., **1628**—MAR., **1629.**

1628. 1. The Petition of Right, reciting the former statutes against

a Arbitrary laying or levying of tallage, or aid (Statutum de Tallagio non concedendo, **1297**).

b Forced loans (authority of Parliament, **1351**, as against reason and the franchise of the land).

c Benevolences (other laws of this realm).

d Imprisonment of a freeman, but by the lawful judgement of his peers or by the law of the land ("The Great Charter of the liberties of England").

e Imprisonment without being brought to answer by due process of law. **(1354)**.

f Adjudging to death but by the laws established in the realm, either by the customs of the said realm, or by Acts of Parliament (The Great Charter, and other the laws and statutes of the King's realm).

g Dispersing of great companies of soldiers and mariners into divers counties of the realm, against the laws and customs of this realm, and to the great grievance and vexation of the people.

And humbly petitioning, as rights and liberties,

a That no man hereafter be compelled to make or yield any gift, loan, benevolence, tax, or such like charge, without common consent by Act of Parliament.

b That none be called to make answer, or take oath, or give attendance, or be confined, or otherwise molested or disquieted concerning the same or for refusal thereof.

c That no freeman, in any such manner as before mentioned, be imprisoned or detained.

d That his Majesty be pleased to remove the said soldiers and mariners, and that his people may not be so burdened in time to come.

e That the commissions for proceeding by martial law be revoked and annulled ; and that hereafter no commissions of like nature may issue forth, lest by colour of them any of his Majesty's subjects be destroyed or put to death contrary to the laws and franchise of the land.

f That his Majesty would further vouchsafe to declare that no award, doing, or proceeding, to the prejudice of his people in any of the premisses, be drawn hereafter into consequence or example.

g That his Majesty be also graciously pleased, for the further comfort and safety of his people, to declare his royal will and pleasure, that in the things aforesaid all his officers and ministers shall serve him according to the laws and statutes of this realm, as they tender the honour of his Majesty, and the prosperity of this kingdom.

2. The replies of the King.
   (*a*) "That right should be done according to the laws and customs of the realm." [The King considered that the right to imprison without cause shown lay legitimately within his "absolute power."] JUNE 2.
   (*b*) Dissatisfaction of the Commons: proposal to present Remonstrance to the King and to demand Buckingham's dismissal. The regular formal consent ("Soit droit fait comme est desiré") conceded by the King. JUNE 7. The Remonstrance however presented.
3. Assassination of Buckingham while preparing to embark for La Rochelle. AUG. 23. Capture of La Rochelle by Richelieu, OCT. [Edict of Grace issued by him to the revolted Huguenots, 1629.]

1629. 4. Second session of Parliament. JAN.
   (*a*) Irritation of the Commons at the favour shown to Montague, Mainwaring, and Laud; and at the continued levying of Tonnage and Poundage [claimed by the King, upon the opinion of the judges, as his legal due not impaired by his signature of the Petition of Right].
   (*b*) The question of the religious innovations raised first; then of the seizure of the goods of Henry Rolle (a member of the House) for non-payment of the Customs dues. Appearance of the farmers of the dues, upon summons, at the bar of the House; their refusal to answer, pleading the King's command.
   (*c*) The discussion interrupted by the Speaker at the King's command. Three resolutions put by Eliot and tumultuously carried:
      (1) That whosoever shall bring in innovation in religion, or by favour seek to extend or introduce popery, or Arminianism, or other opinions disagreeing from the true and orthodox church, shall be reputed a capital enemy to this Kingdom and the Commonwealth.
      (2) Whosoever shall counsel or advise the taking and levying of the said subsidies of Tonnage and Poundage, not being granted by Parliament, he shall likewise be reputed an innovator in the government, and a capital enemy to this Kingdom and Commonwealth.

(3) If any merchant or other person whatsoever shall voluntarily yield or pay the said subsidies of Tonnage and Poundage, not being granted by Parliament, he shall likewise be reputed a betrayer of the liberty of England, and an enemy to the same.

(*d*) Dissolution, MARCH **10**. Imprisonment of Eliot and others. Refusal of Eliot to acknowledge the jurisdiction of any court but Parliament over offences committed in Parliament, and imprisonment till his death (**1632**).

1629-1638. B Personal Government till the Judgement upon Ship-money. 1629-1638.

1. Charles's foreign diplomacy entirely prompted by family, dynastic, considerations.

1629. *a* Treaty of Susa with France after Richelieu's Edict of Grace tacitly accepting the principle that each sovereign should be free to deal with his own subjects; landing of Gustavus Adolphus (JUNE), hesitation of Charles to co-operate with him (AUG.), and peace with

1630. Spain. NOV.

1631. *b* Secret treaty with Spain for the partition of the Dutch territory in hopes of recovering the Palatinate. JAN.

1631-1632. *c* Negotiations with Gustavus ending in their rejection by Gustavus, owing mainly to Charles's refusal to operate with his fleet in order to assure the communication between Gustavus and Sweden, in case of a combined attack upon the Protestant interest by France and Spain. JULY, **1632**.

d Death of Gustavus, NOV. **6**, and of the Elector Frederick, NOV. **19**.

1632-1633. *e* Charles's anxiety that the Spanish Netherlands should not fall wholly into the hands of France and the Dutch, who were already threatening the English naval ascendency; his offers to protect them.

1634-1638. *f* Overtures to Spain for the renewal of the Partition Treaty of **1631**. The arrangement left unfinished owing to outbreak of war between France and Spain. **1635**.

                g Appearance of a splendid English fleet in the Channel claiming the sovereignty of the seas. Publication by the King of Selden's "Mare Clausum."

                h Treaty of Prague between Austria, Bavaria, and Saxony. **1636**.

                i Proposed treaty with France to give naval aid against Spain on condition of the restitution of the Palatinate. **1637**.

          2. Instances of the chief financial expedients to raise money independent of subsidies from Parliament.

              a Within the letter of the law, but vexatious.

                  (1) Fines for not receiving knighthood levied upon freeholders above £40 a year. [Imposed as early as **1626**.]

1630.   (2) Appointment of commissioners to receive composition for defective titles to estates.

1634–1638.   (3) Fines imposed for encroachments made upon forest land.

                  (4) Fines for all cottages built upon less than four acres of land, according to statute of **1570**.

1632.   (5) City of London fined £33,000 for neglect in investigating into the death of Dr. Lamb from ill-usage (**1628**).

              b Measures of disputed legality.

1630.   (1) Proclamation that all gentry leave London and reside upon their estates. Fines for non-compliance.

1630.   (2) City of London fined £100,000 for extension beyond limits set by royal proclamations of Elizabeth (**1602**) and James. Fined £70,000 for breach of conditions on which

1635.   Derry was held, and deprived of the Charter by which Derry was held, finally the fine remitted upon surrender of the Irish land and the payment of £12,000. **1658**.

                  (3) Exaction of Custom dues, and fines for non-payment.

                  (4) Increase of impositions after the death of Weston, Earl of Portland. **1635**.

                  (5) Fines imposed in the Star Chamber, often for offences which should have come before the courts of common law.

    c Measures clearly illegal.

        (1) Selling of patents of monopoly.

        (2) Demands for loans and benevolences.

    d Ship-money.

        (1) A fleet necessary to protect the fisheries from the Dutch, to chastise the pirates from Algiers and the Barbary States, to co-operate with Spain in checking the French designs upon Dunkirk, to maintain the sovereignty of the seas (**1636**), possibly also to make war upon Spain for the restitution of the Palatinate, **1637**.

1634.   (2) First writ for ships or ship-money issued to the seaport towns (at the suggestion of Noy).

1635.   (3) Second writ for ship-money issued to the whole of the country. Partial resistance and declaration by ten of the judges in favour of its legality as a levy upon all. DEC.

1636.   (4) Third writ for ship-money. The question referred by the King to the judges. The writ declared (**1637**) legal in times of danger, and the King the sole judge of danger. ˙FEB. Fourth writ.

        (5) Trial of Hampden (**1637**), for refusal to pay ship-money, and judgment given against him (two judges, Croke and Denham,
1638.   condemning the writ).

    Arguments against Hampden.

        a All laws must give way to necessity. Impossible, in necessity, to consult Parliament. Property not endangered by being used in its own defence. (Lyttelton.)

        b To be the sole judge of danger is innate in the person of an absolute King and in the persons of the Kings of England. (Bankes.)

    The most decisive judgment, that of Finch, "Acts of Parliament to take away the King's royal power in defence of his Kingdom are void."

Arguments used in defence of Hampden.
- *a* Distinction between the levy upon maritime and inland counties not pressed. The King conceded to be the sole judge of the danger, but no money could be legally raised without consent of Parliament, except in sudden and extreme danger; which danger did not exist. (St. John.)
- *b* The King only the proper judge of danger when it is impossible for lack of time to consult Parliament. (Holborne.)

3. Little discontent, however, and general increase of prosperity.
- *a* The carrying trade between Spain and its possessions and dependencies passing into English hands owing to the strain of the European war.
- *b* Manufactures and industrial enterprise at home fostered by the peace.

4. Ireland since the settlement of Ulster.
- *a* St. John, Lord Grandison, Lord Deputy **1615-1622**. Advantage taken of defective titles in Wexford, Leitrim, Longford, and Westmeath, to convert the old Irish tenures into freeholds, the natives being first satisfied before English settlers received allotments.
- *b* Henry Cary, Lord Falkland, Lord Deputy **1622-1629**. The Irish army to be increased to 5,000 foot and 500 horse; the expense to be met by Contributions from each County. The King to grant in return certain Concessions,

1626. called Graces (51 in number), especially
  (1) That recusants might practice in the courts of law upon taking the oath of allegiance only in place of the oath of supremacy.
  (2) That the Title of land be assured after possession for 60 years.
  (3) That the landowners of Connaught be confirmed in their titles which had been recognized by Elizabeth and James, but not inrolled.

1628. *c* Parliament to be called to confirm the "Graces"; but countermanded on the ground that the English Council had not sufficient time allowed to consider of the measures to be laid before Parliament.

1629.   *d* Recall of Falkland; the power of the Deputy vested in Lords Justices, the Lord Chancellor
1629.   and Richard Boyle, Earl of Cork.
   e Wentworth appointed Lord Deputy, JAN. **1632.** Arrival of Wentworth in Ireland, JULY, **1633.**

1633.   The administration of Wentworth in Ireland.

1634.   *a* Discipline and conformity imposed upon the Protestant Church. Puritanism repressed by the addition of the English Articles to the Calvinistic Irish Articles, drawn up **1615.**

   b General enforcement of law, encouragement of trade and manufactures, efficiency of Administration, and suppression of piracy in the Channel.

   c Parliament and the jury system used to strengthen the royal power.

1634.   (1) Parliament summoned. First session occupied with Supply. Six subsidies of £40,000 each voted and apportioned, used largely for the support of an armed force. Second session devoted to consideration of grievances and the Graces already (**1626**) promised by Falkland, The two most important assuring the title to land after sixty years' possession, and confirming the landowners of Connaught in their lands, laid aside by virtue of Poynings' Act.

   (2) The jury system used to conduct an Inquisition into the Titles of Land in Connaught and Clare, preliminary, most probably, to their colonization. An express grant from the Crown had to be proved in each case. Acknowledgment of the King's title to the land obtained in Roscommon, Sligo, Mayo. Resistance of the Galway jury; the sheriff fined, the jurymen summoned before the Castle Chamber, appeal to the Court of Exchequer to set the verdict aside.

1636.   *d* Wentworth's account of his administration in
JUNE.   Ireland before the English Council, showing the improvement in the state of finance, discipline of the Army, administration of justice, suppression of piracy, growth of trade and manufactures, and defending himself

against the charge of severity (especially in the case of Lord Mountmorris, condemned by Council of War for insubordination Dec. **1635**). Permission given him to proceed with the plantation of Connaught

5. Laud and Ecclesiastical Administration.

a Laud, Bishop of London **1628-1633**.

1630. (1) Conformity to the full ritual of the Prayer Book enforced in his diocese.

1631. (2) Funds collected for the restoration of S. Paul's.

1633. (3) The legality of the purchase of impropriate Church livings by the "feoffees for impropriations" (a company of Puritan churchmen) to support a "preaching clergy," referred by Laud to the judges and the society suppressed.

b Laud, Archbishop of Canterbury.

1633. (1) Re-publication of the "Book of Sports" by royal authority. The declaration of Sunday sports ordered to be read in churches.

(2) Pressure upon the bishops to have the communion table moved to the east, placed altar-wise, and railed off.

1634-1636. (3) Archi-episcopal visitations of the province of Canterbury either in person or by the vicar-general; uniformity of ritual enforced, beauty in ritual encouraged. Offenders prosecuted in the Court of High Commission.

(4) Growing suspicions of his disloyalty to the Church of England; encouraged by his sanction of severe penalties to the Puritans, as in the case of Leighton (1630), Prynne (1634), and of Prynne, Burton, and Bastwick, (1637); his requirement of conformity from the children of French and Walloon Protestants settled in England (**1635**); the prohibition to the English envoy in Paris to attend the Huguenot Chapel; the refusal to allow further importation of Calvinistic Geneva Bibles; the reception at court of Panzani, a Papal agent (**1634-1635**); and the changes in the new Scottish service book (**1637**).

6. The migration to America.
- **1620.** *a* Landing of Independent Separatists at Plymouth in the Mayflower. "The Pilgrim Fathers."
- **1629.** *b* Charter granted by Charles to the Company of Massachusetts Bay, transference of the
- **1630.** Company to America. Great migration of Puritans, especially from the eastern counties.
- **1631.** Settlements also in Rhode Island (**1633-1635**) and Connecticut. Episcopacy and the Prayer Book abolished by the settlers.
- **1634.** *c* Attempt to stop emigration by the Privy Council. No man rateable on the Subsidy Books to go to New England without special license from the Council; no poorer person without certificate of orthodoxy.

d Assumption of independent loyalty by the emigrants to New England in spite of the Privy Council, who had succeeded the Council of New England as the central authority by their surrender of their powers to the Crown, **1635.**

e Foundation of Maryland by Lord Baltimore (a Catholic) on the basis of toleration, **1633-1638.**

1637-1640. C **The Scotch Resistance. 1637-1640.**
1. Ecclesiastical measures in Scotland in the reign of James VI.

[**1572.** (*a*) The "Tulchan" Bishops, so called because "the bishop had the title, but my lord got the milk, or commoditie."]

- **1592.** (*b*) Presbyterianism fully established.
- **1599.** (*c*) Titular bishops (appointed by the King) to sit in Parliament (as commissioners of the clergy); the Bishops not acknowledged by the Church.
- **1604.** (*d*) Attempt of James to put a stop to the meetings of the General Assembly.
- **1606.** (*e*) Restitution of a portion of the Church lands annexed to the Crown for the benefit of the bishops.

(*f*) Trial and banishment of six leading ministers for constituting the meeting of ministers at Aberdeen into a General Assembly. Andrew Melville and seven others summoned to confer with the King at London; Melville brought before the English Council for an epigram upon the service in the Royal Chapel, imprisoned and afterwards banished; the other ministers sent to different parts of Scotland.

178   ANALYSIS OF ENGLISH HISTORY.

1610-1612.   (*g*) Ecclesiastical reorganisation. Power of ordination and spiritual jurisdiction placed in the hands of the bishops: establishment of a Court of High Commission in the Archiepiscopal dioceses of St. Andrews and Glasgow.

1617.
1621.   (*h*) The Five Articles (accepted by a General Assembly at Perth, and sanctioned by the Estates), enjoining the kneeling posture at the Lord's Supper, the administration of the Lord's Supper and Baptism in private houses in case of sickness or necessity, episcopal confirmation, and the observance of Christmas, Good Friday, Easter, Whitsunday.

2. Ecclesiastical changes under Charles.

1629.   *a* Measure for the commutation of tithes on payment of a sum calculated at nine years' purchase, or by commutation into a rent charge.

1633.   *b* The election of the Lords of Articles modified so as to increase the political authority of the Crown. The sixteen commissioners of the untitled gentry and burgesses appointed by the sixteen select bishops and peers. The bishops selected by the Peers, and the peers by the Bishops (whereas each division claimed the right to elect its own representatives).

1633.   *c* Coronation of Charles. The enforcement of the surplice as the clerical dress.

1636.   *d* Issue of the Book of Canons (without the consent of the General Assembly) establishing the ecclesiastical and spiritual supremacy of the bishops and the Crown.

1637.   *e* Publication of a new Liturgy based on the English Prayer Book.

3. Resistance of the Scotch.

1637.   *a* Riot in S. Giles, Edinburgh, on the introduction of the new Liturgy. JULY 23.

1638.   *b* Petitions against the new Liturgy forwarded to the King, answered by royal proclamation forbidding meetings and demanding obedience. FEB. 1638.

c Formation of four Tables, or Committees, of the Petitioners against the innovations. FEB. 19. The signature of the Covenant in the church and churchyard of Grey Friars, Edinburgh (FEB. 28-MARCH 2.)

d Marquis of Hamilton sent to Scotland as royal commissioner (MAY). Demands of the Scotch.
  (1) Abolition of the Courts of High Commission and the bishops' courts.
  (2) Withdrawal of the Canons and new Liturgy.
  (3) A Free Parliament and Assembly.
e Preparation for war both on the side of Charles and the Scotch.
f Royal declaration withdrawing Canons and Liturgy, suspending the Five Articles, promising Parliament and Assembly, and inviting signatures to the King's Covenant. SEPT.
g Meeting of the Assembly at Glasgow (144 ministers and 96 laymen). The whole episcopal system attacked. Dissolution of the Assembly by Hamilton, but refusal to separate. NOV.—DEC.

1639. *h* Resolute attitude of the Scotch. Seizure of the fortresses of Edinburgh, Dumbarton, (MARCH), and advance of General Leslie who had come from Sweden, with 20,000 men, many of whom were veterans returned from Germany, to the border (upon the appearance of a royal fleet under Hamilton in the Forth). MAY.
i Advance of the King with a force (raised by impressment), MAY, and "the pacification of Berwick." The Tables to be dissolved and royal castles restored, upon condition of all ecclesiastical matters being settled by Assemblies, and all civil matters by Parliaments (JUNE). Meeting of Assembly and Parliament (AUG.).
j [Destruction of a Spanish fleet (bound for Flanders with promises of protection from the King) by the Dutch at Dover (OCT.).] Negotiations between the Scots and the French ambassador at London.

1639.
1640. *k* Contributions from the Catholic gentry. Eight thousand troops raised in Ireland for the King by Wentworth (now created Earl of Strafford and Lord Lieutenant instead of Lord Deputy of Ireland), and four subsidies obtained from the Irish Parliament. An English Parliament at last summoned (APRIL).

l The Short Parliament. APRIL—MAY.

    (*a*) An intercepted letter, written by the Scots to the French King, Lewis XIII. (**1639**) but not despatched, laid before Parliament but disregarded.

    (*b*) Supply postponed till grievances had been considered. Twelve subsidies (840,000*l.*) demanded by the King as the price for the abandonment of ship-money, in spite of Strafford, who urged the abandonment of ship-money and trusting the Commons for supply. Objection made by the Commons to military charges being imposed by the King's sole authority. Proposed petition against the Scotch war. Dissolution.

m Vain attempts of the King to get loans from Spain, France, the Pope. Petition of Yorkshire gentlemen against the soldiers quartered among them. (JULY.) Refusal of a loan by the city of London.

n Advance of the Scots into England, occupation of Newcastle (AUG.). Council of Peers summoned at York (SEPT.), and writs issued for a Parliament; security given to the city of London by the Peers for a loan; the Treaty of Ripon concluded with the Scots; their demands to be fully considered at London; Northumberland and Durham left in their hands as pledges for the payment of their army (£25,000 per month). OCT. **5**.

D The Long Parliament till the outbreak of the War. NOV. 1640—JULY, 1642.

    1. Temper of London shown by the attack upon Lambeth House (MAY), and upon the Court of High Commission. (OCT.)

    2. Events till the Adjournment. NOV., **1640**—SEPT., **1641**.

1640.
NOV.

    a Attack upon Ministers.

    Strafford impeached of High Treason by Pym, NOV. **11**. The grounds of impeachment not set forth till NOV. **25**, the articles of impeachment not till JAN., **1641**.

    Escape of Windebank (Secretary of State) to France, of Lord Keeper Finch to Holland. (DEC.)

	Prynne, Bastwick, and Burton set free.
DEC.	The Canons of May and the et cetera oath voted to be illegal. Laud put in charge of the Usher.
1641.	DEC. [Imprisoned MARCH, 1641.]
JAN.	*b* Commissions appointed for the removal of tables placed altar-wise and other "reliques of idolatry." Announcement by the King that henceforth judges shall hold office "quam diu se bene gesserint."
FEB.	*c* Royal assent given to the Bill for Triennial Parliaments.
MARCH.	*d* Ship-money and impositions upon merchandize without consent of Parliament declared illegal.
MARCH.	*e* Introduction of Bill to restrain bishops from sitting in the House of Lords and clergy from exercising judicial functions.
	f Commencement of Strafford's trial. Charged with
	(1) Subverting the fundamental laws of the North of England and Ireland. (No mention however made of the proposed plantation of Connaught.)
	(2) Stirring up hostility with Scotland.
	(3) Attempting to subvert authority of Parliament.
	(4) Advising the King to use the Irish army for the reduction of England to obedience.
APRIL. MAY.	None of the charges definitely amounting to treason, Bill of Attainder introduced against him; royal interference, and assent given to his exclusion from place of trust.
MAY.	*g* Marriage of Charles's eldest daughter to Prince William of Orange. Protestation drawn up by the Commons and accepted by the Lords for the security of the King's person, the privileges of Parliament, and the defence of the true Reformed Protestant Religion, expressed in the doctrine of the Church of England. Attempt of the King to seize the Tower, and statement by Pym of the Army Plot set on foot by Jermyn and Goring (with the knowledge, though not the sanction, of the King) to march upon London, enable the King to dissolve Parliament, and set Strafford free : Followed by

	(1) Panic and riot in London. Passing of Bill of Attainder and of a Bill providing that Parliament be only adjourned or dissolved with its own consent.
MAY 10.	(2) Royal assent to both Bills.
MAY 12.	Execution of Strafford.
JUNE.	(3) Poll-tax to pay off English and Scottish armies.
	[The armies disbanded AUGUST.]
MAY 27.	*h* Agreement to exclude clergy from civil functions by the Lords, excepting the Bishops. Proposal in the Commons for the abolition of Episcopacy. [The beginning of a breach in the House, and of the rise of a Church party under Falkland and Hyde.]
JUNE.	*i* Bills declaring the illegality of ship-money (already declared illegal by resolution of the Commons, DEC., and of the Lords, JAN.) and for the abolition of the Courts of Star Chamber and High Commission. [This marks the end of "those judicial powers which the policy of a century and a half had grouped round the Council."] The Councils of Wales (including Gloucester, Worcester, Herefordshire, Shropshire), the North, Lancashire, and Cheshire, previously abolished, declared illegal. Prohibition of compulsory knighthood upon £40 freeholders. Restriction of the jurisdiction of the Stannaries Courts of Devon and Cornwall. Limits of forest-land to be fixed by Commissioners. Second army plot to bring the army up to London if the neutrality of the Scots could be ensured.
AUG.	*j.* Departure of the King for Scotland [accompanied by a Parliamentary Committee], where the Earl of Montrose had quarrelled with Argyle, and was forming a royal party, but had been imprisoned (JUNE). Large concessions by the King to the Scottish Parliament, those failing to win over Argyle, negotiations with the aristocratic party of the nobles.
SEPT.—OCT.	**3.** Events of the recess. SEPT.—OCT.
SEPT.	*a* Adjournment of the Houses. Committees of each House appointed to sit.
OCT.	*b* "The Incident": a plot in Scotland for the arrest, perhaps murder of Hamilton and Argyle (possibly with the King's partial knowledge).

	c Events in Ireland.
	i. Authority, on the departure of Strafford, in the hands of Lords Justices, Sir W. Parsons, and Sir J. Borlase. Abandonment by the King of the Plantation of Connaught, and hopes held out to the Catholic Lords for the toleration of their religion.
OCT. 23, 1641.	ii. Plan of Sir James Dillon and Lord Maguire to seize Dublin Castle discovered in time to save Dublin.
OCT. 24.	iii. Rising of the native Irish in Ulster under Roger More and Phelim O'Neill. Probably no general massacre, but about 4,000 English settlers were slain in cold blood, while about 8,000 may have perished from exposure and ill-treatment.
DEC.	iv. Junction of the Catholic Lords of the Pale with the Ulster rebels. Spreading of the Rebellion to Munster. Landing of English troops in Ireland, of the Scotch troops (spring). Cruelties of the soldiers.
DEC.	

4. Events after the Adjournment, till the breach with the King. OCT. 1641–JAN. 1642.

NOV.	*a* The Grand Remonstrance, detailing the abuses swept away and the necessary securities. Keen debates in the House between the new Royalist party and the Puritans, both as to the presentation and printing of the Remonstrance. Presented DEC. 1.
	b Re-introduction of the Bishops' Exclusion Bill.
DEC.	*c* "Rabbling of the bishops." Abstention of all the Bishops except two from the House of Lords and protest of twelve absenting Bishops against all proceedings in their absence. Committal of the protestors to the Tower.
	d Skirmishes between the King's body-guard and the citizens [hence the the names Cavalier and Roundhead].
JAN. 1642.	*e* Demand of the Commons for a guard. Royal pledge to protect them from violence. Lord Kimbolton, Pym, Hampden, Hazelrigg, Holles, and Strode accused by the King of treasonable correspondence with the Scotch. Their surrender demanded by the King in person from the House, JAN. 4, and from the City aldermen, JAN. 5.

JAN. 10. JAN. 12.	*f* Removal of the King to Hampton Court. The security of Hull, Portsmouth, and the Tower secured by the vote of the Commons.
JAN.	*g* Demand of the Commons for the right to appoint the officers of the Militia.
	h The Bishops' Exclusion Bill passed by the Lords. Royal assent given. [The last Bill to which Charles gave Royal assent.]

5. Preparations for war. JAN.—JUNE.

JAN.	*a* Departure of the Queen for Holland (ostensibly for the marriage of her daughter Mary to William of Orange) and purchase of arms and stores.
MARCH.	*b* The command of the fleet secured by the Commons.
APRIL 23.	*c* The King denied entrance into Hull.
MAY.	*d* Lieutenancies of counties (conferring power to call out the Militia) granted by the Houses. Commissions of Array issued by the King.
MAY.	*e* Secession of Falkland, Hyde, Colepepper, 35 peers, and 60 Members of the Commons to the King at York.
JUNE.	*f* The "Nineteen Proposals" of the Houses to the King, including demands for—

  (1) Parliamentary sanction to appointments to Council.
  (2) Parliamentary control over education and marriage of Royal children.
  (3) Parliamentary control over the command of the Militia.
  (4) Parliamentary control of Church reform.

E The War. JULY, 1642–MAY, 1646.

1642.	THE WAR.
JULY 12.	An army raised by the Houses for "the defence of the King and the Parliament." The Earl of Essex captain-general.
AUG. 22.	Royal standard raised at Nottingham. Failure of Essex to strike a decisive blow by routing and capturing the King.
SEPT. 20.	The King's headquarters at Shrewsbury, to receive levies, and secure Severn Valley. Decision to march on London, and end the war. Overtaken by Essex at Edgehill;
OCT. 23. OCT. 26.	failure to check the King's advance. Oxford occupied, then Reading; proposed conference

Nov. 12.	for peace interrupted by Rupert's capture of Brentford. Retreat of the King before the trained bands of London (under Skippon
Nov. 13.	and Essex) to Oxford. The "Association of
Dec. 2.	the Eastern Counties." A picked regiment of horse raised in these counties by Cromwell.
1643.	
Jan.	All the S.E. of England (from the Humber to the Bristol Channel) held by the Parliament, except Oxfordshire, Berks, part of Wilts and Gloucester, and Cornwall.
	The N.W. held by the King, except Scarborough, the southern districts of Yorkshire, Derbyshire and Staffordshire. (See map in Public Schools Historical Atlas.)
Jan.-April.	1. Fruitless negotiations between the King and Parliament.
Feb. 23.	2. Arrival of the Queen in Yorkshire; Royalist successes in Yorkshire, passage of the Trent.
April 26.	3. Re-capture of Reading by Essex; not, however, followed up.
May.	4. The Cornish rising for the King.
May 16.	The Earl of Stamford defeated at Stratton,
July 5.	and Waller on Lansdown Hill and on
July 13.	Roundway Down (Somersetshire won for the King).
	The conquest of Devonshire completed by Prince Maurice.
May 31.	5. The discovery of "Waller's plot" to introduce the King into London.
June-July.	6. Successes of Prince Rupert.
	Attack from Oxford upon the army of Essex, dispersed in a chain of weak detachments round Thame. Skirmish at Chalgrove. June 18, and death of Hampden, June 24. Retreat of Essex from Thames to Ux-
July 26.	bridge. Capture of Bristol by Rupert.
	7. Gloucester besieged by the king, relieved by
Aug. 10-Sept. 6.	Essex. Return of Essex to London, overtaken by the King and compelled to fight at
Sept. 20.	Newbury (where Falkland was killed), but his march not interrupted.
Sept. 5.	8. Cessation from arms for twelve months with the "Confederate Catholics" in Ireland. Commissioners to be sent by the Confederates to Oxford to treat with the King as to conditions of permanent peace.

SEPT. 25.
9. Commissioners sent from the English Parliament to the Scotch; the Covenant signed by the Parliament in S. Margaret's Church, Westminster, to secure co-operation with Scotland. "The Solemn League and Covenant."

OCT. 11.
10. Successes of the Royalists in Yorkshire. Siege of Hull by Lord Newcastle. Newcastle's advance into Lincolnshire checked by the younger Fairfax and Cromwell at Winceby. Siege of Hull raised, OCT. 12.

DEC. 6.
11. Death of Pym.

1644.

JAN.
All the N., West Midlands, and West of England (except Hull and the West Riding, the N. of Staffordshire, the S. of Derbyshire—the Peak country excluded), Montgomery, Pembroke, Gloucester, Plymouth, Taunton, Lyme Regis, Weymouth in the King's hands.
The Associated Counties, East Midlands (except Newark and Bedfordshire), and the East of Southampton Water held by the Parliament. (See map in Public Schools Historical Atlas.)

JAN.
1. March of the Scotch army across the border.

JAN. 25.
The auxiliaries from Ormond's army annihilated by the younger Fairfax at Nantwich.

FEB. 16.
2. Institution of the Committee of Both Kingdoms for a limited period, with control over foreign affairs, but to conclude no cessation from arms nor treaty with the King without consent of Parliament.

MARCH.
3. Despatch by the King of Lord Glamorgan to Ireland, who promised to the Confederates the repeal of the penal laws, a term of limitation for inquiries into the titles to estates, and the possible establishment of Catholicism in Ireland, in return for military aid to be sent to Montrose in Scotland.

MAR. to JULY.
4. Siege of York by the combined armies of the younger Fairfax, the Associated Counties, and the Scotch. The Royal garrison joined by Prince Rupert. Utter defeat of the Royalists at Marston Moor. Flight of the

JULY 2.
Marquis of Newcastle from the country, and surrender of York. JULY 16.

JUNE.	5. Independent operations of Essex and Waller. March of Essex westwards in spite of the orders of the Committee of Both Kingdoms.
JUNE 29.	Defeat of Waller by the King at Cropredy Bridge. Capitulation of the infantry of the army of Essex at Fowey, SEPT. 2 Victory (on the same day) of the Highlanders and Confederate Catholics under Montrose at Tippermuir.
OCT. 27.	6. March of Charles upon London met at Newbury by the Parliamentary Army of the North. The King's advance checked, but Lord Manchester blamed by Cromwell for the indecisive result. [For the rise into importance of the Independents and Cromwell and their aims, political and military, see Green pp. 553–563.]
1645.	
JAN. 10.	1. Execution of Archbishop Laud.
JAN. 30.—FEB. 12.	2. Negotiation of Uxbridge between the Parliament and the King; the King consenting to a limited Episcopacy (bishops the Presidents of Synods of Presbyters): Parliament limiting its control over the militia to seven years. Broken off possibly by the news of the victory of Montrose at Inverlochy.
FEB. 2.	
FEB. 15. APRIL 3.	3. Organization of the Army of the Parliament on the "New Model," to be placed under the command of Fairfax. The "Self-denying Ordinance," declaring the tenure of a seat in Parliament incompatible with a military command, passed (with a temporary exception in favour of Cromwell).
MAY 15-31.	4. Relief of Chester, and capture of Leicester by the King on his way to the Eastern Counties. The King overtaken by the New Model Army under Fairfax, and defeated at Naseby. Capture of the King's correspondence, and flight of the King to Wales.
JUNE 14.	
MAY—AUG.	5. Continued victories of Montrose in Scotland.
JULY. SEPT. 10. SEPT. 13. NOV. 5.	6. Conquest of the South-West by Fairfax. Bristol surrendered by Prince Rupert, and Montrose defeated at Philiphaugh. Withdrawal of the King to Oxford. Negotiations opened by him with Parliament and with the Scotch.

1646.
APRIL. Siege of Oxford by Fairfax. Flight of the King. Surrender of the King by himself to
MAY 5. the Scotch, near Newark. His return to Scotland as King barred by his refusal to take the Covenant.

1646. F Events till the Execution of the King. MAY, 1646—JAN., 1649.

JULY 14. 1. Terms offered to the King by the Parliament; and pressed upon him by the Scots, who had retreated with him to Newcastle.
  (*a*) Parliamentary control of the militia and fleet for twenty years.
  (*b*) The exclusion of "Malignants" (*i.e.* those who had fought for the King) from public office.
  (*c*) The abolition of Episcopacy and establishment of the Presbyterian order.
  Concessions finally made by the King.
  (*a*) To surrender the military control for ten years.
  (*b*) To recognize the Presbyterian system for three years. A religious settlement then to be made by the King and Houses after further consultation of the Assembly of Divines.

1645-1646. 2. Active measures taken by Parliament, and the assembly of divines at Westminster (convened JUNE 12, 1643) for the organization of church government upon the Presbyterian model.

1647, JAN. 30.
  3. The King delivered up by the Scots to a commission of the Houses upon the payment of £200,000 (with the pledge of an equal sum to be paid afterwards) in discharge of their claims for service in the field. The King guarded at Holmby House, Northamptonshire.

MARCH 8. 4. Vote of the Parliament that the army be reduced in number and that the remainder take the covenant.
  Election by the army of two members of each
APRIL.   regiment to form a council of agitators to act in political matters.

MAY 12. 5. Acceptance by some of the Presbyterian Parliamentary chiefs of the King's concessions that the religious question be reconsidered after three years.

ANALYSIS OF ENGLISH HISTORY.   189

JUNE 4. **6.** The King seized by Cornet Joyce and carried to Cheldersley, near Cambridge, within reach of the army.

JUNE 5-10. **7.** General meeting of the army at Triploe Heath (near Newmarket). Decision not to disband till their pay (a year in arrears) had been received and liberty of conscience secured.

JUNE 25. **8.** The humble representation of the army for liberty of worship under the new Presbyterian discipline. Advance of the army to Uxbridge, and exclusion of eleven members charged by the army with stirring up strife between them and Parliament.

9. Terms of settlement offered by the army to the King.
  1. A general act of oblivion for all but seven leading delinquents.
  2. Withdrawal of all coercive restrictions upon worship (even Catholics exempted from coercion).
  3. Parliamentary control of the armed forces for ten years.
  4. Parliamentary nomination of great officers of State.
  5. A plan of reform for representation, taxation, judicial procedure, commerce.

AUG. 6. **10.** Riot in London in favour of the return of the eleven Members. Flight of Speaker Lenthall, fourteen Peers, and 100 Commoners to the army. Entrance of the army into London. The King moved to Hampton Court.

NOV. 7. **11.** Impatience of the army at the delay of the King in accepting the Act of Settlement restrained by Cromwell and Ireton. Private negotiations of the King with the Duke of Hamilton, and escape from Hampton Court to the Isle of Wight.

DEC. **12.** Renewal of the King's negotiations with Parliament. Final rejection of the Terms by the King (in consequence of his hopes from the Scots), and attempted flight of the King from Carisbrooke.

1648.
JAN. 3. **13.** Vote of Parliament to make no more addresses to the King.

1648. G The Second Civil War; Trial and Execution of the King. FEB., 1648—JAN., 1649.

APRIL to AUG. **1.** Royalist rising in Wales crushed by Cromwell, through the siege and capture of Pembroke; rising in Kent suppressed by Fairfax at Maidstone (June), and by the capture of Colchester (August). Appearance of the Prince of Wales off the Thames with a fleet of 19 ships (July).

JULY 5. **2.** Invasion of England by the Duke of Hamilton in consequence of secret negotiations with the King, and in co-operation with English Royalists who had seized Berwick and Carlisle.
AUG. 17. Scots defeated at Preston; march of the "New Model" over the border; "Whiggamore Raid,"
SEPT.-DEC. and restoration of Argyll and the Covenanters to power.

3. Strict Presbyterian feeling shown by the majority in Parliament during the Royalist rising and
SEPT.-NOV. Scotch War.
  (*a*) Ordinance for the Suppression of Heresies and Blasphemies passed.
  (*b*) The eleven Members excluded (June, 1647) recalled.
  (*c*) Negotiations with the King —"the Treaty of Newport"—reopened.
    i. The militia to be in the hands of Parliament.
    ii. Episcopacy to be abolished.
    iii. The King to take the Covenant, and accept the authority of the Assembly of Divines.
  Refusal of the King to accept ii. and iii.

4. Demand of the army that the King be brought to justice.
NOV. 30. The King seized by the army, and removed to Hurst Castle.
DEC. 5. Vote of Parliament to accept the concessions of the King, as a basis for a Treaty.
DEC. 6, 7. Arrest of 46 and exclusion of 97 Members from the House by orders of the Council of Officers. "Pride's Purge."

1649.
JAN. 1. **5.** Nomination of High Court of Justice of 150 Members under the presidency of John Bradshaw.

JAN. 5.	Upon the refusal of the Peers to concur, the authority of the Commons declared supreme without the concurrence of King or House of Lords.
JAN. 20.	Trial of the King. [Only 67 of the 150 Members being present.] Refusal of the King to plead.
JAN. 30.	Execution of the King at Whitehall.

1649-1660. THE COMMONWEALTH. 1649-1660.

A The Commonwealth till the Declaration of the Protectorate.

1. The establishment of the Commonwealth. FEB. —MAY.

1649.   *a* Charles II. proclaimed at Edinburgh, supported by Holland, and invited by Ormond to land in Ireland. FEB. The Channel plundered by Prince Rupert.

b Abolition of the House of Lords and of the Monarchy. FEB. 5-7. An Executive Council

FEB. 14.   of State elected and entrusted with extensive and nearly absolute powers—military, diplomatic, and judicial. Refusal of twenty-two of the forty-one members to take oath approving of the King's execution. Withdrawal of six out of the twelve judges. FEB. 9.

c Execution of the Duke of Hamilton (under his English title of Earl of Cambridge), Lords Holland and Capel (implicated in second civil war). MARCH 9. Assassination of Dorislaus at the Hague, by some servants of Montrose, a few days after his arrival as Envoy. MAY 12.

d Trouble from the Levellers in Surrey, who seemed aiming at a social revolution, and equal distribution of the land and its produce. Discontent of the Agitators with the new political arrangements, as too aristocratic, and demands for early dissolution of Parliament, biennial Parliaments (with supreme control over legislation, administration, and foreign affairs, but not over matters of religion), redistribution of seats, legal reforms, enforcement of self-denying ordinance. Arrest of Lilburne and three others.

  e Open mutiny of the discontented troops on the order to sail for Ireland (which was looked upon as a political measure and equivalent to a sentence of banishment). The mutiny crushed by Fairfax and Cromwell. MAY. England declared a Commonwealth or Free State without King or House of Lords. MAY 19.

2. Cromwell in Ireland. AUG. 15.
 a Cromwell's aims in Ireland.
  i To reconquer the country.
  ii. To take vengeance for the massacre of 1641.
  iii. To restore and increase English and Protestant ascendency.

 b Charles invited by Ormond. FEB. Defeat of Ormond by General Jones at Rathmines, near Dublin, which had been voluntarily surrendered by Ormond to the Parliamentary generals to prevent it falling into the hands of the natives and the Papal Nuncio Rinuccini (1647). AUG. 2.

AUG. 2.
SEPT. 11. *c* Drogheda stormed by Cromwell. No quarter shown to the garrison; either killed or sent as slaves to the Barbadoes.

OCT. 9. *d* Wexford stormed. The garrison put to the sword (without orders from Cromwell). Conquest of S.E. Ireland except Waterford.

OCT. *e* Rupert's fleet driven from Kinsale by Blake to the Tagus.

MAY 10.
JULY 20. *f* Defeat of Hugh O'Neill, the leader of the Irish, and storming of Clonmel. Arrival of Cromwell in England (Ludlow and Ireton being left behind in Ireland).

3. Events in Scotland.

FEB. 5, 1649. *a* Prince Charles proclaimed King by Argyle. Negotiations delayed by Charles. Hopes in Ireland and from Montrose.

JAN. 1650.
APRIL.
MAY 21. *b* Landing of Montrose in the Orkneys. Attempts to raise a Royalist force for the King in Caithness and Ross; Montrose defeated, captured, and hanged.

JUNE 24. *c* Arrival of Prince Charles in Scotland from Jersey (having been obliged to leave Holland in consequence of the murder of Dorislaus. MAY 12, 1649). Refusal of Fairfax to take the field against the right of the Scotch to order their own government.

JULY 16.	*d* Advance of Cromwell from the border along the coast towards Edinburgh.
AUG. 16.	*e* Signature of the Covenant by Charles.
SEPT. 3. DEC	*f* Cromwell driven to retreat from want of provisions and illness. His road blocked by Leslie at Cockburnspath. Battle of Dunbar. Defeat of the Scots and surrender of Edinburgh town. The Castle surrendered. DEC.
JAN. 1, 1651.	*g* Coronation of Charles by Argyll acting in conjunction with the new Duke of Hamilton and the less rigid Presbyterians and Royalists at Scone.
AUG.	*h* Advance of Cromwell upon Perth, and march of Charles and Hamilton into England. Pursuit by Cromwell and battle of Worcester. SEPT. 3. Flight of Charles to France.
	i Completion of the Conquest of the Lowlands of Scotland by Monk. 1651.

4. Action of Parliament. MAY, 1649 – APRIL, 1653.

OCT.–NOV. 1649.	*a* Prosecution, but acquittal of Lilburne for treasonable writing against Parliament.
1649. MARCH, 1650. 1651.	*b* Re-organization of the navy (in consequence of the Royalist movement of 1648) by Vane. Prince Rupert driven to the Tagus and sheltered by the Portuguese, but finally driven by Blake from the Portuguese, Spanish, and French harbours. The Channel Islands and Scilly Islands captured by Blake.
JAN. 1651.	*c* Rejection by Holland of proposals of political union with England made in consequence of the death of the Prince of Orange (1650).
OCT. 9.	*d* The Navigation Act passed against the importation of goods, except in English vessels or vessels of the producing country. Salutes claimed from all vessels in the Channel, and right of search in Dutch vessels, even if men-of-war. Followed by war with Holland. 1652.
OCT. 1651.– MAY, 1652.	*e* Measures towards settlement of the country. (1) Proposals for disbanding the army. The dissolution of Parliament fixed for Nov. 3, 1654. (OCT. 1651.) (2) Act of Amnesty passed for State offences previous to battle of Worcester. FEB. 24, 1652.

(3) Measures for the political union of England and Scotland. JAN. and SPRING, **1652**.

(4) Appointment of Committee for reform of legal procedure.

MAY, **1652**. *f* Hostilities with the Dutch. Victory of Blake in the Straits of Dover. MAY **19**. Formal declaration of war. JULY **8**. Victory of Blake in the Downs. SEPT. **28**. Blake driven into the Thames, and the Dutch in possession of the Channel. NOV. **28**. Decisive victories of Blake (FEB. **18-21**) and of the English fleet. JUNE **2-3**, and JULY **31**.

1653.

JUNE **2-3**-JULY **29**. *g* Differences between the Parliament and the army.

AUG. **1652**. (1) Renewed proposals for the disbanding or reduction of the army. Petition of the officers for the election of a new representative. Resolution of the House that present Members retain their seats without re-election. Further resolution (after Blake's victory) that present Members constitute a Committee for revising the returns to the new Parliament. Conference with the officers who pressed for an immediate dissolution and revision of returns by the Council of State.

FEB. **1653**.

APRIL.

APRIL **20**. (2) Attempt of the House to pass its own Bill in the middle of the Conference. Forcible dissolution of the Parliament and of the Council of State by Cromwell.

The Protectorate to the Death of Cromwell. 1653-1658.

1. The Puritan Convention (Barebones Parliament). JULY—DEC. **1653**.

APRIL **30**. *a* Nomination of a provisional Council of State of eight officers and four civilians with Cromwell as President. A convention summoned by them, on the advice of Harrison, JUNE **8** (selected from lists sent up by Congregational churches).

JUNE **8**.

JULY **4**. *b* Meeting of the Convention (156 in number, including 5 for Scotland, 6 for Ireland). Resignation to them of Cromwell and the Council. Formation of eleven committees and inauguration of sweeping reforms, *e.g.* proposed abolition of Chancery (in which there were 23,000 cases pending), of tithes, and lay patronage. Establishment of civil

Dec. 11.	marriage. A vote of resignation of its powers obtained by the sudden action of the minority. Dec. 11.
Dec. 16.	2. The Instrument of Government drawn up by the Council of State nominated by the Convention and adopted by the council of officers.

    (*a*) Establishment of a single chief of the state under the title of Lord Protector.

    (*b*) The power of the Protector limited by

        (1) The administrative check of a council of fifteen—nominated but not removable by the Protector, to be consulted in all foreign matters, to give their consent to peace or war, to approve the nomination of great officers of state, and the disposal of the armed force.

        (2) The political check of Parliament—to meet every year and to be re-elected at least every three years, to impose taxes, make laws (even without the assent of the Protector, who could only delay Acts passed by them twenty days), sanction or annul proclamations issued by the Protector in the recesses, not to be prorogued or dissolved till after an interval of five months.

    (*c*) The constitution of Parliament—the electorate.

        (*a*) Parliament to consist of 400 English, 30 Scotch, and 30 Irish members.

        (*b*) Seats transferred from rotten boroughs to larger constituencies, *e.g.* Leeds, Manchester, Halifax, and counties.

        (*c*) General right of suffrage based upon property to the value of £200, except to Catholics and malignants, *i.e.* all who had borne arms against the Parliament since Jan. **1642**.

        [The drawback to the Instrument being that there was no provision for settling opposition between the Parliament and the administration (*i.e.*, Protector and Council).]

Jan.—Sept. **1654**.	3. The Protector's administration till the meeting of Parliament. Sept. **1654**.
April 5.	(*a*) Conclusion of peace with Holland, the salute to the English flag conceded, and compensation paid. The House of Orange excluded from power.

April 12.	(*b*) Completion of the political union between England and Scotland.
July 10.	(*c*) Treaty concluded with Sweden, mainly by the agency of Bulstrode (April), Denmark, and Portugal. Execution of Vowell and Gerard for a conspiracy to assassinate Cromwell.
April—July.	(*d*) The Highlands reduced to tranquillity by General Monk : the General Assembly suppressed (July), but religious freedom protected.
Sept. 4.	4. The Parliament of **1654**.
	a Discussion of the Instrument, clause by clause, in order to settle the Government upon a Parliamentary basis.
Sept. 12.	*b* Interference of the Protector. An engagement "not to alter the Government as it is settled in a single person and a Parliament" demanded from all members. Refused by only 100 members.
	c Continued Parliamentary discussion of the clauses of the Instrument, and growing irritation of the Protector at seeing the codification of the law, the settlement of Ireland, and foreign affairs deferred, and Royalist intrigues increasing.
Jan. 22. 1655.	*d* Dissolution of Parliament at the end of five lunar months (according to which the army and navy received their pay).
	5. The Protector's sole rule. Jan. **1655**—Sept. **1656**.
1655.	*a* The Government at home.
March.	(1) Establishment of Board of Triers to examine fitness of presentees to livings, and of Church Boards (of gentry and clergy) for each county.
	(2) Reform of Chancery procedure by delegation of its arrears to other courts.
	(3) Taxes levied without consent of Parliament.
March.	(4) Major Wildman's declaration against the tyrant Oliver Cromwell. Attempt to seize the judges at Salisbury (Penruddock's plot), and Royalist risings in Devonshire and the Welsh Marches; followed by a division of the country into twelve military districts; the expense defrayed by a tax of ten per cent. upon the royalists.

OCTOBER.	(5) The press placed under the censorship of the Government; Episcopal ministers forbidden to officiate in public or act as tutors.
NOV.	
	(6) Proposals for admitting Jews into England.
	b The settlement of Ireland. **1652-1659.**
1650.	(1) Capture of Limerick and death of Ireton.
1652.	(2) Final suppression of the rebellion. **1652.** The natives who surrendered sent to forced labour in the West Indies: the Catholics of the Pale allowed to enlist in foreign services.
1654–1659	(3) The settlement by Henry Cromwell.
	(*a*) All proved to have taken part in the massacre sentenced to banishment or death.
	(*b*) Catholic proprietors who had borne arms deprived of their estates and settled in Connaught.
	(*c*) Catholic proprietors of suspected loyalty deprived of a third part of their estates.
	(4) Influx of Protestant settlers from Great Britain.
	(5) Thirty members assigned to Ireland in the General Parliament.
	c Foreign policy.
	(1) Relations with Spain and France.
1652.	(*a*) Negotiations between the Commonwealth and the two rival powers of Spain and France, a fortified port being the price of the alliance. Calais demanded from the Spanish, Dunkirk from the French.
1654.	(*b*) Cromwell's demands of Spain—i. Freedom of trade with Spanish South America; ii. Freedom of English merchants in Spain from the Inquisition, both peremptorily refused.
	(*c*) Discontent caused by the Spanish attacks upon the English settlements in the West Indies.
OCT.	(*d*) An offensive alliance concluded with France.

DEC. 1655.	(e) Despatch of an expedition under Penn and Venables to Barbadoes. Failure of the attack on San Domingo; cap- of Jamaica. [During the same winter an expedition despatched under Blake to the Mediterranean; destruction of the pirate fleet in the harbour of Tunis.]
APRIL.	
MAY.	
SEPT. OCT.	(f) Declaration of war by Spain, and commercial treaty with France, after the liberty of worship had been conceded to the Vaudois by the Duke of Savoy owing to French pressure exerted at Cromwell's request. (AUG.
1656. SEPT. 9.	(g) Capture of a Spanish Plate Fleet by Stayner.
	(2) The Northern League. Failure to form a league of the Northern Protestant Powers—England, Holland, Denmark, Sweden—owing to the disputes between Sweden and Denmark, and the ambitious designs of Charles Gustavus of Sweden upon Poland.

1656.   6. The second Parliament. SEPT. 17, 1656.
SEPT. 17.   *a* The formation of the Parliament.

(1) The Irish and Scottish members not elected but appointed by the Government.

(2) One hundred members excluded by the Council for disaffection or want of religion.

JAN.—FEB. 1657.	*c* Trial and condemnation of Sindercombe for a plot (at the instigation of Colonel Sexby, a leveller, who for some time had been intriguing with the Royalists) against the Protector's life.
	d Withdrawal of the powers of the Major-Generals in deference to the feeling of Parliament.
MARCH.	The humble petition and advice that the Protector assume the title of King and govern with the advice of two Houses of Parliament [partly to render Cromwell's life more secure, partly to give his rule a constitutional title and constitutional limits]. Acceptance of the petition, and the right of taxation thus once more confirmed for the Commons. MAY. The title of King, however, refused by Cromwell, owing to the opposition of the army and its rulers, *e.g.* Lambert, Desborough, Fleetwood.
MAY.	

JUNE 26.	*e*	Inauguration of Cromwell as Lord Protector (with power to nominate his successor and select a second House). [The Parliamentary sanction to the Protectorate.] Adjournment of Parliament.
APRIL 20.	*f*	Capture of the Spanish Plate fleet by Blake in the harbour of Santa Cruz in Teneriffe. Capture of Mardyke by the French and English.
SEPT. 23.		
1658. JAN.	*g*	Meeting of Parliament. Delay in granting supplies for the war: discussion as to the respective powers of the two Houses. Dissolution. FEB. 4.
FEB.		

FEB.—SEPT. 1658.   7. The last triumphs of the Protector. FEB.—SEPT. 1658.

FEB.	*a*	Discovery of the preparations for a Royalist invasion and rising under Ormond, Waller, and possibly Fairfax. Election of Slingsby and Hewitt. JUNE.
JUNE 4-17.	*b*	Battle of the Dunes and capture of Dunkirk.
AUG.—SEPT. 3.	*c*	Illness and death of the Protector. AUG.—SEPT. 3.

C   The Fall of the Protectorate.

SEPT.	1. Richard Cromwell recognized as Protector, in spite of the demand of the army for a military Protector.
OCT.	
NOV.	2. Issue of writs for Parliament upon the unreformed basis (as before 1654), and attacks in Parliament upon the late Protector's administration by Vane, and especially by Ashley Cooper.
1659. FEB.	
APRIL.	3. Petition of the army for payment of arrears, and against designs "against the army and the good old cause." Later petition for the dissolution of Parliament. Dissolution. APRIL 22.
MAY 7.	4. Introduction by the army of the remains of the Long Parliament excepting those excluded 1648. [Lenthall still Speaker.] Resignation of the Protectorate by Richard Cromwell.
AUG.	5. Rising of the Royalists in Cheshire defeated by Lambert.
OCT. 13.	6. Violent expulsion of the Parliament by the Government in the hands of a Committee of Safety.
DEC.	7. Dissatisfaction of the soldiers in Ireland and Scotland with the action of the officers at home. Second Restoration of the Long Parliament by soldiers in England.

1660. JAN. **8.** March of Monk from Scotland. Arrival with
FEB. 3. Lord Fairfax at London. The excluded mem-
FEB. 26. bers of the Long Parliament reinstated. Dis-
MARCH 16. solution of the Parliament by its own act.
APRIL 25. **9.** "The Convention" assembled.
APRIL 14. **10.** The declaration of Breda issued by Prince Charles, promising pardon (except to such as shall be excepted by Parliament) and religious toleration; satisfaction of arrears to Monk's army; settlement of confiscated estates to be left to Parliament.
MAY 25. Landing of Charles at Dover.

CHARLES II. 1660-1685.

Charles II. = Katharine of Braganza.

A **Events of the Reign till the Fall of Lord Clarendon.**
 I. The proceedings of the Convention Parliament (mainly in pursuance of the terms of the King's proclamation at Breda, APRIL). MAY-DEC. **1660.**
  a The Act of Indemnity.
   Seven of the regicides originally excluded from pardon; finally twenty-eight brought to trial, ten executed at once, three in **1662** upon their surrender by the Dutch. Twenty others declared incapable of office. Vane and Lambert, though not connected with the King's trial, excepted from pardon, but with an address from both Houses that their lives should be spared. JUNE-OCT.
  b Claims for reparation as preferred by the crown, the Church and private Royalists.
   i. Restitution of crown lands that had been sold.
   ii. Special legislation to confirm the sale, or to give indemnity to the purchasers, of Church lands, delayed by the skill of Hyde. Consequent reinstatement of dispossessed ecclesiastical bodies and Royalists, by ordinary course of law at the dissolution of the Convention. DEC. **1660.**
   iii. No special legislation to compensate Royalists for losses owing to forced sales of their estates.
  c Settlement of the Revenue.
   i. Settlement of £1,200,000 as annual revenue upon the crown.

> ii. Abolition of military tenure of land, wardships, feudal aids and homages, purveyance and pre-emption. Compensation made to crown by excise upon beer and other liquors, amounting to £100,000 per annum, and by tonnage and poundage (now granted to the King for life).
>
> iii. Payment of arrears, and disbandment of the army, no provision made for the maintenance of a standing army in future.
>
> *d* Proposals for the settlement of Church matters.
>
> > i. Episcopal ministers to be restored to their benefices without the intermediate profits. Ministers against whom there was no living claimant, who had been presented on legal vacancies, to retain their livings.
> >
> > ii. Archbishop Usher's model submitted to the King. A suffragan Bishop to be appointed for each rural deanery. Diocesan synods of suffragan bishops and representatives to be held annually, deciding by plurality of voices, but under the presidency of the Lord Bishop of the diocese.
> >
> > iii. The existing Liturgy to be adopted with the omission or modification of certain "superstitious practices."

OCT. 25.   ii. and iii. accepted by the terms of a royal proclamation. OCT. 25. A bill however for carrying out the royal proclamation defeated. Bishops restored to their sees. NOV.

DEC. 29.   *e* Dissolution of the Convention Parliament. DEC. 29.

> II. Interval between the Dissolution of the Convention Parliament and the meeting of the Long Parliament of the Restoration.

1661. *a* Anabaptist conspiracy under Thomas Venner. Retention of Monk's regiment, the Coldstream,
JAN.   and a regiment of horse, as a protection to the Government. Another regiment formed out of troops brought from Dunkirk. JAN. 1661.

JAN.   *b* Cromwell, Ireton, and Bradshaw disinterred and hung in gibbets at Tyburn, JAN. 30 (in accordance with order of Convention Parliament). The bodies of Pym and Blake removed from Westminster Abbey to S. Margaret's Churchyard.

APRIL–JULY. *c* Conferences at the Savoy between the Episcopalian and Presbyterian clergy.

III. The Cavalier Parliament till the fall of Clarendon. MAY, **1661**.

1661. *a* The Act of Indemnity and Acts of the Long Parliament condemning the Star Chamber and High Commission confirmed, the Covenant declared illegal, and burned by the hangman. The militia vested solely in the crown.

b The *Corporation Act*. All municipal officers to receive the Communion after the Anglican use, to renounce the Covenant, to take an oath of non-resistance. **1661**.

1662. *c* A special act directed against Quakers. Renewal of the *Act of Uniformity* (passed in **1559**). The use of the Prayer Book alone enforced in public worship; unfeigned assent and consent to all contained in it demanded from clergy; all schoolmasters and tutors to take the oath of Non-resistance and to renounce the Covenant; all but episcopal orders legally disallowed. MAY **19**.

AUG. *d* Consequent resignation of upwards of 2,000 rectors and vicars. AUG. **24** (S. Bartholomew's Day).

MAY. *e* Marriage of Charles to Katharine of Braganza. Half a million in money, Tangier, Bombay, and a pledge of toleration to English seamen included in the marriage dowry. MAY **20**.

JUNE. *f* Trial of Vane and Lambert. Execution of Vane in spite of the royal pledge to spare his life. JUNE **14**. Lambert imprisoned in Guernsey, afterwards in Plymouth Sound.

NOV. *g* Sale of Dunkirk and Mardyke to France for five millions. NOV.–DEC.

DEC. *h* The first declaration of Indulgence by the King, by the exercise of his Dispensing Power which was based not only on his Royal Prerogative, but also on his spiritual supremacy as transferred at the Reformation from the Papacy. DEC. **1662**.

FEB. **1663.** *i* Resistance by the Commons to the declaration of Indulgence. Withdrawal of the declaration.

j Guineas first coined in England. Difficulties with the Dutch as to the monopoly of the importation of gold dust from the West African coast (in consequence of the formation of the West African Trading Company, **1662**), and money

1664. voted for protection against Holland.

ANALYSIS OF ENGLISH HISTORY. 203

  k Other causes of dispute with Holland.
    i. Commercial jealousy, especially with regard to the Fisheries and Wool.
    ii. The vexation of the King at the exclusion of the House of Orange from power in Holland.
    iii. Quarrel with the Dutch East India Company as to the possession of the island of Polaroon.
    iv. Quarrel with the Dutch West India Company owing to their settlements near New England.
  l *The Conventicle Act*, forbidding meetings of more than five persons beyond those of the household for any act of religious worship beyond those laid down in the Prayer Book, under penalties of fine, imprisonment and transportation upon third offence. **1664**. The Act extended to all over sixteen years of age.

1665.
FEB. 22. *m* War declared against the Dutch. English victory in Solebay off Lowestoft. JUNE **3**. The supplies voted expressly appropriated by the Commons to the purposes of the war.

    n The plague of London carrying off 100,000 in the course of the year (at its height in September when 10,000 died weekly).

SEPT-OCT. *o* *The Five Mile Act*, forbidding any of the clergy driven to resignation by the Act of Uniformity who refused the oath of non-resistance to come within five miles of any borough town, or any place where they had formerly ministered. SEPT-OCT. **1665**.

1666. *p* Support given by Lewis XIV. to the Dutch in consequence of the defeat of 1665, and the fear of English naval supremacy. Doubtful
JUNE. battle in the Downs. JUNE **1-4**. Commissioners appointed by the Commons to inspect
JULY. the public accounts. English victory. JULY **25**.
SEPT. *q* Fire of London destroying the city from the Tower to the Temple. SEPT. **2-6**.

1667. *r* Supineness of the English in prosecuting the war. Opening of negotiations for peace at Breda.
JUNE. MAY. Appearance of the Dutch in the Medway. JUNE 9. The Dutch masters of the Channel. JUNE-JULY **21**.

JULY. *s* Peace concluded: Holland gaining the island of Polaroon on the Bombay coast, England New Amsterdam (New York) on the Hudson. JULY **21**.

t Dismissal of Hyde (created Earl of Clarendon **1661**) from the Chancellorship. AUG. Impeachment. NOV. **12**. Chief Articles.
  i. Illegal imprisonments.
  ii. Raising contributions for a standing army and advising the King to dissolve Parliament.
  iii. Sale of Dunkirk for insufficient value, and to his own private gain.
  iv. Request of money from France.

u Flight of Clarendon to France, in pursuance of the King's advice, and consequent banishment by Parliament. NOV. **29**.

v Commission of Accounts established by law.

IV. The "Cabal" Ministry. The "Cabal" in reality only a commission for foreign affairs. **1667**-JAN. **1674**.

  a Members of the Cabal: Clifford, Lord Treasurer; Lord Ashley (Ashley Cooper) Chancellor of Exchequer; Duke of Buckingham, at first without office; Earl of Arlington (Henry Bennet), Secretary of State; Earl of Lauderdale, at the head of Scotch affairs.

  Clifford a zealous Catholic, Arlington a moderate Catholic, Ashley and to a certain extent Lauderdale Presbyterian in sympathies, and Buckingham (son-in law of Fairfax), a patron of the Independents.

1668. *b* Scheme for a union of Protestants, based upon comprehension for Presbyterians and toleration for others, submitted to Parliament, but rejected.

1667. *c* Alarm excited by the attack of Lewis XIV. upon the Spanish Netherlands JULY-SEPT. **1667** (in consequence of a secret understanding with the Emperor Leopold as to the final division of the Spanish possessions in case the King of Spain died without an heir). Negotiation of the Triple Alliance, by the diplomacy of Sir W. Temple,
1668. between England, Holland, and Sweden. JAN.-APRIL, **1668**. Peace of Aix-la-Chapelle, arresting the progress of French conquests, and causing the surrender of Franche-Comté to Spain.

1669. *d* Conversion of James, Duke of York, to Roman Catholicism. JAN. Commencement of private negotiations between the King and Lewis XIV. (with the knowledge of Clifford and Arlington alone of the ministers). JAN. **1669**–JUNE **1670**.

1670.
MAY.
e The secret Treaty of Dover between the King and Lewis XIV. (negotiated by Henrietta, Duchess of Orleans, Charles's sister).

  i. England and France to declare war against Holland. England to receive Zeeland, and the Prince of Orange's interest to be regarded.

  ii. Charles to support Lewis XIV. in his wife's claim on the Spanish succession. Charles to receive Minorca, Ostend, and a free hand in Spanish South America.

  iii. Lewis XIV. to pay Charles II. an annual subsidy of £300,000.

These clauses were signed by all the Ministers.

  iv. Charles II. to re-establish Catholicism in England and to declare himself a Catholic, receiving from Lewis XIV. an extra annual subsidy of £200,000.

This was known only to Clifford and Arlington.

1671. *f* The consent of the ministers to the attack upon Holland (the clause as to religion being kept secret) secured by the promise of toleration to the nonconforming Protestants. Negotiations with France conducted by Buckingham, now chief minister. **1671**.

 g Adjournment of Parliament. APRIL, **1671**.

1672.
JAN.
h The exchequer closed, and payment of principal suspended for a year. JAN.

 i Second declaration of Indulgence *suspending the whole code* of penal statutes by virtue of the King's ecclesiastical powers. Places to be appointed for the public worship of the Protestant Dissenters; Catholics to be restricted to private
MARCH. worship. MARCH **15**.

MARCH.
AUG.
 j Invasion of Holland by Lewis XIV. and declaration of war by England upon Holland (MARCH **18**). Murder of de Witt; election of William, Prince of Orange, as Stadtholder. AUG. **1672**.

1673. *k* Meeting of Parliament. FEB. Resistance to, and final withdrawal of, the Declaration of Indulgence. First appearance of an organized opposition, *the Country Party*, under Lord Russell, Lord Cavendish, and Sir W. Coventry, to guard against political and religious usurpations of the crown. Passing of *the Test Act*, enforcing

MARCH. the oaths of Allegiance and Supremacy, the declaration against Transubstantiation, and the receiving of the Sacrament according to the rites of the Church of England upon all holding civil or military offices. Prorogation of Parliament. Resignation of the Duke of York (Lord High Admiral), Lord Clifford (Lord Treasurer), and many officers and civil servants.

FEB.—NOV.
l Indignation of Ashley, now Earl of Shaftesbury (Lord Chancellor, **1672**), although still retaining office, at the King's duplicity, and opposition to the King's French policy, and to the marriage of James with Mary of Modena. FEB.-NOV.

MAY—JUNE.
AUG.
m Engagement of the English fleet, under Prince Rupert, with the Dutch. MAY **28**-JUNE **4**. Practical defeat of the English, and failure of the scheme for a landing in Holland. AUG. **11**.

OCT.
NOV.
n Meeting and prorogation of Parliament, after nine days' debate, and dismissal of Shaftesbury from office.

1674. *o* Shaftesbury leader of the Parliamentary opposition. The King called on by the Commons to dismiss Arlington, Buckingham, and Lauderdale; and to disband troops raised since 1664. A bill for Protestant securities (excluding from the succession any prince married to a Roman Catholic) introduced into Parliament but rejected. Apparent submission of the King to the wishes of Parliament. Buckingham and Arlington dismissed from office. Peace made with the Dutch. FEB. Thomas Osborne (Earl of Danby), a loyal Englishman and constitu-

FEB. tional High Churchman, made chief minister. FEB. **1674.**

V. Danby's Ministry. FEB., **1674**—DEC., **1678.**

1674.
a Confirmation of Princess Mary, daughter of the Duke of York, and commencement of negotiations for her marriage to William of Orange, her cousin.

1675. *b* Danby's proposal to impose the oath of non-resistance, and an oath against the introduction of any changes in Church or State, upon both Houses of Parliament. (An attempt to divide the opposition, and to exclude Presbyterian members from Parliament.) The Bill passed by the Lords and sent down to the Commons. Conflict between the Houses upon the appeal of Shirley from the Court of Chancery to the House of Lords against Sir J. Fagg, a member of the Commons.

Nov.
c Prorogation of Parliament. NOV. 22—FEB. 15. **1677.** Claim made in consequence by Charles on Lewis XIV. for payment of promised annual subsidy of 500,000 louis d'or.

Dec.
d Proclamation for closing the coffee-houses in London to stop the spreading of "false, malicious, and scandalous reports." DEC. **29.** Withdrawn in consequence of popular indignation.

1676. *e* Alarm of Charles at French successes abroad, and fear of a separate French treaty with Holland. A secret treaty concluded between the King and Lewis XIV. (in spite of Danby's opposition) pledging England and France to enter into no separate engagements with other Powers.

1677.
Feb.
f Meeting of Parliament, FEB. **15.** Remonstrance of Shaftesbury and others that the long prorogation had dissolved Parliament. Shaftesbury, Buckingham, Salisbury, and Wharton thereupon committed to the Tower for contempt of the House, and imprisoned till FEB., **1678.**

g A Bill for the security of the Church in event of the succession of a King not of the Established Church, introduced by Danby, providing that the children of such King should be under the guardianship of the Archbishop of Canterbury, and that the bishops should be appointed by the body of prelates; but rejected by the Commons. (Possibly considered by the Country Party as inadequate.)

Sept.
h Alarm felt by the Commons at the French successes in the Spanish Netherlands. Apparent submission of the King to the wishes of Parliament. Marriage of William, Prince of Orange, to Princess Mary, SEPT. Withdrawal of the English Ambassador from Paris. **1677.**

1678 *i* Forces raised to the number of 20,000 men, and supply of 1,000,000*l.* voted by Parliament for war against France.

j Secret negotiations between Lewis XIV. and the Country Party to bring about the dissolution of Parliament and the fall of Danby with his Anglican and anti-French policy, and at the same time between Charles and Lewis. Secret treaty between Charles and Lewis (Danby, by the King's order, signing a despatch demanding the payment of six million crowns as the price) MAY. concluded, MAY. Withdrawal of England from opposition to France, and consequent acceptance by Spain and Holland of the Treaty of JULY—SEPT. Nimeguen transferring to France the control of the Spanish Netherlands and Franche Comté.

k The first deposition of Titus Oates as to the existence of a Popish Plot for the subversion of Protestantism, a massacre with the aid of French troops, and the murder of the King. AUG. AUG. **13.** His credibility confirmed by the previous seizure of the letters of Coleman, secretary to the Duchess of York, and by the murder of Sir Edmondbury Godfrey, before OCT. whom the deposition had been made. OCT. **15.**

l Resolution of the Commons that there hath been, and still is a damnable and hellish plot, carried on by the Popish recusants. OCT. **21.**

m Roman Catholics excluded from a seat in either *House* (the Duke of York being however, in spite of Shaftesbury, specially excepted). NOV. NOV.—DEC. **30.** Condemnation and execution of Coleman. DEC.

n Impeachment of Danby upon the information of Montagu, formerly English Ambassador at Paris, as to the signature by Danby of the request for a French pension (as the price of English good offices at the Treaty of Nimeguen), stopped JAN. **1679.** by the dissolution of Parliament. JAN., **1679.**

1679 VI. The progress of the Protestant reaction. JAN., **1679.**

a Progress of the elections distinctly Protestant, in spite of large bribery by the Court. Ten thousand of the troops disbanded. Fresh revelations as to the so-called Popish Plot made by Bedloe. FEB. Departure of the Duke of York for Brussels (MARCH).

b Resumption of the impeachment of Danby in spite of the dissolution of the previous Parliament. Two pleas urged in defence overruled

(i) That the despatch had been signed by order of the King with respect to matters of peace and war which belonged solely to the prerogative.

(ii) That the King's pardon had been obtained. The trial did not proceed, but Danby was committed by order of the House of Lords to the Tower, where he was detained five years. APRIL.

APRIL.

c Formation of a new body of ministers, Shaftesbury being President of the Council, Sir W. Temple Secretary of State.

d Temple's plan for the abolition of the secret Cabala or Cabinet of selected members of the Royal Council, and for the restoration of the whole body to its original office of giving advice to the King. The Council to consist of thirty members, and to represent in a way the different influential bodies of the nation; the bishops "to take care of the Church"; the Lord Chancellor and Chief Justice "to inform the King well of what concerns the laws": it was to include fifteen non-official, influential members of Parliament: it was to derive weight from its collective property, which amounted to £300,000 a year.

e The statute for the regulation of printing, which expired with the dissolution of the last Parliament, not revived. The *Habeas Corpus Act* passed. [First introduced after the fall of Clarendon, **1668**.]

i. Any prisoner committed for a charge, not treason or felony, declared entitled to his writ, even in the vacation of the Courts.

ii. Any prisoner committed for treason or felony to be released on bail, unless indicted at the next gaol delivery, and to be discharged, unless indicted at the sessions which followed.

iii. A gaoler not obeying the writ subject to a penalty of £100 for the first offence, and £200 and banishment for the second offence. A judge denying the writ subject to a penalty of £500.

	iv. No inhabitant or resident of the kingdom of England, dominion of Wales, or town of Berwick-upon-Tweed, to be sent prisoner into Scotland, Ireland, Jersey, Guernsey, Tangier, or into parts, garrisons, islands, or places beyond the seas.
MAY.	*f* The King's proposal for the security of Protestant interests (vesting all civil and military appointments in the hands of Parliament, providing for the filling of ecclesiastical benefices, and excluding Papists from places of trust during the reign of a Roman Catholic prince) rejected as inadequate, and a Bill for the Exclusion of James from the imperial crown of England read a second time by the Commons. Prorogation of Parliament, followed by dissolution. MAY 27.
JUNE.	*g* Defeat of the Covenanters at Bothwell Bridge by Monmouth. JUNE 22. Illness of the King, and recall of the Duke of York; departure of the Duke to Scotland. Continued prosecutions and condemnations in connection with the Popish Plot. The claim of the Duke of Monmouth to the Throne advocated by Shaftesbury. Second dismissal of Shaftesbury from office.
OCT.	OCT. Dismissal of Monmouth from his offices.
DEC.	DEC.
	h The King's determination to postpone the meeting of the New Parliament. Beginning of a reaction in the King's favour; the country divided between the "Petitioners" for the meeting of Parliament, and the "Abhorrers" of the constraint put upon the Crown.
1680.	*i* Attempt of William of Orange to establish an understanding with Charles for joint action abroad, in conjunction with Brandenburg, Denmark, Sweden, and later possibly Spain and Austria, against the predominating influence of France, and for the adoption of a Bill for Protestant securities at home (so as not to exclude the Duke of York or his daughter Mary). Meeting of Parliament.
OCT.	OCT. The Exclusion Bill rejected by the Peers, mainly through the agency of Lord Halifax (George Savile) acting in the interests of William of Orange and Mary.
NOV.	NOV. The Bill for Protestant securities proposed by Halifax (denying the right of veto to a Catholic King and vesting

all patronage in a permanent continuous council of forty-one) rejected by the Commons as inadequate. Trial and condemnation of Thomas Howard, Lord Stafford, by the House of Lords for complicity in the Plot, though not one of the actions of which he was accused was affirmed by more than one witness. DEC.

1681. *j* Refusal by the Commons of supplies till the Exclusion Bill should be passed. Dissolution of Parliament. Secret negotiations carried on with France by the agency of Thomas Hyde, and a renewal of a French subsidy obtained. JAN. A progress through England by the Duke of Monmouth. A new Parliament opened at Oxford. MARCH **21.** Dissolved upon the re-introduction of the Exclusion Bill and the rejection by the Commons of a New Limitation Bill vesting the regency in the next heir. MARCH **28.** Royal Proclamation and appeal to the loyalty of the nation. APRIL **8.** Seizure of Strassburg (OCT.) and siege of Luxemburg by Lewis XIV. NOV.

MARCH.

APRIL.

NOV.

VII. The Royal triumph and tyranny till the death of the King. **1681-1685.**

a Plunket, titular Archbishop of Armagh, tried in England, and condemned, insufficient time being allowed to summon exculpatory witness from Ireland. JULY **1.**

JULY.

b Trial and condemnation of College (a Protestant joiner) at Oxford, for inciting to arms against the King. AUG. Prosecution of Shaftesbury for high treason; the bill rejected by the Grand Jury of London. NOV., **1681.**

AUG.

NOV.

1682. *c* Second progress of the Duke of Monmouth through England; Monmouth arrested at Stafford. SEPT. Friends of the Court nominated as Sheriffs for the City of London. Flight of Shaftesbury from London. NOV. Death of Shaftesbury in Holland. JAN. **1683.**

1683.

d The Charter of the City of London declared forfeited

(i) For imposition of tolls upon goods brought into the city markets by their own ordinances or bye-laws.

(ii) For the petition to the King in favour of the meeting of Parliament (DEC., **1679**) and its publication through the country. JUNE.

June.	*e* Discovery of the Rye-House Plot for the assassination of the King and the Duke of York. Trial and condemnation of William, Lord Russell, June 13 (though no overt act of treason was proved against him either by Lord Howard, who had turned King's evidence, or Rumsey). Suicide of Lord Essex in the Tower. June 13. Execution of Lord Russell. July 21.
July.	The doctrine of passive obedience formally asserted by the University of Oxford, with a public condemnation of the doctrines

(i) That all civil authority is derived originally from the people.

(ii) That there is a compact, tacit or express, between the King and his subjects. July 21. Condemnation of Algernon Sidney (upon the evidence of Lord Howard as to treasonable dealing with the Scots, supported by the production of a revolutionary paper in the handwriting of the accused). Nov. 21. Execution of Sidney. Dec. 7, **1683**.

Nov.
Dec.

1684. *f* Flight of the Duke of Monmouth, after pardon, to Holland. Increase of the Royal army by the withdrawal of the garrison from Tangier, which had been dismantled (Dec., **1683**), owing to constant troubles with the Moors.

g Informations preferred against corporations, and consequent re-modelling of charters upon a more oligarchical basis.

h Refusal of the King to summon another Parliament. James re-appointed Lord High Admiral, and re-admitted to the Council in violation of the Test Act.

1685. VIII. The King's reconciliation to the Roman Church, and his death. Feb. 6, **1685**.

James II. 1685-1688.

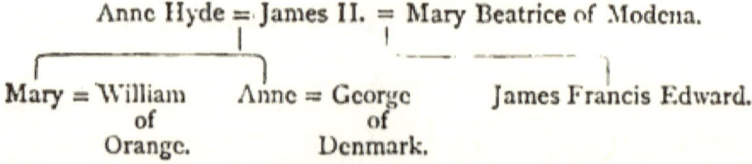

A History of the reign till the dismissal of Halifax, and the Prorogation of the Parliament. (An attempt to rule in co-operation with a Tory Parliament.)

FEB.—MAY.
1. The King's pledge to "preserve this Government both in Church and State as it is now by law established." The customs duties, however, were collected and expended by Royal Proclamation without the sanction of an Act of Parliament.

MAY.
2. Sentence of fine, degradation, whipping, and imprisonment for life, passed upon Titus Oates.

3. Meeting of Parliament (the members for the boroughs largely returned by the re-modelled Corporations). Tonnage and Poundage and other duties on sugar and tobacco to the annual amount of nearly two millions, settled upon the King for life. MAY 19.

4. The rebellions.

MAY—JUNE.
(i) Expedition of Argyll from Holland to Scotland. Failure of the rising mainly owing to the want of harmony among the leaders —Argyll, Patrick Hume, John Cochrane. MAY 2—JUNE. Execution of Argyll upon the former sentence for "leasing making" passed on him in 1682. JUNE 30.

JUNE—JULY.
(ii) Landing of the Duke of Monmouth at Lyme. JUNE 11. Monmouth's proclamation demanding (*a*) Effective Parliamentary Government; (*b*) Freedom of Worship for Protestant Nonconformists, and accusing James of having caused the Fire of London, the murder of Godfrey, and the death of Charles II. Arrival of Monmouth at Taunton, and assumption of the title of king. JUNE 20. Futile attempt to seize Bristol. JUNE 24. The overthrow of Monmouth at Sedgemoor. JULY 6. His capture, JULY 8; and execution, JULY 15.

AUG.—SEPT.
5. The Bloody Assize in Dorsetshire and Somersetshire under Judge Jeffreys. Three hundred and fifty rebels (including women) executed, more than eight hundred sold into slavery for ten years, to the West Indian plantations, besides those whipped and imprisoned. AUG. 24.—SEPT. Jeffreys upon his return made Lord Chancellor, on the death of Lord Guildford. SEPT. 28.

     6. Revocation of the Edict of Nantes by Lewis XIV. OCT. **12.** Flight of the Huguenots from France.

OCT. 7. Dismissal of Lord Halifax from office upon his refusal to co-operate with the King for the repeal of the Test Act. OCT. **21.**

     8. Meeting of Parliament. NOV. **9.** The King's speech reflecting on the inefficiency of the national militia, stating the necessity of a standing military force, and announcing the appointment of certain officers not qualified by the Test Act. Vote of the House that the Militia be made more efficient, coupled, however, with
NOV.   a supply of £700,000 for the temporary support of a standing force. Address of the Commons protesting against the Royal Claim to grant commissions to Roman Catholics, in violation of the Test Act, and to dispense from disabilities which could only be removed by Parliamentary resolution. Opposition of the House of Lords to the dispensing power, and proposed Conference between them and the Judges. Prorogation of Parliament. NOV. **20.**

B From the Prorogation to the dismissal of Rochester and Clarendon (sons of the late Lord Clarendon).

     An attempt to govern by means of the Judges, the High Commission and the Army. NOV. **1685**—APRIL **1687.**

1686. 1. Alteration made by the King in the body of Judges by promotions from the sergeants-at-law.
APRIL. Collusive action brought against Sir Edward Hales, a Roman Catholic officer, for accepting a commission in violation of the Test Act. Decision of the Judges with one dissentient that it was *an inseparable prerogative of the Crown to dispense with penal laws in particular cases, for reasons of which it was the sole*
JUNE. *judge.* JUNE **21.**

     2. Establishment of a court of Ecclesiastical Commission for the exercise of the Royal supremacy over the Church, in violation of an Act of Parliament (**1640** and **1661**). JULY **14.** The Commission consisted of Jeffreys, Sunderland, Rochester, Crewe Bishop of Durham, Sprat Bishop of Rochester, and Chief Justice Herbert. Archbishop Sancroft declined a seat. Compton,

AUG.—SEPT.   Bishop of London, suspended (though the Commission was not unanimous) for not interfering with Dr. Sharp, Rector of S. Giles', who had preached on the claim of the Church of England to be a branch of the Catholic Church. AUG.—SEPT.

JULY.   3. Formation of an armed camp of 13,000 men at Hounslow Heath. JULY.

AUG.

DEC.

4. Dispensation granted to Obadiah Walker, the Roman Catholic Master of University College, Oxford. Appointment of Massey, a Roman Catholic, to the Deanery of Christ Church, Oxford. DEC. 29. 1686.

1687.

JAN.

5. Dismissal of Rochester (Lord High Treasurer), upon his refusal to adopt the Roman Catholic Creed. JAN. 7. Appointment of Lord Bellasyse as first Commissioner of the Treasury, and of Lord Arundel as Privy Seal. (Both Catholics.) Admission of Father Petre to the Privy Council. Dismissal of Lord Clarendon from the Government of Ireland. JAN.—FEB. 1687. Clarendon succeeded by Richard Talbot, Earl of Tyrconnell, a Catholic.

C From the fall of the Hydes to the acquittal of the Bishops. JAN. 1687—JUNE 1688.

An attempt to govern by means of an alliance with the Nonconformists: William Penn being their chief agent.

1687.

APRIL.

1. Publication of a declaration of indulgence, suspending the operation of the penal laws against Nonconformists and Roman Catholics alike, and absolving them from all Tests as qualifications for office (not by letters patent, but in mass). APRIL.

2. Mission of Dykvelt from William of Orange, to ascertain the real feeling of parties in England. SPRING, 1687.

JULY.

3. Dissolution of the 1685 Parliament. Attempt to regulate the Corporations so as to call a Parliament which would repeal the Test Act. JULY. The scheme found impossible, owing to the refusal of the Lords-Lieutenant to co-operate with the King, and consequently abandoned. Dismissal of large numbers of the Lords-Lieutenant.

4. Continued attack upon the Universities.
  a. Deprival of Pechell, Vice-Chancellor of Cambridge, for refusing to confer a degree upon a Benedictine monk. MAY.
  b. Recommendation of an unqualified candidate, Farmer, as President of Magdalen College, Oxford. Upon the election of Dr. Hough by the fellows, forcible installation of Parker, Bishop of Oxford, as President, and upon his death, appointment of Bonaventura Gifford, a Roman Catholic Bishop. Expulsion of the fellows and admission of Roman Catholics to the vacant fellowships. APRIL–DEC. **1687**.

1688. 5. Renewal of the Declaration of Indulgence, APRIL; to be read in churches; MAY **20** and **27** in London; JUNE **4** and **11** in the rest of England. An Appeal to the Nation to support the King in his determination to establish universal liberty of Conscience. Petition of the Archbishop of Canterbury (Sancroft), and six suffragans (Lloyd of St. Asaph, Ken of Bath and Wells, Trelawney of Bristol, Turner of Ely, Lake of Chichester, White of Peterborough), against the order for reading the declaration. MAY **18**. Committal of the Bishops to the Tower. JUNE **8**. Trial for libel by the Court of King's Bench, and acquittal. JUNE **29–30**.

6. Birth of James Francis Edward, Prince of Wales. Secrecy observed as to his birth, hence for a time rumours of his illegitimacy. JUNE **10**.

7. Fresh troops summoned to England from Tyrconnell's Catholic Army.

D The fall of the King. JUNE **30**—DEC. **11**. **1688**.

JUNE.

AUG.

1. Invitation to William, Prince of Orange, to appear in arms for the restoration of English liberty, and the protection of the Protestant religion, signed by the Earl of Danby, the Earl of Devonshire, Bishop Compton, the Earl of Shrewsbury, Lord Lumley, Edward Russell (cousin of William Lord Russell), and Henry Sidney (brother of Algernon Sidney). The invitation carried by Admiral Herbert. JUNE **30**. Promise of support even from Sunderland, James's newly converted Roman Catholic Minister, and Churchill the second in command of the Army.

ANALYSIS OF ENGLISH HISTORY. 217

SEPT.
2. Warning sent to the States, by Lewis XIV., that an attempt upon England involved war with France. Repudiation by the King of interference from Lewis, and encouragement given to the Papal refusal to support Lewis's candidate, Furstenburg, Bishop of Strassburg, for the vacant Archbishopric of Cologne. March of the French troops for the Rhine, followed immediately by William's declaration to the people of England demanding a free Parliament, toleration to Protestant Nonconformists, and freedom of conscience to Roman Catholics, and leaving to Parliament the settlement of the succession, and the inquiry into the legitimacy of the Prince of Wales. SEPT. **27.**

SEPT.-OCT.
3. Attempt of James to renew his old union with the Episcopal Tory party by undoing his illegal acts. SEPT.-OCT. Removal of Sunderland, on suspicion of duplicity, from office.

OCT.

NOV.
4. Departure of William from Holland, OCT. **19.** Return to Holland through stress of weather, OCT. **21.** Second departure and landing at Torbay, NOV. **5.** Appearance of Earls Danby and Devonshire, the Duke of Norfolk, Lord Lumley and others in arms for William. Desertion of Lord Churchill from James at Salisbury, NOV. **22,** and of Princess Anne to join Danby at Nottingham, NOV. **24.**

DEC.
5. Halifax, Nottingham, and Godolphin appointed by the King as Commissioners to treat with William, NOV. **30,** and writs prepared for a new Parliament. Refusal of Lord Dartmouth, in command of the Fleet at Portsmouth, to convey the Prince of Wales across the Channel. Escape of the Queen and Prince of Wales to France, DEC. **10.** Attempted escape of the King in disguise and arrest on the sea coast, DEC. **11-12.** Riots in London; arrest of Jeffreys in disguise. Return of James to London, DEC. **17,** and arrival of William there, DEC. **19.** Final escape of James, DEC. **23.**

E The **Interregnum and Settlement of the Government,** DEC. **11** or **23**-FEB. **13, 1689.**

1. A Convention summoned consisting of the House of Peers, all who had sat in the House of Commons during the reign of Charles II., the Aldermen and Common Councillors of London:

by their advice a new Convention summoned of the House of Peers and elected representatives from the counties and boroughs. DEC.

1689. 2. Meeting of the New Convention. JAN. **22. 1689.**

   a Different plans for the settlement of the Government.

      i. To invite James back, due precautions being taken for the security of liberty and Protestantism. Crushed by the despotic character of James's manifesto, JAN. 4, and not proposed to the Convention.

      ii. Plan for a Regency advocated by Archbishop Sancroft. Defeated by William's refusal to accept a Regency.

      iii.. To proclaim Princess Mary as having become Queen upon James's flight, advocated by the Earl of Danby and Bishop Compton. Defeated by the joint refusal of William and Mary to accept the proposal.

      iv. To declare the throne vacant and proceed to election advocated by the bulk of the Whigs.

   b Proceedings of the Convention.

      i. Vote of the Commons that King James " having endeavoured to subvert the constitution of this Kingdom by breaking the original contract between King and People, and by the advice of Jesuits and other wicked persons having violated the fundamental laws, and having withdrawn himself out of the Kingdom has abdicated the government, and that the throne is thereby vacant."

      ii. Long discussions in the Lords; *deserted* substituted for *abdicated;* the vacancy of the throne denied upon division.

      iii. Letter from Princess Mary to Danby, and declaration of William declining the plans, (*a*) of a Regency, (*b*) of Mary's sole reign.

      iv. Final acquiescence of the Lords (after a conference with the Commons) in the original vote of the Commons.

ANALYSIS OF ENGLISH HISTORY. 219

  v. The Declaration of Right ; denying the right of the Sovereign without the consent of Parliament (i.) to levy taxes, (ii.) to exert suspending or dispensing power, (iii.) to levy troops or keep up standing army in time of peace ; (iv.) to issue Commissions for the creation of Courts for Ecclesiastical causes, and claiming the right of the subject (i.) to elect freely to Parliament, (ii.) to petition the Sovereign, (iii.) to have fair justice, (iv.) to have freedom of debate in Parliament. Acceptance of the declaration and proclamation of William and Mary as King and Queen. FEB. **13, 1689.**

WILLIAM III. and MARY. FEB. **13, 1689**-DEC. **28, 1694.**
William III.—DEC. **28, 1694**-APRIL **12, 1702.**
A Events of the Reign till the Capitulation of Limerick and the end of political danger from Ireland. OCT. **1691.**

  1. The victorious progress of Lewis XIV. in the Palatinate and across the Rhine checked by the news of events in England. Retreat of the French army which had penetrated to Würtemberg, and devastation of the Palatinate, though Bonn and Mainz were rescued from the French.

FEB.-MAY.
  2. Success of William in forming a grand alliance of England, Holland, Spain (in defence of the Spanish Netherlands), Austria (in hopes of establishing its claim to the Spanish succession). FEB.-MAY, **1689.** Victor Amadeus II., Duke of Savoy, to free himself from his dependence on France. OCT. **1690.**

  3. The Revolution in Scotland.
   a Disorders in Scotland, "rabbling of the ministers" and such-like during the winter of **1688-1689.**
   b Summoning of a Scotch Convention. James declared to have forfeited the Crown by
MARCH.   misgovernment.
   c Presentation of the Claim of Right, based upon
APRIL   the English Declaration of Right, with a demand for the abolition of Prelacy.
   d Arrival of Scotch regiments which had come with William from Holland. Revolt of the Episcopalians in the Lowlands and the

JULY.	Highlanders in favour of a Stuart King and against the restoration of the House of Argyll to power, and defeat of the Royal forces at Killiecrankie (counterbalanced however by the death of James Graham of Claverhouse, Viscount Dundee), JULY **27, 1689**. The movement among the Highlanders suppressed by the summer of **1690**, when Fort William was built.
	4. The revolt of Ireland.
1689. MARCH.	*a* Intrigues of Tyrconnell with William till assured of French support. Landing of James at Kinsale, MARCH **12**. Arrival at Dublin, MARCH **14, 1689**.
APRIL–JULY.	*b* The siege of Londonderry by James's army, APRIL **20**–JULY **30**.
	c Meeting of a Parliament at Dublin, MAY **20**. Repeal of the Act of Settlement of Land (**1663**) and attainder (with confiscation of goods) of two thousand five hundred Protestants. MAY.
	d Raising of the siege of Londonderry, JULY **30**, and defeat of James's forces at Newtown Butler. AUG. **2**.
AUG.	*e* Despatch of Marshal Schomberg to Ireland, and landing at Carrickfergus. Formation of an entrenched camp for the winter at Dundalk. Pestilence in Schomberg's army.
	5. Events in England and proceedings of the English Convention, declared a Parliament from the date of the proclamation of William and Mary as King and Queen.
MARCH.	*a* Refusal of the oath of allegiance to William and Mary by Archbishop Sancroft and seven of his suffragans. Commencement of the schism of the nonjurors.
	b William's chief advisers chosen from both Parties; Lord Danby, Lord President; Earl of Shrewsbury and Earl of Nottingham (Finch) Secretaries of State; Lord Halifax, Privy Seal; Charles Mordaunt, First Commissioner of the Treasury.
MARCH.	*c* Passing of the Mutiny Act granting disciplinary powers over the army for six months, in consequence of a mutiny in one of William's Scottish regiments at Ipswich.

d Dispatch of Lord Churchill with English regiments to the Sambre in Flanders, APRIL; and declaration of war against France, in consequence of the French support given to James in Ireland. MAY 13.

e Nottingham's Bill for the Comprehension of Protestant Dissenters referred by the House of Lords to Convocation and finally dropped.

The Toleration Act passed.

MAY 24.
1. Freedom of worship to such as should take the oath of allegiance and subscribe the declaration against Popery.
2. Ministers of separate congregations to sign the Articles of the Church of England (with certain exceptions).
3. Quakers to be allowed on certain occasions to substitute an affirmation for an oath.
4. No part of this toleration extended to Papists, or disbelievers in the Trinity. MAY 24, 1689.

f The Bill of Rights confirming the Declaration of Right, with the additions of :
i. The limitation of the Crown according to the votes of both Houses.
ii. The exclusion from the Crown of all who shall hold-communion with the Church of Rome or shall marry a Papist, it having been found by experience that it is inconsistent with the safety and welfare of this Protestant kingdom to be governed by a Popish Prince. OCT. 25.

1690.
g Objections raised in the Commons to the Bill of Indemnity. Penal clauses against all who had been concerned in or had acquiesced in the forfeiture of Charters introduced into the Bill for Restoring the Corporations, but thrown
JAN. out by the Tories. Prorogation of the Parliament, JAN. 21, 1690, followed shortly by its dissolution. JAN. 27.

6. The campaign in Ireland.
a French auxiliaries sent over to James under the Duke of Lauzun. Attempt of James to fill his treasury by depreciation of the coinage.
b Landing of William at Carrickfergus. JUNE
JULY 1. 14. Battle of the Boyne. Rout of James's forces, and flight of James from Ireland.

SEPT. OCT.

MARCH.

 c Capture of Waterford by William. JULY **25**. Siege of Limerick. AUG. **8-30**. William compelled to raise the siege.

 d Marlborough (Churchill) summoned from Flanders to serve in Ireland. Capture by him of Cork and Kinsale. SEPT. **28**–OCT. **5**.

 7. French descent upon England. Defeat of the English and Dutch fleets off Beachy Head, owing to the treacherous inaction of Lord Torrington (Admiral Herbert). JUNE **30**. Victory of the French over the allies at Fleurus. Ravaging of the English coast by the French, and indignation of the English people.

 8. Proceedings in Parliament. **1690**.

 a Parliament more Tory in feeling. Change in the executive departments in favour of the Tories. Caermarthen (Danby), the King's chief minister; Sir John Lowther, First Lord of the Treasury.

 Act of grace.

 b Settlement and appropriation of the revenue.

  i. £1,200,000 to be the annual revenue of the Crown in time of peace.

  ii. £600,000 to be appropriated to the civil list (*i.e.* the maintenance of the King's government and royal household).

  iii. The revenue consisted of

   (*a*) The hereditary revenue (from the rent of the royal domains, fees, fines, wine licences, first fruits and tenths of benefices, the receipts of the Post Office [first established 1660], and the excise duties which had been voted as compensation for feudal dues (**1660**). Between £400,000 and £500,000.

   (*b*) The rest of the excise duties voted to William and Mary for their joint and several lives. About £300,000.

   (*c*) The customs duties, between £500,000 and £600,000, voted for four years.

  iv. The appropriation of the revenue rendered more strict by the appointment of Commissioners to audit and control the public accounts (on the vote for 64,924 men, exclusive of officers, for the next year). OCT.—NOV.

1691. 9. Deprivation of the nonjuring prelates. FEB. Tillotson appointed Archbishop of Canterbury in the place of Sancroft. MAY **31**.

1691. 10. Progress of the war and conclusion of the Irish campaign.
   a Capture of Mons by the French. APRIL **8**.
   b Defeat of the Irish and French forces at Aughrim by Ginkel. JULY **12**. Siege and capture of Limerick. AUG. **25**.-OCT. **3**. The capitulation of Limerick.
   1. Irish soldiers suffered to retire to France (12,000 in all).
   2. Roman Catholics to enjoy such privileges as were compatible with law, or as they had enjoyed in the reign of Charles II.
   3. Amnesty and possession of former lands promised to all who should take the Oath of Allegiance.

   [The last provisoes practically rendered meaningless by the Irish Parliaments of **1695** and **1698**; which enacted:
   i. That no Catholic be admitted to a corporation, be allowed to bear arms (except those included in capitulations of Limerick and Galway), or be apprenticed to an armourer.
   ii. That no Catholic marry a Protestant heiress, or be guardian to any child.
   iii. That no Catholic be allowed to keep a school; and that no child be sent for education beyond seas.
   iv. That Catholics should conform within six months after any title accrued by descent or settlement on pain of forfeiture to next Protestant heir.]
   End of political danger from Ireland and of the first period of the war.

B Events of the Reign from the Capitulation of Limerick to the Victory of La Hogue, and the removal of the fear of Foreign Invasion. OCT. **1691**-MAY, **1692**.

1692. *a* Treasonable plot of Lord Marlborough to drive William from the throne in favour of Princess Anne. Dismissal of Marlborough from the

JAN.	public service. JAN. **1692**. Alienation between the Queen and Princess Anne, and revival of Jacobite hopes.
FEB. **13.**	*b* Completion of the submission of most of the Highland clans by DEC. **1691**. Massacre of the Macdonalds of Glencoe for delay in tendering submission.
MAY **19.**	*c* A French and Irish force assembled in Normandy for the invasion of England. Fear of invasion removed by the destruction of the French fleet off La Hogue by Admiral Russell (notwithstanding previous intrigues on his part with James). End of the second period of the war.

C Commencement of the System of Party Government and Progress of the War till the Capture of Namur by William (which marked the turn of the tide of success). MAY, **1692**–AUG. **1695**.

AUG. **3.** **1693.**	**1.** Capture of Namur by the French. JUNE **30**. French victory at Steinkirk (with great slaughter among five English regiments, owing to the inaction of Count Solms).
SEPT.-OCT.	**2.** Bill for Triennial Parliaments negatived by the King. Addition of Somers and Trenchard (Whigs) to the Tory Ministers—Caermarthen, Nottingham, Rochester, Lowther, Seymour (MARCH). Advice of Lord Sunderland (the former minister of James) that ministers be chosen exclusively from the party strongest in the House of Commons. This advice gradually adopted.
JUNE **17.** JULY **19.**	**3.** The Smyrna merchant fleet, though escorted by an English and Dutch convoy, scattered by the French, the English Admirals being Killigrew and Delaval. French victory at Landen or Neerwinden.
NOV. **1693**— JAN. **1694.** JAN. **1694.**	**4.** Discussion in new session as to the conduct of Killigrew and Delaval. Dismissal of Nottingham. The Triennial Bill passed again by the Lords, but shelved by the Commons. Bill for excluding Placemen from Parliament vetoed by the King. Votes passed of £2,300,000 for the Fleet, and for an increase to the army of 20,000 men (in all £5,000,000).
1694.	**5.** A loan of £1,200,000 raised for the expenses of the war by public subscription, at 8 per cent. The subscribers, whose interest was secured upon the taxes, incorporated under the name

	of the Governor and Company of the Bank of England, with a charter for eleven years, but with a guarding clause forbidding the advance of money to the crown without the sanction of Parliament. Due to the management of Montague and Michael Godfrey. APRIL.
JUNE.	6. Failure of the English attack on Brest owing to treacherous information conveyed to the French, but French northern coast blockaded and harassed.
JULY.	7. Barcelona secured from the French by Admiral Russell, and French fleet shut up in Toulon. The English fleet ordered by William to winter at Cadiz.
NOV.	8. Final passing of the Triennial Bill, with the omission of the clauses to ensure annual sessions (these being already sufficiently ensured by the annual appropriation of the revenue and the Mutiny Act).
DEC. 28.	9. Death of Queen Mary.
1695.	10. The Whigs now predominant in office (Russell, Chief of the Admiralty Board; Somers, Lord Keeper; Earl of Shrewsbury, Secretary of State; Montague, Chancellor of the Exchequer).
APRIL—MAY.	11. Parliamentary inquiries into the alleged corruption in public offices. Vote of censure on Speaker, Trevor, who was expelled from the House and succeeded as Speaker by Foley (a Whig.) Proposed impeachment of Danby (now Duke of Leeds) for implication in corruption practised by East India Company to obtain renewal of exclusive Charter.
	12. The Act for restraining unlicensed printing (which had lapsed **1679**, and had been re-enacted **1685**) suffered to expire without re-enactment, a proposal to re-enact it being negatived **1697**.

[Growth of the Freedom of Printing.
  i. Printing confined to London, Oxford, Cambridge; the licensing of Publications in the hands of the Primate and Bishop of London, and Printers under the supervision of the Company of Stationers. **1585**.
  ii. Milton's Areopagitica, a speech for the liberty of unlicensed printing to the Parliament of England. **1644**.

   iii. Licensing Act, **1662**. Printing confined to London, York, Oxford, Cambridge. Upon its expiring, **1679**, not renewed.
   iv. Revival of the Licensing Act, **1685**.
   v. Proposal for re-enactment negatived, **1697**.]
  13. Siege and capture of Namur by William. JULY 2-SEPT. 1. Turn of success in the war.

D Progress of Events to the Peace of Ryswick. SEPT. 1695-OCT. 1697.

   1. Dissolution of Parliament (OCT.), Royal progress through the country, and meeting of a new Parliament, mainly Whig in feeling. NOV., **1695**.

1696. 2. Act for the Regulation of Trial in cases of Treason.
    a All indicted for high treason to have a copy of indictment five days before trial, and of the panel of jurors two days before trial.
    b Two direct witnesses to be always produced in evidence of the charge.
    c Prosecutions for treason limited to the term of three years, except in the case of attempted assassination of the King.
    d In the trial of peers, all peers to be summoned who have a right to sit and vote in the House of Lords.
   3. Formation of the Jacobite plots

FEB.
    a For an insurrection, assisted by French force, under the Duke of Berwick (natural son of James II.): on condition of the English rising first. Omission in James's declaration of any pledge for the inviolability of the Test Act.
    b for the assassination of the King at Turnham Green. Revealed FEB. Execution of Charnock, Freind, and their confederates. MARCH-APRIL.
   4. Formation of the Association for the Defence of the King and Country: signature rendered compulsory by Act of Parliament on all officials. APRIL.
   5. Signs of dissension in the Grand Alliance. Secession of the Duke of Savoy upon the cession to him by Lewis XIV. of Pinerola and Casale. Italy thus neutralized, and 30,000 French troops set free. JULY.

6. Abortive attempt of Harley to establish a land bank, which promised to advance the government two and a half millions at 7 per cent. The bank to advance money to country gentlemen on security of mortgage on land. APRIL–AUG.

7. Reform of the debased currency by Montague, the Master of the Mint, Sir Isaac Newton, and John Locke. MAY—AUGUST. (The expense, £1,200,000, borne by the nation and raised by a house duty.)

8. Arrest of Sir John Fenwick for complicity in the assassination plot. JUNE. Fenwick's confession, accusing Marlborough, Godolphin, Russell, Shrewsbury, of treason. Refusal of William to investigate the charges. Fenwick's trial being impossible owing to the escape of one of the witnesses, bill of attainder was brought in against him. Fenwick executed. JAN., **1697**.

1697.

9. Congress for peace at Ryswick. MAY—JUNE. Obstruction from Spain and the Emperor. Private negotiations between England and France, conducted by Portland and Marshal Boufflers. Peace signed. OCT., **1697**.

  a Abandonment by France of all her annexations since the treaty of Nimeguen except Strassburg (retained owing to the delay of the German negotiators), Luxemburg and conquests in the Spanish Netherlands' restored to Spain, Lorraine to the Duke of Lorraine.

  b Abandonment by France of any attempt to subvert the Government of England, and recognition of William as King.

E Tory Re-action, and Progress of Events till the Second Treaty of Partition. OCT. 1697—OCT. 1700.

1. Vote passed in the Commons that the army be reduced to the strength of **1680** (about 7,000 men). DEC. **11**.

1698. Resignation of Sunderland (appointed to the Privy Council **1697**); Civil List increased to £700,000. Attack upon Montague for peculation. FEB.

1698. 2. Departure of William for Holland. Secret negotiations with France to bring about a peaceful solution of the question of the Spanish succession, ending in the First Partition Treaty. The Electoral Prince to succeed to Spain; the Dauphin to the Two Sicilies and Guipuzcoa; Archduke Charles to the Milanese.

Table showing claimants to Spanish Crown:—

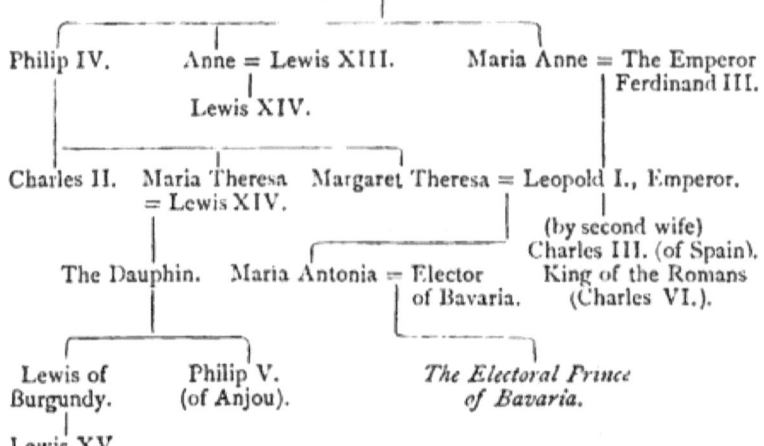

The claim both of the Dauphin and of the Electoral Prince barred by special treaties (but the renunciation of the Dauphin's claim treated as invalid by Spanish law).

3. Meeting of a new Parliament, mainly Tory in tendency. DEC. Vote reducing the army to 7,000 men for England, natural born English subjects. 12,000 men voted for Ireland, 15,000 for the Fleet, but for the Fleet only. FEB.

1699. 1. Dismissal of the Dutch guards in spite of the opposition of ministers and the expressed wishes of the King. MARCH.

4. Death of the Electoral Prince. FEB. **1699.**

5. The Whig Ministers in office, but without authority. Vote for the resumption of the forfeited estates in Ireland, granted by William to his followers. Commission appointed to take account of property forfeited during late troubles. Attack upon Somers for granting a Commission to Captain Kidd, the pirate. Stringent act against " the growth of Popery."

    a £100 reward to any informer against a Romish priest saying mass.

    b Penalty for exercising priestly functions or keeping a school, perpetual imprisonment.

    c All Roman Catholics to take the oaths of allegiance and supremacy, and subscribe the declaration against transubstantiation, under penalty of being incapacitated from purchasing or inheriting land.

Tories admitted into the management of affairs (Lonsdale, Jersey).

6. Indignation in Spain at the news of the First Treaty of Partition, and that a second was in contemplation. AUTUMN.

1700. 7. Bill as to Irish forfeitures passed by both Houses on report of the Commissioners.
  a All property belonging to the Crown in the reign of James II., or since then forfeited, to be placed in the hands of trustees.
  b Grants made by William annulled.

APRIL. 8. Address voted requesting the removal of all foreign councillors (except Prince George of Denmark). APRIL 10. Prorogation of Parliament. APRIL 11.

JULY. 9. Death of the Duke of Gloucester, last surviving child of Princess Anne, rendering new measures for the settlement of the succession necessary.

10. The Second Partition Treaty. Spain, the Indies, and the Netherlands to go to the Emperor's second son, Archduke Charles. All the Spanish
OCT. possessions in Italy to France (Lorraine to be taken in exchange for the Milanese, the Duke of Lorraine being transferred to Milan).

F The Outbreak of War.

OCT. 1. Death of Charles II. of Spain. Philip of Anjou (second son of the Dauphin) nominated by his will as successor to all the Spanish dominions. OCT. 21.

DEC. 2. Rochester and Godolphin chief Ministers; Montague removed to the House of Lords as Lord Halifax, and ascendency of moderate Tories. DEC.

1701. 3. The barrier fortresses in the Netherlands claimed by Lewis XIV. in the name of his grandson, and garrisoned by French troops.

4. Meeting of Parliament. Impeachment of Lord Somers for affixing Great Seal to blank powers for the negotiators of the First Partition Treaty, and for illegal acts. APRIL—MAY. Russell and Montague (Lords Orford and Halifax) also threatened with impeachment. Somers acquitted upon the non-appearance of the Commons at the bar of the Lords. JUNE 17.

5. The Kentish Petition urging the Commons to drop their disputes, and turn their addresses into votes of supply. Imprisonment of the Members who presented it. MAY **8.** Alliance between Holland and England for the security of the Netherlands. The Fleet raised to 30,000 men, the army to 10,000, and an English force sent to Flanders under Marlborough. The "Legion" Memorial. MAY, JUNE. Grand Alliance of England, Holland, and the Emperor, to recover the Low Countries from the French, and obtain for the Emperor the Spanish possessions in Italy. SEPT. [Accession of Prussia, Sweden, the Palatinate, to the Alliance. **1702.**]

SEPT. **6.** Death of James II. SEPT. **6.** James Francis Edward recognised by Lewis XIV. as King of England. Indignation in England, and recall of English ambassador from Paris.

7. The settlement of the Protestant succession, in default of heirs to Anne or William, upon the Electress Sophia and her heirs. **1701-1702.**

Table showing the Hanoverian descent.

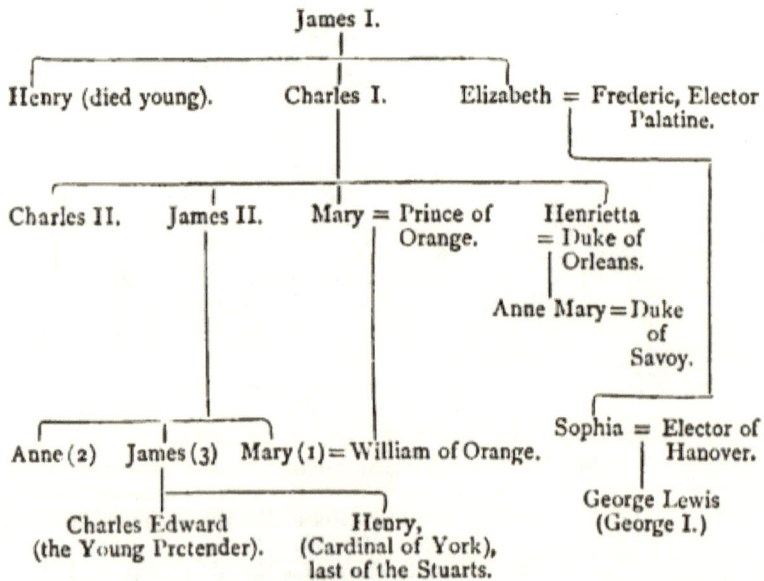

a All future monarchs of England to join in Communion with the Church of England.

  b England not to be obliged to engage in war for the defence of any dominion or territories which may belong to the sovereign but not belonging to the Crown of England, without consent of Parliament.

  c No English sovereign to go out of the dominions of England, Scotland, or Ireland without consent of Parliament.

  d All resolutions upon matters relating to the well-government of the realm to be signed by such of the Privy Council as shall advise and consent to the same.

  e No person not born in the realm or of English parents to enjoy any place of trust.

  f No pensioner or placeman to serve as a member of the House of Commons.

  g Judges to hold their offices *quam diu se bene gesserint*, but removable upon address from both Houses of Parliament.

  h No pardon under the Great Seal to bar impeachment by the Commons.

  8. Meeting of a new Parliament. DEC. National feeling for war with France. Oath of abjuration denying any title or right in the pretended Prince of Wales. FEB.

1702.

  10. Death of the King. MARCH **8.**

ANNE. 1702-1714.

Anne = Prince George of Denmark.

| Four daughters and one son, who died in infancy. | William (Duke of Gloucester). Died July **30, 1700**. |

A Home events till the complete Ascendency of the Whigs. 1702-1708.

  1702. 1. Nottingham, Rochester, and Godolphin in power. Closer union between England and Scotland rendered advisable by the strained relations between the two countries in consequence of the unsuccessful attempt of the Scots to establish a trading settlement at Darien, sanctioned by William **(1695)**, and undertaken **1698, 1699.** Publication of Clarendon's *History of the Rebellion.*

1703. 2. Surrender by Queen Anne to the Church of the First-fruits and Tenths due to the Crown, for the augmentation of the maintenance of the poor clergy (Queen Anne's Bounty). Nov. Introduction of an Act to prohibit Nonconformists for qualifying for office by Occasional Conformity.

1703. 3. Act of Security passed by the Scotch Parliament.
- (i) The Protestant succession guaranteed, but not on the same person as shall succeed to the Crown of England, unless the Scotch were, in the present reign, permitted to share in the advantages of the English trade.
- (ii) The prerogative of declaring peace and war to be exercised subject to the approbation of the Scotch Parliament, and all men capable of bearing arms to be trained by monthly drills.

This was answered by an English Act declaring the Scotch aliens till the Scottish succession was settled in the same way as the English, and prohibiting trade with Scotland.

[**4.** The great storm. Nov. **26**-Dec. **1.**]

5. Occasional Conformity passed by the Commons, but rejected (as again in **1704**) by the Lords. **1703.**

1704. 6. Resignation of Rochester (**1703**), and of Nottingham, and formation of a more moderate Tory Ministry, including Harley and St. John. Royal consent given to the Scotch Act of Succession. **1705.**

1705. 7. New Parliament, Whig in tendency. A combination Ministry, William Cowper (a Whig) being appointed Lord Keeper in place of Wright (a Tory). Passing of the Regency Bill [to provide for a Regency, partly official, partly nominated by the next Protestant heir in the case of the said heir not being in the kingdom at the death of the reigning sovereign].

1706. 8. The Act of Union with Scotland completed, to take effect May **1, 1707.**
- (*a*) The two states to form one United Kingdom of Great Britain; the succession to be ruled by the provisions of the English Act of Settlement.

 (*b*) The Scotch Church and law to remain unaffected.

 (*c*) All rights of trade to be common: taxation and coinage to be uniform.

 (*d*) Forty-five Scotch members added to the 513 English members to form the united House of Commons, and sixteen representative peers added to the 108 English peers.

9. Lord Sunderland (Marlborough's son-in-law), a strong Whig, made Secretary of State; resentment of the Tories. Intrigues between Harley and Abigail Hill (Mrs. Masham) to countermine the influence of the Duchess of Marlborough. **1706.**

1707. 10. Act of union in operation. MAY. The Union Jack appointed as the national flag of Great Britain. JULY. First meeting of the United Parliament of Great Britain. OCT.

1708. 11. Final abandonment by Marlborough and Godolphin of their attempt to govern by means of a Combination Ministry. Dismissal of Harley owing to the revelation of State secrets by Gregg, one of his clerks, and resignation of St. John. Admission of Lords Somers and Wharton, the Duke of Newcastle and Robert Walpole to office. Complete ascendency of the Whigs. OCT.

B Events of the War till the Ascendency of the Whig Ministry, JAN. 1708.

1702. Formal declaration of war against France and Spain. MAY. The French driven by Marlborough out of Venloo, Ruremond, and (in OCT.) Liége, and so cut off from the Lower Rhine. Unsuccessful English attack upon Cadiz (AUG.). Capture of Spanish galleons by Rooke. OCT. **12.** Rising of the French Calvinists (Camisards) under Cavalier, in the Cévennes.

1703. The Methuen Treaty, and accession of Portugal and of Savoy to the Grand Alliance. MAY. Marlborough prevented by the timidity of the Dutch from attacking Antwerp and French Flanders; reduction however by him of Bonn, Huy, and Limburg (commanding the district between the Meuse and the Rhine). Successes of the French upon the Danube threatening the safety of Vienna.

1704. French invasion of Portugal by the Duke of Berwick (the natural son of James II. and nephew of Marlborough). Marlborough's march, to save Vienna, up the Rhine, across the Neckar, through Wurtemberg. Storming of the lines of Donauwörth, JULY **2**, and rout of the French and Bavarian armies at Blenheim by Marlborough and Prince Eugene. AUG. **13.** Capture of Gibraltar by Rooke. JULY **23.**

1705. Marlborough's plan for the invasion of France from the east foiled by the jealousy of the Imperialists, and his operations in Flanders hampered by the timidity of the Dutch.

Capture of Monjuich by Lord Peterborough (SEPT. **6**) and of Barcelona; OCT. **4.** The Archduke acknowledged as Charles III. in Aragon, Catalonia, Valencia. The winter spent by Marlborough in negotiations with the allies.

1706. Further successes on the Spanish coast; reduction of Carthagena, Alicante, Ivica and Majorca.
Victory over Villeroi at Ramillies. MAY **23.** Capture of Brussels, Antwerp, Louvain, Ghent, Bruges, Ostend, Menin, Dendermonde, Aeth; the chief fortresses still in possession of France Mons and Namur. JUNE-OCT. Charles III. acknowledged in Brabant and Flanders.

Entry of the allies into Madrid. JUNE **24.** Evacuation of Madrid by the allies (owing to the steady opposition of the Spaniards). AUG. **5.**

Victory of Prince Eugene over Marsin at Turin. SEPT. **7.** Overtures for peace made by Lewis XIV.

i. Philip to relinquish claim to Spanish throne, but to receive the Milanese, Naples, and Sicily, and to retain the Indies.

ii. Fortresses in the Spanish Netherlands to be granted as a barrier to Holland.

1707. Recall of Peterborough from Spain in consequence of his quarrel with Lord Galway. The allies defeated by the Duke of Berwick at Almanza. APRIL **14.** Unsuccessful English attack upon Toulon. JULY. Indecisive operations between Marlborough and Vendôme in the Netherlands. Sir C. Shovel wrecked on the Scilly Islands. OCT. **22. 1707.**

1708. Attempted invasion of Scotland by James Francis Edward (the Pretender) assisted by a French fleet and force. MARCH.

Victory of Marlborough over Vendôme at Oudenarde. JULY 11. Destruction of the French lines, and invasion of Artois and Picardy. Capture of Port Mahon and Sardinia by Sir J. Leake. The French driven out of Lombardy and Naples. AUG. Capture of Lille. DEC.

C Events till the Fall of the Whigs. OCT. 1710.

1709. 1. Bill for naturalising foreign Protestants settled in England.

2. The English law of treason extended to Scotland, involving the abolition of torture with the exception of the *peine forte et dure* for persons refusing to plead.

3. Terms of peace proposed by Lewis XIV.
    i. Aid to be withdrawn from Philip of Spain.
    ii. Surrender of ten Flemish fortresses including Lille and Tournai as barrier for the Dutch.
    iii. Surrender of Strasburg, Brisach, and Luxemburg to the Emperor.
    iv Acknowledgment of the titles of Anne as Queen, of the Elector of Hanover, and of the King of Prussia, the banishment of the Pretender, demolition of the fortifications of Dunkirk, restoration of Newfoundland to England.

4. Additional demands of the Whig ministers.
    i. The transfer of the whole Spanish monarchy to Charles III.
    ii. Co-operation of French troops to compel Philip to resign the Spanish crown. Refusal of Lewis XIV. and appeal to the French people.

4. Capture of Tournai by Marlborough and Eugene, JULY. Battle of Malplaquet, near Mons, SEPT. 11, unbroken retreat of the French, but capture of Mons by Marlborough. 1709.

5. Quarrel between the Queen and the Duchess of Marlborough, and coldness between Marlborough and the Whigs, owing to their opposition to his appointment as Captain-General for life. 1709.

1710. 6. Impeachment of Dr. Sacheverell (mainly for his sermon upon "Perils from False Brethren" preached before the Lord Mayor Nov. 1709). FEB. 27–MARCH 23. Sacheverell found guilty, but only suspended for three years.

7. Conference for peace at Getruydenberg. i. Agreement by Lewis XIV. to cede all the fortresses in the Austrian Netherlands and the French fortresses of Lille and Valenciennes as a barrier to the Dutch. ii. Agreement to destroy all fortifications on the Rhine from Bâle downwards. iii. Agreement to the former demands of 1709 except to that of making war upon Philip. MARCH 11–JULY 20. Broken off owing to opposition of Austria and Savoy.

8. Victories of the allies in Spain at Almenarao and Saragossa. JULY 10–AUG. 20. Triumphal entry of Charles into Madrid. SEPT. 28.

9. Dismissal of the Whig Ministry. AUG., OCT.

D The Tories in Power.

1. Capitulation of the English in Spain at Brihuega, and of the Imperialists at Villa Viciosa, to the Duke of Vendôme. DEC. 10 and 20, 1710.

1711. 2. Passing of the Occasional Conformity Act (office-holders to attend no conventicle during year of office), owing to a compromise made by the Whig peers with Nottingham in the hope of strengthening themselves.

3. Dispatch of British troops from Flanders under General Hill (brother of Mrs. Masham) for the conquest of Canada. MAY–OCT.

4. Departure of Charles III. from Spain, and election as Emperor (Charles VI.).

5. Breach of Villars's lines by Marlborough and capture of Bouchain. AUG. Marlborough crippled (*a*) by Hill's expedition to Canada, (*b*) by secret negotiations for peace between the Tory ministers and the French, which terminated in two preliminary treaties signed SEPT. 27.

(*a*) A private arrangement between England and France signed by both Powers and not submitted to the allies.

(b) A statement of preliminaries, exclusive of the special concessions to the English, signed only by France and submitted to the allies for consideration.

6. Consequent alienation between Marlborough and the Tories. Accusation of peculation brought against him, and dismissal from his command, DEC.; the Duke of Ormond appointed in his place. **1712.**

1712.

7. Creation of twelve Tory peers to counterbalance Whig majority in the Upper House, DEC., **1711.** Repeal of the Act for the Naturalisation of Alien Protestants. Passing of the Stamp Act upon advertisements to check the license of the Press. Negotiations for peace opened at Utrecht.

8. Terms of peace laid before Parliament, JUNE. Recall of Ormond and the English from Flanders, and consequent successes of the French. JULY–OCT. Death of Godolphin. SEPT.

1713. 9. The Treaty of Utrecht. MARCH–JULY.

a Confirmation of England in the possession of Gibraltar, Minorca, Hudson's Bay, Nova Scotia (Acadia), Newfoundland; grant of the monopoly of the slave trade to the Spanish colonies (for thirty years: England to furnish 4,800 slaves annually to the Spanish colonies in two ships of 500 tons burden); recognition of Anne and the Protestant succession; expulsion of the Pretender from France; demolition of the fortifications of Dunkirk.

b Spain and the Indies retained by Philip.

c Spanish possessions in Italy (Milanese, Naples, and Sardinia) and the Netherlands ceded to Charles (Emperor since 1711).

d Sicily, with the title of King, to the Duke of Savoy, with the promise of succession to the Spanish Crown in the event of the failure of Philip's line.

e No provision made by England for the protection of the provincial liberties of Catalonia.

g Peace of Radstadt between France and the Emperor, SEPT. **1714**; negotiations between the Dutch and the Emperor as to the Barrier Fortresses in the Netherlands not concluded till NOV., **1715**. No formal peace at all between Spain and the Emperor.

10. Increasing divergency of policy between Earl of Oxford (Harley) and Viscount Bolingbroke (St. John), the leader of the extreme Tory, if not Jacobite, party. Introduction by Bolingbroke of the *Schism Act* to punish with imprisonment Nonconformists acting as tutors or keeping schools, except for elementary teaching. Opposition of Harley in conjunction with the Whigs. Election of a New Parliament, Tory in tendency.

1713-1714.

11. Demand by the Whigs of a writ to the House of Lords for the son of the Elector of Hanover (created Duke of Cambridge, afterwards George II.). The writ claimed by the Hanoverian Ambassador APRIL, **1714**. Indignant letter

JUNE. of the Queen to the Electress. JUNE. [Death of the Electress Sophia. JUNE **4**.]

12. Anxiety of the nation as to the succession. Preparations on both sides as if for civil war, the Whigs looking to Marlborough, while Bolingbroke placed the Cinque Ports in the command of Ormond, and Scotland in that of the Earl of Mar. Negotiations between Bolingbroke and the Pretender ending in nothing owing to his refusal to declare himself a Protestant. Dismissal of Harley from office, to make a united Tory Government, followed by the last illness of the Queen. JULY **27**. Appearance of the Dukes of Argyll and Somerset at the Council Table: the appointment of Shrewsbury as Lord Treasurer in the place of Oxford accepted by the Queen.

Death of the Queen, and proclamation of George Lewis, Elector of Brunswick-Lüneburg, as
AUG. King. AUG. **10, 1714**.

13. The government in the hands of those appointed by the Elector, in conformity with the Regency Act of **1705** (eighteen members of the Whig party, Marlborough and Somers being omitted). Bolingbroke dismissed from office. Landing of the Elector, SEPT. **18**.

14. Siege of Barcelona by Philip. APRIL.—SEPT. Fall of Barcelona (SEPT. **11**), and abolition of the provincial liberties of Catalonia.

GEORGE I. 1714-1727.

George I. = Sophia Dorothea of Zell.
  |
  George II.

A The Townshend Administration. Lord Townshend and General (Lord) Stanhope Secretaries of State.

1. Transfer of power to the Whigs. Dissolution of Queen Anne's Privy Council, and formation of a new and smaller one. Bills of attainder against the Duke of Ormond (for alleged treasonable negotiations with Marshal Villars in 1712) of the Earl of Oxford, of Lord Bolingbroke. Flight of Ormond to France; imprisonment of Oxford, **1715-1717**; trial and acquittal, **1717**. Flight of Bolingbroke to France (MARCH) and entrance into the service of the Pretender. SEPT. **1715**. Abandonment of the Pretender's service, **1716**. Return to England, **1723**.

1715.   2. Despatch of the British fleet to the Baltic for the protection of Bremen and Verden (conquered by Denmark **1712**, and sold to Hanover on condition of British participation in the war against Sweden).

3. Deaths of Lords Halifax and Wharton, Bishop Burnet, Lewis XIV.
Regency of the Duke of Orleans in France.

4. Passing of the *Riot Act*, that any assembly of more than twelve persons not separating within an hour after being enjoined to disperse by a Justice of the Peace, and after hearing the Act read, be esteemed felonious.

5. The Jacobite Rebellion.

1715.   James VIII. (James III. of England) proclaimed at Braemar by the Earl of Mar. SEPT. **6**. Unsuccessful attempt of the Jacobites to seize Edinburgh Castle by stratagem. SEPT. **8**. Occupation of Perth by the Earl of Mar. SEPT. **18**. Revolt in Northumberland under Lord Derwentwater and Mr. Forster. OCT. **6**.
SEPT.—DEC.   Meeting of the English Jacobites with Lord Kenmure (commanding the Jacobites of the Borders) and Mackintosh (who had marched from the Highlands, crossing the Forth, and threatening Edinburgh) at Kelso. OCT. **18**. Indecisive battle of Sherriffmuir between Argyll and Mar. NOV. **13**. Retreat of Mar to Perth.

Defeat and surrender of the Southern Jacobites (under Forster and Kenmure) the same day. Nov. **13**. Capture of Inverness from the Jacobites by Lord Lovat. Dec. Landing of the Pretender at Peterhead. Dec. **22, 1715**. Coronation at Scone Jan. **27, 1716**.

1716. Advance of General Carpenter. Retreat of the Highland army from Perth. Jan. **20**. Flight of the Pretender to France. Feb. **4**.

Jan.–Feb.

Two Peers and thirty-four Commoners executed in consequence of the rebellion, and the estates of many Jacobites confiscated, but no measures beyond a Clan Act of **1715** taken to reduce the strength of the Highland clans. Passing of the Septennial Act to avoid a dissolution of Parliament.

Repeal of the clause in the Act of Settlement forbidding the King to leave the kingdom without consent of Parliament. Discontent at the chance of entanglement in fresh foreign war.

B **The Stanhope-Sunderland Administration. 1717**–Feb. **1721.**

1716-1717. 1. Foreign policy (efforts to maintain the Peace of Utrecht).

    a. Treaty for mutual defence between England and the Emperor; coolness between the King and Townshend on Townshend's refusal to declare war upon the Czar for the invasion of Mecklenburg; dismissal of Townshend and Walpole. **1717**.

    b. Compact between Stanhope and the Regent of France to guarantee the succession of the House of Orleans (*i.e.* of the Regent) in France in case of the death of Lewis XV. without an heir; on condition of
        i. Total separation of France from the Pretender.
        ii. The destruction of the newly fortified port at Mardyke.

1717. *c.* Triple Alliance between England, France, and Holland. Jan. **17**.

    d. Designs of Cardinal Alberoni for the revival of the Empire of Spain:

Jan.

        i. Encouragement given to a Northern Confederation of Charles XII. of Sweden and Peter the Great of

Russia for the ruin of Hanover, and restoration of the Stuarts to Great Britain. Arrest of Gyllenburg, Swedish Ambassador in London. JAN. **29**.

AUG.

1718.

ii. Seizure of Sardinia by Alberoni while the Emperor was occupied repelling invasion of the Turks. Peace of Passarowitz between the Emperor and the Turks, owing—

   a. To the victory of Prince Eugene at Belgrade. AUG. **1717**.

   b. To the mediation of Great Britain.

JULY—AUG.

iii. The Quadruple Alliance between Great Britain, the Emperor, France, and Holland for the maintenance of the Peace of Utrecht. JULY—AUG.

   a. Final renunciation by the Emperor of claim to Spain, and of the King of France to the Spanish crown.

   b. Spain to restore Sardinia to the Emperor, which was then to be given to the King of Sicily (Duke of Savoy) in exchange for Sicily, the House of Savoy also acknowledged as next heirs to the crown of Spain, in case of Philip dying without heirs; Spain to obtain, as compensation, the reversion of the Archduchy of Tuscany, and of the Duchies of Parma and Placentia, for the eldest son of Philip's second wife, Don Carlos.

JULY.

AUG.
DEC.
1719.

Attack upon Sicily by Spain, and practical refusal of the terms of the Quadruple Alliance. JULY. Destruction of the Spanish Fleet off Cape Passaro by Byng. AUG. **22**. Death of Charles XII. of Sweden. DEC.

iv. Last efforts of Alberoni.

   a. To stir up a revolt in Brittany against the oppressive taxation, in the hope of securing the recognition there of Philip as heir to the French throne.

R

JUNE.   *b.* To equip Spanish Jacobite expedition: the fleet broken by storms. Those who reached Scotland defeated at Glenshiel.

DEC. 5.   Fall and disgrace of Alberoni. Practically the end, for the time, of European complications.

    2. Home policy.

1717.   *a* Owing to the spirit of Jacobitism among the clergy, and the fierceness of the Bangorian controversy (upon the occasion of Hoadley, Bishop of Bangor, defending the doctrines of religious liberty against the divine authority of the clergy), Convocation prorogued, and not again summoned for business till **1851.**

1717.   *b* Repeal of the Occasional Conformity Act (with he provision that the insignia of office might not be carried to a place of worship other than those of the Established Church), and of the Schism Act. Surplus revenue appropriated for a Sinking Fund, to pay off part of the National Debt.

1719.   *c* Proposal of the Peerage Bill; (i) that exclusive of the Royal Family, no more than six Peers be added to the number of Hereditary Peers then existing. (ii) That the Scotch Peers be increased from 16 to 25; at first selected by the sovereign, then hereditary. Proposed by Sunderland, but rejected mainly owing to Walpole's opposition.

1720.   *d* The South Sea Bubble. A project for the conversion of annuities into South Sea Stock, in the hopes of being able to reduce the interest upon the National Debt from 8 to 4 per cent., and to establish a sinking fund for its extinction out of the profits of the Spanish Trade, the monopoly of which was to be given to the Company; the Company agreeing to give £7,567,000 if all the annuities were converted. Proposed to Parliament. JAN. **22.** Royal assent given. JUNE **11, 1720.** Great growth of projects in imitation of the Company leading to the detection of its unsubstantial basis (the trade with Spain being limited by the Treaty of Utrecht, to the right of sending two ships of 500 tons burden with negroes a year to Spanish America). Alarm and ruin caused by the collapse of

1721.	the Company, accusations of bribery brought against Aislabie (Chancellor of the Exchequer), Charles Stanhope (Secretary to the Treasury), Craggs (the Postmaster-General), and his son the Secretary of State. Death of Lord Stanhope from vexation and grief. FEB. 5.

C **Walpole-Townshend Administration. Walpole, first Lord of the Treasury, Townshend and Carteret, Secretaries of State.**

1. By Walpole's skill the proprietors of South Sea stock received £33 6s. 8d. per cent., and two millions were set apart as Sinking Fund for the diminution of the National Debt.

1720. Nov. 2. Jacobite intrigues stimulated by the birth of the Young Pretender (Charles Edward), Nov. **30, 1720,** and the South Sea disaster. Suspen-
1722. sion of Habeas Corpus, and arrest and exile of Bishop Atterbury; the plot known by his name being made known to the English by the
AUG. Regent of France. Banishment of Atterbury.
1723. (Death of Sunderland and Marlborough.
1724. **1722.**) Resignation of the secretaryship by Carteret, who was appointed Lord-Lieutenant of Ireland.

1724. 3. Attempt to remedy the deficient state of the copper coinage of Ireland by permitting Wood to coin halfpence and farthings (slightly less in weight than those used in Great Britain, though of equally fine metal) to the value of £108,000. Indignation in Ireland increased by Swift's "Drapier's Letters." Abandonment of the attempt.

1725. 4. Pardon of Bolingbroke, and restoration to his estates, but not to the House of Lords.

5. Foreign troubles from **1720.**

1720. *a* Issue of "the Pragmatic Sanction," by the Emperor Charles VI., bequeathing his hereditary possessions in Austria, Hungary, Sicily, and Bohemia, to his daughter, Maria Theresa.

1720. *b* Betrothal of Lewis XV. of France, to the Infanta of Spain; broken off upon the death
1723. of the Duke of Orleans, Regent of France; and arrangements made for the marriage of Lewis to the daughter of Stanislaus, the deposed King of Poland.

1725.   c Alliance between the Emperor and Spain (under the influence of Ripperda).

  i. Spain to guarantee the Pragmatic Sanction, and to put the Ostend Company (trading between the Empire and India), on the footing of the most favoured nation (to the injury of the English and Dutch trade).

  ii. The Emperor to aid in the recovery of Gibraltar and Minorca; by the marriage of Maria Theresa to Don Carlos to unite the Archduchy of Tuscany and the Duchies of Parma and Placentia (secured to Don Carlos) with the Kingdoms of Naples and Sicily, and make the Austro-Spanish influence supreme in Italy; and to secure the election of Don Carlos as Emperor. Adhesion of Russia to this alliance (through enmity of Hanover).

1725-1727.   d Counter-alliance of England, France, and Prussia, by the Treaty of Hanover. SEPT. **1725**. Desertion of Prussia, **1726**, from the alliance, but adhesion of Holland. Siege laid by Spain to Gibraltar, FEB. **1727**; war threatened by the Emperor upon Holland. Troops secured from Sweden, Denmark and Hesse, by a large British and French subsidy; British fleet despatched to the West Indies, but with orders not to begin an attack.

1726.   e European war was mainly averted by the disgrace of Ripperda (MAY), by the accession of Cardinal Fleury to power in France (JUNE) **1726**, and by the death of the Czarina Katharine. MAY, **1727**. Armistice concluded between the Emperor and Great Britain, France, and Holland. MAY **31. 1727**.

Death of George I. JUNE 11, **1727**.

George II. 1727-1760.

George = Caroline of Brandenburg-Anspach.

Frederick, Prince of Wales (died **1751**).   William, Duke of Cumberland.

George III.

Close of British Interference in Foreign Complications.

1. Confirmation of Walpole in power, after a short interval under Spencer Compton.
2. The Treaty of Seville and Vienna. MARCH, **1729** and MARCH, **1731**.

1729-1731.
    a The succession to Archduchy of Tuscany and Duchy of Parma, secured to a Spanish Prince by the introduction of Spanish garrisons.
    b The commercial advantages given to the Ostend Company, revoked.
    c The Pragmatic Sanction guaranteed by Great Britain. MARCH, **1731**.

B Events of Walpole's Internal Government.

1727
1. Annual Acts of Indemnity for breach of the Penal Laws, from **1727**.
2. Financial measures and proposals.
    a Leave to the colonists to export rice to all markets.
    b Schemes of Indirect Taxation, partly as a means of raising money, partly to reconcile the landed gentry to the Government, by diminishing the burdens on land.

1723.
    i. One hundred articles of British manufacture allowed to be imported, and forty articles of foreign manufacture to be imported free of duty.

1732.
    ii. Revival of the Salt Tax.

1733.
    iii. A proposal to collect the duties upon Tobacco and Wines as Excise Duties (payable by the dealers), not as hitherto, as Customs Duties (payable by importers). The goods upon importation to be stored free of duty in bonded warehouses. Withdrawn in consequence of the bitter opposition.

1730.
3. Quarrel between Walpole and Townshend. Resignation of Townshend.

1731.
4. English used instead of Latin in proceedings of Courts of Justice.
5. Growth of opposition to Walpole, partly from his jealous usurpation of power (leading to a coalition of discontented Whigs and Tories, who were not Jacobites, under the name of "Patriots," led by Pulteney in Parliament, and

to a certain extent by Bolingbroke, as well as by Pulteney out of Parliament, and encouraged by Frederick, Prince of Wales, seen first in the publication of "The Craftsman," by Pulteney and Bolingbroke, **1725**); partly from dissatisfaction with his corruption and lack of enthusiasm—hence "The Boys," such as Lyttelton, George Grenville, and William Pitt (who entered Parliament, **1735**).

1738. 6. Beginning of Methodism, and of religious and moral revival in the nation, from **1738**, when Methodism was transferred from Oxford to London.

1737. Death of Queen Caroline, Walpole's steady supporter.

C Fresh Foreign Complications. 1732-1748.

1732. 1. *a* Approximation of France and Spain. War of
Feb. the Polish succession, between Stanislaus, father of the Queen of France, who had been made king by Charles XII., but had been deposed, and Augustus of Saxony, son of the late king. The war (between France, Spain, and Sardinia, nominally on the side of Stanislaus, and the Empire, and Russia on the side of Augustus), brought to an end
1735. by the intervention of Great Britain and Holland.

    i. Augustus elected king.

    ii. Stanislaus compensated with the Duchy of Lorraine, to pass at his death to France.

    iii. Naples and Sicily ceded by the Emperor to Don Carlos, in exchange for the duchies of Parma and Placentia.

    iv. The Duke of Lorraine (betrothed to Maria Theresa) to be compensated with the Grand Duchy of Tuscany.

1733. *b* The family compact between France and Spain, to secure the cession of Gibraltar to Spain, and the transference of the commercial privileges of England regarding the trade with Spanish America to France, delayed in operation by Walpole's refusal to be drawn into the Polish war.

  2. Beginning of troubles between England and Spain.

1738.

a Attempts of the Spaniards, especially after 1733, to restrict English trade with Spanish America to the limits fixed by the Treaty of Utrecht—the monopoly in the slave trade and one ship a year. Excitement produced in England by the story of Jenkins' ear.

b Resistance of Walpole to the cry for war, in order to keep Great Britain free to guard the European settlement in event of the death of the Emperor. Negotiations with Spain leading to a promise of payment of £95,100 as compensation to Great Britain.

1739.

1741.

1740-1744.

c War declared with Spain. Capture of Portobello by Vernon. Formal declaration of France against any English settlement on the mainland. Repulse of the English expedition against Carthagena. Expedition of Commodore Anson for the destruction of Spanish shipping on the western coast of South America.

3. The War of the Austrian Succession.

OCT. 1740.

a Death of the Emperor Charles VI.

1741.

b Attack by Frederick II. of Prussia upon Silesia, defeat of the Austrians at Molwitz, and Prussian invasion of Moravia. Rejection by Maria Theresa of Walpole's advice to cede Silesia, and thus engage Frederick on her side against her other enemies, Spain (claiming the Milanese), France (claiming the Netherlands), Bavaria (claiming Bohemia).

1741.

c British subsidy of £300,000 voted in support of the Pragmatic Sanction. APRIL. Alliance between France and Prussia. JUNE. Treaty of Neutrality signed by George II. guarding Hanover, to the indignation of the British.

1742.

Enthusiasm of the Hungarians for Maria Theresa. Successes against French and Bavarians. SPRING.

d Resignation of Walpole. JAN. 28. Succeeded, upon the refusal of Pulteney to take office, by Lord Wilmington (Compton) with Carteret as Foreign, and Newcastle as Home Secretary; others of Walpole's old colleagues remaining as ministers.

e Treaty of Breslau ceding Silesia to Frederick, and consequent withdrawal of the Prussian army from the war. JUNE. Expulsion of the French from Bohemia. Don Carlos in Naples forced to neutrality by the British fleet; the King of Sardinia won by British subsidy of £200,000.

1743. *f* Carteret's efforts to undo the French encroachments at the end of the Polish war (**1735**). Invasion of Bavaria by the Austrians; advance of George II. and the Earl of Stair to the Main, threatening an invasion of France. "The happy escape" of Dettingen.

JUNE. JUNE **27.** The French compelled however in consequence to evacuate Germany.

JULY. Death of Wilmington. JULY **2.** Henry Pelham, (brother of Newcastle) Prime Minister.

g Ambitious aims of Maria Theresa to seize Naples and transfer it from Don Carlos to the Bavarian Elector (now Emperor) in exchange for Bavaria. Attempted invasion of Great Britain by the French in the interest

1744. of the Pretender. JAN. Formal declaration of war between England and France. MARCH. Intervention of Frederick II. of Prussia on behalf of the Emperor. AUGUST. Defeat of Frederick and expulsion from Bohemia which he had invaded. Severe fighting in the south of Italy between the Austrians and Don Carlos, in the north between the King of Sardinia and the French and Spaniards.

h Carteret (now Lord Granville), forced to resign by the Pelhams who were alarmed at the extension of the war; succeeded as Secretary by Lord Harrington. NOV. **1744.** Tories

1745. for the first time since **1714** admitted to office. "The Broad Bottom Ministry."

i Defeat of the British, Hanoverians and Dutch by Marshal Saxe at Fontenoy. MAY **11.** Capture by the British of Cape Breton, commanding Gulf of St. Lawrence. JUNE.

j The Jacobite rebellion under the Young Pretender. JULY **1745**–APRIL **1746.** James VIII. (his father) proclaimed at Edinburgh. Jacobite victory at Prestonpans. SEPT. **21.** Southward march to Carlisle, NOV. **15**; to Derby, DEC. **4.** Commencement of retreat.

1746. DEC. **6.** Jacobite victory at Falkirk. JAN. **17, 1746.** Final defeat of the rising at Culloden. APRIL **16.** Barbarity of the Duke of Cumberland. The Highlands reduced to order

i. By the abolition of feudal tenures, and the transference to the Crown, for a money equivalent, of the hereditary jurisdictions of the chiefs.

ii. By the prohibition of wearing of the tartan.

iii. By a general Act of Indemnity.

1745. *k* The close of the Austrian war. Death of the Emperor Charles VII., Emperor and Elector of Bavaria. JAN. **18**. Peace between Austria and Bavaria. Election of the Duke of Lorraine, husband of Maria Theresa, as Emperor. SEPT. Peace of Dresden between Austria and Prussia ceding Silesia and Glatz to Prussia. French conquest of the Netherlands, **1745**, and of Holland, **1746**. Austrian successes in Italy. **1746**. British naval victories over the French off Cape Finisterre by Anson, MAY **3, 1746**; and off Belle Isle by Hawke. OCT. **14, 1747**. Capture of Madras by the French. **1746**.

1746.
1747.

1748. *l* The Peace of Aix la Chapelle.

i. France and England to restore conquests made in the war.

ii. France to abandon cause of the Stuarts, expel Pretender, demolish fortifications of Dunkirk towards sea.

iii. Austria to obtain recognition of Pragmatic Sanction, of election of Duke of Lorraine as Emperor, and restoration of lost possessions in Netherlands.

iv. Don Philip of Spain to obtain Duchies of Parma and Placentia.

v. Prussia guaranteed in the possession of Silesia and Glatz. OCT.

D Years of Peace. 1748-1754.

1. Reduction of military and naval forces. Foundation of Halifax in Nova Scotia. Assistance given by the Government to discharged soldiers and sailors willing to settle there.

2. Reduction of the rate of the interest on the National Debt from 4 to 3 per cent.

1751. 3. Reform of the Calendar by the adoption of the new style. (The year to begin JAN. **1** instead of MARCH **25**.)

1753. 4. Lord Hardwicke's Marriage Act—no marriage to be valid in England (Jewish and Quaker marriages excepted) except according to Anglican liturgy, after publication of banns for three consecutive Sundays in the Parish Church or by special license from the Archbishop.

1754. 5. Death of Henry Pelham. MARCH **6.** His brother (Duke of Newcastle) First Lord of the Treasury, Sir Thomas Robinson, Leader of the House of Commons.

E Colonial difficulties between France and England. 1747–1754.

1. In India.

a Attempt of Dupleix, Governor of Pondicherry, to make French influence supreme in Hyderabad and the Carnatic. **1747–1751.**

1751. *b* Capture and defence of Arcot by Clive.

1752–1753. *c* English victories under Lawrence and Clive leading to the destruction of French influence in Southern India. Recall and disgrace of Dupleix. **1754.**

2. In America.

a Rise of the English and French settlements in North America.

1499. i. Discovery of the Continent of North America by John Cabot. JUNE **24.**

1503. ii. Annual visits of Breton fishermen to Newfoundland (whence the name Cape Breton) from **1503.** Discovery of the St. Lawrence and French settlement along its banks.

1606–1608. iii. First successful attempt to make an English settlement in Virginia.

1620–1638. iv. Settlement of New Hampshire, Massachusetts, Connecticut, and Rhode Island by Puritan emigrants. Charter granted to Massachusetts. All four settlements united under the name "New England." **1643.**

1629.
1643.

1628–1634. v. Settlement of Maryland (called after Henrietta Maria) by Lord Baltimore. A Roman Catholic colony based on toleration.

1664–1667. vi. Foundation of the Carolinas. Transference of Dutch possessions to England (New York, New Jersey, Delaware).

1681-1682.　　vii. Quaker settlement of Pennsylvania.
1713.　　viii. The French settlement of Acadia (Nova Scotia) ceded to Great Britain. The British right established to Hudson's Bay and Newfoundland.
1739.　　ix. Settlement of Georgia.
1750-1754.　　x. Attempt of the French to connect their settlements of Canada and Louisiana by a chain of forts along the Ohio Valley. Erection of Forts Duquesne, Niagara, Ticonderoga, to cut off the British from the West. Defeat of the British attempt
1755.　　to capture Fort Duquesne, under General Braddock. JULY. Despatch of French fleet to the St. Lawrence. JUNE.

F **The Seven Years' War.**

1. Secret negotiations between France, Spain (still
1752-1754.　　adhering to family compact of 1733), Austria (anxious for the recovery of Silesia), Saxony, and Russia against Prussia.

2. Compact between Great Britain and Prussia for the neutrality of Prussia and Hanover in event of war between France and England. JAN. 1756. [Robinson succeeded by Fox as Secretary. 1755.]

3. Open alliance between Austria and France.
1756.　　MAY. Alarm in Great Britain as to possibility of French invasion.

4. The war in Europe till the end of 1760.

　　a Declaration of war. MAY 15. Loss of Minorca. JUNE 28. Prussian occupation of Dresden.
1756.　　AUG. [Resignation of Fox., OCT.; and of Newcastle, NOV. The Duke of Devonshire Prime Minister, Pitt, Secretary of State. DEC.]

　　b Two regiments raised by Pitt's advice from the Highland clans; execution of Admiral Byng
1757.　　for having caused the loss of Minorca. MARCH 14. [Dismissal of Devonshire and Pitt, APRIL.] Act for the Organisation of the National Militia, accompanied by discontent and riots. [Newcastle, Prime Minister, Pitt, Secretary for War, JUNE.] Frederick of Prussia defeated at Kolin and driven out of Bohemia. JUNE 18. Defeat of the Duke of Cumberland by the French at Hastenbeck, JULY 26, leading to an engagement to dis-

band the allied forces by the Convention of Closterseven. SEPT. **8**. (Ratification of the Convention refused by Pitt's advice, NOV.) Victories of Frederick of Prussia over the French at Rossbach, NOV. **5**, and over the Austrians at Leuthen. DEC. **5**. [See Public Schools Historical Atlas, 69, 70.]

1758.   *c* Annual subsidy of £700,000 engaged by Great Britain to Prussia. APRIL. Prussian victory over the Russians at Zorndorf. AUG. **25**. Defeat of the Prussians by the Austrians under Daun at Hochkirchen, OCT. **14**. Hostilities between the Hanoverian and British armies under Prince Ferdinand of Brunswick and the French.

1759.   *d* Prussian defeats by the Russians at Kunersdorf. AUG. **12**. Victory of the Hanoverians and British over the French at Minden. AUG. 1. [Public Schools Historical Atlas, 71.]

1760.   *e* Prussian re-occupation of Saxony by the victory of Torgau over the Austrians under Daun. NOV. **3**.

    5. The war between England and France at sea and in America.

1756.   *a* Continued French successes in America.

1757.   *b* Unsuccessful British Expedition against Rochefort.

1758.   *c* Siege and capture of Louisburg, and conquest of Cape Breton and St. John's. JULY. Capture of Fort Duquesne by the British and Colonists (Pittsburg). Failure of General Abercomby to take Ticonderoga. Capture of Goree, and Senegal.

1759.   *d* British capture of Ticonderoga, Fort Niagara, and of Quebec. SEPT. **17**. French projects for the invasion of England defeated by the bombardment of Havre by Rodney, JULY, by the victory of Boscawen over the Toulon Fleet at Lagos, by Hawke's blockade of Brest, and finally by Hawke's decisive victory over the French fleet in Quiberon Bay. NOV. **20**.

1760.   *e* Capture of Montreal by Amherst, and submission of Canada to the British.

    6. English conquests in India.

1756.   *a* Attack of Surajah Dowlah upon Calcutta and tragedy of the Black Hole. JUNE.

1757.   *b* British occupation of Calcutta. JAN. 2. Battle of Plassey. JUNE 23.

1758.   *c* Arrival of the French General Lally to recover lost French supremacy in Southern India. APRIL. French capture of Fort St. David. JUNE. Decisive and final defeat of the French under Lally by Eyre Coote at Wande-

1759.   wash. DEC. 22, 1759.

1761.   *d* British capture of Pondicherry   JAN. 16, 1761.

Death of the King. OCT. 25, 1760.

GEORGE III. = Charlotte of Mecklenburg-Strelitz.

GEORGE III. = CHARLOTTE OF MECKLENBURG.

George IV. = Caroline of Brunswick.   Frederick (Duke of York).   William IV. (Duke of Clarence).   Edward (Duke of Kent) = Victoria of Saxe-Coburg.

Charlotte = Leopold of Saxe-Coburg.   Victoria.

Ernest (King of Hanover).   Augustus (Duke of Sussex).   Adolphus (Duke of Cambridge).   Charlotte = King of Wurtemberg.   Augusta.

Elizabeth = Frederick of Hesse-Homburg.   Mary = Duke of Gloucester.   Sophia.   Amelia.

A   Events to the resignation of the Duke of Newcastle.

1760.
OCT. 25.
OCT. 28.

1. Succession of George III. Admission of John Stuart, Earl of Bute, to the Privy Council. The Royal Speech to the Council drawn up by the King and Bute without communication with the Cabinet.

2. Commissions of the Judges, upon the recommendation of the King, rendered independent of the demise of the Sovereign.

1761.
MARCH.
JUNE 7-11.

3. General Election and meeting of New Parliament. Appointment of Bute as Secretary of State. Capture of Belleisle by Admiral Keppel and General Hodgson.

4. "The Family Compact."

(*a*) Negotiations for peace with France. Spanish demands with reference to the restitution of ships bearing the Spanish flag, the fisheries upon the banks of Newfoundland, and the British settlements in the Bay of Honduras presented by the French. Rupture of the negotiations for peace.

Aug. 15. (*b*) Signature of the Family compact between France and Spain, involving close offensive and defensive alliance of the two branches of the House of Bourbon (as in 1733).

Sept. 18

Oct. 5.

(*c*) Information of the Compact conveyed to Pitt by Stanley, British negotiator at Paris. Pitt's proposed measures of retaliation: to withdraw British Ambassador from Madrid, to occupy Isthmus of Panama, to intercept the Spanish treasure ships, and attack Spanish dominions in America. Resignation of Pitt and Earl Temple on the rejection of these plans by the Cabinet. This action was partly due to the discontent of the ruling class with the popular support and confidence claimed by Pitt. Title of Baroness Chatham accepted by Pitt for his wife. [Marriage of the King, Sept. 1761.]

Dec. 10.
Dec. 31.

5. Avowal of the alliance between France and Spain. Recall of the British Ambassador from Madrid; declaration of war against Spain.

1762. Feb. 6. Capture of Martinico from the French, followed by that of Grenada, St. Lucia, St. Vincent, and of Havana.

May. 7. Resignation of the Duke of Newcastle upon Bute's determination to withdraw the British subsidy from Frederick of Prussia.

June 6.
Aug. 14.
Oct. 6.

8. Continued British successes. Siege and capture of Havana; surrender of Manilla and the Philippines to Sir W. Draper.

1765. Feb. 9. Conclusion of the seven years' war by the Treaty of Paris, the terms of which had been settled by the Duke of Bedford, British ambassador at Paris before the news of the capture of Havana and Manilla (Nov. 1762).

Spain to concede all points in dispute with Great Britain.

France and Great Britain to retire from the war in Germany.

In Europe: Minorca to be exchanged for Belleisle, and Dunkirk to be dismantled.

In America: Canada, Nova Scotia, Cape Breton, to be ceded to Great Britain, but France to retain right of fishing off Newfoundland and in the Gulf of St. Lawrence.

In the West Indies: Tobago, Dominica, St. Vincent, Grenada, to be retained by Great Britain; Guadaloupe, Martinico, St. Lucia, to be restored.

In Africa: Senegal to be retained by Great Britain, and Goree restored to France.

In India: the French Military Establishment to be given up.

In exchange for Havana, Florida to be surrendered by Spain to Great Britain.

Manilla restored to Spain without equivalent.

10. Dissatisfaction with the Peace, in spite of the bribery and intimidation practised by Bute and Henry Fox.

APRIL 8. Resignation of Bute. Elevation of Fox to Peerage as Lord Holland.

[Notice.—Bute's policy with regard to the American colonies as represented by Charles Townshend, President of the Board of Trade:

i. Despatch of a British fleet to insist upon the execution of the Navigation Laws and to stop clandestine trade between the Colonies and the Spanish islands.

ii. Proposal to increase the revenue from the Colonies by a Stamp Tax.

iii. Establishment of ten thousand British troops quartered on the colonists at the conclusion of the war, and proposals entertained for converting the district round the lakes of St. Lawrence into a military settlement.

iv. Proposal to make all the public officers in the Colonies dependent on the Crown, and thus to remodel the colonial governments.]

B The Grenville Ministry. April 1763–July 1765.

April 23. **1.** Appearance of "Number 45" of the *North Briton* attacking the Royal Speech at the close of the last session. Issue of a general warrant of arrest by Lord Halifax; arrest of Kearsey the publisher, and Balfe the printer of "Number 45," and upon their information of Wilkes.

April 30–May 2. Imprisonment of Wilkes in the Tower upon his refusal to answer interrogatories till released upon Habeas Corpus as a Member of the House of Commons. Action brought by Wilkes and printers against the messengers:

July. condemnation of general warrants of arrest by Lord Chief Justice Pratt.

Aug. **2.** Conflict of opinion and temper between the King and Grenville; appeal of the King by means of Bute to Pitt to form a ministry; Pitt's proposal to reinstate the Cabinet of 1761, with the exception of Bedford, rejected by the King. Consequent triumph of Grenville and retirement of Bute from political activity. Resignation of Shelburne, and addition of Bedford to the Ministry.

Nov. 15. **3.** Continued action against Wilkes.

(*a*) Wilkes denied his privilege by the House of Commons; "Number 45" ordered to be burned as a "false, scandalous, and malicious libel." The "Essay on Woman" voted a breach of privilege by the Lords, on the ground of the notes being attributed to Bishop Warburton, and ordered to be burned along with the paraphrase of the "Veni Creator" as "scandalous, obscene, and impious."

Nov. 16. Wilkes wounded in a duel with Mr. Martin, a member of the House of Commons.

Dec. (*b*) Wilkes' action against the Under Secretary of State. Verdict given for Wilkes with damages of £1,000. Withdrawal of Wilkes to Paris.

1764. Jan. (*c*) Expulsion of Wilkes from the House of Commons, Jan. **19.** Condemnation of Wilkes by the Court of King's Bench for reprinting "Number 45" and for printing the "Essay on Woman."

Feb. Upon his non-appearance sentence of outlawry pronounced against him.

4. Unconstitutional action of Grenville and the King in dismissing political opponents—Earl Temple, Lord Shelburne, General Conway, Colonel Barré—from civil and military commissions.

5. Grenville and America.

(i) Grenville's policy towards America.

(*a*) To enforce strictly the trade laws which had fallen into disuse.

(*b*) To establish a portion of the British army in the Colonies—rendered apparently necessary by the irruption of the Ottawa Indians under Pontiac into the Ohio valley that for a time threatened the forts of Detroit and Fort Pitt. **1763.**

(*c*) To raise by parliamentary taxation of the Colonies part of the funds necessary for the support of this force.

(*d*) On the other hand no attempt made to carry out Bute's and Townshend's scheme of remodelling the colonial constitutions.

MARCH. (ii) Bill modifying the existing Trade laws but providing for the stricter execution of those retained, accompanied with the proposal of a Stamp Tax—all legal documents to bear stamps varying in price from 3*d*. to £10. Petition of the Assembly of Virginia and of New York against Parliamentary taxation ; resistance threatened by Massachusetts, Rhode Island, North Carolina. Remonstrance from the assembly of Pennsylvania presented by their agent Benjamin Franklin.

1765. FEB. (iii) The Stamp Act passed, in spite of this opposition, almost unanimously.

APRIL. 6. Illness of the King. Introduction upon his recovery of a Regency Bill limiting the right of becoming regent to the Queen and the descendants of the late King, then residing in England. The name of the Princess Dowager, thus excluded by the Bill, added by the Commons. Vexation of the King with his advisers.

S

MAY.   7. Negotiations of the King with Pitt, through the Duke of Cumberland, offering him power on his own terms—the return of the Ministry of 1761, the abolition of general warrants, and a Protestant system of German alliances to check the power of the House of Bourbon. Failure of the negotiations owing to the refusal of Earl Temple—Pitt's chief parliamentary supporter—to co-operate. Renewal of the negotiations in June without effect.

MAY 15.   8. Riot of the Spitalfields' silk-weavers upon the rejection by the Lords of a Bill for the protection of their trade. Attack upon the Duke of Bedford and Bedford House.

JULY.   9. Negotiations of Cumberland with the old Whig leaders: return of the main body of the Whigs to office under Lord Rockingham.

C The Rockingham Ministry. JULY 1765—JULY 1766.

MAY.

MAY—JUNE.

OCT.
1. Continued opposition in America. Proposal of five resolutions in the Assembly of Virginia by Patrick Henry, declaring that the Colonies could not be taxed without their own consent. Proposal of Massachusetts to convoke Congress of delegates from all the assemblies. Meeting of Congress of deputies from nine of the Colonies expressing allegiance to the Crown, subordination to the Parliament of Great Britain, but claiming as "inseparably essential to the freedom of a people and the undoubted right of Englishman that no taxes be imposed on them but with their own consent."

DEC.

766. FEB.

MARCH 18.
2. Meeting of Parliament. Firm attitude of Pitt in justification of the American resistance. Passing of a Declaratory Act maintaining the authority of Parliament to make laws for the Colonies "in all cases whatsoever," including imposition of taxes, followed by introduction of a Bill for the Repeal of the Stamp Act.

APRIL.   3. General warrants, already condemned by Lord Mansfield in the Court of King's Bench, declared illegal by resolution of the House of Commons.

JULY.   4. Resignation of Rockingham: his Ministry having been constantly undermined by the influence of the "King's friends."

ANALYSIS OF ENGLISH HISTORY. 259

D **The Grafton Ministry.** JULY 1766—JUNE 1770.

    1. Return of Pitt to power in defiance of party connexion. The Ministry composite, including, as well as Pitt and his supporters, the Duke of Grafton, Lord Shelburne, Lord Camden, Conway and Barré, and two great supporters of Colonial taxation Lord North and Charles Townshend.

JULY.   2. Pitt's sudden loss of popularity on his elevation to the peerage as Lord Chatham. Proposed alliance of England, Prussia, and Russia rejected by Frederick. Motion for inquiry into the affairs of the East India Company preliminary to a proposal for transferring their territories to the jurisdiction of the Crown.

NOV.
1767.

MARCH.   3. Illness of Chatham, lasting till OCT. 1769.
MAY 13.   Townshend's Colonial policy.

    (*a*) Suspension of the Assembly of New York for refusal to support British troops according to Mutiny Act.

    (*b*) Appointment of Board of Commissioners to superintend the execution of the Trade Laws.

    (*c*) Imposition of import duties upon glass, red and white lead, painters' colours, paper, and tea imported into the Colonies, in ·order to furnish Civil List for payment of governors and judges in the Colonies and a fund for the protection of the Colonies in war.

[Death of Townsend from fever SEPT. **4.**]

    4. Reconstruction of the Ministry by the retirement of Conway, the admission of the Duke of Bedford's friends, and the appointment of Lord Hillsborough as Secretary for the Colonies.

1768. FEB.   5. General Election. Wilkes returned for Middlesex. Wilkes released from his sentence of outlawry, but condemned for his original offence to imprisonment for twenty-two calendar months. His appeal to the House of Commons, accusing Lord Mansfield of having altered the record on his trial, and claiming his privilege against further imprisonment, rejected (NOV.). Expulsion from the House for having published a letter from Lord Weymouth to the magistrates of Surrey prefaced
1769.   by observations of his own. (FEB. **1769.**) Re-

elected for Middlesex, but declared incapable of being returned, once expelled, to the same Parliament. Again returned without opposition, and the election declared void. Returned for a third time over his Court opponent, Colonel Luttrell, but Luttrell declared elected in spite of the pleading of Wedderburn, Burke, and Grenville. (MAY **1769**.) Wilkes elected an alderman of the City of London.

1767-1768. 6. Circular of the Assembly of Massachusetts to the other Colonies to obtain the repeal of the Acts of 1767. Dissolution of the Assembly by Lord Hillsborough upon its refusal to recall the circular; similar dissolution of the Assemblies of Virginia, Maryland, Georgia, North Carolina,
1768. OCT. 1. New York. Despatch of two British regiments and seven ships of the line to Boston.

7. Domestic difficulties of the Government.
   (*a*) Resignation of Chatham. OCT. **1768**.
   (*b*) Purchase of Corsica from Genoa by France in spite of remonstrance from British Ambassador. **1768**.
   (*c*) Expulsion of the British from the Falkland Islands by Spain. **1769**.
   (*d*) Appearance of the letters of Junius to the Duke of Grafton, the Duke of Bedford, the King, Lord Mansfield, Lord North. NOV. **21, 1768**—JAN. **21, 1772**.
   (*e*) Opposition of Conway and Camden to the rest of the Ministry.

8. Reappearance of Chatham in the House of Lords, and changes in the Ministry.
1770. Attack of Camden on the conduct of the Government and dismissal from office. Resignation
JAN. 17. of the Commander-in-Chief, Lord Granby, and
JAN. 28. of the Duke of Grafton, the Prime Minister. Grafton succeeded by Lord North.

E Lord North's Ministry and the American War of Independence.

1770. 1. Attempts of Chatham, Rockingham, and others to obtain from Parliament a condemnation of the proceedings against Wilkes. JAN. **1770**–APRIL **1771**. Petition of the City for the dissolution of Parliament. Condemnation of the King's reply by Chatham as dangerous to the right of free-petitioning.

MARCH 5 2. Collision between the soldiers and people at
MAY 1.   Boston, commonly called "the Boston Massacre." Repeal by the Parliament, on the suggestion of Lord North, of all the import duties to the Colonies except 3*d.* in the pound on tea. Circular of Lord Hillsborough pledging the British Government to raise no further Colonial revenue; the Quartering Clause of the Mutiny Act not re-enacted, and the British troops recalled from Boston.

MAY 14. 3. Chatham's motion for parliamentary reform that a third member be added to every county. (A similar but more comprehensive scheme proposed by Wilkes, **1776**.)

1771.   4. Contest of the House of Commons with the
FEB. 8-MARCH 12. printers and establishment of freedom of reporting. Complaints of Col. Onslow against Thompson, Wheble, and six others for misrepresenting speeches, and reflecting on Members of the House. Refusal of Wheble and Thompson to attend; issue of warrants
MARCH 14. for their apprehension. Wheble taken before Alderman Wilkes, Thompson before Alderman Oliver, and both discharged. The Messenger
MARCH 15. of the House committed by the City magistrates. The Lord Mayor and Alderman Oliver heard in their places in the House and com-
MARCH 25. mitted to the Tower, till set free by Prorogation
MAY 8.   of Parliament. Publication of debates thenceforth permitted, though still asserted to be a breach of privilege.

1772.   5. The Royal Marriage Bill to prohibit members of the Royal Family marrying before the age of twenty-five without the King's consent under the Great Seal, and after twenty-five without a year's notice to the Privy Council and assent of Parliament.

6. Renewal of the contest with the American Colonies.

1772.   (*a*) Pecuniary difficulties of the East India Company, owing to the war with Hyder Ali of Mysore and Nizam Ali of Hyderabad (**1767-1769**), and to the famine in Bengal (**1770**). Permission given by Parliament to the Company to export teas to the American colonies free from English duties, and subject only to the duty payable by the Colonies.

1773.
Dec. 16.
 (*b*) Arrival of three tea-ships at Boston. The cargo—340 chests of tea—seized and emptied into the harbour. Other tea-ships refused admittance at New York and Philadelphia; the cargo of a tea-ship confiscated at Charleston.

1774.
 (*c*) Measures of the British Government against Boston.
  (i.) The harbour at Boston closed till compensation should be given to the East India Company, and satisfaction of future good conduct to the Crown (to come into operation June 1).
  (ii.) The Charter of Massachusetts remodelled. The Council to be appointed by the Crown, and the judicial officers by the royal governor.
  (iii.) Persons accused of murder or other capital offence to be sent for trial, at discretion of Governor, to Nova Scotia or to Great Britain.
  (iv.) General Gage appointed Governor of Massachusetts, and British troops quartered in Boston.
  [Here may be mentioned the Quebec Act, maintaining the French law and virtually establishing the Roman Catholic form of worship in Canada. (In order to secure the loyalty of the French Canadians in case of a struggle with the colonies.)]

Sept. 5.
 (*d*) Meeting at Philadelphia of Congress of Deputies from all the colonies except Georgia.
  (i.) The right of Parliament to tax the Colonies denied, while its right to general legislative authority was admitted.
  (ii.) The colonies pledged to have no commercial dealings with Great Britain after Dec. 1.
  (iii.) A petition addressed to the King, and a memorial to the British people.
  (iv.) An address published to the people of Quebec, warning them against the despotic authority claimed by Great Britain.

 (*e*) Proceedings in the British Parliament.

1775. Feb. 1.
 (i.) Chatham's scheme of conciliation, providing for the removal of British troops from Boston, it being illegal to send troops to the Colonies without the assent of the

colonial assemblies; for the abandonment of the claim of taxation, provided that the "supreme legislative authority and superintending power of the Parliament of Great Britain" was acknowledged; for the suspension of the late Acts, and for the confirmation of the security of the colonial charters. Colonial contributions towards the public debt to be referred to a colonial assembly. The scheme rejected by the Lords without discussion.

1775. (ii.) Lord North's proposals.
FEB. 3. (*a*) Measures of coercion; the British force in Boston to be raised to 10,000. The New England States (and afterwards Pennsylvania, New Jersey, Maryland, Virginia, South Carolina) to be excluded from trade with Great Britain, Ireland, the West Indies, and from the Newfoundland fisheries. Massachusetts declared in a state of rebellion.

FEB. 20. (*b*) Measure of conciliation. That any colony voting a contribution for imperial purposes, satisfactory to the British Parliament, be exempted from all imperial taxation for the purpose of revenue. Carried after opposition.

MARCH 22. (iii.) Burke's proposal in the Commons: To repeal the recent Acts, and leave colonial taxation to the colonial assemblies. Rejected.

MAY 15. (iv.) Remonstrance of the Legislature of New York presented by Burke, disclaiming "the most distant desire of independence"; acknowledging the superintending power of the British Parliament; expressing readiness to contribute " full proportion of aids to the Crown for public service"; asserting, however, the sole right of the Colonies to tax themselves, and protesting against the recent Acts. Refusal of the House to receive it.

[To these may be added a petition from the City of London to the King as to the injury to trade resulting from the colonial policy. APRIL **10.**]

7. The war with the Colonies.

1775, Attempt of General Gage, Governor of Boston,
FEB. to seize cannon and ammunition at Salem.

April 19.	Skirmish at Lexington, and struggle at Concord.
May 10.	Seizure of Ticonderoga, on Lake Champlain, by a force of New Englanders under Ethan Allen, and of Crown Point.
May.	Meeting of Congress at Philadelphia.
	(*a*) Committees appointed to draw up petition to the King and remonstrance to the people of Great Britain.
	(*b*) The force raised by Massachusetts recognized as the Colonial or Continental Army, and raised to 15,000 men.
	(*c*) The Colonies advised to call out their militia; money coined and loan raised in the common name of the Colonies.
	(*d*) Washington appointed as Commander-in-Chief.
June 17.	Battle of Bunker's Hill or Braid's Hill.
	Attack on Canada under Richard Montgomery.
Nov.	Capture of St. John's and Montreal. Defeat
Dec. 31.	and death of Montgomery before Quebec.
	Home events affecting the Colonies, **1775**.
August.	(*a*) Arrival of Penn with the petition of Congress (called the Olive Branch Petition); the petition rejected with indifference by King and Ministers.
Oct.	(*b*) Resignation of Grafton, who had accepted Privy Seal without a seat in the Cabinet after the death of Lord Halifax in 1771.
	(*c*) German troops hired to serve in America.
1776. Jan. 1.	Destruction of Norfolk, the wealthiest town in Virginia, by the British.
March 4.	Attack of Washington on Boston, and evacua-
March 16.	tion of Boston by the British.
March.	Outbreak of hostilities in North Carolina.
	Gradual formation of Independent State go-
Autumn, **1775**—	vernments in New Hampshire, South Caro-
May, **1776**.	lina, Rhode Island, and Virginia.
July 4.	The Declaration of Independence, based upon Declaration of Rights issued by Virginia in May.
	(i) Assertion of the original rights of man, as to life, liberty, pursuit of happiness.
	(ii) Enumeration of "injuries and usurpations having in direct object the establishment of absolute tyranny."

	(iii) Declaration that these united Colonies "are and of right ought to be free and independent States," with full power to levy war, make peace, and contract alliances. [The Articles of Confederation were settled by Congress in 1777, but not finally signed till March, 1781.]
JUNE 28.	Unsuccessful attempt of Admiral Parker and General Clinton on Charleston.
AUGUST 27. SEPT. 15.	British victory, and evacuation of Long Island by the continental forces. British occupation of New York. (The dilatory action of Sir W. Howe, the British Commander, possibly due to his desire for conciliation shown by his consenting to meet commissioners from Congress.)
SEPT.	Enlistment by Congress of 88 battalions, of 750 men each, to serve for the duration of the war, the engagement of most of the present troops closing with the end of the year.
NOV.—DEC.	Retreat of Washington behind the Delaware into Pennsylvania.
	Removal of the Congress from Philadelphia to Baltimore.
DEC.	Occupation of Rhode Island by Parker and Clinton.
DEC. 25.	Crossing of the Delaware by Washington, and surprise of a German detachment of the British army at Trenton.
1777.	Recovery by Washington of New Jersey, *i.e.* the country between the Delaware and Hudson, except Brunswick and Ambry.
SEPT. 11.	British victory by Howe at Brandywine Creek, and British occupation of Philadelphia.
OCT. 4.	Repulse of Washington's attack upon the British position at Germanstown on the Schuykill covering Philadelphia.
	Washington in winter quarters at Valley Forge, twenty miles from Philadelphia.
	Meanwhile, a movement in combination with Clinton from New York was made from Canada by Burgoyne to seize the Hudson
JUNE.	Valley, and cut off New England from the rest of the Colonies. Capture of Ticonderoga.

AUG. 16.	Burgoyne checked at Bennington.
SEPT. 19.	Burgoyne again checked at Stillwater.
OCT.	Capture by Clinton of Forts Clinton and Montgomery.
OCT. 17.	Capitulation of Burgoyne at Saratoga. The Convention of Saratoga.
1778. JAN.	Howe recalled at his own request. Succeeded in chief command by Clinton.
FEB.	Offensive and defensive alliance between the Colonies and France.
	(Proceedings in the British Parliament affecting the Colonies.
	(*a*) Re-appearance of Chatham. His remonstrance against the employment of Indians in warfare.
FEB.	(*b*) Lord North's measures.
	(i) No direct tax to be imposed on the Colonies.
	(ii) Five Commissioners to be sent out with full powers to suspend all Acts passed since 1763.
	(*c*) Chatham's last appearance in the Lords.
APRIL 7.	His death, MAY 11.)
JUNE.	Abandonment of Philadelphia by the British, and concentration at New York to meet
AUG.	French invasion. Unsuccessful attack of the French and Colonists on Rhode Island.
JULY.	Indecisive action between English and French fleets off Ushant.
NOV.—DEC.	Capture of Savannah for the British by Colonel Campbell, and reduction of Georgia.
DEC.	(Acceptance by the King of the resignation of Lord Barrington, Secretary of War, who had for long been opposed to the war.)
1779. JUNE.	Union of Spain with France against England. Siege of Gibraltar, **1779-1783**.
SEPT.	Continued British successes in the south. Failure of the French and Colonists to recover Savannah.
	Defeat and almost complete destruction of the Massachusetts fleet in Penobscot Bay.
1780. JAN. 16.	Battle of St. Vincent: provisions and supplies safely convoyed to Gibraltar by Rodney.
MAY 11.	British capture of Charleston.
JUNE.	Attempt of the Spanish to destroy English squadron at Gibraltar by fire ships.

JULY 10.	Arrival of French fleet and force of 6,000 men at Newport.
SEPT.	Treasonable attempt of the Colonial General Arnold to surrender Westport to the British. Negotiations with him carried on by means of Major André. André captured by the Americans in disguise and hung as a spy. Escape of Arnold to the British.
OCT. 2.	
DEC.	Declaration of war by Great Britain against Holland.
	(Notice in this year the desolation of the Carnatic by Hyder Ali of Mysore, who had allied himself with the French, the Nizam of Hyderabad, and the Mahrattas.)
1781. JAN.	Mutiny of Colonial troops in Pennsylvania owing to arrears of pay, and afterwards in New Jersey.
FEB.	British capture of St. Eustatius from Holland, and confiscation of all the property of the island to the Crown.
MARCH 1.	The Articles of Confederation between the Colonies, settled by Congress 1777, finally signed.
	Proposed march of Lord Cornwallis through North Carolina and Virginia to effect junction with Clinton.
MARCH 15.	Battle of Guildford.
AUG. 1.	Fortification of York Town by Cornwallis, Clinton being compelled to remain at New York to resist probable attack from French invading force.
AUG. 30.	Arrival of French fleet under De Grasse, not, as expected, at New York, but in Chesapeake Bay.
SEPT.	March of Colonial and French forces into Virginia to attack Cornwallis.
SEPT. 8.	Engagement at Entaw Springs, near Charleston, between the Colonial General Greene and Colonel Stewart. Victory of the British, but with such loss that they could not protect South Carolina and Georgia from Greene's ravages.
OCT. 17.	Surrender of Lord Cornwallis at York Town.
	[Notice in this year the great bombardment of Gibraltar by the Spanish for six weeks after it had been again relieved by Darby; the French attack upon Jersey; and the defeats of Hyder Ali at Porto Novo, July 1, and at Pollilore, AUG. 27.]

Dec.	Recapture of St. Eustatius by French fleet and Irish brigade.
1782. Jan. Feb.	French capture of Demerara, Essequibo, and loss of all British possessions in the West Indies except Jamaica, Barbadoes, and Antigua.
	Surrender of Minorca to French and Spanish fleet.
March 20.	Resignation of Lord North. Succession of Lord Rockingham as Premier. Clinton superseded in command by Sir Guy Carleton to carry on measures of conciliation.
April 12.	Victory of Rodney over De Grasse between Guadeloupe and Dominique, and annihilation of the French fleet.
May 24.	Death of Lord Rockingham. Succession of Lord Shelburne as Prime Minister.
Sept. 13. Oct.	Failure of the last grand attack on Gibraltar. Third relief of the fortress by Lord Howe.
Nov. 30.	Preliminary articles of peace between Great Britain and the Colonies signed; assented to by the King Dec. 5.
1783. Jan. 20.	Preliminary articles of peace between Great Britain, France, and Spain.

The Peace.

(a) The Independence of the Colonies acknowledged, and the right of the Newfoundland and St. Lawrence Fisheries conceded; the Colonists dropping claims to Canada, Nova Scotia, New Brunswick, Newfoundland, Hudson's Bay.

(b) The islands of St. Pierre and Miquelon near the fisheries of Newfoundland, St. Lucia and Tobago in the West Indies, Senegal in Africa, establishments in Orissa, Bengal, Pondicherry, Carical, Fort Mahé on the Malabar coast, and Surat, restored or ceded to *France*, and the demand for the demolition of the fortress of Dunkirk dropped.

(c) Florida and Minorca ceded to *Spain*, but Gibraltar retained by Great Britain, and the Bahamas restored, and the disputed right of cutting log-wood in Honduras Bay ceded.

F Domestic Affairs during the American War.

1778. 1. The Catholic Relief Act of Sir George Savile and Dunning repealing perpetual imprisonment of priests for celebrating mass, forfeiture of estates in the case of Catholic heirs educated abroad, prohibition to acquire land by purchase. Followed by

1778.   (*a*) Riots and "Protestant associations" in Scotland.

1780.   (*b*) The "No Popery riots" under Lord George Gordon in London. Meeting at Coachmakers' Hall for the repeal of the Relief Act. MAY 29. Houses of Parliament invested by the mob. JUNE 2. Destruction worked by the mob (the Bank threatened, Lord Mansfield's Library burned, JUNE 2–JUNE 7) till stopped by the prompt action of the King. Twenty-one of the rioters executed.

1779-1780. 2. Public meetings of the freeholders of Yorkshire and other counties to discuss measures of reform, economical and parliamentary.

        3. Growing dissatisfaction with the undue influence of the Crown and of the "King's friends" in Parliament.

1780.   (*a*) Dunning's resolution passed by the Commons, "That it is necessary to declare that the influence of the Crown has increased, is increasing, and ought to be diminished."

1781.   (*b*) Complaints of the undue influence of the Crown made in the Lords by Shelburne and Rockingham.

1782.   (*c*) Civil List Act abolishing useless offices and restraining use of secret service, introduced by Rockingham.

1782. 4. Rejection of Pitt's motion for a committee of inquiry into the necessity of Parliamentary reform.

G The Coalition Ministry.

JULY **1782.**   (*a*) Fall of the Shelburne Ministry. Resignation by Fox of the Secretaryship of State, followed by that of Keppel, Lord Carlisle, the Duke of Grafton.

1783.

FEB.   (*b*) Coalition of Fox and Lord North to make a united and independent administration formed under the Duke of Portland, and including Fox, North, Keppel, Carlisle, Burke. Refusal of Pitt to join the Coalition.

APRIL.

      (*c*) Rejection of Pitt's resolutions for reform.
1783.   i. Recommending measures to prevent bribery.
May.   ii. Disenfranchising corrupt boroughs.
      iii. Increasing the number of county members and members for Metropolis.
     (*d*) Fox's India Bill.
      i. A Supreme Council to regulate political affairs to be appointed in England of seven commissioners named by the Legislature and irremovable for four years except upon address from either House. After four years the commissioners to be named by the King; the King also from the beginning to nominate to any vacancies.
      ii. A subordinate Council to be chosen by Parliament from among the largest proprietors to regulate commerce.
     (*e*) The India Bill passed by the Commons. The King's assurance conveyed by Lord Temple "that whoever voted for the India Bill was
Dec. 11.   'not only not his friend, but would be considered by him as an enemy." The Bill
Dec. 17.   rejected by the Lords. The Ministry dismissed by the King. Dec. **18**.

[H Summary of the History of the East India Company and of the British in India.

     1. Charter granted by Queen Elizabeth to the Governor
1600.   and Company of the Merchants of London trading into the East Indies. The Charter made perpetual,
1609.   unless national detriment be at any time found to ensue.
1623. 2. Massacre of English sailors by the Dutch at Amboyna, in the Moluccas; English adventure checked in the direction of the Indian Archipelago.
1640-1642. 3. Foundation of Fort St. George, Madras; cession
1661.   of Bombay to the Crown by Portugal on the marriage of Charles II., and by the Crown trans-
1698.   ferred to the Company. Fort William (Calcutta) erected on land rented from the Great Mogul. Fort St. David erected on land purchased near Madras. Establishment of a rival company
1698.   "The General East India Company." Union of the two companies. **1708**.
     4. Death of Aurungzebe and break-up of the Mogul
1707.   power.

ANALYSIS OF ENGLISH HISTORY. 271

1744-1754. 5. First stage of the struggle between Great Britain and France.

(a) The two great French presidencies Isle de France and Pondicherry. Isle de France under command of La Bourdonnais, Pondicherry under that of Dupleix. Capitulation
1746. of Madras to La Bourdonnais to be restored on payment of £440,000. Claimed by Dupleix as a French conquest, but surrendered by
1748. treaty of Aix-la-Chapelle.

(b) Scheme of Dupleix to make French influence supreme in Southern India, by establishing Mirzapha Jung as Nizam of the Dekkan, and Chunda Sahib as Nawab of the Carnatic. Success by Dupleix in the Dekkan and found-
1750-1751. ation of the city "Dupleix Fatihabad." Success of the French candidate in the
1751-1752. Carnatic; capture and defence of Arcot by Robert Clive; destruction of Dupleix Fatihabad. Pacification with France; the British
1754. candidate, Mahomed Ali, recognised as Nawab of the Carnatic.

1755. Nov. 6. Arrival of Clive in India, as Governor of Fort St. David.

(a) Attack of Surajah Dowlah, Nawab of Bengal,
1756. upon Calcutta; 146 British confined in the
June 20. Black Hole.

(b) Arrival of Clive and Admiral Watson at Calcutta; alliance favourable to the Company
1757. Feb. concluded with the Nawab. Intrigues of
June 23. the Nawab with the French. Battle of Plassey; Meer Jaffier created by Clive Nawab of Bengal, Orissa, and Bahar.

(c) Subjugation of the Northern Circars; capture
1758-1759. of Masulipatam; successful hostilities against the Dutch at Chinsurah.

(d) Second stage of the struggle between Great Britain and France for supremacy in Southern India. Capture and destruction of Fort St.
1758. June 2. David by Lally Tollendal. Siege of Madras
1759. Feb. 16. (Dec.) by Lally: Madras relieved by Admiral
1760. Jan. 22. Pocock. Decisive defeat of Lally by Eyre
1761. Jan. 16. Coote at Wandewash; surrender of Pondicherry, and fall of the French power in India.

1760-1765. 7. Return of Clive to England, and events during his absence.

		(a) Massacre of British traders at Patna by Meer

1763. OCT. 5.   (a) Massacre of British traders at Patna by Meer Cossim, son-in-law of Meer Jaffier, and appointed by the Company as Nawab in his place. Mutiny of the Company's sepoys crushed by Hector Munro; victory of Buxar

1764. OCT. 23.   by Munro over Meer Cossim and Sujah Dowlah, Vizier of Oudh. Shah Allum, the Great Mogul, under the protection of the Company.

    (b) Misery in Bengal caused by the greed and despotism of the Company's servants; clamour among the Proprietors for high dividends, and bitter struggles at the India House, principally between Sulivan and Lord Clive. Final victory of Clive's party.

1765–1767. 8. Last return of Clive to India. His measures of reform.

    (a) Oudh restored to Sujah Dowlah, as Nawab Vizier, except Kora and Allahabad which were reserved for the Emperor Shah Allum. Sole right of financial administration in Bengal, Orissa, Behar, granted to the Company by the Emperor, as well as territorial jurisdiction over the Northern Circars. Mahomet Reza Khan appointed by Clive as director of the revenue department, resident at Moorshedabad, but responsible at Calcutta.

    (b) Dealings of Clive with the civil servants of the Company. Private trade and acceptance of presents from native princes prohibited; salaries, on the other hand, increased out of the salt monopoly.

    (c) Mutiny among the Company's soldiers (in consequence of the abolition of Double Batta, *i.e.*, the double allowance granted by Meer Jaffier after Plassey) crushed by Clive.

1767. JAN.   Final return of Clive to England.

    9. Disorder in finances of the Company, produced by

1767–1769.   (a) The attack of Hyder Ali, Sultan of Mysore, on the Carnatic and Madras.

1770.   (b) The great famine in Bengal.

Loan of a million asked from the Government by the Company. Appointment of two Committees of the House, resulting in the Regulating Act of

1773.   Lord North.

    i. A Loan of £1,500,000 granted to the Company for four years.

ANALYSIS OF ENGLISH HISTORY.

ii. No dividend to exceed 6 per cent. till repayment of loan, nor 8 per cent. while profits were confined to the Company.

iii. The Government of Bengal to be supreme over the other Presidencies, and to be vested in a Governor-General and four councillors, the Governor to have a casting vote in case of equality. Warren Hastings nominated by Parliament as the Governor; Barwell, Clavering, Monson, Francis, as the Council. The term of office to be five years; the Governor and Council to be irremovable except by the Crown upon address from the Court of Directors; future appointments to be made by the Court of Directors subject to the approbation of the Crown.

iv. Supreme Court of Justice constituted at Calcutta, consisting of a Chief Justice and three Puisne Judges appointed by the Crown but paid by the Company.

v. The Court of Directors to be elected for four years only, one fourth—*i.e.* 6—retiring annually; the qualification for a vote raised from the possession of £500 to £1,000 stock, with more votes in proportion up to four.

vi. All proceedings of the Company, military, political, financial, to be laid before one of the Secretaries of State.

1773. Vote of censure moved upon Clive; passed in part with the addition "that Robert Lord Clive did at the same time render great and meritorious services to his country."

1774. Nov. Suicide of Clive.

10. Warren Hastings.

1772. (*a*) Hastings as Governor of Bengal.
Arrest and trial of Mahomed Reza Khan, and transference of the financial department from Moorshedabad to Calcutta. Reduction by one-half of the allowance paid to the Nawab of Bengal (£32,000 to £16,000).

1773. Resumption of the districts of Kora and Allahabad from the Emperor Shah Allum and cession to the Nawab Vizier of Oudh for the payment of fifty lakhs of rupees (£500,000). Company's troops lent to the Vizier of Oudh

1774. for the annexation of Rohilchund on payment of forty lakhs of rupees (£400,000).

T

(b) Hastings as Governor-General of India.
  i. Differences between Hastings and his Council. Accusation brought by Rajah Nuncomar against Hastings of having received a bribe to acquit Mahomet Reza Khan. Arrest of Nuncomar on the charge of having forged a bond; his condemnation by the Supreme Court. Rajah Nuncomar hanged.

1775. AUG. 5.

  ii. Indignation of Lord North at the iniquity of the Rohilla war. Presentation by Col. Maclean of a letter of resignation left by Hastings. The resignation declared invalid by the Supreme Court at Calcutta. Death of Monson (SEPT. **1776**), and of Clavering (AUG. **1777**). Consequent diminution of opposition in the Council.

1776. OCT.
1777.

  iii. The First Mahratta war. (The great Mahratta chiefs—the Peishwa at Poonah; Scindia at Gwalior; Holkar at Indore; the Guicowar of Guzerat at Baroda; the Rajah of Berar, at Nagpore. In addition to these was the Rajah of Satara, the lineal descendant of Sivaji, whose power was at this time nominal.)

Differences between the Bombay presidency and the Mahratta confederacy owing to the shelter given to Rao Ragoba a deposed and exiled Peishwa. Intrigues of the Mahrattas with the French. News of the declaration of war between Great Britain and France. Capture of Pondicherry from the French by Hector Munro.

1778.

Capitulation of a British force to the Mahrattas at Wurgaum near Poonah. Despatch by Hastings of Goddard with a force from Bengal.

1780. APRIL. 14.
1780.

Defeat of the forces of Scindia and Holkar by Goddard. Capture of Gwalior, the great fortress of Scindia, by Popham. Negotiations for peace begun, but not concluded till **1782**.

  iv. Resumption of war in the south by Hyder Ali.

1780. SEPT. 10.

Defeat of Baillie by Hyder Ali, and retreat of Munro. Capture of Arcot by Hyder Ali. Suspension by Hastings of the Governor of Madras, and despatch of Sir Eyre Coote from Bengal.

1781. JULY 1.
AUG. 27.

Victories of Coote at Porto Novo and Pollilore.

	v. Financial dealings of Hastings to raise money for these war expenses.
	(a) With Cheyte Sing. Demand made upon Cheyte Sing, as tributary to the Company, for Five Lakhs of Rupees (£50,000) for the expenses of the
1778.	Mahratta War. Delay of Cheyte Sing; private present by him to Hastings of two Lakhs, transferred afterwards by Hastings to the Company. Visit of
1781. AUG. 21.	Hastings to Benares to extort the amount which the Rajah had been eventually fined, £500,000. Imminent danger of Hastings at Benares; his relief; defeat and deposition of Cheyte Sing and seizure of his treasure (£250,000).
	(b) With the Nawab Vizier of Oudh, Asaf ul
1782.	Dowlah. A million sterling extorted from the Begums of Oudh—the mother and grandmother of Asaf ul Dowlah —by means of the starvation of their attendants and their own confinement. The money accepted in liquidation of the arrears of money due to the Company by the Nawab.
1780.	vi. Transference of the judicial powers of the Supreme Council to a Judge appointed by the Governor and Council.
	vii. Appointment of two committees of the House
1781.	of Commons; one "select" to consider the administration of justice in Bengal; the other "secret" to consider the causes of the war in the Carnatic.
1782. MAY.	Resolution of the House that the Court of Directors should recall Hastings. The order for recall passed by the Court of
OCT.	Directors, but rescinded by the Court of Proprietors.
	viii. Successful war against the Dutch settlements at Sadras, Pulicat, and Trincomalee in Ceylon; and conclusion of the war in the Carnatic.
1782. FEB.	Surprise of a British force by Tippoo Sahib, son of Hyder Ali, in Tanjore. Indecisive
1782. FEB.-JUNE 1783.	naval engagements between British and French squadrons. Death of Hyder Ali (DEC. 1782) and of Eyre Coote (APRIL 1783). Conclusion of the Treaty of Versailles, and peace with Tippoo Sahib upon

1783. AUG.   the mutual restitution of conquests made during the war.

1785.   Departure of Hastings from India.]

¶ Pitt's Ministry to the outbreak of the War of the French Revolution.

1784. JAN. 12.–MAR. 25. 1. Pitt in a minority in the Commons.

     JAN. 14.   (*a*) Pitt's India Bill.
- i. A Board of Control in England, to check the policy of the Court of Directors, but without patronage.
- ii. A Court in England with power to try Indian offences. The bill rejected by 8.

     JAN. 23.

(*b*) Fox's demand that his own India Bill, if re-introduced, be not interrupted by a dissolution.

(*c*) Continued efforts of the Opposition to guard against dissolution. Popular reaction in favour of Pitt.

     MARCH 8.   (*d*) Representation to the King stating the Constitutional case of the Opposition carried by 1. After passing of the Mutiny Act
     'MARCH 25.   and voting of supplies Parliament dissolved.

2. Pitt's Ministry till the question of the Regency. Pitt at the head of a large majority; 160 members losing their seats.

     1784.   (*a*) Fox returned for Westminster over Sir Cecil Wray, a Government candidate, by 236. A scrutiny demanded and granted by the High Bailiff as returning officer. Fox kept out of his seat for Westminster till MARCH **1785**.

     1784.   (*b*) Passing of Pitt's India Bill.
- (i) A Board of Control, consisting of a Secretary of State, the Chancellor of the Exchequer, and four members of the Privy Council, unpaid and without patronage, to superintend, control, and amend the civil and military government.
- (ii) A Committee of Secrecy, of not more than three, to be formed out of the Directors, to transmit to India, when necessary, secret orders of the Board of Control.

(iii) The Court of Proprietors to lose rescinding power with regard to decisions of Board of Directors when approved by Board of Control.

(iv) A Court established at home to try offences committed in India.

1785. (c) Pitt's proposal for the reform of the Representation.

(i) 72 members, returned by 36 decayed boroughs, to be distributed among the counties and the metropolis.

(ii) No boroughs to be disfranchised, except with the consent of their proprietors. One million to be granted as compensation, to be distributed by a Committee of the House.

(iii) A second fund to be applied to the purchase of other boroughs that might afterwards be decayed.

The proposals negatived.

1785. (d) Commercial proposals with reference to Ireland, securing reciprocal freedom of trade. Ireland to pay a contribution towards the British Navy, and to be bound by future British regulations affecting trade. The proposals rejected in Ireland, owing to the latter claim.

1786. (e) Commercial treaty with France, securing liberty of navigation and of commerce, and granting to the two countries respectively the advantages of "the most favoured nation."

1786. (f) Establishment of a sinking fund—one million per annum—to accumulate at compound interest, for the extinction of the national debt.

1787. (g) Opposition of Pitt to the motion for a Bill to repeal the Test and Corporation Acts—as

JUNE. again in 1789 and 1790.

1788. [Commencement of the Impeachment of Warren Hastings, FEB. **13**, under the management of Fox, Burke, and Sheridan, lasting till APRIL **23, 1795**, when Hastings was acquitted.]

[Here may be noticed the private marriage of the Prince of Wales with Mrs. Fitzherbert, a Roman Catholic lady, in defiance of the Royal Marriage Act and of the Act of Settlement (**1785**). The marriage denied in the House by Fox on "direct authority" (**1787**).]

3. Pitt's Ministry from the Regency dispute till the outbreak of the war.

1788.
Nov.
(*a*) The King's illness. Meeting of Parliament without Royal summons after prorogation. Claim advanced by Fox that the right to exercise sovereignty during the King's incapacity devolved by right upon the Prince of Wales.

1789.
Jan. **31.**
Letters patent under the Great Seal for the opening of Parliament authorized by Parliament. Introduction of the Regency Bill, forbidding the Prince, as Regent, to bestow peerages except on royal princes, restricting his patronage to "his Majesty's pleasure," and entrusting the care of the King's person to the Queen.

Feb. **19-27.** Rapid recovery of the King.

April.
(*b*) Attack by the Spanish upon the British settlement of Nootka Sound, Vancouver's Island. Reparation made by the Spanish, the British engaging not to approach existing Spanish settlements, and both British and Spaniards engaging to form no settlement south of the Spanish settlements, all to the northward being left free to both nations. [Publication of Burke's "Reflections on the French Revolution." Oct.]

1790. Oct.

1790.
(*c*) Flood's motion for Reform. One hundred members to be added to the House, elected by resident householders of every county. (Motions for Reform subsequently brought forward by Mr. Grey, supported by the Society of the Friends of the People. **1792, 1793, 1797.**)

1790.
(*d*) Vote of the House, with reference to the Impeachment of Warren Hastings, that the dissolution of Parliament does not terminate an impeachment.

1791.
(*e*) Bill for the Relief of "Protesting Catholic Dissenters," securing to Catholics who should take the oath of allegiance, freedom of education and worship, and opening to them the legal profession from the rank of barrister downwards.

1791.
(*f*) The Quebec Government Act.
   i. Canada divided into Upper and Lower Canada (*i.e.* English and French Canada).

	Each province to have a Legislative Council, appointed by the Crown, and a Representative Assembly, elected for seven years by freeholders, and £10 leaseholders.
1791-1792.	(*g*) Fox's Libel Act, empowering the jury to give a general verdict on the whole question, instead of being limited to a verdict as to the fact of publication and the signification of allusions.
	(*h*) Affairs in the East of Europe.
	[1772. First partition of Poland. Polish Livonia and all east of the Duna and Dnieper to Russia. West Prussia to the kingdom of Prussia. Galicia to Austria.
1774.	Treaty of Kainardji terminating the war of 1768-1774, between Russia under Katharine the Second and Turkey, recognizing the Tartars of the Crimea as independent of Turkey, and acknowledging Russia as the protector of the Christian provinces of Turkey.
1783.	Incorporation of the Crimea with Turkey.]
1787.	Declaration of war by Turkey against Russia (AUG.) and by Austria under Joseph the
1788.	Second against Turkey (FEB.).
	Triple alliance of Great Britain, Prussia, and Holland, to preserve the balance of power, and preserve integrity of Sweden and Turkey, both threatened by Russia.
1789.	Ulterior designs of Prussia to restore Galicia to Poland in exchange for Dantzig and Thorn, and to separate the Austrian Netherlands from the Empire.
1790. FEB.	Death of Joseph II. and accession of his brother Leopold. Offensive alliance between Prussia and Turkey. Practical withdrawal of Austria from the war with Turkey. Consequent Peace of Warela between Russia and
AUG.	Sweden.
1791. AUG. 1792. JAN.	Treaty of Sistova between the Emperor and Turkey, followed by that of Jassy between Russia and Turkey, ceding the fortress of Oczakow to Russia, and advancing the Russian frontier to the Dniester. Belgrade, however, ceded by the Emperor to Turkey.
	(*i*) Affairs in France, from May, **1789** to the end of **1791**.

1789. May 4. Meeting of the States-General at Versailles.

20. Shutting of the Hall of Assembly. "Oath of the Tennis-court" taken by the deputies of the Third Estate to meet in all places till the Constitution is made.

22-27. The States-General declared to be a "National Assembly," and fused into one Chamber.

July 11-14. Dismissal of Necker, and attack upon and capture of the Bastille.

Oct. 3. Dinner of the officers of the Regiment de Flandre. Insurrection of women. The King
5-7. and royal family brought to Paris. Removal of the Assembly to Paris.

1790. July 14. Feast of Pikes. Mutual oath of all Frenchmen. The Constitution.

    i. France divided into eighty-three departments.
    ii. Citizens divided into "active" and "passive."
    iii. Appropriation of Church property by the State. Civil constitution of the clergy.
    iv. Judicial reforms, including abolition of torture, a new penal code, securities against arbitrary arrest, trial by jury in criminal cases, and the abolition of the old courts of justice.

1791. April 2. Death of Mirabeau.

June 20. The King's flight to Varennes. His return to
25. Paris as a practical captive.

Aug. 25-Aug. 27. Convention of Pilnitz between Emperor Leopold II., Frederick William II. of Prussia, and Emigrant Princes of France, to call upon all Governments to co-operate in prompt action to enable the King of France to establish the foundations of monarchical government.

Sept. 30. Close of the National Assembly.

Oct. 1. Meeting of the Legislative of 745 members (all members of the National Assembly being excluded).

Oct. 16. Annexation of Avignon to France, followed by resistance and massacres of "aristocrats."

(*j*) Events in Great Britain, and in France till beginning of war.

1792. Jan. 31. Pacific speech of King in opening Parliament. Reduction of British sailors and marines to 16,000, and of the army in England. Pitt's anticipations of fifteen years of peace.

ANALYSIS OF ENGLISH HISTORY. 281

FEB. 7. Treaty between Emperor Leopold and King of Prussia to keep down disturbance, and to assist one another in case of attack.

APRIL 20. War declared by the French Assembly against Leopold, followed by an unsuccessful French invasion of the Austrian Netherlands.

JUNE 20. Capture of the Tuileries by the people of Paris.

JULY 24. Declaration of war by Prussia upon France, and Manifesto of the Duke of Brunswick from Coblentz, summoning the city of Paris, the National Assembly, and the National Guard, to submit to their King on pain of "losing their heads pursuant to military trials without hope of pardon."

AUG. 10. Second attack of the people of Paris on the Tuileries. Massacre of the Swiss Guard. Escape of the King, Queen, Dauphin, to the
AUG. 13. Hall of the Assembly. Conducted thence to the Temple. Decree for the summoning of a National Convention.

AUG. Re-organization of the Commune of Paris, which by degrees exercised supreme power.

SEPT. 2-6. The September massacres.

20. Battle of Valmy.

22. Meeting of National Convention and proclamation of Republic.

30. Retreat of the Allies. Invasion of Sardinia by the French, and conquest of Savoy and Nice;
SEPT.—OCT. invasions of the Empire, and capture of Spier, Worms, and Mainz.

NOV. 6. Defeat of the Austrians by the French at Jem-
NOV. 7. 14. mappes, and capture of Mons and Brussels.
NOV. Surrender to the French of Liége, Aix-la-Chapelle, Antwerp.

NOV. 16. The treaty rights of the Dutch to the exclusive navigation of the Scheldt and Meuse declared by the French to be abolished; French commanders authorized to pursue the Austrians into Holland.

NOV. 19. Assistance promised by the Convention to all nations revolting against their rulers.

NOV. 28. Congratulatory deputation from British democratic societies to the Convention.

DEC. 1. Proclamation to call out and embody the British militia, followed by an Alien Bill subjecting foreigners to supervision.

11–16.	Trial of the French King.
1793. Jan. 15–17.	Sentence of the French King to death. His execution, Jan. 21.
Feb. 1.	War declared by France against Great Britain and Holland; against Spain March 7.
1793.	Panic in Great Britain showed by the trials of Frost, Winterbotham, Briellat, Hudson, in England; and of Muir, Fyshe Palmer, in Scotland.
	[Second partition of Poland by Russia and Prussia.]

J The War of the French Revolution.

1. The War of the Revolution to the Rupture of the First Coalition against France.

1793.

Feb. 11.	Invasion of Holland by the French under Dumouriez.
March 7.	War declared by the Republic against Spain.
March 18.	Defeat of the French at Neerwinden. Flanders laid open to the Austrians.
	Treasonable negotiations of Dumouriez with the Austrians, ending in his flight to their lines.
	Revolt of La Vendée against the levy of men ordered by the Convention.
July 10. July 16. July 26.	Surrender of Condé to the Austrians, and of Valenciennes to the Duke of York. Re-capture of Mainz from the French.
Aug. 28.	Occupation of Toulon by Lord Hood.
Sept. 8.	Repulse of the Duke of York from before Dunkirk with the loss of his artillery. .
Oct. 15.	Victory of Jourdan over the Austrians at Wattignies.
Dec. 19.	Re-occupation of Toulon by the French; the main part of the French Mediterranean fleet destroyed or carried off by Hood.
Dec. 23–26.	Storming of the Austrian positions at Wörth and Weissenburg by Hoche and Pichegru.
	Conquest of La Vendée by Kleber, British aid arriving too late.
1794.	[Revolt in Poland under Kosckiusko. April.]
April—May.	French struggle for the passage of the Sambre.
June 1.	Victory of Admiral Earl Howe over the French fleet off Ushant.

JUNE 26. French victory at Fleurus, between Namur and Charleroi, over the Prince of Coburg and the Austrians. Retreat of the Austrians from the Netherlands.
OCT. 6. Entry of the French army into Cologne.
DEC. Holland overrun and conquered by Pichegru. Capture of the Dutch fleet by French cavalry.
JAN. **1795**.
Notice in this year the British successes at sea— the capture of Tobago, Martinique, St. Lucia, Guadaloupe—and the revolt of Corsica from the Republic.
1795. APRIL 5. Treaty of Basel between France and Prussia.
JULY 20. Invasion of royalist emigrants in British ships crushed by Hoche at Quiberon.
JULY 22. Treaty of Basel between France and Spain. The Republic recognized by Sweden and the Protestant Cantons of Switzerland. End of the First Coalition, one of the chief causes of its failure being illustrated by the third and final partition of Poland amongst Russia, Prussia, and Austria. **1795.**

2. Internal History of France from the Execution of the King till the Rise of the Directory.

1793.
MARCH-APRIL. Appointment of a Committee of Public Safety to superintend the Administration.
MARCH. Commencement of the struggle between the Mountain and the Girondists.
JUNE 2. Arrest of twenty-two leading Girondists "in their own houses."
JULY 3. Assassination of Marat by Charlotte Corday.
SEPT. 17. Fixing of a maximum price for corn, most raw and many manufactured materials, and for wages. The Revolutionary Committees empowered to imprison all "suspected" persons. Commencement of the Reign of Terror.
OCT. 16. Execution of Marie Antoinette.
OCT. 31. Execution of the Girondists.
NOV. Execution of Philippe Egalité (Duke of Orleans), Madame Roland, Barnave, Bailly (ex-mayor of Paris). Adoption of a new Republican Calendar.
NOV. 10. Installation of the Goddess of Reason in Notre Dame.

1794. Mar. 24. Execution of Hébert and eighteen Hébertists.
  April 5. Execution of Danton and Camille Desmoulins.
  June 8. Proclamation of the belief of the French people in a Supreme Being and in the immortality of the soul.
  July 28. Execution of Robespierre and close of the Reign of Terror.

1795.
April 1–May 20. Struggles of Jacobinism in the insurrections of Germinal and Prairial.
  July–Sept. Formation of a new Constitution,
    i. A Directory of five, chosen by the Assemblies, to direct administration.
    ii. A Chamber of 500 to propose legislative measures.
    iii. A Chamber of 250 Ancients (over forty years), to approve or reject legislative measures.
    iv. Neither Chamber to interfere with the Executive.
    v. One Director and a third part of each Chamber to retire every year.
    vi. Two-thirds of each Chamber to consist of Members of the National Convention.
  Oct. 5. Insurrection of Vendémiaire against the New Constitution suppressed by artillery.
  Oct. 6. Commencement of the Directory.

3. Continuation of the War, mainly by Great Britain and Austria, to the Peace of Campo Formio.

1795. Dec.—
1796. March. Overtures for peace made by Great Britain in consequence of the hope that the establishment of the Directory implied restoration of Constitutional rule.

  April. Triple aggressive movement by the French armies against Austria by the Main, the Danube, and Lombardy.

  Aug. 17. (*a*) The attack by the Main crushed by the defeat of Jourdan by Archduke Charles.

  (*b*) Consequent abandonment of the attack by the valley of the Danube under Moreau, which so far had been successsful, and re-
  Oct. treat of the French behind the Rhine.

  (*c*) Success of the attack through Lombardy under Buonaparte.

APRIL.	Armistice with Sardinia leading to the secession of the King of Sardinia from Great Britain and Austria.
MAY.	
MAY 10.	French victory at the Bridge of Lodi, and entry of Buonaparte into Milan.
MAY 15.	
MAY 29.	Battle on the Mincio, and evacuation of Lombardy by the Austrians.
JUNE.	Submission of Naples and of the Pope to a suspension of hostilities, and entry of the French into Leghorn.
	Arrival of a relieving Austrian army in Lombardy; the Austrians again defeated at Lonato and at Castiglioni.
JULY 30.	
AUG. 3.	
AUG. 5.	Secret treaty between France and Prussia.
OCT.	Despatch of Lord Malmesbury to Paris to conclude a general peace.
	i. The conquests of Great Britain (to which this year were added Grenada, Essequibo, Demerara, Ceylon, Malacca, Cochin) to be surrendered.
	ii. The Netherlands to be surrendered by France to Austria.
	Declaration of war by Spain against Great Britain.
	Modena, Reggio, Bologna, Ferrara, formed by Buonaparte into the Cispadane Republic.
NOV. 10.	Death of Katharine, Empress of Russia.
NOV. 15-17.	Renewed defeat of the Austrians by Buonaparte after heavy fighting at Arcola.
DEC. 15-31.	Failure of the attempt to invade Ireland by Hoche owing to stormy weather.
1797.	
JAN. 14-15.	Victory of Buonaparte over the Austrians at Rivoli.
FEB. 2.	Surrender of Mantua to the French.
FEB. 14.	Defeat of the Spanish fleet off Cape St. Vincent by Admiral Jervis.
FEB. 19.	Peace between France and the Pope: the Papal Government ceding Bologna, Ferrara, Ravenna.
FEB. 26.	Run for gold upon the Bank, and cash payments suspended in Great Britain by an Order in Council.
APRIL 15-	Mutiny in the Channel fleet against impressment, the severity of discipline, the unequal distribution of prize-money, and for an increase of wages by statute, pacified by Lord Howe.
MAY 7.	

APRIL 18.	Armistice of Leoben between France and Austria.
MAY 22.	Mutiny in the fleet at the Nore (for a revision of the Articles of War and the dismissal of unpopular officers), and blockade of the Thames, in which the fleet at the Texel under Duncan joined, JUNE 7.
JUNE 15.	Submission of the fleet at the Nore and execucution of the ringleaders.
MAY-JUNE.	Seizure of the Ionian Islands by the French.
JULY 9.	Death of Edmund Burke.
OCT. 11.	Destruction of the Dutch fleet, which had been designed to co-operate with the French for the invasion of Great Britain, by Admiral Adam Duncan at Camperdown.
OCT. 17.	Treaty of Campo Formio.

    i. The Austrian Netherlands and the Ionian Islands ceded to France. Lombardy, the "Cispadane Republic," and Italy north of the Rubicon united in the "Cisalpine Republic."

    ii. Venice, Istria, Dalmatia, ceded to Austria.

    iii. A Congress to meet at Rastadt to settle terms of peace between France and the German Empire; it being understood that the Emperor would secure the extension of France to the Rhine.

4. Events Abroad from the Peace of Campo Formio to the Peace of Amiens.

1798.

FEB.	Entry of the French into Rome, and declaration of the Roman Republic.
APRIL 12.	Rising in Basle and Vaud against the Senate at Berne. Switzerland formed by the French into the Helvetic Republic.
MAY 19.	Departure of Buonaparte from Toulon for Egypt (part of the threefold attack of France upon Great Britain (*a*) through Ireland; (*b*) by a naval confederacy of French, Dutch, and Spanish fleets; (*c*) through India).
JULY 21.	Battle of the Pyramids and defeat of the Mameluke cavalry.
	French occupation of Cairo.
AUG. 1.	The battle of the Nile and destruction of the French fleet in Aboukir Bay by Nelson.

Nov.	*Second coalition* of Russia, Austria, Turkey, Great Britain, and Naples against France.
Nov. Dec. 6-13.	Invasion of Naples by the French, and defeat of the Austrian general, Mack. The Parthenopœan Republic declared at Naples.
1799. March 25.	Defeat of the French army of the Rhine under Jourdan, advancing upon Vienna by the Danube valley, by the Archduke Charles at Stockach, near the Lake of Constance.
April 5.	Defeat of the French army of Italy at Magnano.
June 17-19.	Victory of the Russians under Suvaroff over the French on the Trebbia; rising of Southern Italy against the French.
Aug. 14.	Defeat of the French by Suvaroff at Novi; evacuation of Northern Italy by the French.
Sept. 26.	The Russian attack upon the French in Switzerland checked by Massena at the battle of Zurich.
Aug. Aug. 28.	Attack upon the French in Holland by Great Britain and Russia. First successes under Sir Ralph Abercromby and Admiral Story. Surrender of the remains of the Dutch fleet to the allies.
	Capture of the Ionian Islands by Russian and Turkish fleets.
Sept.	The chief command in Holland taken by the Duke of York.
Oct. 8.	Failure of the expedition, and evacuation of Holland by the British.
	Retreat of Suvaroff from Switzerland over the Grisons from Glarus into the valley of the Rhine.
Oct. 8.	Return of Buonaparte from the East after invading Syria (Feb.), besieging Acre, defended by the Turks and the British Captain, Sir Sidney Smith (March 16-May 20), and defeating a Turkish force which had disembarked in Egypt at Aboukir.
Nov. 9-10.	Coup d'état of Brumaire 18. End of the Directory, and beginning of the Consulate.
	The New Constitution.
-	i. 500,000 elected by the nation eligible to offices in the Communes, to elect 50,000 eligible to offices in the departments, to elect 5,000 eligible to offices in the Government and to the Legislature.

ii. The Legislature to be appointed from the 5,000 by the Executive, and to consist of:

    (*a*) A Council of State to draft measures proposed by the Executive.

    (*b*) A Tribunate to discuss the measures when drafted.

    (*c*) The Legislative to pass or reject the measures but without power of debate.

    (*d*) A senate to guard the Constitution, with the power of annulling laws passed by the Chambers.

    The members to hold office for life.

iii. The Executive to consist of Three Consuls, the First Consul to wield executive authority with the advice of the others. Buonaparte, Siéyès, and Ducos; afterwards Buonaparte, Cambacérès, Lebrun, appointed Consuls. Talleyrand, minister of foreign affairs; Fouché, minister of police.

1800. MAY **15.** Crossing of the Great S. Bernard by Buonaparte.
20. JUNE **14.** Battle of Marengo; armistice granted to the Austrians on the cession of all Lombardy west of the Oglio.

SEPT. Renewal of the armistice till NOV. **25** by the surrender of Ulm and Ingolstadt to the French under Moreau who were advancing on Vienna by the Danube; Austria being pledged not to make peace separately from Great Britain before MARCH **1801.**

Proposal of Buonaparte to put Malta, which was blockaded by Great Britain, under the guardianship of Czar Paul as Grand Master of the Maltese order of S. John of Jerusalem. Refusal of Great Britain. Surrender of Malta to the British.

DEC. **5.** Battle of Hohenlinden; utter defeat of the Austrians and commencement of negotiations for peace.

DEC. **16.** Revival of the Armed Neutrality of 1780 by the Northern Powers (Russia, Sweden, and Denmark), against the right of search claimed by Great Britain with respect to neutral ships. " Free ships make free goods."

1801. JAN. War between Great Britain and the Northern Powers.

ANALYSIS OF ENGLISH HISTORY. 289

FEB. 9. Peace of Lunéville between Austria and France.
  i. The left Bank of the Rhine definitely ceded to France.
  ii. Modena annexed to the Cisalpine Republic, and Tuscany ceded to the Duke of Parma.
  iii. The compensation to the Dukes of Modena, Tuscany, and the Princes dispossessed west of the Rhine, to be approved by France.
MARCH 21. Defeat of the French in Egypt at Alexandria by Sir Ralph Abercromby.
MARCH 23. Murder of Czar Paul at S. Petersburg, and accession of Alexander.
APRIL 2. Battle of Copenhagen; destruction of the Danish fleet and batteries by the British, and armistice between Great Britain and Denmark.
JUNE 17. Abandonment of the Armed Neutrality by the Northern Powers.
JUNE 27. Surrender by the French of Cairo and of Alexandria to the British.
AUG. 30.
OCT.-MARCH Negotiations for peace between Great Britain and
1802. France.
1802. MARCH 27. The Peace of Amiens.
  i. All British conquests surrendered except Trinidad and Ceylon. The Cape of Good Hope restored to Holland as a free port, Malta to the Knights of S. John, and Egypt to the Porte. The Ionian Isles recognized as a Free Republic.
  ii. The French to withdraw from Naples and the States of the Church and to guarantee the integrity of Portugal.
  iii. No attempt made by Great Britain to modify the Continental arrangements of the Peace of Lunéville.

5. Domestic Events in Great Britain from 1794 to 1802.

1794. MAY-1801. Suspension of the Habeas Corpus Act.
  AUG.-SEPT. Trial and condemnation of Watt and Downie in Scotland for high treason; Watt executed.
  OCT.-DEC. Trial and acquittal of Hardy, Horne Tooke and Thelwall for treasonable connexion with the Corresponding Society of London.
1795. OCT. 29. Bread riots in London, and attack of the population upon the King at the opening of Parliament.

U

Nov.	Passing of the Treasonable Practices Bill, dispensing with proof of overt acts of treason, and punishing as a high misdemeanour and on a second conviction with banishment or transportation all writing or speaking tending to excite to contempt of the King or of the established Constitution.
	Passing of the Seditious Meetings Bill.
	i. Meetings of more than fifty persons for considering alterations of matters in Church or State to be licensed and attended by a Magistrate.
	ii. The power of arrest and of dispersal of the meeting to be vested in the Magistrate.
	iii. Lecture rooms to be licensed and supervised by Magistrates.
Nov.	Public meetings held by the Whig Club, by the London Corresponding Society, and in Palace Yard under Fox, to express opposition to the Bills.
1797. Feb.	Suspension of specie payments by Bank of England by Order in Council.
May 14.	Defeat of Fox's motion for the repeal of the Treasonable Practices and Seditious Meetings Bills.
May 26.	Defeat of Mr. Grey's motion for Reform.
1798.-May 1801.	Secession of the Whigs under Fox from Parliament. Tierney the one remaining leader of opposition.
1799.	Suppression of the London Corresponding Society and others by name. All debating clubs and reading rooms to be licensed, and printing presses to be registered.
1801. Feb. 1.	Resignation of Pitt on the question of Catholic Emancipation in Ireland; succession of Addington as Prime Minister.

6. Union of Ireland with Great Britain, and Summary of Events in Ireland from the Treaty of Limerick, 1691.

1. The Penal Code.

1695.	*a* No Catholic to keep a school; no children to be sent abroad for education.
1695.	*b* No Catholic to be in the possession of arms.
1697. 1704.	*c* Catholic Priests in correspondence with Rome expelled; all Catholic Priests to be registered.

1698.	*d* No Catholic to practise as a solicitor.
1704.	*e* The lands of Catholics to be divided among all the sons by "gavelkind," except in the case of the eldest son professing Protestantism, when the father became merely a life-tenant and the lands passed in entirety to the eldest son.
	f No Catholic to inherit or purchase land, or lease it for more than thirty-one years, or to settle in Limerick or Galway. Catholic minors to be under Protestant guardians.
	g All holders of office to subscribe the oaths of allegiance and abjuration (of the Stuarts), and the declaration against Transubstantiation.
1709.	*h* Informers of the breach of the provisions as to lease and inheritance of lands to be put in possession of the property.
1727.	*i* No Catholic to have either Parliamentary or municipal vote.
1696–1699.	2. Prohibition of export of Irish woollen goods to the Colonies, **1696**; to England, **1698**; to Continental countries, **1699**. Remonstrance of Molyneux in favour of the independence of the Irish Parliament burnt by the common hangman.
1724.	3. Publication of the "Drapier's Letters" by Swift on the occasion of the introduction of "Wood's Halfpence."
1768.	4. Octennial Bill limiting the duration of Parliament which before had lasted for the lifetime of the Sovereign. Claim of the first octennial House of Commons to originate Money Bills.
1769–1773.	
	5. Effect upon Ireland of the struggle between Great Britain and the American Colonies.
1776.	i. Declaration of Rights brought forward by Grattan claiming the independence of the Irish Parliament.
1778–1779.	ii. Removal of restrictions upon Irish commerce, limited by the opposition of English merchants.
1778 Dec.–1781.	iii. Formation of Irish volunteers for the defence of the country against privateers, notably Paul Jones.
1782, Feb.	iv. Convention of Dungannon and demand of the volunteers for Parliamentary independence, Freedom of Trade, the repeal of the Act of 1780 making the Mutiny Act permanent in Ireland.

1782. May.	v.	Renunciation by the British Parliament of legislative and judicial authority over Ireland: renunciation of the power of disallowing statutes passed by the Irish Parliament conferred on the Council by Poynings' Act, **1495**; repeal of the Perpetual Mutiny Act. Habeas Corpus Act for Ireland passed by the Irish Parliament.
1784.	**6.**	Defeat of Flood's motion for Reform—which did not include Catholics; and rejection by the Irish Parliament of Free Trade with Great Britain, owing to the British claim that Ireland should be bound by any future British legislation as to trade, and to the withdrawal of concessions as to trade with India and the foreign West Indies.
1785.		
1791.	**7.**	Formation of the Society of United Irishmen by Wolfe Tone for Reform and Catholic Emancipation.
Jan.-April. **1793.**	**8.**	Passing by the Irish Parliament of a bill to open to Catholics the Municipal Franchise, and the political franchise to Catholic 40s. freeholders.
1793		Passing of the Convention Bill against "the Representatives of the Nation," an attempt of the United Irishmen to convene a Representative Assembly.
1795.	**9.**	Disturbances and faction fights between the Protestant "Peep of Day Boys" and the Catholic "Defenders." Arrival of Lord Fitzwilliam as Viceroy (Jan.). Introduction by Grattan of a bill for the admission of Catholics into Parliament (Feb. **12**). Recall of Lord Fitzwilliam (Feb. **23**).
	10.	The Irish Rebellion.
1796.	i.	Opening of negotiations with the French Directory by Lord Edward Fitzgerald and Wolfe Tone. "Insurrection Act" passed by the Irish Parliament to secure Tithes, and against unlawful oaths.
1796. Dec.**15-31.**	ii.	French expedition to Ireland under Hoche. Its failure owing to stormy weather.
1797.	iii.	Misconduct of the British troops sent to Ireland under General Lake, except during the command of Sir Ralph Abercromby who resigned, April **1797**. The outrages covered by a Bill of Indemnity passed by the Irish Parliament.

1798.	iv. Arrest of the leaders of the United Irishmen, of Lord Edward FitzGerald. Outbreak of the Irish Rebellion. Capture by the Rebels of Wexford, and formation of a camp on Vinegar Hill, near Enniscorthy. Storming of Vinegar Hill by Lake, and recapture of Wexford.
MARCH 12–MAY 19.	
MAY 24.	
MAY 21.	
JUNE 26.	
AUG.	v. Landing of the French general Humbert at Killala. Defeat of Lake by the French at Castlebar; capitulation of the French force at Longford to Lord Cornwallis. Failure of a second French expedition under General Hardi; arrest and death of Wolfe Tone.

11. The Union of Ireland with Great Britain.

1799. JAN.   i. Rejection by the Irish Parliament of the proposal of Union by one vote. (Carried in the British House of Commons by 149 to 24, in the Lords without a division.)

1799.   ii. Purchase by the British Government of 84 boroughs which would be disfranchised by the Union at £7,500 for each seat. Total compensation, £1,260,000.

Twenty-eight Irish peerages created in connexion with the Union; twenty Irish peers promoted; six English peerages granted for Irish services.

1800. JAN.   iii. Passing of the Union by the Irish Parliament.

iv. The terms of the Union.

Ireland to be represented by "four spiritual lords sitting in rotation of Sessions, twenty-eight temporal peers elected for life, and by a hundred members of the House of Commons."

v. Pitt's proposal to the British Cabinet for Catholic Emancipation.

(*a*) To remove all religious tests limiting exercise of franchise, admission to Parliament, to the Bar, to municipal offices, to the army, to the public service.

(*b*) To substitute for the Sacramental Test an oath of allegiance and fidelity to the Constitution.

(*c*) To grant State aid to the Catholic Clergy, the Crown being granted by the Irish Bishops a "veto" on their nomination. Similar concessions and aid to be made to the Protestant Dissenters.

	(*d*) To commute Tithes into a Land-tax.
	(*e*) To increase the stipends of the poorer clergy of the Established Episcopal Church.
1800. SEPT.	Hostility displayed by the King upon the disclosure of the plan to him by Lord Loughborough while still under discussion by the Cabinet. Continued refusal of the King to make concessions. Resignation of office by Pitt. Pitt's
1801. FEB.	pledge to the King not to revive the question of Catholic Emancipation.

K European affairs to the Conclusion of the Peace of Tilsit, and the Outbreak of the Peninsular War.

1802. JUNE.	Demand by Buonaparte that Great Britain should expel all the French princes and their adherents, and all whose political principles and conduct occasion jealousy to the French Government, and should adopt effectual measures for the suppression of seditious publications.
	Refusal of the British Government to entertain his demands.
SEPT.	Annexation of Piedmont to France.
OCT.-JAN. 1803.	Intervention of Buonaparte in Switzerland; re-construction of the Swiss Constitution, La Valais (with the Simplon Route) being created into a separate republic.
1803. MARCH.	Refusal of the British to cede Malta to the Knights lest it should fall into the hands of France.
MAY.	Declaration of war by Great Britain upon Buonaparte, and invasion of Hanover by the French.
1804. MARCH 15-20.	Arrest and murder of the Duke of Enghien on the charge of connexion with the Assassination Plot of Cadoudal and Pichegru.
MAY 12.	Return of Pitt to office as Prime Minister. Failure of his scheme to form a comprehensive ministry.
MAY 18.	Buonaparte Emperor of the French.
AUG. 16.	Appearance of Napoleon in the camp formed at Boulogne for the invasion of Great Britain.
OCT. 5.	Capture of Spanish Treasure Ships from America by the British, and declaration by Spain of
DEC.	war upon Great Britain. (Coronation of Napoleon as Emperor, DEC. 2.)
1805.	(*a*) Napoleon's scheme for the invasion of Great Britain by the junction of the three French Squadrons of Toulon, Rochefort, and Brest with the Spanish Fleet.

APRIL.	The British Blockade of Cadiz forced by Admiral Villeneuve. Arrival of Villeneuve at Martinique, followed by Nelson; his departure to raise the British Blockades of Ferrol and Rochefort and join the squadron of Brest. Discovery of Villeneuve's departure by Nelson at Antigua.
MAY 28.	
JUNE 13.	Arrival of Nelson's despatch in London. The blockades of Ferrol and Rochefort raised by the British, and the advance of the French Fleet checked off Cape Finisterre by Sir Robert Calder. Blockade of Villeneuve at Cadiz by Nelson.
JULY 9.	
JULY 22.	
OCT. 19.	Attempt of Villeneuve to sail from Cadiz to carry out Napoleon's plan. Annihilation of French and Spanish Fleets N.W. of Trafalgar. (See plan in Public Schools' Historical Atlas.) Death of Nelson.
OCT. 21.	

(b) Pitt's scheme for a *third* Coalition against France.

APRIL.	Treaty between Great Britain and Russia, to expel the French from Piedmont, Switzerland, and Holland; and to unite Belgium and Holland as a barrier against France.
MARCH 31.	Proclamation of Napoleon at Milan as King of Italy.
MAY 26.	Coronation of Napoleon at Milan with the Iron Crown of Lombardy—placed on his head by his own hands.
JUNE 9-30.	Annexation of Genoa to France.
AUG.	The Coalition joined by Austria and Sweden.
SEPT. 1.	The Army of England marched from Boulogne against Austria.
OCT. 19.	Capitulation of the Austrian General Mack at Ulm. Prussia drawn to the side of the Coalition by the march of Napoleon through Prussian territory at Anspach (OCT.) and treaty of Potsdam between Russia and Austria for joint action against France.
NOV. 3.	
NOV. 13.	Entry of the French into Vienna.
DEC. 2.	Defeat of the Austrians and Russians at Austerlitz.
DEC. 4.	Armistice between Napoleon and the Allies.
DEC. 15.	Conclusion by the Prussian Envoy Hangwitz of a treaty with Napoleon, accepting Hanover from him.

Dec. 26.		Treaty of Presburg between France and Austria
	i.	Venetia ceded to the Kingdom of Italy.
	ii.	The Tyrol ceded to Bavaria.
	iii.	The Electors of Bavaria and Würtemberg recognized as Kings and made independent of the Emperor.
	iv.	£1,600,000 exacted as war indemnity.

1806. Jan. 8. Second capture of the Cape of Good Hope by the British.

Jan. 23. Death of Pitt: accession to power of the "Ministry of all the Talents," Fox, Lord Grenville, and Lord Sidmouth (Addington).

March 28. British ships excluded by Prussia from Prussian and Hanoverian ports.

April-July. Negotiations opened by Napoleon with the British Cabinet on the terms of the restoration of Hanover to the British King, and the cession of Malta, the Cape of Good Hope, if Sicily were surrendered to King Joseph of Naples.

April 14 and June 5. Two brothers of Napoleon, Joseph and Louis Buonaparte, made Kings of Naples and Holland respectively.

June 28. Capture of Buenos Ayres by the British; recapture by the Spanish Aug. 12; Blockade of Buenos Ayres by the British.

July 6. Victory of a British force over the French at Maida in Calabria.

July 12. Confederation of the Rhine. Bavaria, Würtemberg, Baden, Hesse, Darmstadt and other minor States, declared severed from the Empire. End of the Holy Roman Empire. Resignation

Aug. 6. of the title of Roman Emperor by Francis of Austria (who had assumed the title of Emperor of Austria, July **1804**).

Aug. Determination of Prussia to make war upon Napoleon in consequence of his offer of the restoration of Hanover to Great Britain after bestowing it upon Prussia. Declaration of war by Russia upon the Porte in consequence of the deposition by the Sultan of the Princes of Moldavia and Wallachia.

Sept. 13. Death of Fox.

Oct. 14. Defeat of the Prussians at Jena and Auerstädt.

Oct. 27. Entry of the French into Berlin.

Nov. 21.	The Berlin Decree prohibiting Spain, Italy, Holland, and all French territory from commerce direct or indirect with Great Britain; answered by the British Order in Council forbidding all vessels, under pain of capture, from trading with any French port, or ports under the influence of France. JAN. **7, 1807.**
DEC.	March of the French into East Prussia against Russia.
1807. FEB. **8.**	Napoleon's advance checked by the Russians at Eylau.
FEB.-JULY.	British expedition to South America, ending in the capture of Monte Video and capitulation of the British at Buenos Ayres.
FEB.-MARCH. MARCH-SEPT.	British expedition to the Dardanelles, ending in a repulse before Constantinople. Unsuccessful British attack upon Egypt.
MARCH **24.** APRIL.	Fall of the Grenville Ministry. Accession to power of the Duke of Portland, with Canning as Foreign Minister. Fourth coalition of Russia, Prussia, Great Britain, Sweden against France.
MAY **7.**	Treaties of Napoleon with Turkey and Persia.
MAY **27.**	French capture of Dantzig after a close siege, MARCH-MAY.
JUNE **14.**	Defeat of the Russians at Friedland.
JUNE **25.**	Meeting of Napoleon and the Czar Alexander at Tilsit.
JULY **7-9.**	Treaties of Tilsit between France, Russia, and France and Prussia.

    i. Prussian dominions west of the Elbe ceded by Prussia, and formed into the Kingdom of Westphalia under Jerome Buonaparte.

    ii. Prussian provinces won from Poland ceded to the King of Saxony, as the Grand Duchy of Warsaw.

    iii. Finland, Moldavia, Wallachia, granted to the Czar: in the case of refusal by the Porte, France to assist Russia in taking possession of all Turkish dominions in Europe except Roumelia and Constantinople.

    iv. Russia to join in the prohibition of commerce with Great Britain and to "summon the courts of Stockholm, Copenhagen, Lisbon, to declare war against Great Britain."

    v. Prussia to declare war against Great Britain if Napoleon were still at war with the British on DEC. **1.**

JULY 1807.	British expedition against Denmark and demand for the surrender of the Danish fleet to the British till the conclusion of peace.
SEPT. 2.	Bombardment of Copenhagen, and capture of the Danish fleet by the British.
OCT. 16.	Alliance between Denmark and France.
OCT. 27.	Treaty at Fontainebleau between France and Spain for the partition of Portugal; invasion of Portugal by the French under Junot; flight of
NOV. 29.	the Prince-Regent of Portugal to Brazil.
NOV.	Fresh Orders in Council forbidding trade with ports subject to France. Met by Napoleon's Milan decree, declaring all vessels bound to or coming from Great Britain or British Colonies liable to seizure.

L. The Peninsular War.

1808. MARCH 17.	Riot at Aranjuez against Godoy, the King's favourite, and abdication of the King of Spain, Charles IV. His son Ferdinand proclaimed King.
APRIL.	Ferdinand enticed to Bayonne to meet Napoleon. Arrival of Charles IV. at Bayonne.
MAY.	Ferdinand and Charles compelled by Napoleon to surrender their rights upon the Crown of Spain.
JUNE.	Rising of Spain against French intervention. Joseph Buonaparte declared King by an assembly of Spanish notables at Bayonne.
JULY 19.	Defeat of the French under Dupont at Baylen.
JULY.	Alliance between Spain and Great Britain. Despatch of British expeditions under Sir Arthur Wellesley and Sir John Moore.
AUG. 21. AUG. 30.	Defeat of Junot at Vimieiro. The Convention of Cintra, permitting the French to retreat from Portugal with arms and stores, signed by Sir Harry Burrard.
NOV. 10. DEC. 4.	Defeat of the Spaniards at Espinosa upon the Ebro by Napoleon. Entry of Napoleon into Madrid.
NOV.	Advance of Moore from Lisbon to Salamanca. Advance of Moore from Salamanca upon Valladolid, in consequence of information sent by Frere, the British agent at Madrid.
DEC. 9.	Information received by Moore of the fall of Madrid.

	Retreat of Moore northwards, followed by Napoleon.
1809. JAN. 11.	Arrival of Moore at Corunna. Defeat of Soult
16.	at Corunna, death of Moore, safe embarkation of the British army.
19.	Departure of Napoleon from Spain.
MARCH.	Capture of Zaragoza by the French, after being besieged in the summer of 1808, and from DEC. 20, 1808, to MARCH, 1809.
MAY 12.	Soult driven by Wellesley from Oporto into Galicia.
JUNE 27.	March of Wellesley on Madrid. Defeat by him
JUNE 27–28.	of Marshal Victor and King Joseph at Talavera.
AUG. 2.	Retreat of Wellesley before Soult, Mortier, and Ney into winter quarters in Portugal.
1810.	Attack of Massena upon Portugal. Capture of Ciudad Rodrigo (JULY 11), of Almeida (AUG. 27).
SEPT. 27.	Massena repulsed by Wellesley (now Lord Wellington) at Busaco.
OCT. 8–15.	Retiring of the British behind the lines of Torres Vedras thrown up by Wellington after Talavera and the retreat which followed, for the defence of Lisbon.
NOV. 14.	Abandonment by Massena of his position before the lines, and retreat to Santarem.
1811. FEB. 2.	Retreat of Massena from Santarem towards Almeida.
FEB. 19.	Capture of Badajoz by Soult.
MARCH 5.	Defeat of Marshal Victor at Barosa by General Graham.
APRIL 9.	Blockade of Almeida by Wellington.
MAY 4.	French relieving army under Massena defeated by Wellington at Fuentes d'Onoro.
MAY 10.	Destruction and evacuation of Almeida by the French.
MAY 16.	Victory of Beresford over Soult at Albuera, near Badajoz. Abandonment by the British of the siege of Badajoz on the advance of the con-
JUNE 10.	joined armies of Soult and Marmont.
SEPT.	Blockade of Ciudad Rodrigo by the British. Failure of the French attempt under Dorsenne
SEPT. 24–27.	and Marmont to succour it.
OCT.–JAN. 1812.	Conquest of Valencia for the French by Suchet.
1812. JAN. 19.	Storming of Ciudad Rodrigo by Wellington.

April 7.		Storming of Badajoz by Wellington.
July 22.		Defeat of Marshal Marmont and the French army of the north at Salamanca. Entry of Wellington into Madrid.
Aug. 12.		
Sept. 19.–Oct.		Siege of Burgos by Wellington. Retreat of Wellington, with much disorder and loss, on Ciudad Rodrigo, and evacuation of Madrid by the British, before a combined advance of Clausel, Soult, and Drouet.
Oct. 21.		
Nov. 2.		
1813.	March.	Unsuccessful attack by the French under Suchet upon Sir John Murray at Castalla, near Alicante.
	May 22.	Advance of Wellington (now Generalissimo in Spain), and retreat of the French beyond the Ebro to Vittoria.
	June 21.	Utter defeat of King Joseph and the French at Vittoria.
July 25–Aug. 1.		Battles of the Pyrenees.
	Aug. 31.	Storming of San Sebastian by the British after being besieged from June 29, and capitulation of the citadel, in spite of the efforts of Soult to relieve it, Aug. 30–31.
	Sept. 9.	
	Sept. 7.	Crossing of the Bidassoa by Wellington, and invasion of France.
	Nov. 9.	Defeats of Soult on the Nivelle, on the Nive, and at St. Pierre.
Dec. 9–10, 13.		
1814.	Feb. 27.	Defeat of Soult at Orthes, and investment of Bayonne by the British.
	April 10.	Last battle of the Peninsular war at Toulouse, and preparations of Soult for retreat.

M Affairs in the rest of Europe during the Peninsular War.

1809.	April. a	War between Austria and France. Appeal of the Austrians "to the German people," and rising of the Tyrol against the French.
	April 20–22.	Defeats of the Austrians by the French at Abensberg, Landsput, and Eggmuhl, in Bavaria.
	May 13.	Second entry of Napoleon into Vienna.
	May 20–22.	Napoleon's advance across the Danube checked at Aspern, and the French army cut off in the island of Lobau.
	July 4–6.	Second passage of the French across the Danube, and great French victory at Wagram.
		[For both Aspern and Wagram see plans in Public Schools' Historical Atlas.]

JULY 28.	British expedition against Antwerp under Lord Chatham to divert part of the French forces from Austria. Delay in Walcheren at the siege of Flushing till AUG. 16. Failure of the attempt upon Antwerp, and evacuation of Walcheren owing to the disease in the army. [Duel in consequence between Canning, the Secretary for Foreign Affairs, and Lord Castlereagh, the Minister for War.]
OCT. 14.	Peace of Vienna or Schönbrunn between France and Austria.
	i. Austrian acquisitions in the last partition of Poland ceded to Russia and to the Grand Duchy of Warsaw (*i.e.* to the King of Saxony).
	ii. Trieste and the Adriatic seaboard (Carniola, Fiume, Croatia, and part of Dalmatia) ceded to the Kingdom of Italy.
	iii. Salzburg, and a frontier in Upper Austria ceded to Bavaria, and the Tyrol restored.
NOV. 1810. JAN.	Suppression of the revolt in Tyrol. Condemnation, and execution at Mantua of Hofer, the chief leader of the revolt.

b Napoleon's dynastic plans.

1810. APRIL 1.	Marriage of Napoleon to Marie Louise, daughter of the Emperor Francis.
JULY.	Annexation of Holland upon the resignation of the Dutch throne by Louis Buonaparte. [The Papal States had been annexed to France MAY 17, 1809].
	Annexation of La Valais, the Hanseatic Towns, and the North German seaboard as far as the Elbe.

c The struggle between Napoleon and Russia.

1810. DEC.	Secession of Czar Alexander from Napoleon's system of commercial blockade.
1812. FEB.	Prussia, in spite of reviving energy (shown by the emancipation of the peasants by Stein, 1807, the formation of the "Tugendbund" and the military reforms of Gneisenau and Schnarhorst) compelled to an alliance with Napoleon.
JUNE 23.	Crossing of the Niemen by the French.
SEPT. 7.	Battle of the Borodino.
SEPT. 14.	Moscow evacuated and fired by the Russians.
OCT. 19.	Commencement of the French retreat.
NOV. 28–	Passage of the Beresina, and the Niemen.

Dec. 13.	*d* The War of Liberation.
1813. Feb. 3.	Appeal of Frederick William to the Prussian youth to arm in defence of the fatherland.
Feb. 27.	Treaty of Kalisch between Prussia and Russia against Napoleon. The territory gained by Prussia in the partitions of Poland in 1793-1795 to be ceded to Russia, in exchange for additions to its dominions in West Germany.
March 15.	War declared by Prussia against Napoleon.
May 2	Battle of Lützen, and retreat of the Allies towards Silesia.
May 14.	Entry of Napoleon into Dresden.
May 21.	Battle of Bautzen on the Spree. Defeat of the Allies, but their retreat conducted in good order.
June 4.	Armistice for seven weeks.
June 27.	Treaty of Reichenbach pledging Austria to join the Allies in case of the refusal of Napoleon to consent to Austrian mediation. i. Restoration of the Illyrian Provinces and of the States of the Church. ii. Suppression of the Grand-Duchy of Warsaw. iii. Restoration of the German sea-board annexed in 1810.
July 15–Aug. 10.	Failure of the attempt to agree upon terms of peace at the Congress of Prague, and union of Austria with the Allies.
Aug. 22-23.	French advance upon Berlin under Oudinot checked at Gross-Beeren.
Aug. 26.	Defeat of Marshal Macdonald by Blücher at the Katzbach.
Aug. 26-27.	Defeat of the Allies at Dresden.
Aug. 29-30.	Defeat of the French general Vandamme at Kulm, near Töplitz: capture of Vandamme and 10,000 men.
Sept. 6.	Failure of a second attempt of Napoleon to advance upon Berlin through the defeat of Marshal Ney at Dennewitz.
Oct. 14.	Arrival of Napoleon at Leipzig from Dresden.
Oct. 16-19.	Great battle at Leipzig. Retreat of Napoleon and entry of the Allies into Leipzig.
1814. Jan.	Invasion of France by the Allies, under Schwartzenberg, by Basle, Bülow by the Netherlands, and Blücher between Mainz and Coblentz.
Feb. 1.	Defeat of Napoleon by Blücher and Schwartzenberg at La Rothière, near Brienne.

ANALYSIS OF ENGLISH HISTORY. 303

FEB. 5-9. Failure of the attempt to agree upon terms of peace at the Congress of Châtillon.
FEB. 10-14. Advance of Blücher by the Marne checked by Napoleon.
MARCH 1. Treaty of Chaumont; "of union, concert, and subsidy," between Great Britain, Austria, Prussia, Russia.
MARCH 4. Junction of Blücher with Bülow's army from the Netherlands.
MARCH 9-10. Defeat of the French by the combined armies at Laon.
MARCH 23. Attempt of Napoleon to march to the rear of the Allies and cut off their communication with the Rhine. Advance of the Allies on Paris.
MARCH 31. Entry of the Allies into Paris.
APRIL 3. Abdication of Napoleon in favour of his son rejected.
APRIL 6. Unconditional abdication of Napoleon.
MAY 3. Entry of Lewis XVIII. into Paris.
MAY 30. Treaty of Paris.
    i. France limited to the frontier of 1791 except in the direction of Savoy, and so as to have a defensible frontier in the north and north-east (Landau, Saar Lewis, Philipville, Marienburg.)
    ii. Holland restored to the House of Orange. Switzerland declared free. The Austrian provinces in Italy restored.
    iii. No indemnity exacted from France.
    iv. The Isle of France, Tobago, St. Lucia, and Malta ceded to Great Britain. All other British conquests from France surrendered.
    v. A Congress of European Powers to meet at Vienna to settle all other European questions.

N The Congress of Vienna, and Escape of Napoleon from Elba.

SEPT. 25. Opening of the Congress.
    i. Proposal that Austria, Prussia, Russia, and Great Britain should alone be admitted as principals to the Congress defeated mainly through Talleyrand, the representative of France.

      ii. Difficulties owing to the demand of Czar Alexander for the restoration of Polish nationality under himself as King, and owing to the demand of Prussia for the annexation of Saxony.

      iii. Opposition—threatening to become armed—of France, Austria, and Great Britain against Russia and Prussia.

1815. FEB. 26. Escape of Napoleon from Elba; landing in the gulf of St. Juan. Secession of Marshal Ney to the side of Napoleon. Flight of Lewis XVIII. from Paris, and arrival of Napoleon.
MARCH 1.
MARCH 14.
MARCH 20.

MARCH 25. Coalition between the Powers represented at Vienna. The British and Prussians to invade France from the Netherlands; the Austrians and Russians by the Rhine.

    JUNE 11. Departure of Napoleon for the Netherlands.
    JUNE 16. Defeat of the Prussians at Ligny, and attack of Ney upon the British position at Quatrebras.
    JUNE 17. Retreat of the British from Quatrebras to Waterloo.
    JUNE 18. Battle of Waterloo. Final overthrow of Napoleon by the British and Prussians.
    JUNE 22. Second abdication of Napoleon.
    JULY 7. Second entry of the Allies into Paris.
    JULY 13. Surrender of Napoleon to Capt. Maitland of the *Bellerophon*. Exile of Napoleon to St. Helena.
    NOV. 20. The second Treaty of Paris.

      i. Indemnity of 700,000,000 francs exacted from France, to be paid in five years.

      ii. The art treasures taken under Napoleon to be restored.

      iii. The frontier fortresses in the north to be held by the Allies under Wellington for five years.

      iv. The additions made in **1814** to the boundary of **1791** revoked, but Alsace and Lorraine left to France.

    JUNE 10. Final Act of the Congress of Vienna, and changes made by it.

      i. Austrian possessions in Illyria and Italy restored to Austria, and the Tyrol, Salzburg, and Vorarlberg ceded.

      ii. Prussian possessions restored, and Posen, Swedish Pomerania, the northern part of Saxony, Westphalia, and the Rhine from Mainz to Aix-la-Chapelle (Aachen) ceded.

iii. Würzburg, Aschaffenburg, and the upper Rhenish Palatinate ceded to Bavaria.
iv. Hanover recognized as a kingdom.
v. The States of Germany joined into a Confederation with a permanent Diet to sit at Frankfurt under the presidency of Austria.
vi. Holland and Belgium united under the House of Orange as a bulwark against France; and Norway separated from Denmark and put under the rule of the King of Sweden, though not incorporated with Sweden.
vii. Genoa ceded to the King of Sardinia.
viii. Heligoland taken from Denmark and ceded to Great Britain, and Malta retained by the British, all claim on Minorca being dropped. The Ionian Islands ceded to Great Britain.
ix. The Slave Trade condemned as "an odious traffic."

O **War between Great Britain and the United States.**

(i.) Causes of the War.

1806. Seizure of deserted British subjects and of American citizens on board American ships: vexatious rights of search exercised according to British
1807. Orders in Council.
1808. Embargo laid by the Americans upon trade with Europe.
1809. Removal of the embargo by President Madison, and attempt to carry out a Non-Intercourse Act with France and Great Britain. Repeal of the Act owing to the difficulty of its execution.
1810. Withdrawal by Napoleon of the Berlin and Milan Decrees as far as regarded American trade with Great Britain.
1811. All intercourse between the United States and Great Britain or British colonies and dependencies declared at an end.

(ii.) The War.

1812. JUNE **18.** Declaration of War between the United States and Great Britain (the Orders in Council being repealed too late—JUNE **23**).

Unsuccessful American attack on Canada, but successful actions of the Americans at sea.

x

1813.		Capture of Toronto by the Americans, and reduction of Upper Canada.
		Action between the *Chesapeake* and *Shannon*.
		Recovery of Upper Canada by the British.
1814.	MAY.	Capture of Oswego on the American side of Lake Ontario by the British.
	JUNE.	Defeat of the advance-guard of the British at Chippewa by the invading American army.
	JULY **28.**	Indecisive action between the whole of the British and American forces in Canada at Lundy's Lane, near Niagara.
	AUG.	British descent on Chesapeake Bay; march on Washington; capture of Washington, and destruction of the Capitol.
SEPT. **12**– JAN. **8, 1815.**		Unsuccessful attempt of the British to take New Orleans.
	DEC. **24.**	Treaty of Ghent between Great Britain and the United States.

P Domestic Affairs from the Resignation of Pitt to the Treaty of Paris.

1801.
FEB.–MAR. Third illness of the King. Pitt formally succeeded by Addington as Prime Minister (MARCH).

DEC. Expiry of the Act for the Suspension of Habeas Corpus, and introduction of a Bill of Indemnity for all concerned in the apprehension of any suspected of high treason since FEB. **1793.**

1802. Sir R. Peel's "Health and Morals" Act (the first of the series of Factory Acts).

i. Factories to be whitewashed twice a year, and adequately ventilated.

ii. Legally bound apprentices (many of whom had been sent by the poor-law overseers from the southern to the northern and manufacturing districts) not to be worked more than twelve hours a day; night-work for apprentices forbidden; and measures taken to secure their instruction in reading, writing, and arithmetic—as well as greater decency and wholesomeness in their life, *e.g.* male and female apprentices not to sleep in the same room, and not more than two apprentices in one bed.

	Refusal of Buonaparte's demand for the expulsion of French exiles from Great Britain, and for more stringent restrictions upon the liberty of the British Press.
1803. Feb.	Trial of Jean Peltier for libelling Buonaparte. A verdict of "guilty" found, but sentence not pronounced owing to the outbreak of hostilities with France in May.
	An addition of £60,000 made to the income of the Prince of Wales, and his debts paid off (as before in **1787** and **1795**).
1804. Feb.-April.	The King's fourth illness.
April.	Resignation of Addington and succession of Pitt to the Premiership. His attempt to form a comprehensive Cabinet, including Fox, thwarted by the King; refusal of Lord Grenville and Pitt's old adherent Windham to take office without Fox.
1805. April.	Vote of censure on Henry Dundas, Lord Melville, for misappropriation of public funds while Treasurer to the Navy, in Pitt's former Ministry, passed by the Speaker's casting vote. (The censure reversed by the Lords, **1807**.)
	Establishment of the British and Foreign School Society, teaching the Bible without "note or comment."
May.	Presentation of a petition from the Roman Catholics of Ireland by Lord Grenville; motions in their favour made by Grenville and Fox rejected in both Houses.
1806. Jan. 23.	Death of Pitt. Accession to power of the Ministry of All the Talents, under Lord Grenville —including Fox, Erskine, Windham, Lord Sidmouth (Addington), Lord Fitzwilliam, Lord Howick (Grey), and Lord Ellenborough.
1807. Feb.	Abolition of the Slave Trade with all possessions, British or foreign, by the General Abolition Act (the completion of an Order in Council, **1805**, forbidding the trade with possessions acquired in the war, and of a Bill in **1806** confirming the Order, and extending the prohibition to foreign countries) [see article in *Dictionary of English History* (Cassell)].
March.	Introduction, with the King's "reluctant assent," of the Army and Navy Service Bill, extending the Irish Act of **1793** (admitting Catholics to hold commissions in the army up to the rank of

colonel) to Great Britain, to both services, and without restriction as to rank. Resignation of Sidmouth, and withdrawal of the Bill, owing to the marked opposition of the King.

Demand by the King of a pledge from the Ministers never again to propose concessions to the Catholics; refusal of the pledge by the Ministers; dismissal of the Ministry, and formation of a new Ministry under the Duke of Portland, with Spencer Perceval as Chancellor of the Exchequer, and George Canning as Foreign Secretary.

APRIL. Dissolution of Parliament, and appeal of the King to the People on the Catholic Question. [Bill for the establishment of parochial schools chargeable on local rates levied by vestries, introduced by Whitbread, passed by the Commons, but rejected by the Lords.]

1808. Abolition of the punishment of death for stealing from the person to the value of five shillings. carried by Romilly. (Similarly, abolition of capital punishment for stealing from bleaching-grounds carried by Romilly, **1811**; his other proposals to abolish death for stealing from shops to the value of five shillings, and for stealing to the value of £2 from houses, being lost in one of the two Houses, **1810-1811-1813**.)

1809. Trial and condemnation of Cobbett for an attack upon the German Legion and upon flogging in the army. Cobbett fined £1,000 and imprisoned for two years (**1810**).

Duel between Lord Castlereagh and Canning arising out of the failure of the British expedition against Antwerp. Resignation of Castlereagh, Canning, and the Duke of Portland owing to failing health. Perceval Prime Minister, with Lord Liverpool succeeding Castlereagh as War Minister, and the Marquess of Wellesley succeeding Canning as Foreign Minister.

1810. MAY–JUNE. Revival of the subject of Catholic claims by Earl Grey, and Grattan.

OCT. 5. The King's Jubilee.

NOV. 2. Death of the King's daughter Amelia, and fifth and final illness of the King.

1811.	JAN.-FEB.	Passing of the Regency Bill, with restrictions similar to those of **1788-1789** on grant of peerages and patronage, and committing the care of the King's person to the Queen. The restrictions only to remain in force for one year. Uncertain support given by the Regent to the Tory Ministry.
1812.	JAN.-APRIL.	Fresh motions brought forward on the Catholic claims owing to the state of Ireland by Lord Fitzwilliam, and Grattan, supported by Brougham and Canning.
	MAY 2.	Assassination of Perceval by Bellingham in the lobby of the House. Failure of Wellesley and Canning to come to satisfactory terms with Earl Grey and Lord Grenville as to the formation of a new Ministry. Failure of Lord Moira to satisfy Grey and Grenville as to the support of the Regent, and final breach between the Regent and the Whigs. Succession of the Liverpool Ministry, with Lord Castlereagh as Foreign Minister and Lord Sidmouth as Home Minister; the Catholic Question regarded by the Ministry as an open question.
	JUNE 23.	Canning's motion for the consideration of the Catholic claims passed by the Commons; a similar motion in the Lords lost by one (JULY 1).
	JUNE 23.	Repeal of the British Orders in Council (though too late to stop the war with the United States).
		Luddite machine-breaking riots, beginning **1811**.
1813.		Extension to Great Britain of the Irish Act of **1793**, enabling Catholics to hold commissions in the army up to the rank of colonel.
1815.		Proposal to grant the Catholic claims, reserving for the Crown a veto on the appointment of the Catholic Bishops, rejected in Ireland through the influence of Daniel O'Connell.

Q **The Last Years of the Reign from the Conclusion of the Treaty of Paris.**

    1. Internal affairs in Great Britain.

1815.	Corn Law: the ports closed against importation of foreign corn till British wheat should have risen to 80s. the quarter.

1816. March 17. Defeat of the Government on the proposal to retain half the income-tax, *i.e.* to reduce the tax on all incomes over £60 (first imposed for war purposes in **1799**), from 10 per cent., which it had reached in **1806**, to 5 per cent. [The tax dropped till **1841**.]

May 2. Marriage of the Regent's daughter Charlotte Augusta to Leopold of Saxe-Coburg.

May. Revival of the Luddite riots of **1811–1812**, at London, Manchester, and other towns; and risings of the labourers in Norfolk and Suffolk.

May 21. Select Committee granted Mr. Brougham to inquire into the state of education among the poor in London.

July. March of unemployed colliers and miners from Bilston to the Regent at London stopped at St. Albans by the magistrates and constables.

Formation of "Hampden Clubs" for sweeping Parliamentary Reform, including universal suffrage and annual Parliaments.

Institution of the Society of Spencean Philanthropists for community of land.

Dec. 2. Spa Field Riot; the riot suppressed by the Lord Mayor (Mr. Wood), Sir James Shaw, and six others.

1817. Jan. 28. Attack on the Prince Regent on his return from opening Parliament.

Feb. 3–19. Sitting of a Secret Committee to collect evidence and give advice on the condition of the country.

March 3. Habeas Corpus Act suspended.

March 10. Meeting of operatives at St. Peter's Field in Manchester, "the Blanketeers," with the intention of marching to London to make known their complaints; the majority dispersed by the reading of the Riot Act, 180 getting as far as Macclesfield.

March 27. Circular of Lord Sidmouth, as Home Secretary, to the Lords Lieutenant of counties, that justices had the power of arresting any charged upon oath with the publication of blasphemous or seditious libels and holding them to bail. Its legality disputed in the Lords by Earl Grey, and in the Commons by Romilly.

June 8–10. The Derbyshire Insurrection finally crushed by Mr. Rolleston near Nottingham. Execution in consequence of the ringleaders, Brandreth, Turner, Ludlam.

JUNE 16.	Trial and acquittal of Watson, Preston, Thistlewood, and others, for high treason in connexion with the Spa Field Riot.
[NOV. 6.	Death of the Regent's newly-married daughter Charlotte.]
DEC. 18.	Trial of Hone " for libelling the Lord's Prayer, the Ten Commandments, and the Catechism, and thereby bringing into contempt the Christian religion."
DEC. 19.	Second trial of Hone for a profane libel, "the Litany."
DEC. 19.	Third trial of Hone before Lord Ellenborough, the Chief Justice, for a parody on the Athanasian Creed. Hone acquitted on each trial.

1818.

JAN. 28-29.	Repeal of the Suspension of Habeas Corpus Act. The repeal followed, as in **1801**, by a Bill of Indemnity (MARCH).
FEB.	Secret Committees of both Houses appointed to report upon papers relative to the state of the country in **1817**.
MARCH.	Motion to inquire into the use made of spies (notably one called Oliver) by the Government rejected in the Commons.
	Announcements of proposed Royal marriages :—
APRIL 7.	i. Proposed marriage of the King's daughter Elizabeth to the Landgrave of Hesse-Homburg.
APRIL 13.	ii. Proposed marriage of the Duke of Clarence to Adelaide of Saxe-Meiningen.
APRIL 13.	iii. Proposed marriage of the Duke of Cambridge to Augusta of Hesse.
MAY 13.	iv. Proposed marriage of the Duke of Kent to Mary Louisa Victoria of Saxe-Coburg-Saalfeld, sister of Prince Leopold.
MAY.	Re-enactment of the Alien Act (placing aliens under the supervision of the Secretary of State, and making them liable to removal at his discretion) for two years (as before in **1814** and **1816**), after much opposition. Aliens not
JUNE 9.	to be considered naturalized by holding Bank shares.
JUNE 10.	Dissolution of Parliament.
JUNE–SEPT.	Strike of the Manchester cotton-spinners.
NOV. 2.	Death of Sir R. Romilly by his own hand.
NOV. 17.	Death of the Queen.

1819. May. Government proposals (based upon the principle of Ricardo) for the resumption of cash payments by the Bank of England, suspended since Feb. **1797**, that the Bank should from Feb. **1, 1820**, exchange its notes for gold ingots at the rate of 81 shillings per ounce, and at lowering rates till gold should descend to the Mint price of £3 17s. 10½d. the ounce. [Cash payments really resumed by the Bank, May **1, 1821**, though the date finally fixed by Parliament was May **1, 1822**.]

Second Factory Act (applicable only to cotton mills).

   i. No children under nine to be allowed to work in cotton mills.

   ii. Between nine and sixteen the working day not to exceed twelve hours, exclusive of mealtimes.

   iii. Night-work prohibited for all under sixteen.

May–June. Meetings of operatives throughout the country to consider the low rate of wages.

Aug. Commencement of drilling in connexion with meetings of the operatives or reformers.

Aug. 16. Great meeting of reformers in St. Peter's Field under the presidency of "Orator" Hunt. The meeting attacked first by a troop of Manchester Yeomanry in order to execute a warrant of arrest upon Hunt, then by two squadrons of the 15th Hussars. "The Peterloo massacre."

Nov. 23. Meeting of Parliament for special autumn session.

Nov.–Dec. The Six Acts.

   i. An Act to prevent Delay in the Administration of Justice in cases of Misdemeanour; defendants deprived of the right of traversing, *i.e.* of objecting to the framing of the accusation, but not to be brought to trial after a period of twelve months. (The second clause of the Act due to Lord Holland.)

   ii. An Act for the more effectual Prevention and Punishment of Blasphemous and Seditious Libels: upon conviction all copies of the libel to be seized; the publisher liable upon second conviction to imprisonment, banishment, or transportation.

   iii. An Act to prevent the Training of Persons to the Use of Arms, and to the Practice of Military Evolutions and Exercise.

iv. An Act to authorize Justices of the Peace, in certain disturbed Counties, to seize and detain Arms collected and kept for Purposes dangerous to the Public Peace. (Sixteen counties named as disturbed.)

v. An Act to subject certain Publications to the duties of Stamps upon Newspapers, and to make other Regulations for restraining the Abuses arising from the Publication of Blasphemous and Seditious Libels. (Publishers to enter into recognizances for the payment of any penalty.)

vi. An Act for more effectually preventing Seditious Meetings and Assemblies.

(*a*) No meeting of more than fifty to be held without six days' notice to a Justice of the Peace.

(*b*) None but freeholders or inhabitants to attend, and no adjournment allowed.

(*c*) Proposed time and place of meeting to be changed at discretion of Justice.

(*d*) All meetings declared unlawful that tended to incite to hatred and contempt of the King's person, or of the constituted Government, and rendered liable to summary dispersion.

(*e*) No banners or flags to be allowed.

(*f*) All lecture and debating rooms liable to inspection.

Act i. due to the Lord Chancellor, Lord Eldon.

Act v. due to the Foreign Minister, Lord Castlereagh.

Acts ii., iii., iv., and vi. due to the Home Secretary, Lord Sidmouth.

1820. Jan. 29. Death of King George III.

2. Foreign affairs from the Treaty of Paris to the death of the King.

1815. Sept. 26. [i. The Treaty of Holy Alliance between Russia, Prussia, Austria, Naples, Sardinia, Spain, France.]

Nov. 20. ii. Treaty between Great Britain, Russia, Prussia, Austria, to keep Napoleon from returning to power, and to maintain a settled government in France.

1818. Oct. iii. Conference of Aix-la-Chapelle.
    (a) France to be at once evacuated, the sum remaining to be paid by France as war indemnity fixed at 265 millions of francs.
    (b) The Quadruple Alliance of **1815** to guard against French disorders renewed.
    (c) Proposal to form a sort of International Council of the five Great Powers thwarted by the opposition of Great Britain.

iv. State of the South American States.
    (a) La Plata and Chili independent of Spain and proclaimed as republics.
    (b) Spanish rule still recognized in Mexico, New Grenada, Venezuela, in spite of attempts to shake it off, between **1807** and **1815**, and in Peru.
    (c) Brazil the home of the Portuguese monarchy since **1807.**

GEORGE IV.

George IV. = Caroline of Brunswick-Wolfenbüttel.
    |
    Charlotte = Leopold of Saxe-Coburg (d. **1817**).

A Internal Affairs till the Illness and Retirement of Lord Liverpool.

1820. Feb. Proposals of Lord J. Russell for Reform.
    i. That corrupt boroughs should cease to return members.
    ii. That their rights be transferred to big towns or large counties.
    iii. That Grampound be disfranchised.

Feb. Plot by Thistlewood and others to murder the Ministers while at dinner at Lord Harrowby's, to seize the Bank and Tower, and proclaim a Provisional Government. The plot betrayed by Edwards; the conspirators attacked and disarmed by the police in a stable in Cato Street.

April–May 1. Thistlewood and four others executed, and five others of the conspirators transported.

May 9. Motion for a Select Committee of the House of Commons to inquire into the conduct of the informer Edwards and his employment by the Government rejected.

APRIL 5.	Dispersal of a seditious rising in Stirlingshire to seize the Carron Ironworks in conjunction with rioters from Glasgow. "The Battle of Bonnymuir."
APRIL.	Imprisonment of "Orator" Hunt for two years and six months, and of Sir Charles Wolseley for eighteen months.
[FEB.-NOV.	Proceedings against Queen Caroline.
FEB.	Anxiety of the King to obtain a divorce from the Queen, who had lived abroad since June 1814. Promise of the Ministers to support him in the event of the Queen's return to Great Britain. Orders meanwhile given that she should not be recognized at foreign Courts and that her name should be omitted from the Liturgy.
JUNE 6.	Return of the Queen to Great Britain and landing at Dover.
JUNE 19.	Failure of negotiations with the Queen that she should live abroad on an annuity of £50,000, but without the insertion of her name in the Liturgy or formal recognition at foreign Courts.
JULY.	Introduction by Lord Liverpool of a Bill of Pains and Penalties against the Queen and to dissolve the marriage. Production of evidence before the House of Lords. Passing of the Pains and Penalties Bill through the Lords by a majority of nine. Dropping of the Bill and illuminations in London. (The Queen's defence before the Lords managed by Brougham and Denman, the King's Commissioners being the Duke of Wellington and Lord Castlereagh.)
AUG. 17-SEPT. 8. and OCT. 3-NOV. 2. NOV. 10.	
NOV. 29.	The Queen's solemn thanksgivings at St. Paul's.
(1821.	An annuity of £50,000 voted by Parliament to the Queen. JULY 19. Exclusion of the Queen from the Coronation. AUG. 7. Her death.)]
JUNE 4.	Death of Henry Grattan.
JUNE 28.	Brougham's proposals for the education of the poor in England and Wales rejected through the opposition of the Dissenters.
	i. Rates for education to be raised by vestries and disbursed by the magistrates of quarter sessions.
	ii. All teachers to be members of the Church of England, and to be certified in all cases by the clergyman of the parish.

Reforms in the criminal law effected by Sir James Mackintosh.
  i. Abolition of death-punishment for stealing from shops to the value of five shillings.
  ii. Abolition of death-punishment for mutilation of cattle and writing threatening letters.
  iii. Gipsies to be dealt with by the vagrant laws.

DEC. Formation of the "Constitutional Association," or "Bridge Street Gang," to prosecute for seditious, libellous, and blasphemous publications.

1821. MAY 1. Resumption of cash payments in full by the Bank of England.

MAY 4. Dinner of Reformers at the London Tavern. The beginning of the continuous agitation for Reform of Parliament.

MAY 23. Attack by Brougham upon the Constitutional Association, leading to its abandonment.

MAY 30. Disfranchisement of Grampound, its franchise being transferred to Yorkshire.

JUNE 14. The Bishop of Peterborough (Dr. Marsh) attacked in the House of Lords for setting up a new test of orthodoxy by means of questions and written answers.

NOV. ? Resignation of the Home Office by Lord Sidmouth, Peel becoming Home Secretary.

1822. Canning appointed as Governor-General of India in succession to Lord Hastings (Lord Moira).

APRIL–MAY. Canning's Bill to enable Catholic peers to sit in the House of Lords passed by the Commons, but rejected by the Lords.

AUG. 9. Death of Lord Londonderry (Castlereagh) by his own hand.

SEPT. 11. Accession of Canning to power as Foreign Secretary in succession to Londonderry.

Lord Amherst sent to India.

1823. JAN. Mr. Huskisson appointed President of the Board of Trade.
  i. Proposal of Huskisson to remit the import duty on raw cotton defeated by the reluctance of the manufacturers to submit to the free exportation of manufactured cotton.
  ii. Introduction of a Bill to free the silk-manufacturers of Spitalfields from the power of magistrates to fix the wages of the trade in that quarter. The Bill dropped owing to the

opposition of the Spitalfields operatives (11,000 petitioning against it), and of the House of Lords.

JUNE 6. iii. Reciprocity of Duties Bill introduced by Huskisson and passed. The Bill, practically the repeal of the old Navigation Act (which was formally repealed, though with restrictions on non-European goods, **1826**), rendered necessary by the retaliatory measures adopted by Prussia, the Netherlands, and Portugal.

Presentation of the Yorkshire petition for Reform, signed by two-thirds of the freeholders (17,000).

MAY 24. Adoption of Canning's resolutions on Slavery, that slaves should be prepared for freedom, and that their condition should be improved; the colonists urged to abandon the flogging of
AUG. 18-20. women. Rising of the slaves in Demerara against restrictive measures on religious worship issued by the Governor; trial and condemnation to death by court-martial of John Smith, an Independent missionary; death of Smith in prison before the decision of the British Government could arrive (FEB. **6, 1824**). New regulations issued by the Colonial Office.

  i. Prohibiting the use of the whip in the field, and flogging of women.
  ii. No flogging to be inflicted within twenty-four hours of offence.
  iii. No slave to receive more than twenty-five lashes a day.
  iv. Married slaves not to be separated from their children.

JUNE 4. Motion in the Commons for inquiry into the arrears in the Court of Chancery, followed by a Commission of Inquiry moved for by the Lord
JULY. Chancellor.

1824. FEB. **4.** Establishment of the "Catholic Rent," *i.e.* a subscription raised in Ireland by the Catholic Association (started by Daniel O'Connell, **1823**).

Further commercial changes in the direction of Free Trade made by Huskisson.

  i. The power of magistrates to fix the wages of the silk trade in Spitalfields abolished.

              ii. Duty on raw silk reduced to 3*d.* in the pound (while before it had been 4*s.* if coming from Bengal, and 5*s.* 7½*d.* from other countries). Foreign silk to be admitted on an *ad valorem* duty after JULY, **1826**.

             iii. Duty on foreign wool reduced from 6*d.* to 1*d.* or ½*d.* the pound. Wool to be exported on a duty of 1*d.* the pound.

             iv. Artisans allowed freely to leave the country.

             v. The combination laws, rendering it illegal for workmen to combine and agree as to the wages for which they should labour, abolished. (The number of these laws dating from Edward I. about thirty-five in number.)

NOV.-JAN.**1825.** Commercial failures and breaking of banks owing to over-speculation in trade.

    1825. FEB. Measures of the Government to meet the commercial panic.

             i. The issue of small notes (*i.e.* under £5) by private banks in England and Wales suppressed, and their circulation after a fixed date prohibited ; a large quantity of sovereigns issued from the Mint.

            ii. The limitation of six, imposed in **1708**, on the number of partners in a private bank, removed from all banks beyond sixty-five miles from London. The beginning of Joint-Stock Banks. The Bank of England allowed in return to establish branches in large towns.

            iii. Arrangement finally made with the Bank of England to make advances up to three millions on deposits of merchants' goods.

    FEB. **10.** The Catholic Association suppressed by Parliament (still, however, carried on in another form).

    FEB. **28.** Sir F. Burdett's motion to substitute for the relief of Catholics a new oath in place of the oath of supremacy, that recognized the Sovereign as "in all causes and over all persons as well ecclesiastical as civil supreme," and thus debarred Catholics from office. Passed by the
    MAY. Commons, but rejected by the Lords.

    APRIL. Further motions in the House of Commons with regard to the Catholics.

             i. To raise the qualification of freeholders for voting from 40*s.* to £10. Abandoned after the second reading on the rejection of the Relief Bill by the Lords.

ii. To declare the expediency of making State provision for the secular priests in Ireland.

MAY 18. Chancery Reform Bill based on the Report of the Commission appointed 1823, moved for by the Attorney-General.

MAY 31. Dissolution of Parliament.

AUG. Commencement of riots, continuing through the winter and spring of 1826. [An Assistant Under-Secretary of State appointed for the Colonies.]

1826. MAY. 300,000 quarters of corn in the ports to be let out of bond to meet the distress; a further supply of 500,000 quarters to be imported, if necessary, in two months, at price and duty, to be fixed by Ministers.

SEPT. Order in Council issued by Ministers for the admission of foreign oats, rye, beans, and peas.

NOV. 21. Meeting of the new Parliament. An Act of Indemnity for opening the ports in September passed in favour of Ministers.

1827. JAN. 5. Death of the Duke of York.

FEB. 16-17. Lord Liverpool seized with apoplexy, from which he never recovered.

B Foreign Affairs during the Reign.

1. Naples.

1820. Rising of the Carbonari in the kingdom of Naples, and grant of a Constitution by King Ferdinand (JULY 13).

OCT. Conference of the Czar, the King of Prussia, and the Emperor of Austria, at Troppau, in Bohemia. King Ferdinand summoned to Laybach, in Carniola, and a circular sent to the other Powers asking for federative intervention.

DEC. Protest of Great Britain.

1821. JAN. Meeting at Laybach. Austria empowered to march an army against Naples. Entry of the Austrians into the city of Naples, and restoration of Ferdinand's absolute rule; Great Britain remaining neutral. Meeting of the Powers fixed for the next year at Verona

2. Spain.

1820. MARCH. Acceptance by Ferdinand of Spain, owing to a revolt for freedom in the army assembled at Madrid for the subjugation of the revolted Spanish colonies in South America, of the Constitution of **1812**.

1820-1822. Conspiracy of Ferdinand against the Constitution, and civil war in Spain.

1822. SEPT. Canning appointed as British Foreign Secretary.

OCT. Meeting of the Congress at Verona. Results of Canning's efforts.

    i. No declaration made jointly by the Powers against Spain; a blow thus given to the doctrine of federative interference.

1823. APRIL.   ii. British protest at once but ineffectually entered against French interference with Spanish
1823-1824. affairs. French invasion of Spain, and restoration of absolute rule.

    iii. Refusal of Canning to take part in a Congress at Paris to discuss jointly the question of the revolted Spanish colonies.

1824.   iv. The independence of Buenos Ayres, Mexico, Columbia, recognized by Great Britain. "I resolved that if France had Spain, it should not be Spain with the Indies. I called the New World into existence, to redress the balance of the Old."

3. Portugal.

1826. Attack of Don Miguel upon the Regency and Constitution of Portugal with the sanction of Spain. Appeal of the Portugese Regency for aid to Great Britain, as pledged by treaty to support Portugal if attacked. Immediate
DEC. despatch of British troops to Lisbon.

4. Greece.

1821. Insurrection of Greece and of the Danubian Provinces against the Porte.

1824. The help of Mehemet Ali, Pasha of Egypt, called in by his Suzerain the Sultan to crush the Greek revolt.

1825. Death of Czar Alexander, and understanding arrived at between Czar Nicholas, his successor, and Great Britain. Joint representation of Great Britain and Russia to the Porte that
1826. Greece should be autonomous but tributary to the Sultan.

	Treaty of Ackermann concluded by the Porte, granting virtual independence to Moldavia and Wallachia and partial independence to Servia.
1827. JULY.	Union of France with Russia and Great Britain in demanding the tributary independence of Greece. Despatch of a joint squadron to enforce an armistice.
OCT. 1829.	The Battle of Navarino, and the destruction of the Egyptian fleet, leading along with the Russo-Turkish War of **1828-1829** to the Treaty of Adrianople, by which the independence of Greece, though within somewhat narrow geographical limits, was recognized.

5. France in **1830**.

1824-1829.	Reactionary Government of Charles X.
1829. AUG.	Formation of a Ministry under Prince Polignac. The elections of **1830** being unfavourable to
JULY 26.	the Ministry, the following ordinances published:—

    i. No journal to be published without Royal permission.

    ii. The Chamber of Deputies dissolved.

    iii. The property qualification for a vote raised, double election established, the initiative in all legislation confined to the Government.

JULY 28–31.	Revolution in Paris, ending in the abdication and departure of Charles X.
AUG. 7.	Louis-Philippe, Duke of Orleans, son of Philippe Égalité, made King of the French.
[**1824-1826.**	Attack of the Ashantees on the Fantees, who were under the protection of the British. Sir Charles MacCarthy, Governor of Cape Coast Castle,
JAN. **1824.**	surprised and killed by the Ashantees. The
AUG. **1826.**	Ashantees finally defeated by the British at Dudowah.]

C **Internal Affairs from the Accession of Canning to Power, till the Death of the King.**

1827. APRIL 10.	Canning Prime Minister. Resignations of the Duke of Wellington (who also withdrew from the offices of Master of the Ordnance and Commander-in-Chief), Mr. Peel, Lord Eldon, Lord Bathurst, Mr. Wallace (Master of the Mint), Sir C. Wetherell (Attorney-General), and Lord Melville, First Lord of the Admiralty.

Y

May 10.	Attack upon Canning by Earl Grey in the House of Lords.
Aug. 8. 1828.	Death of Canning. Dissensions in the Cabinet, and resignation of Lord Goderich (Robinson), who after Canning's death had succeeded him as Premier.
Jan. 8.	
Jan.	The Wellington Cabinet, with Peel as Home Secretary, Lord Aberdeen as Foreign Secretary, the Marquess of Anglesey as Viceroy of Ireland, and Huskisson as Secretary for the Colonies.
	The Battle of Navarino described in the King's Speech as an "untoward event."
Feb. 26.	Repeal of the Test and Corporation Acts of 1673 and 1661 moved by Lord J. Russell. The Repeal passed by the Commons, and by the Lords with the concurrence of many of the Bishops, but with the addition to the Declaration to be taken of the words, "on the true faith of a Christian."
April.	
May.	Bills introduced for disfranchising Penryn and East Retford. Misunderstanding between the Duke of Wellington and Huskisson as to the latter's proffered resignation. Resignation along with Huskisson of other "Canningites"—Lord Palmerston, Mr. Lamb (Lord Melbourne), and Mr. Grant (Lord Glenelg).
May.	Sir F. Burdett's motion in favour of the Catholics passed by the Commons, but abandoned after a conference with the Lords.
June-July.	The Clare election. Defeat of Mr. Vesey Fitzgerald, the new President of the Board of Trade, although favourable to the Catholic claims, by Daniel O'Connell.
July.	Revival in full activity of the Catholic Association and of new Orange Associations, the Act of 1825 having expired.
	Attempts made by the Ministers to sound the King and the Bishops as to the possibility of granting the Catholic claims.
1829. Feb. 4.	Recommendation in the King's Speech to Parliament, the King having finally assented to the measure, to consider whether the Catholic claims could be granted "consistently with the full and permanent security of our establishments in Church and State."

FEB. 4.   Resignation by Peel of his seat for Oxford University. Sir R. Inglis elected over him to represent the University.

The Government measures as to Catholic Emancipation.

FEB.   i. A Bill for the suppression of dangerous associations or assemblies in Ireland.

MARCH 5.   ii. A Bill for Catholic relief: Catholics admitted, on taking a new oath instead of the oath of supremacy, to Parliament, to all judicial offices except in Ecclesiastical Courts, to all corporate offices, to all political offices except those of Regent, Lord Chancellor in England and Ireland, and Lord-Lieutenant in Ireland; Catholic Bishops not to assume the titles of existing sees, the insignia of office to be taken to no place of worship except those of the Established Church, Jesuits to be registered, the admission of Jesuits to be prevented, and monastic orders to be discouraged.

iii. The franchise in Ireland to be remodelled by the substitution of a £10 freehold for a 40s. freehold as qualification for a vote.

[Notice that on MARCH 3 the King renewed his objections to the Bill for relief, which were only overcome by the resignation of the Duke of Wellington, Lord Lyndhurst (the Lord Chancellor), and Mr. Peel. Their resignation withdrawn the same day at the King's request, and with the King's written consent to the Bill.

MARCH.   Notice also the duel between the Duke of Wellington and Lord Winchilsea on account of the Bill.]

Resignation of the office of Lord High Admiral by the Duke of Clarence owing to the Duke of Wellington's objections to the amount of his travelling expenses. The last Lord High Admiral of England.

JUNE 2.   Reform motion brought forward by Lord Blandford to disfranchise close or corrupt boroughs to prevent them being purchased by Catholics.

1830.   [Notice the creation of a new Metropolitan police force by Peel, and of an office of police under the Secretary of State.]

April 5. Motion by Mr. Grant for the removal of Jewish disabilities, increased by the addition of "on the true faith of a Christian," added by the Lords to the Declaration of **1828**.

April. The punishment of death for forgery restricted to cases of forgery of the great seal, the privy seal, the sign manual, wills, bank-notes, or other representatives of money.

April. Renewal of Lord Blandford's proposals for the disfranchisement of rotten boroughs, supported by O'Connell. Rejection of Lord J. Russell's proposal to enfranchise Leeds, Birmingham, Manchester.

June **26**. Death of the King.

THE END.

www.ingramcontent.com/pod-product-compliance
Lightning Source LLC
Chambersburg PA
CBHW030002240426
43672CB00007B/794